SELECTED WRITINGS ON MARXISM

Stuart Hall: Selected Writings

A series edited by Catherine Hall and Bill Schwarz

SELECTED WRITINGS ON MARXISM

Edited, introduced, and with commentary by
Gregor McLennan

Stuart Hall

DUKE UNIVERSITY PRESS | DURHAM AND LONDON | 2021

All essays © Stuart Hall Estate
All other material © 2021, Duke University Press
Printed and bound by CPI Group (UK) Ltd, Croydon, CR0 4YY
Designed by Amy Ruth Buchanan
Typeset in Minion Pro by Westchester Publishing Services

Library of Congress Cataloging-in-Publication Data
Names: Hall, Stuart, 1932–2014, author. | McLennan, Gregor, editor. | Hall, Stuart, 1932–2014. Works. Selections. 2016.
Title: Selected writings on Marxism / Stuart Hall ; edited, introduced, and with commentary by Gregor McLennan.
Description: Durham : Duke University Press, 2021. | Series: Stuart Hall: selected writings | Includes index.
Identifiers: LCCN 2020021730 (print)
LCCN 2020021731 (ebook)
ISBN 9781478000273 (hardcover)
ISBN 9781478000341 (paperback)
ISBN 9781478002154 (ebook)
Subjects: LCSH: Hall, Stuart, 1932–2014—Political and social views. | Communism.
Classification: LCC HX40.H355 2021 (print) | LCC HX40 (ebook) | DDC 335.4—dc23
LC record available at https://lccn.loc.gov/2020021730
LC ebook record available at https://lccn.loc.gov/2020021731

Cover art: Photo provided by the Open University.

"Black Crime, Black Proletariat" from Stuart Hall, Chas Critcher, Tony Jefferson, John Clarke, and Brian Roberts, *Policing the Crisis: Mugging, the State, and Law and Order* © 1978, SpringerNature. Reprinted by permission.

CONTENTS

vii   A Note on the Text

ix   Acknowledgments

1   Editor's Introduction: Mediating Marxism

Part I | THEORETICAL READINGS

19   **ONE** Marx's Notes on Method: A "Reading" of the "1857 Introduction" [1974]

62   **TWO** Rethinking the "Base and Superstructure" Metaphor [1977]

91   **THREE** The "Political" and the "Economic" in Marx's Theory of Classes [1977]

134   **FOUR** The Problem of Ideology: Marxism without Guarantees [1983]

158   *Editor's Discussion of the Part I Writings*

Part II | THEMATIC OVERVIEWS

179   **FIVE** Subcultures, Cultures and Class: A Theoretical Overview (with John Clarke, Tony Jefferson, and Brian Roberts) [1975]

199   **SIX** Black Crime, Black Proletariat (with Chas Critcher, Tony Jefferson, John Clarke, and Brian Roberts) [1978]

227   **SEVEN** Variants of Liberalism [1986]

247   *Editor's Discussion of the Part II Writings*

Part III | POINTS OF DEPARTURE

261 **EIGHT** Nicos Poulantzas: State, Power, Socialism [1980]

273 **NINE** In Defence of Theory [1981]

282 **TEN** Authoritarian Populism: A Reply to Jessop et al. [1985]

293 **ELEVEN** When Was "the Post-colonial"? Thinking at the Limit [1996]

316 **TWELVE** The Centrality of Culture: Notes on the Cultural Revolutions of Our Time [1997]

335 *Editor's Discussion of the Part III Writings*

351 Index

363 Place of First Publication

A NOTE ON THE TEXT

Hall's publications and papers did not follow a consistent method of presentation, nor was his referencing as precise as nowadays would be expected of fully polished texts. There were also many inadvertent author or printer slippages of grammar and spelling that Hall would certainly have ironed out in a thoroughgoing editorial process, had this been a priority for him. In bringing together the work for this volume as uniformly and accessibly as possible, numerous matters of those kinds have been attended to and further details supplied, though obvious gaps and glitches remain, especially when it is unclear which editions of Marx and Engels's texts Hall was working with. Moreover, chapters 5, 6, 7, and 12 have been abridged, both for reasons of general economy/readability and to ensure best fit with the overarching theme of this selection of Hall writings. The nature and extent of the cuts to the originals are indicated in the editor's introduction and discussions. Some of the original subheadings have been adjusted as part of this process.

ACKNOWLEDGMENTS

Thanks are due to Palgrave Macmillan for permission to reproduce part of *Policing the Crisis: Mugging, the State, and Law and Order* (1978) in chapter 6, and to *New Left Review* for the essays in chapters 8 and 10. I'm grateful to Chas Critcher, Tony Jefferson, John Clarke, and Brian Roberts for allowing the collective work of *Policing the Crisis* and *Resistance through Rituals* to be presented as part of this Stuart Hall volume. Amelia Horgan and Keith McClelland kindly helped to source the original texts and convert them into a new format. Enjoyable exchanges with Nick Beech on points of bibliographic detail unexpectedly turned into larger matters of interpretation. Reviewers' comments on both the initial proposal and the completed manuscript were much appreciated. At Duke University Press, Senior Executive Editor Ken Wissoker was encouraging and receptive, and the editorial team provided ongoing expertise. Series editors Catherine Hall and Bill Schwarz were hugely supportive throughout the process of development of the book. Bill's unfailing responses to drafts and to strategic issues as they arose were invaluable. A special thanks to him.

EDITOR'S INTRODUCTION

Mediating Marxism

Rationale

Architect of contemporary cultural studies; New Left analyst of British political moments and movements; radical educator *sans pareil*; herald of new ethnicities and hybrid social selves; critical race theorist and diasporic voice: Stuart Hall (1932–2014) can be characterized in many ways. The purpose of this volume of Hall's writings is to help decide how centrally the designation "Marxist thinker" should be placed within, or ranged right across, that protean spectrum of endeavor.

I should say at once: "help further decide," because the basic proposition at issue has been aired before in various collections of papers, commentaries, and interviews geared toward identifying Hall's fundamental contributions. Not least, it features within other publications in the Hall series by Duke University Press. Thus, in framing *Essential Essays*, editor David Morley underlines Hall's "lifelong intellectual investment in Marxism," and many of his selections, not only those assigned to the most ostensibly relevant section, provide ample testimony to the influence of Marxism on Hall.[1] Similarly, introducing *Cultural Studies 1983*, Larry Grossberg and Jennifer Daryl Slack depict that brilliant course of Hall lectures as undertaken in order to clarify "Marxism's contribution to the interpretation of culture," resulting in a superb record of Hall's ongoing "'wrestling with the angels' of Marxist theory."[2] Likewise, the editors of *Selected Political Writings* insist that "Hall's engagement with politics cannot be fathomed without acknowledging this long presence of Marxism in his thought," the contours of which are then briefly traced in Michael Rustin's afterword to that book.[3]

The goal of the present work is to extend the evidence and angle of those previous volumes by gathering another group of Hall's central texts—writings that do not appear together elsewhere—and by giving undivided attention to the Hall/Marxism issue. If Marxism is agreed to have been—albeit in a complex way—at the forefront of Hall's thought over the years, then we should track this through as many of his emblematic compositions as possible. We should also bear in mind that some presentations of Hall's thought make it difficult to conclude that Marxism *was* central to him. Indicatively, a collection of essays on Hall involving close associates was entitled *Without Guarantees*, referring to what many see as his signature attitude toward the politics of theory.[4] That catchphrase was culled from a Hall essay (our chapter 4) the full title of which ("The Problem of Ideology: *Marxism* without Guarantees") conveyed a specific anchorage for the relevant sense of openness. The truncation was therefore questionable; but even so, it was fit for purpose, because across the four hundred pages of that tribute volume, Hall's Marxism received only a smattering of passing mentions. More recently, in Homi Bhabha's stylized conversation with Hall beyond the grave, the cultural critic describes that same Hall trademark—"without guarantees"—as our consciousness of how "affect registers and regulates the subject's ambivalent and anxious responses as it faces what is new, partially known . . . at the same time it provides the agent with an imminent sense of sensory and bodily attentiveness to the task of change." To this rather nebulous end, Hall is construed by Bhabha as "deftly recast[ing] Antonio Gramsci in the spirit of poststructuralism," transforming the latter's "concept of conjunctural analysis into an active rhetorical practice" in conditions of "multifaceted contingency." Hall is thereby positioned as having little to do with the totalizing "*Marxisant* narrative."[5]

Twenty years earlier, from an unequivocal Marxist standpoint, Colin Sparks handed down a surprisingly similar verdict: that Hall, never having been a Marxist, was always a poststructuralist-in-waiting.[6] Preempting any rejoinder to the effect that during the 1970s Hall's governing concepts were demonstrably influenced not only by Marx himself but also by Louis Althusser, Antonio Gramsci, and other Western Marxists, Sparks ruled that some of those figures, and Althusser above all, were philosophical idealists and social conservatives, not proper materialists and true radicals. More recently, while coming from the same straight-left political camp as Sparks and having in the 1970s registered his own closely worked criticisms of Althusser, Alex Callinicos begged to differ, exempting Hall from the charge of being a non-Marxist discourse theorist.[7]

This volume invites readers to participate in such debates by providing indispensable Hall material about which we can make our own judgements; by organizing the material in a particular way; by offering an overall conception of Hall's distinctive intellectual persona; and by providing further textual and contextual commentary and discussion.

Structure of the Volume

The first part of the book is the longest, providing four core papers from the decade in which Hall's relationship to Marxism was at its closest. One indication of this is the level of sheer detail in his engagement with the works of Marx and Engels. Chapters 1–3 are very much *studies* in their thought, on the thoroughgoing basis of which Hall subsequently—as in chapter 4—synthesized in a more strategic way. Determined fully to plumb the depths of the "classic" Marxist statements and wholly absorbed by the surrounding disputation, Hall's coverage is extensive: the early as well as the mature Marx texts; the philosophical and the economic; the letters as well as the treatises; the contrasting modes of the political writings (interventionist here, observational there). Hall's first aim here is to get to grips, soundly, with the totality of Marx's thought. Notwithstanding their considerable thematic overlap and some commonality of reference, in these essays Hall makes canny, specialist use of different canonical works, and different slices of the same works, to illuminate each problem under examination. In all this, naturally, Hall has his own take on Marx, the works under examination, and the key issues. But it is not as though his preferred interests—the relative autonomy and constitutive role of the superstructures (ideology, culture, politics)—are independently projected on to, or pulled out of, his encounter with Marx and others. Expressed so consistently in that terminology, they could not be. Rather, Hall sees his concerns as intimately woven into the layered, checkered bulk of Marx's oeuvre and legacy.

A second observation seems almost too obvious to press, except that it is not quite the same as the previous point and is seldom stated plainly: that these writings exhibit a clear intent on Hall's part to *defend* Marx, to embody commitment to his ideas. Undoubtedly, Hall was a critical, revisionist Marxist. In these pieces it is the "best Marx," not every bit of Marx, that Hall is after, and this was a shared motivation at the Centre for Contemporary Cultural Studies, University of Birmingham, of which Hall was director throughout the 1970s. Thus, *The Communist Manifesto*, despite its rhetorical brilliance and provocative intent, was ultimately regarded as too crudely teleological to make the cut. Yet the extent to which Hall constructively elucidates Marx, goes along with Marx's stated intentions, brings out his depth of insight, and refuses to indulge in easy putdowns is notable. More will be said about these writings in my later discussion, especially concerning the quasi-foundational status of Hall's reading of Marx's 1857 "Introduction" to the *Grundrisse*.

Meanwhile, the very title of chapter 1 signals something central to Hall's conception of method that has perhaps gone under-remarked and gives this first part its heading: his approach to questions of theory by way of detailed close readings. This inclination reflects something of the "practical criticism" of English literature in which Hall first trained, where the discourse develops— at least at first—in elucidatory-interpretative rather than propositional mode. Hall has described this methodological "imperative" or "idiom" as it developed in Raymond Williams's work in the 1960s—which was formative for Hall—as "the preference for text over general argument . . . the privileging of 'complexity of response' over position."[8] Though always more analytically inclined than Williams, Hall retained from the older thinker that strong sense of the need for attention to detail, text, and timbre. As Hall practices it, the close-up method also incorporates something of the collective spirit of the many radically minded and educationally driven "reading groups" of the late 1960s and 1970s, aiming to share basic understandings of a particular author-text in pursuit of a common interpretation or "line" that would have wider interventionist ramifications. In relation to both author-text and fellow inquirers, then, Hall wants us to "think with" as part of thinking better, and that is how he proceeds with Marx.

Part II showcases three thematic overviews of demarcated problem areas. Although it is hard to see the part I pieces as anything other than concentrated theoretical scholarship, Stuart Hall did not regard himself primarily as a theorist in any system-building sense. Rather, his characteristic mode, incorporating his practice of "reading," was the critical interpretive survey of standpoints within a politically relevant field. Yet the overview genre as Hall and his coauthors developed it was certainly theoretically driven and conceptually creative—it was not just a matter either of political contestation or applying to urgent social matters theories developed elsewhere. There are many outstanding reviews of this sort distributed across Hall's work. In the first volume of *Essential Essays*, for example, Hall's defining discussions of cultural studies (e.g., "Cultural Studies: Two Paradigms"); his journey through the sociology of knowledge in search of "ideology" ("The Hinterland of Science"); and his critique of communications studies ("Culture, The Media, and the 'Ideological Effect'") are eminent cases in point, all closely aligned with our own selections.[9] It is necessary to add that Hall's overviewing talent is also evident in later writings on race and difference, in which the presence of specifically Marxist concepts is hard to discern—for example, in "The Multicultural Question" of 2000, which appears in the second volume of *Essential Essays*.[10]

Two of the part II selections come from collective works that are often taken to be quintessential Hall—and quintessential "Birmingham school." One is from *Resistance through Rituals: Youth Subcultures in Post-war Britain*, the other from *Policing the Crisis: Mugging, the State, and Law and Order*.[11] These works are designed to illuminate specific sociological realities and to facilitate political change. Accordingly, their conjunctural positioning is crucial. At the same time, many of their pages were preoccupied with developing the right (chiefly Gramscian) Marxist or neo-Marxist theoretical framework, and they have been edited with that in mind.

The third (also abridged) item in this part, "Variants of Liberalism," is one of Hall's lesser-known excursions, deriving from a set book for the Open University (OU) course "Beliefs and Ideologies." Hall's writing in thematic-overview vein stocked a remarkable stream of OU teaching materials, some conventionally published as thematic compilations, others produced in-house and sent directly to the large numbers of students. Hall composed hundreds of thousands of words (plus a great many broadcasts and audio guides) during his time as the principal figure within such large-scale collective OU productions as the "Social Sciences Foundation Course," "Crime and Society," "State and Society," "Popular Culture," "Understanding Modern Societies," and several others. Altogether, Hall's work for that nontraditional university represents a truly unique contribution to cultural politics.

His forays into political discourse, and about political discourse, were numerous, and by their nature were short. They were often fed, however, by longer investigations such as his consideration of the multisided political tradition of liberalism. This selection is interesting for us in two main ways. It shows Hall holding on—sometimes at a pinch—to historical materialist analysis in order coherently to place the emergence, heyday, and signal ideological expressions of the defining political tradition of Western modernity.

The essay also lays the groundwork for Hall's excoriating contribution of 2011, "The Neo-liberal Revolution."[12] Fans of the latter are many, some seeing it as a return to uncompromising Left analysis on Hall's part; but they may not be aware of its connection to the earlier study.

The chapters in part III represent different sorts of points of departure regarding Marxism, theory, and politics. Chapter 8 is an appreciative review of the Greek Marxist Nicos Poulantzas's final book. Poulantzas worked in Paris and very much in the structuralist-Althusserian mode, albeit with considerable drive of his own. He committed suicide in 1979, aged forty-three. Hall's significant reservations about his theory of class, as detailed in our chapter 3, are by no means erased in this review of Poulantzas's foreboding last work, *State, Power, Socialism*, but they are not foregrounded because Hall is equally concerned to reach out to a kindred spirit: someone who continually felt the pull of systematic Marxism, but who was lately beginning to lever away from it in ways that could not be completely rationalized. Hall is especially perceptive on the tensions that emerge when the ideas of Michel Foucault on the saturating microeffects of "power-knowledge" are brought into contact with Marxist perspectives (whether traditional or structuralist) on class interests and the coercive role of the state. Those comments of Hall's are doubly interesting for us, because while he incisively identifies sources of inconsistency in Poulantzas, these increasingly had to be grappled with in his own thinking in the years ahead, as he sought to incorporate aspects of Foucault that his 1970s work held at a distance. In that regard, Hall's phrasing, in this piece, of the problems facing the Marxist theorization of power as constituting an intractable "knot" is telling.

The debates with E. P. Thompson and with Bob Jessop, Kevin Bonnett, Simon Bromley, and Tom Ling in chapters 9 and 10 were highly charged and were received at the time as politically consequential. Never comfortable with personal polemic or high-handed dismissal, Hall typically sought out some basis for commonality, even at times of strenuous disagreement. However, this residual quality of Hall's was sorely tested in both these exchanges.

The first originated in the History Workshop conference of 1979. The circumstances of its delivery were in themselves dramatic. The occasion was a discussion of Thompson's polemical *The Poverty of Theory*, which had recently been published.[13] The venue was a church in Oxford, where the electrical power had failed, replaced only by dim candlelight. The church was packed out, and the atmosphere crackled. Not only had Thompson, in Hall's view, unjustly caricatured Althusser's contribution to Marxism, Thompson had, at the conference, gratuitously taken to task Richard Johnson, Hall's Birmingham colleague, for seeking out a constructive middle ground between theorists and historians, between conceptual and substantive work. Though himself suspicious of stand-alone exercises in abstraction, Hall reacted to Thompson unambiguously, by opposing to the "poverty of theory" thesis the case for its vital necessity in giving depth and shape to the empirical surfaces of history and society. This brief exchange, we should note, is freighted throughout with the sense that a longer-term process of reckoning had come to a head. Thompson's substantive studies and formidable critical powers had long been admired by Hall, which he routinely deployed in teaching, along with the work of the much less combative Raymond Williams, as touchstones for the central issues defining the cultural studies field. But now, after nearly a decade in which Hall's own Marxism and (explicitly qualified) commitment to "theory" had been serially developed, Thompson's stress on the primacy of "experience" had to be challenged.

Williams makes no appearance in chapter 9, but that unwitting founder of "cultural studies" looms large on the horizon. Hall often drew attention to the irony of Thompson defending the richness of "experience" against the political blight of flinty abstraction, given that Thompson himself had previously lambasted what he saw as Williams's romanticized exaggeration, in *The Long Revolution*, of the intrinsic value of "lived experience" and "whole ways of life."[14] Although loyal to Williams in many ways, Hall agreed with the substance of Thompson's evaluation, as neatly summarized in a piece written, coincidentally, at the very time of his standoff with the great historian. Hall felt that even when Williams, like himself, turned more explicitly to Gramscian Marxism in the early 1970s—to the extent, we should note, of each writing keynote essays on "base and superstructure," having similar purposes and arguments—"concrete experience" and "structure of feeling" remained too central to Williams's problematic for Hall's liking. Evocative and essential though they may be in terms of humanistic appreciation, these fulsome notions struck Hall as too vague—"uninspected" and "unsatisfactory"—for purposes of conceptual analysis, with "the question of determination" in particular being "the theoretical thorn" in Williams's side. Thereafter, Hall could not bring himself to disagree with those who categorized Williams ultimately—though the disparagement bothered him—as a "culturalist."[15]

A few years later, a variant of the charge of "culturalism" was laid against Hall himself, in a stinging critique in *New Left Review* by Bob Jessop and colleagues of Hall's alleged "ideologism" in his analysis of Thatcherism.

Ideologism, for Jessop and others, meant exaggerating the strength of commitment—whether on the part of elites or in popular "common sense"—to Thatcher's "regressive modernization" worldview, and correspondingly underemphasizing endemic socioeconomic contradictions. In his vigorous rejoinder—our chapter 10—Hall insists that he was not discounting such structural factors; rather, he was underlining the fact that the Left was still insufficiently attuned to the way political projects seek hegemony through ideological—imagined, moral—imperatives and identities, even if that hegemony turns out to be partial and contested. It was the tone of the attack as much as its content that struck Hall as inappropriate, not least since Jessop's perspectives on the state, on structuralist Marxism, and on Marx's "method of articulation" were close to Hall's own.[16] With some magnanimity given the provocation, Hall allowed that his delineation of "authoritarian populism" might have been more precise. What he was offering, we might again say, was a certain way of reading Thatcherism, seeking illumination rather than comprehensive validity.

The remaining texts push further into this growing mood of possible departure from Marxism, though in notably different ways. Chapter 11—"When Was 'the Post-colonial'? Thinking at the Limit"—is by any reckoning a significant discussion, deserving its place in any selection seeking to exemplify both Hall's range and his best. It goes untampered with here for that reason and also because its implications for Marxism are indirect, being strewn across both topic and treatment. It registers the definite tensions that arise—manifestly there in Hall too—when historical-materialist discourses on modernity, capitalism, and imperialism become interwoven with postcolonial purposes and concepts. Relatedly, Hall's incremental interest in Jacques Derrida's ideas reaches a peak in this essay, the effects of which are interestingly debatable.

The final chapter is an extract from one of the Open University books comprising the bumper "Culture, Media and Identities" course of 1997. In keeping with the latter's decisive platforming statement concerning the growing substantive and epistemological centrality of culture, Hall's "Notes on the Cultural Revolutions of Our Time" take him to the threshold where—perhaps contrary to the circumscribed relative autonomy accorded to ideologies and subjectivity throughout his previous work—"culture" finally strikes out to achieve not only political and investigative centrality but also a more comprehensive theoretical primacy. I return to this issue of incipient "culturalism" in the relevant discussion.

What Kind of Marxism?

Alignment with Marxism comes in many varieties and palpably changes over time, including our own. As an ideal type, or maximum program, we might think of Marxism as containing the following elements:

- a philosophical anthropology, in which the activity and creativity of *labor* define humanity's "species being" in its practical encounter with nature;
- a conception/methodology of history, outlining the course of social development from so-called primitive communism at one end to (anticipated) advanced communism at the other, with a handful of epochal stages in between characterized by different types of labor exploitation and class division (modes of production);
- a dialectical materialist philosophy, or scientific epistemology, capable of orientating all major questions of human understanding;
- an account of the structural logic of capitalism, being the current and most crucial mode of production, based on the formally free sale of workers' capacity to labor to owners of capital, the dynamic contradictions of which form the material and social preconditions for socialism;
- a socioeconomic sociology highlighting—for any epoch, but especially the capitalist one—the centrality of *class* positions, relationships, and experiences;
- a revolutionary politics based on (working-)class struggle, without which the transition to socialism cannot be realized;
- an analysis, working from those tenets, of the nature and function of institutional and informal social spheres such as politics and the state, culture and ideology, consciousness and belief systems.

Heuristically useful, the need for such a comprehensive package has always been contested among Marxists themselves, as has the nature and scope of each presumed component element. Crucial questions arise at all levels. For example, does the analysis of capitalism and class today require strict adherence to the labor theory of value? Must Marxist historians conform to the idea of a given sequence of modes of production when seeking to explain the dynamics of their chosen period and focus? Does Marxism really require a distinctive, superior form of epistemology? And so on. In any case, the very content of Marxist thinking has always been thoroughly overdetermined by strategic geopolitical factors: the dominance, first, of German gradualist social democracy in the later nineteenth century; through the phases of Leninist and Stalinist consolidations of authoritarian Marxist "orthodoxy" (with Trotskyist and libertarian alternatives consistently in opposition); and on again to the markedly more pluralistic, predominantly academic Western Marxism of the later 1960s and beyond. In turn, these currents came to be significantly challenged by feminist, postcolonial, and environmentalist perspectives and priorities.

According to Göran Therborn's convenient terminology, the situation today is that the original hallmark "triangle" of Marxist understanding—philosophical-historical theorizing; the structural analysis of capitalism; revolutionary class politics—now lies damaged and perhaps even irretrievably broken, though "resilient" Marxists still strive to hold it all together.[17] At the least, each of the component sides of that triangle seems to require considerable stretching and bending to hold up. Ironically perhaps, this uncertain predicament of Marxism has fed a revival of interest in, and respect for, the person of Karl Marx himself. Following the global financial crash of 2008, commentators of all stripes rediscovered the incisiveness and wit with which Marx pilloried capitalism's fundamental irrationality and spiraling inequalities. In parallel, within networks like cultural studies, the residual sense of embarrassment through the 1990s regarding its own previous Marxist proclivities gave way, toward and beyond the millennium, to a definite awkwardness about *that*. Yet if Marx has returned to the seminar rooms, to activist vocabularies, and even to the arts—during 2017 the "Young Marx" was in the movies and on the London theater stage—his rehabilitation has been limited. Indicatively, Gareth Stedman Jones's heavyweight intellectual biography of 2016, *Karl Marx*, was even-handedly subtitled "greatness and illusion," yet the emphasis was firmly on the second of those terms.[18]

Stuart Hall developed a highly qualified approach to Marxism, and he is often considered, reasonably enough, to be a "neo-Marxist." But the brunt of my sketch of the Marxist problematic is that neo-Marxisms are intrinsic to the history and health of Marxism, not something external, far less necessarily hostile. Moreover, Hall's work and example have done more than anyone's to justify such an inclusive, self-critical remit as a valid expression of contemporary Marxism.[19]

One interpretative difficulty in locating Hall in relationship to Marxism concerns his own (ever-growing) canonicity and aura within cultural theory and politics. This led, from the mid-1980s on, to Hall giving a stronger impression of distance and equivocation than may be warranted—certainly if we have the 1970s texts in front of us (such as our part I). To take a single example: There is no doubt that Hall found Althusser's prioritizing of philosophical thought within Marxism excessive. This was recast later by Hall himself, and picked up by others accordingly, in overly gladiatorial terms, as a "warring to the death," with Hall taking his stand, refusing to be beaten down, and going not one inch further.[20] What is occluded by this dramatization is, first, that very many Marxist academics—philosophers, historians, sociologists, political theorists—were also routinely both critiquing residual Marxist reductionism and wrestling hard with the theorists of Western Marxism, not least Althusser. Second, the depiction plays down how crucial—if never wholesale—Althusser's influence on Hall was. Many of the phrasings that within cultural studies came to be associated almost exclusively with Hall himself, peppering so many of his writings and interviews, were taken directly from Althusser: articulation, problematic, the specific effectivity of the superstructures, the "matrix" conception of mode of production, "both ends of the chain," determination and relative autonomy, theory as a (necessary) "detour," "bending the stick" to achieve due balance, avoiding at all costs the traps of "essentialism" and any philosophy of "guarantees." As Hall put it in *Cultural Studies 1983*, Althusser's injection of structural complexity into Marxism was a "genuine moment of transformation," such that cultural studies thereafter could not be contemplated outside the effects of that contribution.[21]

By the later 1980s, Hall's relationship with Marxism had become not just complex but agonistic. In the discussion section of his contribution to the landmark conference (and later megavolume) *Marxism and the Interpretation of Culture*, Hall stated: "I no longer believe in the Marxist notion of connections being 'given' in the origins of the social formation."[22] Yet this is curious, because Hall never *did* believe in that, and we may doubt whether many "dogmatic" Marxists themselves ever did. Related slippages occur when Hall runs "classical" Marxism alongside other terms designating the brands of Marxism he is dissociating himself from—vulgar, mechanical, traditional, orthodox, reductionist, and so on. This is problematical because several chapters in the present volume witness Hall arguing that neither Marx's classic works, nor key contemporary Marxist authors, *are* seriously reductionist. During the conference discussion, Hall aired the thought that Marxism's "whole classical edifice begins to rock" as soon as we "abandon that teleological structure" whereby "the economy" is always assumed to determine everything, at least when Saint Peter arrives and the last trumpet sounds. However, by this time not only were there relatively few devotionally religious Marxists left, but Hall's own work had emphatically shown that it is erroneous to describe the primacy in Marxism of the mode of production as the direct causal effect of "the economy" as such. Despite drifting into overstatement in this way, however, Hall did not go on to conclude that it was time to leave Marxism behind. On the contrary, he ended the paper by depicting himself as engaged in "unfashionable salvage work," retaining from Marx the "notion of classes," "the capital/labour contradiction," "the social relations of production, *etc.*"[23] That is a lot to recover. So when Hall says occasionally that he was only ever within "shouting distance" of Marxism; that Marxism was more of a problem for cultural studies than a central theory or problematic; that reductionism is "intrinsic to sophisticated and vulgar Marxism alike," we need to tread carefully.[24]

What Style of Intellectual Mediation?

Such oscillations in outlook and phrasing can best be resolved, in my view, by thinking about Hall's Marxism in relation to the type of intellectual that he exemplified. This goes beyond accounting for his success in terms of his uniquely winning personality, tempting though that is. One natural move would be to portray Hall as a Gramscian in every respect, not least because what he says about Gramsci could surely be said of Hall himself:

> He understood that the general framework of Marxist theory had to be constantly developed theoretically; applied to new historical conditions; related to developments in society which Marx and Engels could not possibly have foreseen; expanded and refined by the addition of new concepts. . . . Not that he *ever* forgot or neglected the critical element of the economic foundations of society and its relations. But he contributed little by way of original formulations to *that* level of analysis. However, in the much-neglected areas of conjunctural analysis, politics, ideology and the state . . . [he] has an enormous amount to contribute.[25]

Yet this commonality between Gramsci and Hall is more about the high degree of substantive theoretical affinity between the two thinkers than with the kind of intellectual *modality* that I am trying to bring out here.

Placing Hall within Gramsci's own theory of intellectuals is another possibility. Gramsci distinguished between "traditional" and "organic" intellectuals, the former encompassing professions that carried over essentially premodern roles and class configurations into capitalist modernity. By contrast, the organics are projected as the leading layers of the new industrial working class, or at any rate are closely connected to the "fundamental social groups" of the present day (Gramsci was talking of course about the 1920s). However, from where we sit now, Gramsci's categories seem too anachronistic, too class-specific, and too intimately bound up with his abiding concern for the role of the "Modern Prince," a.k.a. the Communist Party, to apply to Hall. In his paper "Theoretical Legacies," Hall does invoke Gramsci's concepts to convey the way that the Birmingham CCCS understood its academic endeavors as political. But his conclusion that "we were organic intellectuals without any organic point of reference" implicitly concedes that the category did not really fit.[26]

At this point, we can turn to Jean-Paul Sartre for useful prompts. Sartre makes relatively few appearances in Hall's written work, but they are all positive, as they were in his graduate cultural theory course at Birmingham—Sartre's *Search for a Method* (alternatively translated as *The Problem of Method*) being one of the key readings for that module. For example, in the first issue of *Working Papers in Cultural Studies*, Hall "quarrelled" with what he saw as the phenomenological subjectivism of a fellow contributor, citing Sartre's formulations in *Search for a Method*.[27] Let me be clear: I am not suggesting that Hall is a "Sartrean." Rather, Sartre's account of the predicament and pluralism of Marxism in that short book serves to illuminate defining aspects of Hall's mode and practice as a political intellectual. For Sartre, Marxism was "the one philosophy of our time which we cannot go beyond": only Marxism, with its unrivaled comprehensiveness and totalizing sequence of investigation—think back to those bullet points on Marxism listed above—enables us to situate all manner of cultural phenomena and human aspirations in historical-materialist terms. Sartre called this explanatory armory the "regressive" part of a two-step methodological process, regressive only in the sense of retrospectively accounting for how things come to be as they are, historically speaking, and what the range of class positions and interests is at any given time.[28]

But Sartre also warned that "lazy Marxism" stands as a constant danger, treating as "concrete truths" what should be "regulative ideas."[29] Correspondingly, good Marxists will understand that the work of totalization is never complete, only "perpetually in process." In order to grasp the totality, at any given time, in its full complexity, Sartre goes on, more "mediations" are required than simplistic formulas can ever cope with. And the mediations of Marxism which most exercised him were existentialism, psychoanalysis, sexuality, and microsociology. He regarded these as enclaves operating *within* the orbit of Marxism, but somehow simultaneously both "engendering" and "rejecting" it.[30] Of course, Sartre was probably even more controversial a Marxist than Hall, and to repeat, I am not drawing a parallel between them in any substantive or political sense. But like Sartre, Hall was vitally concerned with problematical enclaves that both mediated and disturbed an overarching Marxist perspective. He too would have flagged up sexuality/psychoanalysis as one such zone of engagement, but he had other concerns too—race and ethnicity, feminism, postcolonialism, and cultural studies itself.

Sartre identifies a second, "progressive" form of social and political understanding: appreciation of the richness and singularity of "projects." I take him to be referring here to action-orientated phenomena such as social movements, local popular initiatives, subcultural contestations, organization building, campaigns and protests, inventive artistic or philosophical currents. Being future- and possibility-oriented, projects cannot be grasped only in causal-explanatory Marxist terms. Rather, they require an acceptance of historical contingency and identification with what Sartre calls "the profundity of the lived."[31] Again, this insightfully encapsulates Hall's habitual interest in cultural specifics, in the grounding of theory in the politics of people's creativity and adaptability as they make their way in the world, nothing of which renders any less important the constraints set by socioeconomic conditions. In the Sartrean sketch, dialectical mediators are those who make sense of both universals and particulars; who develop a varied trail of connections and dislocations, "from the broadest determinations to the most precise." The relative autonomy—Sartre uses that term too—of cultures, movements, and politics means having the "power of mediation" vis-à-vis larger structural forces, and *new* mediations can be expected to arise at every juncture.[32] Hall, I want to suggest, can best be appreciated as a peerless dialectical mediator of that kind. He mediated *within* Marxism—structuralism/culturalism; economism/ideologism; class/nonclass social forces—and he mediated *between* Marxism and various non- and post-Marxist discourses and movements. For all his reservations, Hall embraced Marxism; and arguably he needed it, too, because without the anchorage that Marxism provided—a committed baseline from which to branch out—the risk was that Hall's theoretical and political mediations might become too thinly pluralistic.

NOTES

1 "General Introduction," in Stuart Hall, *Essential Essays*, vol. 1, *Foundations of Cultural Studies*, ed. David Morley (Durham, NC: Duke University Press, 2019), 4.
2 "Editors' Introduction," in Stuart Hall, *Cultural Studies 1983: A Theoretical History*, ed. Jennifer Daryl Slack and Lawrence Grossberg (Durham, NC: Duke University Press, 2016), ix.
3 "Introduction," in Stuart Hall, *Selected Political Writings*, ed. Sally Davison, David Featherstone, Michael Rustin, and Bill Schwarz (Durham, NC: Duke University Press, 2017), 5.
4 Paul Gilroy, Lawrence Grossberg, and Angela McRobbie, eds., *Without Guarantees: In Honour of Stuart Hall* (London: Verso, 2000).
5 Homi K. Bhabha, "'The Beginning of Their Real Enunciation': Stuart Hall and the Work of Culture," *Critical Inquiry* 42, no. 1 (2015): 1–30, 1–3, 6–8.
6 Colin Sparks, "Stuart Hall, Cultural Studies and Marxism," in *Stuart Hall: Critical Dialogues in Cultural Studies*, ed. David Morley and Kuan-Hsing Chen (London: Routledge, 1996), 71–101.
7 Alex Callinicos, "Stuart Hall in Perspective," *International Socialism: A Quarterly Review of Socialist Theory*, no. 142 (2014); and Alex Callinicos, *Althusser's Marxism* (London: Pluto Press, 1976).
8 Stuart Hall, "The Williams Interviews," *Screen Education*, no. 34 (1980): 98.
9 Chapters 2, 4, and 10, respectively, of Hall, *Essential Essays*, vol. 1.
10 Chapter 5 of Stuart Hall, *Essential Essays*, vol. 2, *Identity and Diaspora*, ed. David Morley (Durham, NC: Duke University Press, 2019).
11 "Resistance through Rituals: Youth Subcultures in Post-war Britain," *Working Papers in Cultural Studies*, nos. 7–8 (Birmingham: Centre for Contemporary Cultural Studies, University of Birmingham, 1975); Stuart Hall, Chas Critcher, Tony Jefferson, John Clarke, and Brian Roberts, *Policing the Crisis: Mugging, the State, and Law and Order* (London: Macmillan, 1978).
12 Reproduced in Hall, *Selected Political Writings*, chap. 21.
13 E. P. Thompson, *The Poverty of Theory and Other Essays* (London: Merlin, 1978).
14 E. P. Thompson, "The Long Revolution" (in two parts), *New Left Review* I/9 (May–June 1961): 24–33; and I/10 (July–August 1961): 34–39; Raymond Williams, *The Long Revolution* (London: Chatto and Windus, 1961).
15 Hall, "The Williams Interviews," 101, 103. Hall was reflecting on Raymond Williams, *Politics and Letters: Interviews with New Left Review* (London: New Left Books, 1979). See also Raymond Williams, "Base and Superstructure in Marxist Cultural Theory," *New Left Review* I/82 (November–December 1973): 3–16. Perhaps just because of their otherwise close concerns and trajectories, Hall took some time fully to work through those aspects of Williams's "culturalism," and his Marxism, that he accepted, and those from which he took due distance. The most considered version of that assessment is given in *Cultural Studies 1983*. Into the 1990s, Hall noted further "difficulties" with Williams's affirmation of "whole ways of life" as the basis of social belonging. This time, Hall's worry was about

its conservative, and perhaps even ethno-nationalist implications for questions of cultural identity, diversity, and selfhood. See Hall, "Our Mongrel Selves," in his *Selected Political Writings*, 275–82, 280. The paper was originally given as the Raymond Williams Memorial Lecture, 1992.

16 Bob Jessop, *The Capitalist State: Marxist Theories and Methods* (Oxford: Martin Robertson, 1982), 213–20.
17 Göran Therborn, *From Marxism to Post-Marxism?* (London: Verso, 2008), 116–20.
18 Gareth Stedman Jones, *Karl Marx: Greatness and Illusion* (London: Allen Lane, 2016).
19 By "neo-Marxist" I do not mean anything as vague as "vaguely Marxist." Some of the standard dictionary connotations of *neo-* are more precise and appropriate, even as they chafe against one another: new, contemporary, revised, extended, adapted, modified, revived.
20 Hall, "Cultural Studies and Its Theoretical Legacies," in *Essential Essays*, 1:75–76.
21 Hall, *Cultural Studies 1983*, 114.
22 Stuart Hall, "The Toad in the Garden: Thatcherism among the Theorists," in *Marxism and the Interpretation of Culture*, ed. Cary Nelson and Lawrence Grossberg (Houndmills, UK: Macmillan, 1988), 60.
23 Hall, "The Toad in the Garden," 72–73.
24 Hall, "Cultural Studies and Its Theoretical Legacies," 74–75.
25 Stuart Hall, "Gramsci's Relevance for the Study of Race and Ethnicity," in *Essential Essays*, 2:22, 25–26.
26 Hall, "Cultural Studies and Its Theoretical Legacies," 77. For Gramsci's notion of the intellectuals, see *Selections from the Prison Notebooks*, ed. and trans. Quintin Hoare and Geoffrey Nowell Smith (London: Lawrence and Wishart, 1971), 4–14.
27 Stuart Hall, "A Response to People and Culture," *Working Papers in Cultural Studies* 1 (1971): 97–102.
28 Jean-Paul Sartre, *Search for a Method* (New York: Vintage Books, 1968), xxxiv. Part III of *Search* is devoted to "The Progressive-Regressive Method."
29 Sartre, *Search for a Method*, 35, 53.
30 Sartre's idea of mediations is set out in part II of *Search for a Method*, "The Problem of Mediations and Auxiliary Disciplines."
31 Sartre, *Search for a Method*, 145.
32 Sartre, *Search for a Method*, 49, 66.

PART I | THEORETICAL READINGS

CHAPTER 1

Marx's Notes on Method:
A "Reading" of the "1857 Introduction"

PREFATORY NOTE: *This is a shortened version of a paper on Marx's 1857 "Introduction" presented and discussed in a series of seminars at the Centre for Contemporary Cultural Studies. It has been somewhat revised in the light of those discussions, though I have not been able to take account of some further, more substantive criticisms generously offered by John Mepham, among others. The 1857 "Introduction" is Marx's most substantial text on "method," though even here many of his formulations remain extremely condensed and provisional. Since the "Introduction" presents such enormous problems of interpretation, I have largely confined myself to a "reading" of the text. The positions taken by Marx in the "Introduction" run counter to many received ideas as to his "method." Properly grasped and imaginatively applied—as they were in the larger corpus of the* Grundrisse *to which they constantly refer—they seem to me to offer quite striking, original and seminal points of departure for the "problems of method" which beset our field of study, though I have not been able to establish this connection within the limits of the paper. I see the paper, however, as contributing to this on-going work of theoretical and methodological clarification, rather than as simply a piece of textual explication. I hope this conjuncture will not be lost in the detail of the exposition.*

The 1857 "Introduction" is one of the most pivotal of Marx's texts.[1] It is also one of his most difficult, compressed and "illegible." In his excellent Foreword to the *Grundrisse*, Nicolaus warns that Marx's Notebooks are hazardous to quote, "since the context, the grammar and the very vocabulary raise doubts as to what Marx 'really' meant in a given passage."

Pierre Vilar observes that the 1857 "Introduction" is one of those texts "from which everyone takes whatever suits him."[2] With the growing interest in Marx's method and epistemology, the "Introduction" occupies an increasingly central position in the study of Marx's work. I share this sense of its significance, while differing often from how many of Marx's explicators have read its meaning. My aim, then, is to inaugurate a "reading" of this 1857 text. It is, of course, *not* a reading *tabula rasa*, not a reading "without presuppositions." It reflects my own problematic, inevitably. I hope it also throws some undistorted light on Marx's.

In a famous letter of 14 January 1858, Marx wrote to Engels:

> I am getting some nice developments. For instance, I have thrown over the whole doctrine of profit as it has existed up to now. In the *method* of treatment the fact that, by mere accident, I have glanced through Hegel's *Logic* has been of great service to me—Freiligrath found some volumes of Hegel which originally belonged to Bakunin and sent them to me as a present. If there should ever be use for such work again, I should greatly like to make accessible to the ordinary human intelligence in two or three printer's sheets, what is rational in the method which Hegel discovered but at the same time enveloped in mysticism.[3]

It was not the only time Marx expressed that hope. In 1843, Marx made notes for a substantial critique of Hegel's *Philosophy of Right*. The "Critique of the Hegelian Dialectic and Philosophy as a Whole," usually printed together with the other *1844 Manuscripts*, also aimed at an exposition and critique of Hegel's dialectic, now in relation to the *Phenomenology* and the *Logic*, though, in the final event, largely confined to the former. As late as 1876, he wrote to Joseph Dietzgen:

> When I have shaken off the burden of my economic labours, I shall write a dialectic. The correct laws of the dialectic are already included in Hegel, albeit in a mystical form. It is necessary to strip it of this form.[4]

These hopes were not to be fulfilled, the burden of the economics never laid aside. Thus, we do not have, from the mature Marx, either the systematic delineation of the "rational kernel," nor the method of its transformation, nor an exposition of the results of that transformation: the Marxian dialectic. The 1857 "Introduction," and the compressed 1859 "Preface" to the *Contribution to the Critique of Political Economy*, together with other scattered asides, have therefore to do duty for the unfulfilled parts of Marx's project. The 1857 "Introduction" in particular represents his fullest methodological and theoretical summary text. Decisive, however, as this text is, we must not handle it as if it were something other than it is. It was written as an "Introduction to the Notebooks," themselves enormously comprehensive in scope, digressive and complex in structure; and quite unfinished—"rough drafts." Roman Rosdolsky remarked that the *Grundrisse* "introduces us, so to speak, into Marx's economic laboratory and lays bare all the refinements, all the bypaths of his methodology." The "Introduction" was thus conceived as a résumé and guide, to "problems of method" concretely and more expansively applied in the Notebooks themselves. It was not, therefore, intended to stand wholly in its own right. Moreover, the tentative character of the text was signified by Marx's decision in the end *not* to publish it. The "Introduction" was replaced by the terser "Preface": and some of the central propositions of the "Introduction" are modified, or at least suspended, in the later "Preface." An immediate contrast of the "Introduction" with the "Preface" (where a classical conciseness is everywhere in play, quite different from the linguistic playfulness and conceit of the "Introduction") reminds us that, despite its dense argumentation, the 1857 "Introduction" remains, even with respect to Marx's method, provisional.

In the "Introduction," Marx proceeds via a critique of the ideological presupposition of political economy. The first section deals with production. The object of the inquiry is "material production." Smith and Ricardo begin with "the individual and isolated hunter or fisherman." Marx, however, begins with "socially determinate" individuals, and hence "socially determined individual production." Eighteenth-century theorists, up to and including Rousseau, find a general point of departure "the individual" producer. Smith and Ricardo found their theories upon this ideological projection. Yet "the individual" cannot be the point of departure, but only *the result*. Rousseau's "natural man" appears as a stripping away of the contingent complexities of modern life, a rediscovery of the natural, universal human-individual core beneath. Actually, the whole development of "civil society" is subsumed in this aesthetic conceit. It is not until labour has been freed of the dependent forms of feudal society, and subject to the revolutionary development it undergoes under early capitalism, that the modern concept of "the individual" could appear at all. A whole historical and ideological development, then, is already presupposed in—but hidden within—the notion of the Natural Individual and of universal "human nature."

This is an absolutely characteristic movement of thought in the "Introduction." It takes up the "given" points of departure in political economy. It shows by a critique that these are not, in fact, starting points but points of arrival. In them, a whole historical development is already "summed up." In short: what appear as the most concrete, common-sense, simple, constituent starting points for a theory of political economy, turn out, on inspection, to be the sum of many, prior, determinations.

Production outside society is as absurd as language without individuals living and talking together. It takes a gigantic social development to produce "the isolated individual" producer as a concept: only a highly elaborated form of developed social connectedness can appear as—take the "phenomenal form"—men pursuing their egoistic interests as "indifferent," isolated, individuals in a "free" market organised by an "invisible hand." In fact, of course, even this individualism is an "all sided dependence" which appears as mutual indifference:

> The reciprocal and all-sided dependence of individuals who are indifferent to one another forms their social connection. The social bond is expressed in *exchange value*.[5]

This concept—that the capitalist mode of production depends on social connection assuming the "ideological" form of an individual disconnection—is one of the great, substantive themes of the *Grundrisse* as a whole. But its working-out also has consequences for the problems of method. For the displacement of real relations via their ideological representations requires—for its critique, its unmasking—a method which reveals the "essential relations" behind the necessary but mystifying inversions assumed by their "surface forms." This method—which, later, Marx identifies as the core of what is *scientific* in his dialectic—forms the master methodological procedure, not only of the Notebooks, but of *Capital* itself. This "methodological" procedure becomes, in its turn, a theoretical discovery of the utmost importance: in its expanded form (there are several provisional attempts to formulate it in the *Grundrisse*) it constitutes the basis of the pivotal section in *Capital* I, on "The Fetishism of Commodities."[6]

The "Introduction," then, opens with a methodological argument: the critique of "normal" types of logical abstraction. "Political economy" operates as a theory through its categories. How are these categories formed? The normal method is to isolate and analyse a category by abstracting those elements that remain "common" to it through all epochs and all types of social formation. This attempt to identify, by means of the logic of abstraction, which remains the core of a concept stable through history is really a type of "essentialism." Many types of theorising fall prey to it. Hegel, the summit of classical German philosophy, developed a mode of thought that was the very opposite of static: his grasp of movement and of contradiction is what raised his logic above all other types of logical theorising, in Marx's eyes. Yet, because the movement of Hegel's dialectic was cast in an idealist form, his thought also retained the notion of an "essential core" that survived all the motions of mind. It was the perpetuation of this "essential core" within the concept which, Marx believed, constituted the secret guarantee within Hegel's dialectic of the ultimate harmoniousness of existing social relations (e.g., the Prussian state). Classical political economy also speaks of "bourgeois" production and of private property as if these were the "essence" of the concepts, "production" and "property" exhaust their historical content. In this way, political economy too presented the capitalist mode of production, not as a historical structure, but as the natural and inevitable state of things. At *this* level, even classical political economy retained an ideological presupposition at its "scientific" heart: it reduces, by abstraction, specific historical relations to their lowest common, trans-historical essence. Its ideology is inscribed in its method.

On the contrary, Marx argues, there is no "production-in-general": only distinct forms of production, specific to time and conditions. One of those distinct forms is—rather confusingly—"general production": production based on a type of labour, which is not specific to a particular branch of production, but which has been "generalised": "abstract labour." (But we shall come to that in a moment.) Since any mode of production depends upon "determinate conditions," there can be no guarantee that those conditions will always be fulfilled or remain constant or "the same" through time. For example: except in the most common-sense way, there is no scientific form in which the concept, "production," referring to the capitalist mode, and entailing as one of its required conditions, "free labour," can be said to have an "immediate identity" (to be "essentially the same as") production in, say, slave, clan or communal society. (Later, in *Capital*, Marx reminds us that this transformation of feudal bondsmen into "free labour," which is assumed here as a "natural" precondition for capitalism, has, indeed, a specific history: "the history of... expropriation... written in the annals of mankind in letters of blood and fire.")[7] This is one of the key points-of-departure of historical materialism as a method of thought and practice.

Nothing in what Marx subsequently wrote allows us to fall behind it. It is what Karl Korsch called Marx's principle of "historical specification."[8] The "unity" which Marx's method is intended to produce is not *weak* identity achieved by abstracting away everything of any historical specificity until we are left with an essential core, without differentiation or specification.

The "Introduction" thus opens, as Nicolaus remarks, as the provisional, extended answer to an unwritten question: political economy is our starting point, but, however valid are some of its theories, it has not formulated scientifically the laws of the inner structure of the mode of production whose categories it expresses and theoretically reflects. It "sticks," despite everything, inside its "bourgeois skin."[9] This is because, within it, historical relations have "already acquired the stability of natural, self-understood forms of social life."[10] Its categories, then (in contrast with vulgar political economy), "are forms of thought expressing with social validity the conditions and relations of a definite, historically determined mode of production."[11] But it presents these relations as "a self-evident necessity imposed by Nature as productive labour itself." Thus, though classical political economy *has* "discovered what lies beneath these forms," it has not asked certain key questions (such as the origin of commodity-production based in labour-power: "the form under which value becomes exchange-value") which are peculiar to specific historical conditions (the forms and conditions of commodity-production). These "errors" are not incidental. They are already present in its presuppositions, its method, its starting points. But, if political economy is itself to be transcended, *how? Where to begin?*

The answer is, with "production by social individuals," "production at a definite stage of social development." Political economy tends to etherealise, universalise and de-historicise the relations of bourgeois production. But what follows if, as Marx does, we *insist* on starting with a principle of historical specification? Do we then, nevertheless, assume that there is some common, universal practice—"production-in-general"—which has always existed, which has then been subject to an evolutionary historical development which can be steadily traced through: a practice which, therefore, we can reduce to its common-sense content and employ as the obvious, uncontested starting-point for analysis? The answer is, no. Whatever other kind of "historicist" Marx may have been, he was definitively *not* a historical evolutionist. Every child knows, he once remarked, that production cannot cease for a moment. So, there must be something "in common," so to speak, which corresponds to the idea of "production-in-general": all societies must reproduce the conditions of their own existence. This is the type of abstraction, however, which sifts out the lowest common characteristics of a concept and identifies this unproblematic core with its scientific content. It is a mode of theorising that operates at a very low theoretical threshold indeed. It is, at best, a useful time-saver. But, to penetrate a structure as dense and overlaid with false representations as the capitalist mode of production, we need concepts more fundamentally dialectical in character. Concepts that allow us to further refine, segment, split and recombine any general category: which allow us to see those features which permitted it to play a certain role in this *epoch*, other features which were developed under the specific conditions of *that* epoch, distinctions which show why certain relations appear *only* in the most ancient and the most developed forms of society *and in none in between*, etc. Such concepts are theoretically far in advance of those which unite under one chaotic general heading the quite different things which have appeared, at one time or another, under the category, "production-in-general": conceptions which *differentiate* in the very moment that they reveal hidden connections. In much the same way, Marx observes that concepts which differentiate out what makes possible the specific development of different languages are more significant than "abstracting" a few, simple, basic, common "language universals."

We must observe—it is a common strategy throughout the "Introduction"—that Marx establishes his difference here *both* from the method of political economy *and* from Hegel. The "Introduction" is thus, simultaneously, a critique of both. It is useful, in this context, to recall Marx's earlier procedure in the famous chapter "The Metaphysics of Political Economy," in *The Poverty of Philosophy*, where he, again, simultaneously offers a critique of "Hegelianised political economy" via an attack on Proudhon. The terms of this critique of Proudhon are particularly germane to this argument against "abstraction," for they remind us that something more than a methodological quibble is involved, namely the exaltation of mental operations over the content of real, contingent historical relations; it was not surprising that

> if you let drop little by little all that constitutes the individuality of a house, leaving out first of all the materials of which it was composed, then the form that distinguishes it, you end up with nothing but a body; that if you leave out of account the limits of this body, you soon have nothing but a space—that if, finally, you leave out of account the dimensions of this space, there is absolutely nothing left but pure quantity, the logical

category. If we abstract thus from every subject all the alleged accidents, animate or inanimate, men or things, we are right in saying that in the final abstraction, the only substance left is the logical categories. . . . If all that exists, all that lives on land and under water can be reduced by abstraction to a logical category—if the whole real world can be drowned thus in a world of abstractions, in the world of logical categories—who need be astonished at it?

Apply this method to the categories of political economy, Marx argues:

and you have the logic and metaphysics of political economy . . . the categories that everybody knows, translated into a little-known language which makes them look as if they had newly blossomed forth in an intellect of pure reason. . . . Up to now we have expounded only the dialectics of Hegel. We shall see later how M. Proudhon has succeeded in reducing it to the meanest proportions. Thus for Hegel, all that has happened and is still happening is only just what is happening in his own mind. . . . There is no longer a "history according to the order in time," there is only the "sequence of ideas in the understanding."[12]

Marx had long ago noted[13] Hegel's "outstanding achievement": his recognition that the different categories of the world—"private right, morality, the family, civil society, the state, *etc*."—had "no validity in isolation," but "dissolve and engender one another. They have become 'moments' of the movement." However, as we know, Marx radically criticised Hegel for conceiving this "mobile nature" of the categories as a form of "self-genesis": Hegel "conceives them only in their thought form." Thus "the whole movement . . . ends in absolute knowledge."[14] In Hegel, the constitution of the real world becomes "merely the appearance, the cloak, the exoteric form" of movement and contradiction, which, in the speculative conception, never really deserts the ground of thought. "The whole history of alienation and of the retraction of alienation is therefore only the history of the production of abstract thought, i.e., of absolute, logical, speculative thought." This was certainly not the simple, trans-historical, external connections established by vulgar forms of political economy, but an equally unacceptable alternative: the ultimate identity of Mind with itself "only in . . . thought form." Marx added, "This means that what Hegel does is to put in place of these fixed abstractions the act of abstraction which revolves in its own circle." He put the same point even more clearly in *The Holy Family*:

> The *Phenomenology* ... ends by putting in place of all human existence "absolute knowledge." ... Instead of treating self-consciousness as the self-consciousness of real men, living in a real objective world and conditioned by it, Hegel transforms men into an attribute of self-consciousness. He turns the world upside down.

And in *The Poverty of Philosophy*:

> He thinks he is constructing the world by the movement of thought, whereas he is merely reconstructing systematically and classifying by the absolute method the thoughts which are in the minds of all.

The core of these earlier critiques is retained by Marx here in the 1857 "Introduction." Hegel *did* understand "production," he did understand "labour": but ultimately, it was what Marx called, "labour of the mind, labour of thinking and knowing."[15] However dialectical its movement, the historical production of the world remains, for Hegel, "moments" of the realisation of the Idea, the "external appearances" of thought—stations of the cross in the path of Mind towards Absolute Knowledge. The method which Marx proposes in the "Introduction" is not of this kind: it is not merely a mental operation. It is to be discovered in real, concrete relations: it is a method which groups, not a simple "essence" behind the different historical forms, but precisely the many determinations in which "essential differences" are preserved.

Marx ends this argument with an illustration. Economists like Mill start from bourgeois relations of production and extrapolate them as "inviolable natural laws." All production, they assert, despite historic differences, can be subsumed under universal laws. Two such "laws" are (a) production requires private property, (b) production requires the protection of property by the courts and police. Actually, Marx argues, private property is neither the only nor the earliest form of property: historically, it is predated by communal property. And the presence of modern, bourgeois legal relations and the police, far from indexing the universality of the system, shows how each mode of production requires, and produces, its own legal-juridical and political structures and relations. What is "common" to production, then, as produced by the process of mentally abstracting its "common" attributes, cannot provide a method which enables us to grasp, concretely, any single, "real historical stage of production."

How then, *are* we to conceptualise the relations between the different phases of production—production, distribution, exchange, consumption? Can we conceive them "as organically coherent factors"? Or simply as "brought into haphazard relation with one another, i.e., into a simple reflex connection"? How, in short, are we to analyse the relations between the parts of a "complexly structured whole"? Throughout his later work, Marx insists that the superiority of the dialectical method lies in its ability to trace out the "inner connection" between the different elements in a mode of production, as against their haphazard, and extrinsic "mere juxtaposition." The method which merely sets opposites together in an external way, which assumes that, because things are neighbours, they must therefore be related, but which cannot move from oppositions to contradictions, is "dialectical" only in its surface form. The syllogism is one of the logical forms of an argument by external juxtaposition. Political economy "thinks" production, consumption etc., in this syllogistic form: production produces goods; distribution allocates them; exchange makes the general distribution of goods specific to particular individuals; finally, the individual consumes them. This can also be interpreted as almost a classical Hegelian syllogism.[16] There are many ways in which Marx may be said to have remained a Hegelian; but the use of Hegelian triads (thesis, antithesis, synthesis) and syllogisms (general, particular, singular) is *not* one of them. The coherence such syllogisms suggest remains conceptually extremely shallow. Even the critics of this position, Marx adds, have not taken their critique far enough. The critics assume that the syllogism is wrong because it contains a logical error—a textbook mistake. For Marx, the error consists in a taking over into thought of the mystifications which exist in the real relations of bourgeois production, where production, distribution and consumption do indeed, *appear* "phenomenally" as "independent, autonomous neighbours," but where this appearance is false, an ideological inversion. Conceptual mistakes cannot be clarified by a theoretical practice alone, "wholly within thought."

In his "Critique of the Hegelian Dialectic and Philosophy as a Whole," Marx had remarked that, in Hegel, the supersession of one category by another *appears* to be a "transcending of the thought entity." However, in Hegel, thought treats even the objectively-created moments as "moments" *of itself*—"because the object has become for it a moment of thought, thought takes it in its reality to be a self-confirmation of itself." Thus, "this superseding in thought, which leaves its object standing in the real world, believes that it has really overcome it." There is no true "profane history" here, no "actual realisation for man of man's essence and of his essence as something real."[17] Thus, "the history of man is transformed into the history of an abstraction" (*The Holy Family*). The movement of thought therefore remains ultimately confined within its own circle:

> Hegel has locked up all these fixed mental forms together in his *Logic* laying hold of each of them first as negation—that is, as an alienation of human thought—and then as negation of the negation—that is, as a superseding of that alienation, as a real expression of human thought. But as even this still takes place within the confines of the estrangement, this negation of the negation is in part the restoring of these fixed forms in their estrangement.[18]

Thus, "the act of abstraction . . . revolves within its own circle." The language here remains headily Hegelian-Feuerbachian. How much cleaner the blow is in the 1857 text: "as if the task were the dialectical balancing of concepts, and not the grasping of real relations." "As if this rupture had made its way not from reality into the textbooks, but rather from the textbooks into reality."[19]

Thus, neither the functional disconnectedness of political economy nor the formal supersessions of the Hegelian Logic will serve to reveal the inner connection between processes and relations in society, which form "a unity" of a distinct type, but which must be grasped as real, differentiated processes in the real world, not merely the formal movement of the act of abstraction itself. It is because, in the "real relations" of capitalist production, the different parts of the process *appear*, simply, as independent, autonomous "neighbours" that they appear, in the textbooks, as linked by an accidental connection: not vice versa. But, how then to think the relations of identity, similarity, mediateness and difference which could produce, at the conceptual level, in thought, a "thought-concrete" adequate in its complexity to the complexity of the "real relations" which is its object?

The most compressed and difficult pages of the "Introduction," which immediately follow, provide an answer to this question. This section deals with the relations between production, distribution, consumption and exchange. Start with production. In production, individuals "consume" their abilities, they "use up" raw materials. In this sense, there is a kind of consumption *inside* production: production and consumption *are* here "directly coincident." Marx seems to have thought this example of "immediate identity" "right enough," though—as he says earlier and later of other formulations[20]—"trite and obvious," or "tautologous"; true at a rather simple level, but offering only a "chaotic conception," and thus requiring "further determinations," greater analytical development. The general inadequacy of this type of "immediate identity" *is* clearly signalled by Marx's reference here to Spinoza, who showed that an "undifferentiated identity" cannot support the introduction of more refined "particular determinations." However, insofar as "immediate identities" reign, at this simple level, identical propositions can be reversed: if A = B, then B = A. Marx, then, reverses the proposition. If there is a consumption-inside-production, there is also, "immediately," production-inside-consumption. The consumption of food, for example, is the means whereby the individual produces, or reproduces his physical existence. Now political economy recognises these distinctions but simply in order to separate out the consumptive aspects of production (e.g., the consumption of raw materials) from production proper. Production, as a distinct category, remains. The "immediate identity" thus leaves their "duality intact." (This type of identity is thus open to the criticism which Marx originally delivered on Hegel in the 1844 fragment on the Critique of the Hegelian Philosophy as a Whole": "This superseding in thought which leaves its object standing in the real world, believes it has really overcome it.")

Marx now adds a second type of relation: that of *mediation*: the relation of "mutual dependence." Production and consumption also mediate one another. By "mediate" here, Marx means that each cannot exist, complete its passage and achieve its result, without the other. Each is the other's completion. Each provides within itself the other's object. Thus, production's product is what consumption consumes. Consumption's "needs" are what production is aimed to satisfy. The mediation here is "teleological." Each process finds its end in the other. In this mediating movement, Marx later observes,[21] each side is "indispensable" to the other; but they are *not* identical—they remain necessary but "external to each other."

Marx now expands on *how* this mediation works. Consumption "produces" production in *two* ways. First, production's object—the product—is only finally "realised" when it is consumed.[22] It is in the passage of the forms, from productive activity to objectified product, that the first mediating movement between production and consumption is accomplished. Second, consumption produces production by creating the need for "*new* production." It is crucial, for the later discussion of the determinacy of production in the process as a whole, that what consumption now does, strictly speaking, is to provide the "ideal, internally impelling cause," the "motive," "internal image," "drive," "purpose" for *re*-production. Marx stresses "*new* production"; strictly speaking, and significantly, it is the need to *re*-produce for which consumption is made mediately responsible.

"Correspondingly" production "produces" consumption. Marx notes *three* senses in which this is true. First, production furnishes consumption with its "object." Second, production specifies the *mode* in which that object is consumed, but, third, production produces the need which its object satisfies. This is a difficult concept to grasp, for we normally think of consumption's needs and modes as the property of the consumer (that is, belonging to "consumption"), separate from the object which, so to speak, satisfies. But as early as 1844 Marx had pointed to the way in which needs are the product of an objective historical development, not the trans-historical subjective property of individuals:

> The manner in which they (objects) become his depends on the nature of the objects and on the nature of the essential power corresponding to it: for it is precisely the determinate nature of this relationship which shapes the particular, real mode of affirmation. To the eye an object is another object than the object of the ear.

If consumption of the object produces the subjective impulse to produce anew, the production of the object creates, in the consumer, specific, historically distinct and developed modes of "appropriation," and, simultaneously, develops the "need" which the object satisfies. "Music alone awakens in man the sense of music."

Thus the "forming of the senses" is the subjective side of an objective labour, the product of "the entire history of the world down to the present."[23] "The production of new needs is the first historical act," he observed in *The German Ideology*. Here, "the object of art ... creates a public which is sensitive to art."[24] Production, then, *forms* objectively the modes of appropriation of the consumer, just as consumption reproduces production as a subjectively experienced impulse, drive or motive. The complex shifts between objective and subjective dimensions which are tersely accomplished in this passage seem incomprehensible without the gloss from the 1844 *Economic and Philosophic Manuscripts* even if, here, the language of "species being" has altogether vanished.

The general argument is now resumed.[25] There are *three* kinds of identity relation. First, *immediate* identity—where production and consumption are "immediately" one another. Second, *mutual dependence*—where each is "indispensable" to the other, and cannot be completed without it, but where production and consumption remain "external" to one another. Thirdly, a relation, which has no precise title, but which is clearly that of an *internal connection* between two sides, linked by the passage of forms, by real processes through historical time. Here, in contrast with relation (2), production not only proceeds to its own completion, but is *itself reproduced again* through consumption. In this third type of relation, each "creates the other in completing itself and *creates itself* as the other." Here we find not only what distinguishes the third type of relation from the second; but also, what permits Marx, on the succeeding page, to give a final determinacy to production over consumption. Production, he argues, initiates the cycle: in its "first act," it forms the object, the mode and the need to consume: what consumption can then do is to "raise the inclination developed in the first act of production through the need for repetition to its finished form." Production, then, requires the passage through consumption to commence its work anew; but in providing "the act through which the whole process again runs its course," production retains a primary determination over the circuit as a whole. Some of Marx's most crucial and sophisticated distinctions, developed later in *Capital*—such as those between simple and expanded reproduction—achieve a gnomic, philosophic, first-formulation in this elliptical passage. In this third relation, production and consumption are no longer external to each other: nor do they "immediately" merge. Rather, they are linked by an "inner connection." Yet this "inner connection" is *not* a simple identity, which requires only the reversal or inversion of the terms of the syllogism into one another. The inner connection here passes through a distinct process. It requires what Marx, in his earlier critique of Hegel, called a "profane" history: a process in the real world, a process through historical time, each moment of which requires its own determinate conditions, is subject to its own inner laws, and yet is incomplete without the other.

Why is relation 3 not an "immediate identity" of the Hegelian type? Marx gives three reasons. First, an immediate identity would assume that production and consumption had a single subject. This identity of the "subject" through all its successive "moments" of realisation—a pivotal aspect of Hegel's "essentialism"—allowed Hegel to conceive the historical world as, ultimately, a harmonious circuit. In the real historical world, however, the "subject" of production and consumption are *not* one. Capitalists produce: workers consume. The production process links them: but they are not "immediate." Second, these are not Hegelian "moments" of a single act, temporary realisations of the march of World Spirit. These are the circuits of a *process*, with "real points of departure": a process with specific forms through which value is prescribed to pass "for its realisation." Third, whereas Hegel's identities form a self-engendering, self-sustaining circuit, in which no one moment has priority, Marx insists that the historical process through which production and consumption pass *has* its breaks, its moment of determinacy. Production, not consumption, initiates the circuit. Consumption, the necessary condition for value's "realisation," cannot destroy the "overdeterminacy" of the moment from which realisation departs.

The significance of these distinctions is delivered in the closing paragraph—the distinction between a Marxian and a Hegelian analysis of the *forms* of capitalist production.[26] Capitalism tends to reproduce itself in expanded form *as if* it were a self-equilibrating and self-sustaining system. The so-called "laws of equivalence" are the necessary "phenomenal forms" of this self-generating aspect of the system: this is precisely the beauty and greatness of it: this spontaneous interconnection, this material and mental metabolism which is independent of the knowing and willing of individuals.[27]

But this constant tendency to equilibrium of the various spheres of production is exercised only in the shape of a reaction against the constant upsetting of this equilibrium.[28] Each "moment" has its determinate conditions—each is subject to its own social laws: indeed, each is linked to the other in the circuit by quite distinct, determinate, forms—processes. Thus, there is no guarantee to the producer—the capitalist—that what he produces will return again to him: he cannot appropriate it "immediately."

The circuits of capital "depend on his relation to other individuals." Indeed, a whole, intermediate or "mediating movement" now intervenes— "steps between"—producers and products—determining, but again "in accordance with social laws," what will return to the producer as his share in the augmented world of production. *Nothing except the maintenance of these determinate conditions can guarantee the continuity of this mode of production over time.*

> Just as the exchange value of the commodity leads a double existence, as the particular commodity and as money, so does the act of exchange split into two mutually independent acts: exchange of commodities for money, exchange of money for commodities; purchase and sale. Since these have now achieved a *spatially* and *temporally separate* and *mutually indifferent* form of existence, their immediate identity ceases. They *may* correspond or not; they *may* balance or not; they *may* enter into disproportion with one another. They will, of course, always *attempt* to equalise one another;

but in the place of the earlier immediate equality there now stands the constant *movement of equalisation*, which evidently presupposes constant non-equivalence. It is now entirely possible that consonance may be reached only by passing through the most extreme dissonance.[29]

It is, in short, a *finite* historical system, a system capable of breaks, discontinuities, contradictions, interruptions: a system *with limits*, within historical time. It is a system indeed, which rests on the mediating movement of other processes not yet named: for example—distribution: production—(distribution)—consumption. Is distribution, then, "immediate with" production and consumption? Is it inside or outside production? Is it an autonomous or a determinate sphere?

In the first section,[30] Marx examined the couplet production/consumption in terms of an immediate Hegelian unity: opposites/identical. He then dismantled the production/consumption couplet—by the terms of a Marxian transformation: opposites—mediated—mutually dependent—differentiated unity (not identical). In part, this is accomplished by wresting from apparently equivalent relations a moment of determinacy: *production*. In the second section (from page 94) the second couplet production/distribution is dismantled by means of a different transformation: determined—determining—determinate.

In political economy, Marx wrote, everything appears twice. Capital is a factor of production: but also a form of distribution, (interest + profits). Wages are a factor of production, but also a form of distribution. Rent is a form of distribution: but also a factor of production (landed property). Each element appears as both *determining* and *determined*. What breaks this seamless circle of determinations? It can only be deciphered by reading back from the apparent identity of the categories *to their differentiated presuppositions* (determinate conditions).

Here, once again, Marx is concerned to establish the moments of *break*, of *determinacy*, in the self-sustaining circuits of capital. Vulgar economy assumed a perfect fit between the social processes of capital. This was expressed in the Trinitarian formula. Each factor of production was returned its just rewards in distribution: Capital—profits; Land—ground rent; Labour—wages. Thus each bit "appeared twice," by grace of a secret assumed "natural harmony" or compact with its identical opposite. Distribution appears to be, in common sense, the prime mover of this system. Yet, Marx suggests, behind the obvious forms of distribution (wages, rent, interest) lie, not simply economic categories, but real, historic relations, which stem from the movement and formation of capital under specific conditions. Thus, wages presuppose, not labour, but labour *in a specific form*: wage-labour (slave labour has no wages). Ground rent presupposes large-scale landed property (there is no ground rent in communal society). Interest and profit presuppose capital in its modern form. Wage-labour, landed property and capital are not independent forms of distribution but "moments" of the organisation of the capitalist mode of production: they *initiate* the distributive forms (wages, rent, profits), not vice versa. In this sense, distribution, which is, of course, a differentiated system, is nevertheless "overdetermined" by the structures of production. Before distribution by wages, rent, profits can take place a *prior* kind of "distribution" must occur: the distribution of the means of production between expropriators and expropriated, and the distribution of the members of society, the classes, into the different branches of production. *This* prior distribution—of the means and of the agents of production into the social relations of production—belongs to *production*: the distribution of its *products*, its *results*, in the form of wages or rent, *cannot* be its starting point.[31] Once this distribution of instruments and agents has been made, they form the starting conditions for the realisation of value within the mode; this realisation process generates its own distributive forms. This second type of distribution, however, is clearly *subordinate* to production in this wider, mode-specific sense, and must be considered as overdetermined by it.

In the third section, on exchange, the demonstration is even briefer.[32] Exchange, too, is an "aspect of production." It mediates between production and consumption, but, again, as its presupposition, it requires determinate conditions which can only be established within production: the division of labour, production in its private exchange form, exchanges between town and country, etc. This argument leads, almost at once, to a conclusion—it is a conclusion, not simply to the section on exchange, but to the whole problem posed on page 88. Production, distribution, consumption and exchange are not adequately conceptualised as immediate identities, unfolding, within the essentialist Hegelian dialectic, to their monistic categorical resolution. Essentially, we must "think" the relations between the different processes of material production as "members of a totality, distinctions within a unity." That is, as a complexly structured differentiated totality, in which distinctions are not obliterated but preserved—the unity of its "necessary complexity" precisely *requiring* this differentiation.

Hegel, of course, knew that the two terms of a relation would not be *the same*. But he looked for the identity of opposites—for "immediate identities" *behind* the differences. Marx does not altogether abandon the level at which, superficially, opposite things *can* appear to have an "essential" underlying similarity. But this is not the principal form of a Marxian relation. For Marx, two different terms or relations or movements or circuits remain specific and different: yet they form a "complex unity." However, this is always a "unity" formed by and requiring them to preserve *their difference*: a difference which does not disappear, which cannot be abolished by a simple movement of mind or a formal twist of the dialectic, which is not subsumed into some "higher" but more "essential," synthesis involving the loss of concrete specificity. This latter type of "non-immediacy" is what Marx calls a *differentiated unity*. Like the notion to which it is intimately linked—the notion of the concrete as the unity of "many determinations and relations"— the concept of a "differentiated unity" is a methodological and theoretical key to this text, and to Marx's method as a whole. This means that, in the examination of any phenomenon or relation, we must comprehend *both* its internal structure—what it is in its differentiatedness—as well as those other structures to which it is coupled and with which it forms some more inclusive totality. Both the specificities and the connections—the complex unities of structures—have to be demonstrated by the concrete analysis of concrete relations and conjunctions. If relations are mutually articulated, but remain specified by their difference, this articulation, and the determinate conditions on which it rests, has to be demonstrated. It cannot be conjured out of thin air according to some essentialist dialectical law. Differentiated unities are also therefore, in the Marxian sense, *concrete*. The method thus retains the concrete empirical reference as a privileged and undissolved "moment" within a theoretical analysis without thereby making it "empiricist": the concrete analysis of concrete situations.

Marx gives an "overdeterminacy" to production. But how does production determine? Production specifies "the different relations *between* different moments" (our italics). It determines the *form* of those combinations out of which complex unities are formed. It is the principle of the formal articulations of a mode. In the Althusserian sense, production not only "determines" in the last instance but determines the form of the combination of forces and relations which make a mode of production a complex structure. Formally, production specifies the system of similarities and differences, the points of conjuncture, between all the instances of the mode, including which level is, at any moment of a conjuncture, "in dominance." This is the *modal* determinacy which production exercises in Marx's overall sense.

In its more narrow and limited sense—as merely one moment, forming a "differentiated unity" with others—production has its own spark, its own motive, its own "determinateness" derived from other moments in the circuit (in this case, from consumption). To this argument—the nature of the relations of determinacy and complementarity or conjuncture between the different relations or levels of a mode of production—Marx returned at the end of the "Introduction." One of its results, already foreshadowed here, is the "law of uneven development."

Marx now goes back to the beginning: the method of political economy.[33] In considering the political economy of a country, where do we begin? One possible starting position is with "the real and concrete," a given, observable, empirical concept: e.g., population. Production is inconceivable without a population which produces. This starting point, however, would be wrong. Population, like "production," is a deceptively transparent, "given" category, "concrete" only in a common-sense way.[34] Already it presupposes the division into classes, the division of labour, and thus wage-labour, capital, etc.: the categories of a specific mode of production. "Population" thus gives us only "a chaotic conception of the whole." Further, it triggers off a methodological procedure which moves from the blindingly obvious to "ever more simple concepts," "ever thinner abstractions." This was the method of abstraction of the seventeenth century economists. It is also the "metaphysical" method of Proudhon which Marx pilloried so brilliantly and brutally in *The Poverty of Philosophy*. Later economic theorists begin with simple relations and trace their way back to the concrete. This latter path, Marx calls "the obviously scientifically correct one." This "concrete" is *concrete* in a different sense from the first formulation. In the first case, "population" is "concrete" in a simple, unilateral, common-sense way—it manifestly exists; production cannot be conceived without it, etc. But the method which *produces* the "complex concrete" is concrete because it is "a rich totality of many determinations and relations." The method, then, is one which has to *reproduce in thought* (the active notion of a practice is certainly present here) the concrete-in-history. No reflexive or copy theory of truth is now adequate. The simple category, "population," has to be reconstructed as contradictorily composed of the more concrete historical relations: slave-owner/slave, lord/serf, master/servant, capitalist/labourer. This clarification is a specific practice which theory is required to perform upon history: it constitutes the first part of theory's "adequacy" to its object. Thought accomplishes such a clarification by decomposing simple, unified categories into the real, contradictory, antagonistic relations which compose them. It penetrates what "is immediately present on the surface of bourgeois society," what "appears" as "the phenomenal form of"—the necessary form of the appearance of—"a process which is taking place behind."[35]

Marx sums up the point. The concrete is concrete, in history, in social production, and thus in conception, not because it is simple and empirical, but because it exhibits a certain kind of necessary complexity. Marx makes a decisive distinction between the "empirically-given," and the *concrete*. In order to "think" this real, concrete historical complexity, we must reconstruct in the mind the determinations which constitute it. Thus, what is multiply determined, diversely unified, in history, already "a result," appears, in thought, in theory, not as "where we take off from" but as *that which must be produced*. Thus, "the abstract determinations lead towards a reproduction of the concrete by way of thought." Let us note at once, that this makes the "way of thought" *distinct* from the logic of history as such, though it does not make thought "absolutely distinct." What is more, for Marx, the concrete-in-history makes its appearance once again, now as the historical substratum to thought. Though the concrete-in-history cannot be the point of departure for a theoretical demonstration, it is the absolute precondition for all theoretical construction: it *is* "the point of departure in reality and *hence also* the point of departure for observation and conception" (our italics).

Marx's formulations here[36] are seminal; the more so since they have, in recent years, become the *locus classicus* of the whole debate concerning Marx's epistemology. The "way of thought," Marx seems to be arguing, must "lay hold upon historical reality"—"appropriate the concrete"—and produce, by way of its own distinct practice, a theoretical construct adequate to its object ("reproduce it as the concrete in the mind"). It is important, however, to see that, right away, Marx addresses himself directly to the much-vexed question as to whether this "theoretical labour" can be conceived of as a practice which "takes place entirely in thought," which "is indeed its own criterion," and which "has no need for verification from external practices to declare the knowledges they produce to be 'true.'"[37] Significantly, his remarks here are, once again, embedded in a critique of Hegel, a procedure which appears to warn us explicitly against any final, idealist bracketing. Because "thought" has its own mode of appropriation, Marx argues, therefore Hegel made the error of thinking that "the real" was the product of "thought concentrating itself, probing its own depths, and unfolding itself out of itself." From this, it was an easy step to thinking of thought as absolutely (not relatively) autonomous, so that "the movement of the categories" became "the real act of production." Of course, he continues, thought *is* thought and not another thing; it occurs in the head; it requires the process of mental representations and operations. But it does not, for that reason, "generate itself." It is "a product of thinking and comprehending," that is, a product, rather, of the working-up of observation and conception into concepts. Any theory of "theoretical practice," such as Althusser's, which seeks to establish an "impassable threshold" between thought and its object, has to come to terms with the concrete reference (it is not, in our view, an empiricist reduction) embodied in Marx's clear and unambiguous notion, here, that thought proceeds from the "*working-up* of *observation and conception*" (our italics). This product of theoretical labour, Marx observes now, is, of course, a "totality of thoughts" *in the head*. But thought does not dissolve "the real subject"—its object—which "retains its autonomous existence outside the head." Indeed, Marx caps the argument by briefly referring to the relation of thought to social being, a reference consonant with his position as previously stated in the *Theses on Feuerbach*. The object, "the real" will *always* remain outside the head, so long as "the head's conduct is merely speculative, merely theoretical." That is, until the gap between thought and being is closed *in practice*. As he had argued, "Man must prove the truth i.e., the reality and power, the this-sidedness, of his thinking, in practice. The dispute over the reality or non-reality of thinking, that is isolated from practice is a purely scholastic question." There is no evidence here for Marx having fundamentally broken with this notion that, though thinking "has its own way," its truth rests in the "this-sidedness" of thinking, *in practice*. In fact, the 1857 text makes the point explicit: "Hence, *in the theoretical method too*, the subject, society, must always be kept in mind as the presupposition."[38] On this evidence, we must prefer Vilar's brief but succinct gloss over Althusser's complex but less satisfying ones:

> I admit that one ought neither to mistake thought for reality nor reality for thought, and that thought bears to reality only a "relationship of knowledge," for what else could it do? Also that the process of knowledge takes place entirely within thought (where else on earth could it take place?) and that there exists an order and hierarchy of "generalities" about which Althusser has had really major things to say. But on the other hand I fail to see what "astounding" mistake Engels was committing when he wrote (in a letter, incidentally, as a casual image) that conceptual thought progressed "asymptotically" towards the real.

As Vilar remarks, "When reading the 1857 'Introduction,' if one should 'hear its silences,' one should also take care not to silence its words."[39]

Thought, then, has its own distinct, "relatively autonomous" mode of appropriating "the real." It must "rise from the abstract to the concrete" not *vice versa*. This is different from "the process by which the concrete itself comes into being." The logic of theorising, then, and the logic of history do *not* form an "immediate identity": they are mutually articulated upon one another, but remain distinct within that unity. However, lest we immediately fall into the opposite error that, therefore, thinking is its own thing, Marx, as we have seen, immediately turned, as if in the natural course of the argument, to the critique of Hegel, for whom of course, the march of the categories was precisely the only motor. In so doing, Marx offered a critique of every other position which would transpose the *distinctiveness* of thought from reality (in terms of the modes of their production) into an *absolute distinction*. His qualifications on this "absolute" break are pivotal. Thought *always* has built into it the concrete substratum of the manner in which the category has been realised historically within the specific mode of production being examined. Insofar as a category already exists, albeit as a relatively simple relation of production, not yet with its "many sided connections," then that category can already appear "in thought," because categories are "the expression of relations." If, then, turning to a mode in which that category appears in a more developed, many-sided form, we employ it again, but now to "express" a more developed relation, then, in that sense, it *does* remain true that the development of the theoretical categories *directly mirror* the evolution of historic relations: the "path of abstract thought, rising from the simple to the combined," does indeed "correspond to the real historical process." In this *limited case*, the logical and historical categories *are indeed parallel*. The notion that Marx has prescribed that the logical and the historical categories *never* converge is shown to be incorrect. It is a matter of cases.

In other cases, however, the two movements are *not* identical in this way. And it is these instances which concern Marx, for this was precisely Hegel's error. Marx's critique of any attempt to construct "thinking" as wholly autonomous is that *this constitutes an idealist problematic*, which ultimately derives the world from the movement of the Idea. No formalist reduction—whether of the Hegelian, positivist, empiricist or structuralist variety—escapes this stricture. The distinctiveness of the mode of thought does not constitute it as absolutely distinct from its object, the concrete-in-history: what it does is to pose, as a problem remaining to be resolved, precisely *how* thought, which is distinct, forms "a unity" with its object: remains, that is to say, nevertheless determined "in the last instance" (and, Marx adds, in the "first instance, too, since it is from 'society' that thinking derives its 'presupposition'"). The subsequent passages in the 1857 "Introduction" in fact constitute some of Marx's most cogent reflections on the dialectical relation of thought, of the "theoretical method," to the historical object of which it produces a *knowledge*: a knowledge, moreover, which—he insists—remains "merely speculative, merely theoretical" (there is no mistaking that "merely") so long as practice does not, dialectically, realise it, *make it true.*

If thought is distinct in its mode and path, yet articulated upon and presupposed by society, its object, how is this "asymptotic" articulation to be achieved? The terms are here conceived as neither identical nor merely externally juxtaposed. But what, then, is the precise nature of their unity? If the genesis of the logical categories which express historical relations differs from the real genesis of those relations, what is the relation between them? How does the mind reproduce the concreteness of the historical world in thought?

The answer has something to do with the way history, itself, so to speak, enters the "relative autonomy" of thought: the manner in which the historical object of thought is rethought inside Marx's mature work. The relation of thought to history is definitively *not* presented in the terms of a historical evolutionism, in which historical relations are explained in terms of their genetic origins. In "genetic historicism," an external relation of "neighbourliness" is posited between any specific relation and its "historical background": the "development" of the relation is then conceived lineally, and traced through its branching variations: the categories of thought faithfully and immediately mirror this genesis and its evolutionary paths. This might sound like a caricature, until one recalls the inert juxtapositions, the faithful tracing out of quite unspecified "links," which has often done justice for modern instances of the Marxist method. It is crucial to distinguish Marx from the evolutionism of a positivist historical method. We are dealing here neither with a disguised variant of positivism nor with a rigorous a-historicism but with that most difficult of theoretical models, especially to the modern spirit: a *historical epistemology.*

Marx now employs again the distinctions he has made between different types of "relation": immediate, mediated, etc. Previously, these had been applied to the categories of a theoretical analysis—"production," "distribution," "exchange." These distinctions are now applied again; but this time to the different types of relations which exist between thought and history.

He proceeds by example. In the *Philosophy of Right*, Hegel begins with the category "possession." Possession is a simple relation which, however, like "production," cannot exist without more concrete relations—i.e., historical groups with possessions. Groups can, however, "possess" without their possessions taking the form of "private property" in the bourgeois sense. But since the historico-judicial relation, "possession," *does* exist, albeit in a simple form, we can think it. The simple relation is the "concrete substratum" of our (relatively simple) concept of it. If a concept is, historically, relatively undeveloped (*simple*) our concept (of it) will be *abstract*. At this level, a connection of a fairly reflexive kind *does* exist between the (simple) level of historical development of the relation and the relative (lack of) concreteness of the category which appropriates it.

But now Marx complicates the theory/history couplet. Historically the development of the relation is not evolutionary. No straight, unbroken path exists from simple to more complex development, either in thought or history. It is possible for a relation to move from a dominant to a subordinate position within a mode of production as a whole. And this question of dominant/subordinate is not "identical" with the previous question of simple/ more developed, or abstract/concrete. By referring the relation to its articulation *within a mode of production*, Marx indicates the crucial shift from a progressive or sequential or evolutionary historicism to what we might call "the history of epochs and modes": a structural history. This movement towards the concepts of *mode* and *epoch* interrupts the linear trajectory of an evolutionary progression, and reorganises our conception of historical time in terms of the succession of modes of production, defined by the internal relations of dominance and subordination between the different relations which constitute them. It is a crucial step. There is, of course, nothing original whatever in drawing attention to the fact that Marx divided history in terms of successive modes of production. Yet the *consequence* of this break with genetic evolutionism does not appear to have been fully registered. The concepts "mode of production" and "social formation" are often employed as if they are, in fact, simply large-scale historical generalisations, within which smaller chronological sections of historical time can be neatly distributed. Yet, with the concepts of "mode of production" and "social formation," Marx pinpoints the structural interconnections which cut into and break up the smooth march of a historical evolutionism. It represents a rupture with historicism in its simple, dominant form, though this is not, in our view, a break with *the historical* as such.

Take money. It exists before banks, before capital. If we use the term, "money," to refer to this relatively simple relation, we use a concept which (like "possession" above) is still abstract and simple: less concrete than the concept of "money" under commodity production. As "money" becomes more developed so our concept of it will tend to become more "concrete." However, it is possible for "money" in its *simple* form to have a *dominant* position in a mode of production. It is also possible to conceive of "money" in a more *developed*, many-sided form, and thus expressed by a more *concrete* category, occupying a *subordinate* position in a mode of production.

In this double-fitting procedure, the couplets simple/developed or abstract/concrete refer to what we might call the diachronic string, the developmental axis of analysis. The couplet dominant/subordinate points to the synchronic axis—the *position* in which a given category or relation stands in terms of the other relations with which it is articulated in a specific mode of production. These latter relations are always "thought" by Marx in terms of relations of dominance and subordination. The characteristic modern inflexion is to transfer our attention from the first axis to the second, thus asserting Marx's latent structuralism. The difficulty is, however, that the latter does not bring the former movement to a halt but *delays* or (better) *displaces* it. In fact, the line of historical development is always constituted within or behind the structural articulation. The crux of this "practical epistemology," then, lies precisely in the necessity to "think" the simple/developed axis and the dominant/subordinate axis as dialectically related. This is indeed how Marx defined his own method, by proxy, in the second "Afterword" to *Capital*: "What else is he picturing but the dialectic method?"

Take another case. Peru was relatively developed but had no "money." In the Roman Empire, "money" existed, but was "subordinate" to other payment relations, such as taxes, payments-in-kind. Money only makes a historic appearance "in its full intensity" in bourgeois society. There is thus no linear progression of this relation and the category which expresses it through each succeeding historical stage. Money does not "wade its way through each historical stage." It *may* appear, or not appear, in different modes; be developed or simple; dominant or subordinate. What matters is not the mere appearance of the relation sequentially through time, but its *position* within the configuration of productive relations which make each mode *an ensemble*. Modes of production form the discontinuous structural sets through which history articulates itself. History moves—but only as a *delayed and displaced trajectory*, through a series of social formations or ensembles. It develops by means of a series of *breaks*, engendered by the internal contradictions specific to each mode. The theoretical method, then, to be adequate to its subject, society, must ground itself in the specific arrangement of historical relations in the successive modes of production, not take its positions on the site of a simple, linearly constructed sequential history.[40]

Now Marx defines the articulation of thought and history. The "most general abstraction"—in the main sense—of general (i.e., many-sided) development appears only when there is, in society, in history, "the richest possible concrete development." Once this has happened "in reality," the relation "ceases to be thinkable in its particular (i.e., abstract) form alone." Labour, as a loose, catch-all, concept (such as "all societies must labour to reproduce") has thus been replaced by the more *concrete* category, "labour-in-general" (generalised production), but only because the latter category now refers in bourgeois society to a real, concrete, more many-sided, historical appearance. The "general concept" has, Marx strikingly asserts, "become true in practice." It has achieved that specificity, "in thought," which makes it capable of appropriating the concrete relations of labour in practice. It has "achieved practical truth as an abstraction only as a category of the most modern society." Thus, "even the most abstract categories ... are nevertheless ... themselves likewise a product of historical relations and possess their full validity only for and within these relations."[41]

It is for this reason especially that bourgeois society, "the most developed and the most complex historic organisation of production," allows us insights into vanished social formations: provided we do not make over-hasty "identities" or "smudge over all historical differences." For, it is only insofar as older modes of production survive within, or reappear in modified form within, capitalism, that the "anatomy" of the latter can provide "a key" to previous social formations.[42] Again, we must "think" the relation between the categories of bourgeois social formations and those of previous, vanished formations, *not* as an "immediate identity," but in ways which preserve their appearance in bourgeois society (that is, the relations of developed/simple and of dominant/subordinate in which *new* and *previous* modes of production are *arranged* or combined within it). From this basis, Marx can make his critique of simple, historical evolutionism: "The so-called historical presentation of development is founded, as a rule, on the fact that the latest form regards the previous ones as steps leading up to itself."

This is to regard the matter "one-sidedly." This does not, however, abolish "history" from the scheme. If thought is grounded in social being, but not in social being conceived "evolutionarily," then it must be *present social reality*—modern bourgeois society, "the most developed and complex historic organisation of production"—which forms thought's presupposition, its "point of departure." The object of economic theorising, "modern bourgeois society," is "always what is given in the head as well as in reality."[43] And it is *this point*—it "holds for science as well"—which is "decisive for the order and sequence of the categories."

It has recently been argued that, with this observation about the distinction between the historical and the logical succession of the categories, Marx makes his final rupture with "historicism." It is often forgotten that the point is made by Marx in the context of a discussion about the fundamentally relativised epistemological origins of thought itself: a discussion which specifically draws attention to the dependence of the logical categories on the relations, the "forms of being," which they "express." Thus, not what thought produces by its own "mechanisms" from within itself, but what is concretely "given in the head as well as reality" is Marx's starting point here for his discursus on the epistemological foundations of method.

"The order and sequence of the economic categories," then, do not "follow one another in the sequence in which they were historically decisive": not because—as was true for Hegel—the logical categories engender themselves above or outside the "real relations," but because the epistemological reference for thought is *not the past but the present historic organisation of production* (bourgeois society). This is a quite different argument. Thus, what matters is not the historical sequence of the categories but "their order within bourgeois society." In bourgeois society, each category does not exist as a discrete entity, whose separate historical development can be traced, but within a "set," a *mode*, in relations of dominance and subordination, of determination, and determinateness to other categories: *an ensemble of relations*. This notion of an ensemble does indeed interrupt—break with—any straight historical evolutionism. The argument has then, sometimes, been taken as supporting Marx's final break with "history" as such—a break expressed in the couplet, historicism/science. Marx, in my view, is drawing a different distinction, signalling a different "break": that between a sequential historical evolutionism determining thought/and the determinateness of thought within *the present historic organisation of social formations*. The relations of production of a mode of production are articulated *as an ensemble*.

There are complex internal relations and connections between them. In each mode, moreover, there is a level of determination "in the last instance": one specific production-relation which "predominates over the rest... assigns rank and influence to the others... bathes all other colours and modifies their particularity."[44] Marx insists that we attend to the specificity of each ensemble, and to the relations of determination, dominance and subordination which constitute each epoch. This points towards the Althusserian concept of a social formation as a "complexly structured whole" "structured in dominance" and to the complementary notions of "overdetermination" and "conjuncture." The full theoretical implications of this modal conception take Marx a good deal of the way towards what we may call a "structural historicism." But, since thought, too, takes its origins from this "reality," which is "always given in the head," it too operates by way of an epistemology determined in the first-last instance by the "present historical organisation of production."

Marx now develops this argument, again by way of examples. In bourgeois society, "agriculture is progressively dominated by capital." What matters for the order and sequence of categories is not the evolution of any one relation—say, feudal property—into industrial capital: though, in *Capital*, Marx does at certain points provide just such a historical sketch. It is the relational position of industrial capital and landed property, or of "capital" and "rent," in the capitalist mode as against their relational position in, say, the feudal mode, which matters. In the latter, "combination" provides the starting point of all theorising. This is "anti-historicist" if by that term we mean that the method does not rest with the tracing of the historical development of each relation, singly and sequentially, through time. But it is profoundly *historical* once we recognise that the starting-point—bourgeois society—is not outside history, but rather "the present historic organisation of society." Bourgeois society is what "history" has delivered to the present as its "result." The bourgeois ensemble of relations is the present-as-history. History, we may say, realises itself progressively. Theory, however, appropriates history "regressively." Theory, then, starts from history as a developed result, *post festum*. This is its presupposition, in the head. History, but only in its realisation as a "complexly structured totality," articulates itself *as the epistemological premise*, the starting point, of theoretical labour. This is what I want to call Marx's historical—not "historicist"—epistemology. However undeveloped and untheoreticised, it marks off Marx's method sharply both from a philosophically unreflexive traditional mode, including that final reference to the self-generating "scientificity" of science which indexes the lingering positivist trace within structuralism itself. Lucio Colletti has expressed the argument succinctly when he observes that much theoretical Marxism has shown a tendency

> to mistake the "first in time"—i.e., that from which the logical process departs as a recapitulation of the historical antecedents—with the "first in reality" or the actual foundation of the analysis. The consequence has been that whereas Marx's logico-historical reflections culminate in the formation of the crucial problem of the contemporaneity of history (as Lukács once aptly said, "the present as history") traditional Marxism has always moved in the opposite direction of a philosophy of history which derives its explanation of the present from "the beginning of time."[45]

Marx's "historical epistemology," then, maps the mutual articulation of historical movement and theoretical reflection, not as a simple identity but as differentiations within a unity. He retains—in, as it were a displaced form—the historical premise, thoroughly reconstructed, inside the epistemological procedure and method, as its final determination. This is not thought and reality on infinitely parallel lines with "an impassable threshold" between them. It signifies a convergence—what Engels called an *asymptotic movement*—on the ground of the given: here, bourgeois society as the ground or object both of theory and practice. It remains an "open" epistemology, not a self-generating or self-sufficient one, because its "scientificity" is guaranteed only by that "fit" between thought and reality—each in its own mode—which produces a knowledge which "appropriates" reality in the only way that it can (in the head): and yet delivers a critical method capable of penetrating behind the phenomenal forms of society to the hidden movements, the deep-structure "real relations" which lie behind them. This "scientific" appropriation of the laws and tendencies of the structure of a social formation is, then, *also* the law and tendency of its "passing away": the possibility, not of the proof, but of the *realisation* of knowledge in practice, in its practical resolution—and thus, the self-conscious overthrow of those relations in a class struggle which moves along the axis of society's contradictory tendencies, and which is something more than "merely speculative," more than a theoretical speculation. Here, as Colletti has remarked, we are no longer dealing with "the relationship 'thought-being' within thought, but rather with the relation *between* thought and reality."[46]

It is worth referring this methodological argument in the "Introduction" to passages in the *Grundrisse* itself where the distinctions between the "historical origins" of the capitalist mode, and capitalism as "the present historic organisation of production" are elaborated.[47] The capitalist mode, Marx is arguing, depends on the transformation of money into capital. Thus, money constitutes one of "the antediluvian conditions of capital, belongs to its historic presuppositions." But once this transformation to its modern form in commodity production is accomplished—the establishment of the capitalist mode of production proper—capitalism no longer depends directly upon this recapitulation of its "historic presupposition" for its continuation. These presuppositions are now "past and gone"—they belong to "the history of its formation, but in no way to its contemporary history, i.e., not to the real system of the mode of production ruled by it." In short, the historical conditions for the appearance of a mode of production *disappear into its results*, and are reorganised by this realisation: capitalism now posits "in accordance with its immanent essence, the conditions which form its point of departure in production," "posits the conditions for its realisation," "on the basis of its own reality." It (capitalism) "no longer proceeds from presuppositions in order to become, but rather it is itself presupposed, and proceeds from itself to create the conditions of its maintenance and growth." This argument is again linked by Marx with the error of political economy, which mistakes the past conditions for capitalism becoming what it is, with the *present* conditions under which capitalism is organised and appropriates: an error which Marx relates to political economy's tendency to treat the harmonious laws of capitalism as natural and "general."

In the face of such evidence from the *Grundrisse*, and later from *Capital*,[48] it cannot be seriously maintained for long that, with his brief remarks on the "succession of the categories" in the 1857 "Introduction," Marx wholly relinquishes the "historical" method for an essentially synchronic, structuralist one (in the normal sense). Marx clearly is sometimes unrepentantly concerned, precisely, with the most delicate reconstruction of the *genesis* of certain key categories and relations of bourgeois society. We must distinguish these from the "anatomical" analysis of the structure of the capitalist mode, where the "present historic organisation of production" is resumed, analytically and theoretically, as an ongoing "structure of production," a combination of productive modes. In the latter, "anatomical" method, history and structure have been decisively reconstructed. The methodological requirement laid on his readers is to maintain these two modes of theoretical analysis—a view eloquently endorsed in the "Afterword" to *Capital* I. This injunction constitutes both the comprehensiveness, and the peculiar difficulty, of his dialectical method. But the temptation to bury one side of the method in favour of the other—whether the historical at the expense of the structural, or *vice versa*—is, at best, an evasion of the theoretical difficulty Marx's own work proposes: an evasion for which there is no warrant in the 1857 "Introduction." As Eric Hobsbawm has remarked:

> A structural model envisaging only the maintenance of a system is inadequate. It is the simultaneous existence of stabilising and disruptive elements which such a model must reflect. . . . Such a dual (dialectical) model is difficult to set up and use, for in practice the temptation is great to operate it, according to taste or occasion, either as a stable functionalism or as one of revolutionary change; whereas the interesting thing about it is, that it is both.[49]

The problem touched on here goes to the heart of the "problem of method," not only of the 1857 "Introduction," but of *Capital* itself: a question which the "Introduction" throws light on but does not resolve. Maurice Godelier, for example, argues for "the priority of the study of structures over that of genesis and evolution": a claim, he suggests, inscribed in the very architecture of *Capital* itself.[50] Certainly, the main emphasis in *Capital* falls on the systematic analysis of the capitalist mode of production, not on a comprehensive reconstruction of the genesis of bourgeois society as a social formation. Thus, the long section in *Capital* III on "Ground Rent" opens: "The analysis of landed property in its various historical forms belongs outside of the limits of this work. . . . We assume then that agriculture is dominated by the capitalist mode of production."[51] This does not contradict the centrality of those many passages which *are* in fact directly historical or genetic in form (including parts of this same section of *Capital* III). Indeed, there are important distinctions between different *kinds* of writing here. Much that seems "historical" to us now was, of course, for Marx immediate and contemporary. The chapter on "The Working Day," in *Capital* I, on the other hand, contains a graphic historical sketch, which *also* supports a theoretical argument—the analysis of the forms of industrial labour under capitalism, and the system's ability, first, to extend the working day, and then, as labour becomes organised, the movement towards its limitation ("the outcome of a protracted civil war"). Both are modally different from "the task of tracing the genesis of the money-form . . . from its simplest . . . to dazzling money-form," announced early in the same volume:[52] a genesis which Marx argues "shall, at the same time, solve the riddle presented by money," but which in fact is not cast in the form of a "history of money" as such, but an analysis of "the *form* of value" (own italics), as expressed in the money-form, a quite different matter. And all of these differ again from the substantive historical material in *Capital* I, addressed explicitly to the question of "origins" but which Marx deliberately put after, not before, the basic theoretical exposition. None of these qualifications should be taken as modifying our appreciation of the profoundly historical imagination which informs *Capital* throughout. Decisively, the systematic form of the work never undercuts the fundamental historical premise which frames the whole exposition, and on which Marx's claim for its "scientificity," paradoxically, rests: the historically specific, hence transitory, nature of the capitalist epoch and the categories which express it. As early as 1846, he had said this to Pavel Annenkov, *a propos* Proudhon: "He has not perceived that economic categories are only abstract expressions of these actual relations and only remain true while these relations exist."[53] He never changed his mind.[54]

It is certainly the case that, *in extenso*, *Capital* deals with the forms and relations which the capitalist system requires to reproduce itself on an expanded scale: that is, with the "structure and its variations." Some of the most dazzling parts of the manuscript consist, precisely, of the "laying bare" of the forms of the circuits of capital which enable this "metamorphosis" to take place. But Marx's method depends on identifying two dialectically related but discontinuous levels: the contradictory, antagonistic "real relations" which sustain the reproductive processes of capitalism, and the "phenomenal forms" in which the contradictions appear as "equalised." It is the latter which inform the consciousness of the "bearers" of the system and generate the juridical and philosophic concepts which mediate its movements. A *critical* science must unmask the inverted forms of the metamorphosis of the structure of capital and lay bare its antagonistic "real relations." The difficult but magnificent opening sections on commodity fetishism (which it is now sometimes fashionable to dismiss as another Hegelian trace) not only lay the base, substantially, for the rest of the exposition; they also stand as a dramatic demonstration of the logic and method by which the other discoveries of the work are produced.[55] Thus, though for Marx one of the truly staggering aspects of capitalism was, exactly, its self-reproduction, his theory transcended political economy only insofar as he could show that the "forms of the appearance" of this structure could be read through, read behind, read back to their presuppositions—as if one were "deciphering the hieroglyphic to get behind the secret of our own social products." And one of the sources of these permanent, self-reproducing "appearances" of capitalism to which

Marx drew our attention was, precisely, the "loss" (misrecognition) of any sense of its movements as socially created, historically produced forms:

> Man's reflections on the forms of social life, and consequently also his scientific analysis of these forms, take a course directly opposite to that of their actual historical development. He begins *post festum* with the results of the process of development already to hand. The characters that stamp products as commodities, and whose establishment is a necessary preliminary to the circulation of commodities, have already acquired the stability of natural, self-understood forms of social life before man seeks to decipher, not their historical character, for in his eyes they are immutable, but their meaning.

"So too," he added, "the economic categories, already discussed by us, bear the stamp of history." They are "socially valid and, therefore, objective thought-forms which apply to the production-relations peculiar to this one historically determined mode of social production."[56] But, this decipherment (which is, in its "practical state," *his method*: "all science would be superfluous if the outward appearance and the essence of things directly coincided")[57] is not *just* a critique. It is a critique *of a certain distinctive kind*—one which *not only* lays bare the "real relations" behind their "phenomenal forms," but does so in a way which *also* reveals as a contradictory and antagonistic necessary content what, on the surface of the system, appears only as a "phenomenal form," functional to its self-expansion. This is the case with each of the central categories which Marx "deciphers": commodity, labour, wages, prices, the equivalence of exchange, the organic composition of capital, etc. In this way, Marx *combines* an analysis which strips off the "appearances" of how capitalism works, discovers their "hidden substratum," and is thus able to reveal how it *really* works: with an analysis which reveals why this functionalism in depth *is also* the source of its own "negation" ("with the inexorability of a law of Nature").[58] The first leads us to the ideological level, at which the "phenomenal forms" are taken at their justificatory face-value: they "appear directly and spontaneously as current modes of thought"—i.e., as the prevailing forms of common-sense perceptions. The second penetrates to "the essential relation manifested within," to "their hidden substratum": they "must first be discovered by science." Classical political economy provides the basis—but only via a *critique*—of this second, scientific level, since it "nearly touches the true relation of things, without however consciously formulating it."[59] Marx's critique transcends its origins in political economy, not only because it formulates consciously what has been left unsaid, but because it reveals the antagonistic movement concealed behind its "automatic mode," its "spontaneous generation."[60] The analysis of the double form of the commodity—use-value, exchange-value—with which *Capital* opens, and which appears at first as merely a formal exposition, only delivers its first substantive conclusion when, in the chapter on "The General Formula for Capital," the "circuit of equivalence" (M-C-M) is redefined as a circuit of disequilibrium (M-C-M′), where "this increment or excess over the original value I call 'surplus value.'" "It is this movement that converts it (value) into capital."[61] Thus, as Nicolaus has argued:

> Exploitation proceeds behind the back of the exchange process. . . . Production consists of an act of exchange, and, on the other hand, it consists of an act which is the opposite of exchange. . . . The exchange of equivalents is the fundamental social relation of production, yet the extraction of non-equivalents is the fundamental force of production.[62]

To present Marx as if he is the theorist, solely, of the operation of "a structure and its variations," and not, also and simultaneously, the theorist of its limit, interruption and transcendence is to transpose a dialectical analysis into a structural-functionalist one, in the interest of an altogether abstract scientism.

Godelier is aware that an analysis of the variations of a structure must embrace the notion of contradiction. But the "functionalist" shadow continues to haunt his structuralist treatment of this aspect. Thus, for Godelier, there are two, fundamental contradictions in Marx's analysis of the system: that between capital and labour (a contradiction *within* the structure of the "social relations of production") and that between the socialised nature of labour under large-scale industry and the productive forces of capital (a contradiction *between* structures). Characteristically, Godelier exalts the latter (deriving from the "objective properties" of the system) over the former (the struggle between the classes). Characteristically, Marx intended to connect the two: to found the self-conscious practice of class struggle *in* the objective contradictory tendencies of the system.[63] The neat, binary contrast offered by Godelier between a "scientific" contradiction which is objective material and systemic, and the practice of class struggle which is epiphenomenal and teleological disappears in the face of this essential internal connectedness of theory to practice. Korsch long ago, and correctly, identified the attempt "to degrade the opposition between the social classes to a temporary appearance of the underlying contradiction between the productive forces and production-relations" as "Hegelian."[64] Marx ended his letter outlining the theoretical argument of *Capital* III thus: "Finally, since these three (wages, ground rent, profit) constitute the respective sources of income of the three classes ... we have, in conclusion, the *class struggle*, into which the movement of the whole *Scheisse* is resolved."[65]

Yet, when Godelier quotes Marx's letter to Ludwig Kugelmann[66]—"I represent large-scale industry not only as the mother of antagonism, but also as the creator of the material and spiritual conditions necessary for the solution of this antagonism"—he appears unable to *hear* the second half of Marx's sentence at all. Yet, for Marx, it was exactly the interpenetration of the "objective" contradictions of a productive mode with the politics of the class struggle which alone raised his own theory above the level of a "Utopia" to the status of a science: just as it was the coincidence of an adequate theory with the formation of a class "for itself" which alone guaranteed the "complex unity" of theory and practice. The idea that the unity of theory and practice could be constituted on the ground of theory alone would not have occurred to Marx, especially after the demolition of Hegel.

There remain the extremely cryptic notes[67] which conclude the "Introduction": notes on notes—"to be mentioned here ... not to be forgotten," nothing more. The points rapidly touched on in these pages are, indeed, theoretically of the highest importance: but there is scarcely enough here for anything that we could call a "clarification." They are at best, *traces*: what they tell us is that—significantly enough—Marx already had these questions in mind. What they hardly reveal is what he thought about them. They primarily concern the superstructural forms: "Forms of the State and Forms of Consciousness in Relation to Relations of Production and Circulation, Legal Relations, Family Relations." What would the modern reader give for a section at least as long as that on "The Method of Political Economy" on *these* points. It was not to be.

We can, then, merely, *note* what the problems here seemed to him to be. They touch on the question as to how, precisely, we are to understand the key concepts: "productive forces," "relations of production." Moreover, they specify these concepts at the more mediated levels: the relation of these infrastructural concepts to war and the army; to cultural history and historiography; to international relations; to art, education and law. Two conceptual formulations of the first importance are briefly enunciated. First, it is said again, that the productive-forces/relations-of-production distinction, far from constituting two disconnected structures, must be conceived dialectically. The boundaries of this dialectical relation remain to be specified in any theoretical fullness ("to be determined'): it is a dialectic which connects, but which is *not* an "immediate identity"—it does not "suspend the real difference" between the two terms. Second, the relation of artistic development, of education and of law to material production is specified as constituting a relation of "uneven development." Again, a theoretical note of immense importance.

The point about artistic development and material production is then briefly expanded. The "unevenness" of the relation of art to production is instanced by the contrast between the flowering of great artistic work at a point of early, indeed, "skeletal" social organisation—Greek civilisation. Thus, the epic appears as a *developed* category in a still simple, ancient, mode of production. This instance parallels the earlier example, where "money" makes its appearance within a still undeveloped set of productive relations. Though Marx is here opening up a problem of great complexity—the graphic demonstration of the "law of the uneven relations of structure and superstructures"— he is less concerned with developing a specifically Marxist aesthetics, than with questions of method and conceptualisation. His argument is that, like "money" and "labour," art does not "wade its way" in a simple, sequential march from early to late, simple to developed, in step with its material base. We must look at it in its "modal" connection at specific stages.

His concrete example—Greek art—is subordinated to the same theoretical preoccupation. Greek art presupposes a specific set of "relations." It requires the concrete organisation of the productive forces of Ancient society—it is incompatible with spindles, railways, locomotives. It requires its own, specific modes of production—the oral art of the epic is incompatible with electricity and the printing press. Moreover, it requires its own forms of consciousness: mythology. Not *any* mythology—Egyptian mythology belongs to a different ideological complex and would not do. But mythology as a form of thought (at the ideological level) survives only to the degree that the scientific mastery over and transformation of Nature is yet not fully accomplished. Mythology lasts only so long as science and technique have not overtaken magic in their social and material pacification of Nature. Thus, mythology is a form of consciousness which is only possible at a certain level of development of the productive forces—and hence, since this mythology forms the characteristic content and mode of imagination for the epic, the epic is connected—but by a complex and uneven chain of mediations—to the productive forces and relations of Greek society. Is this historical coupling, then, not irreversible? Do not ancient society and the epic disappear together? Is the heroic form of Achilles imaginable in the epoch of modern warfare?

Marx does not end his inquiry with this demonstration of the *historical* compatibility between artistic and material forms. The *greater* theoretical difficulty, he observes, is to conceive how such apparently *ancient* forms stand in relation to the *"present* historic organisation of production" (emphasis added). Here, once again, Marx gives a concrete instance of the way he combines, in his method, the analysis of *concrete instances*, the epochal development of complex structures *through time*, and the structural "law" of the mutual connection and interdependence of relations *within the present mode of production*. The demonstration, though brief and elliptical, is exemplary. The answer to the question as to why we still respond positively to the epic or Greek drama—in terms of the "charm" for us of "the historic childhood of humanity"—is, however, unsatisfactory in almost every respect: a throwaway line. The resolution to these perplexing, (and, in our time, progressively central and determining) theoretical issues is achieved stylistically, but not conceptually.

What light, if any, does the 1857 "Introduction" throw on the problem of "theoretical breaks" in Marx? Marx considered classical political economy to be the new science of the emergent bourgeoisie. In this classical form, it attempted to formulate the laws of capitalist production. Marx had no illusions that political economy could, untransformed, be made theoretically an adequate science for the guidance of revolutionary action: though he did, again and again, make the sharpest distinction between the "classical" period which opened with Petty, Boisguillebert and Adam Smith and closed with Ricardo and Sismondi, and its "vulgarisers," with whom Marx dealt dismissively, but whom he read with surprising thoroughness and debated intensively to the end of his life. Yet some of his sharpest criticism was reserved for the "radical" political economists—the "left-Ricardians," like Bray, the Owenites, Rodbertus, Lasalle and Proudhon—who thought political economy theoretically self-sufficient, though skewed in its political application, and proposed those changes from above which would bring social relations in line with the requirements of the theory. The socialist Ricardians argued that, since labour was the source of value, all men should become labourers exchanging equivalent amounts of labour. Marx took a harder road. The exchange of equivalents, though "real enough" at one level, was deeply "unreal" at another. This was just the frontier beyond which political economy could not pass. However, merely knowing this to be true did not, in Marx's sense, make it real for men in practice. These laws could only be thrown over in practice: they could not be transformed by juggling the categories. At this point, then, the critique of political economy, and of its radical revisionists, merged with the metacritique of Hegel and *his* radical revisers—the left-Hegelians: for Hegel, too, "conceived only of abstractions which revolve in their own circle" and "mistook the movement of the categories" for the profane movement of history; and his radical disciples thought the Hegelian system complete, and only its application lacking its proper finishing touch. Certainly, when Marx said of Proudhon that he "conquers economic alienation only within the bounds of economic alienation," it was a direct echo, if not a deliberate parody, of the critique he had already made of Hegel.[68]

It is this point—that bourgeois relations must be overthrown in practice before they can be wholly superseded in theory—which accounts for the complex, paradoxical, relations Marx's mature work bears to political economy: and thus for the extreme difficulty we have in trying to mark exactly where it is that Marxism, as a "science," breaks wholly and finally with political economy. The difficulty is exactly that which has in recent years so preoccupied the discussion of Marx's relation to Hegel: and it may be that we must tentatively return the same kind of answer to each form of the question.

The whole of Marx's mature effort is, indeed, the *critique* of the categories of political economy. The critique of method is positively opened, though not closed, in the 1857 "Introduction." Yet political economy remains Marx's only theoretical point-of-departure. Even when it has been vanquished and transformed, as in the case of the dismantling of the Ricardian theory of wages, or in the break-through with the "suspended" concept of surplus value, Marx keeps returning to it, refining his differences from it, examining it, criticising it, going beyond it. Thus even when Marx's theoretical formulations lay the foundations of a materialist science of historical formations, the "laws" of political economy still command the field, theoretically—because they dominate social life in practice. To paraphrase Marx's remarks on the German "theoretical conscience," political economy cannot be realised in practice without abolishing it in theory, just as, on the other side, it cannot be abolished in practice until it has been theoretically "realised."

This is in no sense to deny his "breakthroughs." In a thousand other ways, *Capital*, in the doubleness of its unmasking and reformulations, its long suspensions (while Marx lays bare the circuits of capital "as if they were really so," only to show, in a later section, what happens when we return this "pure case" to its real connections), its transitions, lays the foundation of a "scientific" critique of the laws of capitalist production. Yet it remains a *critique* to the end: indeed, the critique appears (to return to the 1857 text) as paradigmatically, *the form of the scientificity of his method*.

The nature of this "end" toward which his critique pointed must be spelled out. It was not an attempt to erect a scientifically self-sufficient theory to replace the inadequate structure of political economy: his work is not a "theoreticist" replacement of one knowledge by another. In the aftermath of the 1848 upheavals, Marx's thought did, clearly, increasingly cast itself in the form of theoretical work. No doubt the systematic and disciplined nature of this work imposed its own excluding and absorbing rhythms: the letters eloquently testify to that. Yet for all that, the theoretical labour of which the successive drafts and predrafts of *Capital* were the result, had, as its prospective "end"—paradoxically—something other than the "founding of a science." We cannot pretend, as yet, to have mastered the extremely complex articulations which connect the scientific forms of historical materialism with the revolutionary practice of a class in struggle. But we have been right to assume that the power, the historical significance, of Marx's theories are related, in some way we do not yet fully understand, precisely to this *double articulation* of theory and practice. We are by now familiar with a kind of "reading" of the more polemical texts—like the *Manifesto*—where the theory is glimpsed, so to speak, refracted through a more "immediate" political analysis and rhetoric. But we are still easily confused when, in the later texts, the movement of the classes in struggle is glimpsed, so to speak, refracted through the theoretical constructs and arguments. It is a strong temptation to believe that, in the latter, only Science holds the field.

Marx's mature method—we would argue—does not consist of an attempt to found a closed theoreticist replacement of bourgeois political economy. Nor does it represent an idealist replacement of alienated bourgeois relations by "truly human" ones. Indeed, great sections of his work consist of the profoundly revolutionary, critical task of showing exactly how the laws of political economy *really worked*. They worked, in part, through their very formalism: he patiently analyses the "phenomenal forms." Marx's *critique*, then, takes us to the level at which the real relations of capitalism can be penetrated and revealed. In formulating the nodal points of this *critique*, political economy—the highest expression of these relations grasped as mental categories—provided the only possible starting point. Marx begins there. *Capital* remains "A Critique of Political Economy": not "Communism: An Alternative to Capitalism." The notion of a "break"—final, thorough, complete—by Marx with political economy is, ultimately, an idealist notion: a notion which cannot do justice to the real complexities of theoretical labour—*Capital* and all that led up to it.

Much the same could be said of Marx's relation to Hegel, though here a substantive "break" is easier to identify—for what it is worth, it is identified time and again for us by Marx himself. It is the relation to Hegel in terms of *method* which continues to be troubling. Early and late, Marx and Engels marked the thoroughgoing manner in which the whole idealist framework of Hegel's thought had to be abandoned. The dialectic in its idealist form, too, had to undergo a thorough transformation for its real scientific kernel to become available to historical materialism as a scientific starting-point. It has been argued that Marx and Engels cannot have meant it when they said that something rational could be rescued from Hegel's idealist husk: yet, for men who spent their lives attempting to harness thought to history in language, they appear peculiarly addicted to that troubling metaphor of "kernel" and "husk." Could something remain of Hegel's *method* which a thoroughgoing transformation would rescue—when his *system* had to be totally abandoned as mystification and idealist rubbish? But that is like asking whether, since Ricardo marked the closure of a bourgeois science (and was a rich banker to boot), there was anything which the founder of historical materialism could learn from him. Clearly, there was; clearly he did. He never ceased to learn from Ricardo, even when in the throes of dismantling him. He never ceased to take his bearings from classical political economy, even when he knew it could not finally think outside its bourgeois skin. In the same way, whenever he returns to the wholly unacceptable substance of the Hegelian system, he always pinpoints, in the same moment, what it is he learned from "that mighty thinker," what had to be turned "right-side-up" to be of service. This did not make the mature Marx "a Hegelian" any more than *Capital* made him a Ricardian. To think this is to misunderstand profoundly the nature of the *critique* as a form of knowledge, and the dialectical method. Certainly, as far as the 1857 "Introduction" is concerned, time and again, Hegel is decisively abandoned and overthrown, almost at the very points where Marx is clearly learning—or re-learning—*something* from his dialectical method. One of the traces of light which this text captures for us is the illumination of this surprisingly late moment of supersession—of return-and-transformation.

NOTES

This essay first appeared in "Cultural Studies and Theory," *Working Papers in Cultural Studies* 6 (Birmingham: Centre for Contemporary Cultural Studies, University of Birmingham, 1974), 132–70.

1. I have used the translation of the 1857 "Introduction" by Martin Nicolaus, in his edition of Karl Marx, *Grundrisse: Foundations of the Critique of Political Economy (Rough Draft)* (Harmondsworth, UK: Pelican, 1973).
2. Pierre Vilar, "Writing Marxist History," *New Left Review* I/80 (1973).
3. In *Marx-Engels Selected Correspondence*. [The date of this letter from Marx to Engels is not certain; some scholars give it as written on or around January 16.—Ed.]
4. *Sämtliche Schriften*, vol. 1. Translated in Sidney Hook, ed., *From Hegel to Marx* (Ann Arbor: University of Michigan Press, 1962).
5. Marx, *Grundrisse*, 156–57.
6. On the "real relations/phenomenal form" distinction, see John Mepham, "The Theory of Ideology in *Capital*," in "Cultural Studies and Theory," *Working Papers in Cultural Studies* 6 (1974); and Norman Geras, "Essence and Appearance: Aspects of Fetishism in Marx's *Capital*," *New Left Review* I/65 (1971).
7. Karl Marx, *Capital* I, 745. [Edition uncertain.—Ed.]
8. Karl Korsch, *Three Essays on Marxism* (London: Pluto Press, 1971).
9. Marx, *Capital* I, 542.
10. Marx, *Capital* I, 75.
11. Marx, *Capital* I, 76.
12. Karl Marx, *The Poverty of Philosophy* (Moscow: Foreign Languages Publishing House, n.d.), 118–19, 121.
13. Karl Marx, "Critique of the Hegelian Dialectic and Philosophy as a Whole," in *Economic and Philosophic Manuscripts of 1844* (London: Lawrence and Wishart, 1964). [Edition uncertain.—Ed.]
14. Marx, *Economic and Philosophic Manuscripts*, 190.
15. Marx, *Economic and Philosophic Manuscripts*, 44.
16. Note Marx's ironic use of the terms. *Grundrisse*, 450.
17. Marx, *Economic and Philosophic Manuscripts*, 186–87.
18. Marx, *Economic and Philosophic Manuscripts*, 190.
19. Marx, "Introduction," *Grundrisse*, 90.
20. Marx, "Introduction," *Grundrisse*, 88, 100.
21. Marx, "Introduction," *Grundrisse*, 93.
22. See Marx's more developed notion of how the "activity" of labour appears in the product as a "fixed quality without motion": *Capital* I, 180–81.
23. Marx, *Economic and Philosophic Manuscripts*, 140–41.

24 Marx, "Introduction," *Grundrisse*, 92.
25 Marx, "Introduction," *Grundrisse*, 93: the distinctions between the three types of identity-relation are not as clearly sustained as one could wish.
26 Marx, "Introduction," *Grundrisse*, 94.
27 Marx, *Grundrisse*, 161.
28 Marx, *Capital* I, 356.
29 Marx, *Grundrisse*, 148. [Italics are Hall's.—Ed.]
30 Marx, "Introduction," *Grundrisse*, 90, 93.
31 [Hall's footnote number 29 is missing, but the relevant text was given as "Cf. the dismantling of the theory of wages in *Capital* II and of the 'Trinity Formula' in *Capital* III." I have therefore placed the footnote where it seems most fitting, though anywhere in the paragraph would work well enough.—Ed.]
32 Marx, "Introduction," *Grundrisse*, 98.
33 Marx, "Introduction," *Grundrisse*, 100.
34 On Hegel's and Marx's usage of "concrete," see G. L. Kline, "Some Critical Comments on Marx's Philosophy," in *Marx and the Western World*, ed. N. Lobkowicz (Notre Dame, IN: Notre Dame University Press, 1967).
35 Marx, *Grundrisse*, 255.
36 Marx, "Introduction," *Grundrisse*, 101.
37 Louis Althusser, *For Marx* (London: Allen Lane, 1969), 42, 58.
38 Marx, "Introduction," *Grundrisse*, 102.
39 Vilar, "Writing Marxist History," 74–75.
40 Marx's discussion of a further example—labour—has been omitted here.
41 Marx, "Introduction," *Grundrisse*, 105.
42 Marx, "Introduction," *Grundrisse*, 105.
43 Marx, "Introduction," *Grundrisse*, 105–6.
44 Marx, "Introduction," *Grundrisse*, 107.
45 Lucio Colletti, *Marxism and Hegel* (London: New Left Books, 1973), 130–31.
46 Colletti, *Marxism and Hegel*, 134.
47 See Marx, *Grundrisse*, 459.
48 See Marx, *Capital* I, 762.
49 E. J. Hobsbawm, "Marx's Contribution to Historiography," in *Ideology and Social Science*, ed. Robin Blackburn (Glasgow: Fontana, 1972).
50 See Maurice Godelier, "Structure and Contradiction in *Capital*," in Blackburn, *Ideology and Social Science*, and developments of the same argument in Godelier, *Rationality and Irrationality in Economics* (London: New Left Books, 1972).
51 Karl Marx, *Capital* III, 720. [Edition uncertain.—Ed.]
52 Marx, *Capital* III, 48.
53 Reprinted in Marx, *The Poverty of Philosophy*, 209.
54 Marx quoted his reviewer in the *European Messenger* to the same effect, without demur: in the "Afterword" to the second edition of *Capital* I.
55 For a recent, and striking, reassertion of the centrality of "fetishism" to *Capital* from an "anti-historicist" interpreter of Marx, see "Interview with Lucio Colletti," *New Left Review* I/86 (1974).

56 The quotes are from Marx, *Capital* I, 74–75, 169, 42. See also Engels to F. A. Lange, in Karl Marx and Friedrich Engels, *Selected Correspondence* (London: Lawrence and Wishart), 198.
57 Marx, *Capital* III, 797.
58 Marx, *Capital* I, 763.
59 On this point, see also "Interview with Lucio Colletti."
60 Marx, *Capital* I, 542.
61 Marx, *Capital* I, 150.
62 In Blackburn, *Ideology and Social Science*, 324–25.
63 The two strands are beautifully and inextricably combined in passages such as, e.g., *Capital* I, 763.
64 Karl Korsch, *Karl Marx* (1938; repr, London: Universale Laterza, 1969), 201.
65 To Engels, 30 April 1868, Marx and Engels, *Selected Correspondence*, 245.
66 Dated 11 July 1868, only three months later.
67 Marx, "Introduction," *Grundrisse*, 109–11.
68 Marx, *The Holy Family* (Moscow: Foreign Languages Publishing House, 1956), 213. [Edition uncertain.—Ed.]

CHAPTER 2

Rethinking the "Base and Superstructure" Metaphor

Of the many problems which perforce Marx left in an "undeveloped" state, none is more crucial than that of "base and superstructure." The manuscript of the third volume of *Capital* breaks off at the opening of the tantalising passage on "classes." The promised volume on the state, which appears in several of the schemes for *Capital* which he prepared, was left unwritten. Both, if completed, would have thrown the light of his mature reflection on the base/superstructure question. As it is, we have a very substantial part of his mature thought on the "laws of motion" of the capitalist mode of production, but nothing from the same period which takes as its theoretical object a capitalist social formation as a whole, encompassing all its levels and the relation between them, including the "superstructures."

There is a view that everything that Marxism needs is already there in *Capital*: and that, if you stare hard enough at it, it will—like the hidden books of the Bible—yield up all its secrets, a theory of everything. I don't subscribe to this thesis in its literal form. Apart from anything else, it denies one of the central premises of *Capital*—that the capitalist mode of production is constantly developing, and this in turn requires a continuous labour of theoretical development and clarification. "There is no royal road to science," Marx warned the French.[1] Besides, it smacks too much of the religious attitude. Of course, Marx's work on the laws of the capitalist mode of production contains many profound hints and pointers which await further theoretical development. What is more, *Capital* unravels the essential movements of that level which precisely Marx insisted was "determining." Hence, the problem of base/superstructure must be "thought" within the terrain of concepts elaborated in that fundamental work. But it is a different proposition to imagine that it will be resolved by slavishly repeating the "logic of *Capital*." This too often results in an exercise which may be logically elegant but is, in the larger theoretical sense, abstract: reducing everything to "political economy." To rethink the base/superstructure problem, within the framework of Marx's problematic as evidenced in *Capital*, requires difficult theoretical labour. This paper addresses itself, of necessity, to some starting points only.

What is fundamentally at issue here is: How does Marxism enable us to "think" the complexities of a modern capitalist social formation? How can we conceptualise the relationships between the different levels which compose it? Further, can we "think" this problem in such a way as to retain a key premise of historical materialism: the premise of "determination in the last instance" by what is sometimes misleadingly referred to as "the economic"? Can this be done without losing one's way in the idea of the *absolute* autonomy of each of its levels? For Marx insists that we must think the "*ensemble* of relations," its complex unity: and quoted with unqualified approval, in a text which Althusser unwarrantably defines as "gestural," his Russian reviewer, who pointed to Marx's concern with "that law of movement . . . which governs these phenomena, in so far as they have a definite form and mutual connexion within a given historical period." Can it be done without succumbing to the notion of a capitalist social formation as a functional "whole," without antagonism or contradiction ("the contradictions inherent in the movement of capitalist society . . . whose crowning point is the universal crisis")?[2] Can it be done without falling back into the essentially relativistic sociological notion of a social formation as composed of a multivariate interaction-of-all-sides-on-one-another, without primacy of determination given or specified at any point? Can *determination*—one of the central themes of Marx's theoretical work—be thought without simplifying what it is that "determines" (the economic?), when (in the last instance?) or how that determination operates (one-directionally)? In essence, those are the problems posed by the central position in Marxism occupied by the topographical metaphor of base/superstructure.

I want to look, briefly, at some of the key formulations in Marx's and Engels's own work, which throw light on the base/superstructure question: noting not only the hints they throw out, but the developments in them and the shifts between them. Secondly, I examine one or two key developments in recent theoretical work which mark significant moments of further clarification; and attempt to estimate how far they take us, and what remains to be done.

The German Ideology

The first texts are taken from formulations offered in and around the period of *The German Ideology*. It is important to situate this text itself, and thus the conceptual field and the theoretical problematic in which the formulations are offered. This is the text where the "species-being" perspective of the *Economic and Philosophical Manuscripts* is replaced, in often a simple but thorough-going manner, by a historical, often an evolutionary *genetic* materialism. It registers the "break" with the problematic of Feuerbachian sensuous materialism. It constitutes a "settling of accounts," by Marx and Engels, with German "critical criticism"—the speculative philosophy of the Left Hegelians. Its whole thrust—including its "materialism"—is *polemical*. This polemical, reasonably simplifying, thrust of the text must be borne in mind if we are properly to situate the reductive simplification which appears sometimes to intrude.

> The production of life, both of one's own by labour and of fresh life by procreation, appears at once as a double relationship, on the one hand as a natural on the other as a social relationship. By social is meant the cooperation of several individuals, no matter under what conditions, in what manner or to what end. It follows from this, that a determinate mode of production, or industrial stage, is always bound up with a determinate mode of cooperation or social stage, and this mode of cooperation is itself a "productive force." It also follows that the mass of productive forces accessible to men determines the condition of society, and that the "history of humanity" must therefore always be studied and treated in relation to the history of industry and exchange. (Marx and Engels, *The German Ideology*)

There are two key points to note here: both are re-stated in only a slightly different form at several other points in the text. The first is the proposition— the reverse of the Hegelian premise—that it is "the mass of productive forces accessible to men" which "determines the condition of society." The second point is slightly more complex; but just as important. It just concerns the "double relationship." For Marx and Engels, "men" (this is the general, historically undifferentiated, way in which people are referred to in this text) intervene in Nature in order to produce and reproduce their material conditions of life. This intervention is accomplished through human labour and the use of tools. Human labour, ever since its first rudimentary historical appearance, is only possible through social co-operation between men: these "relations," which develop between men, and constitute the "determinate mode of co-operation," result from the historically specific mode of men's social intervention in Nature—their mode of production. The basis of all history is the successive modes of production, including the modes of social co-operation dependent on them. As Marx puts it in another similar passage: "We are bound to study closely the men of the eleventh century and those of the eighteenth, to examine their respective needs, their productive forces, their mode of production, the raw materials of their production, and finally the relations of man to man which resulted from all these conditions of life."[3] Each "mode of production," each "mode of cooperation" is "determinate": historically specific. The latter "results from" or "is bound up with" the former. The premise of historical specificity in this relation between the two relations—the "double relationship"—is insisted on throughout: but always in a very general, epochal, way. One way of measuring the distance—and the difference—between the Marx of this period and the Marx of *Capital* is precisely by comparing these general formulations with the chapters on "Co-operation" and "The Division of Labour and Manufacture" in *Capital* I (Chapters XIII and XIV) to see how far the concept of historical specificity could itself be further specified.

The premises which inform these ways of attempting to "expound" the relations between the different levels of a social formation are stated in an admirably simple and clear way, elsewhere in the same text. They constitute the working analytic principles of Marx's "historical materialism," as this was developed by this point in time:

> This conception of history, therefore, rests on the exposition of the real process of production, starting out from the simple material production of life and on the comprehension of the form of intercourse connected with and created by this mode of production, i.e., of civil society in its various stages as the basis of all history, and also in its action as the State. From this starting point, it explains all the different theoretical productions and forms of consciousness, religion, philosophy, ethics, etc., and

traces their origins and growth, by which means the matter can of course be displayed as a whole (and consequently, also the reciprocal action of these various sides on one another). Unlike the idealist view of history, it does not to have look for a category in each period, but remains constantly on the real ground of history; it does not explain practice from the idea but explains the formation of ideas from material practice, and accordingly comes to the conclusion that all forms of and products of consciousness can be dissolved, not by intellectual criticism, not by resolution into "self-consciousness," or by transformation into "apparitions," "spectres," "fancies," *etc.*, but only by the practical overthrow of the actual social relations which gave rise to this idealist humbug; that not criticism but revolution is the driving force of history, as well as religion, philosophy, and all other types of theory. (*The German Ideology*)

The passage is too well known to require much comment. It contains the easily recognised anti-Hegelian "inversion": "not practice from the idea but . . . the formation of ideas from material practice." It begins to identify the different levels of a social formation. Note that these—constituting the germ of the base/superstructure metaphor—appear, if anything, as *three* levels, not two. The difference is important, even though the text, in its compression, tends to run them together. First, the "material production of life . . . and the form of intercourse connected with and created by this mode of production." Then—at, as it were, a different though related level of representation—"i.e.," civil society . . . and also its action as the State." Then—another half-distinction worth remarking: "all the different theoretical productions and forms of consciousness, religion, philosophy, ethics, *etc*." Note here, also, the variety of ways in which the principle of "determination" is rendered: "connected with": "created by"; "in its action as"; etc.

The classic formulation, in its tightest and most succinct form, and clearly resting on the same conceptual terrain, appears again in the often quoted passage (but written nearly a decade later, and by a Marx already into his second draft, at least, of what is to become the first book of *Capital*): from the 1859 "Preface" to the *Contribution to the Critique of Political Economy*, replacing the longer, more complex, more theoretical and difficult 1857 "Introduction" to the *Grundrisse*.

In the social production which men carry on they enter into definite relations that are indispensable and independent of their will; these relations of production correspond to a definite stage of development of their material powers of production. The totality of these relations of production constitutes the economic structure of society, the real foundation on which legal and political superstructure arise and to which definite forms of social consciousness correspond. The mode of production of material life determines the general character of the social, political, and spiritual processes of life. It is not the consciousness of men that determines their being, but, on the contrary, their social being determines their consciousness.[4]

This clarifying but over-condensed paragraph contains all the elements of the base/superstructure problem as Marx formulated it in the middle, transitional period of his work up to the verge of the preparation of the first volume of *Capital*. Here, not only is material production and its relations the determining factor: but the "corresponding" social relations are *given*—definite, indispensable and independent of men's will: objective conditions of a social mode of production. These, under determinate conditions, constitute a *stage*. This—material mode, relations of production—is what is designated as "the economic structure." It forms the base, the "real foundation." From it arise the legal and political superstructures. And, *to this* correspond theoretical productions *and* definite forms of social consciousness.

Marx's "Historicism"

The formulations in both *The German Ideology* and the 1859 "Preface" clearly exhibit what would now be identified as the traces of Marx's *historicism*. That is to say, a determining primacy is given to the base basis, real foundation—and the other levels of a social formation are seen to develop in close correspondence with it: even if this is not phrased uni-directionally ("and consequently, also, the reciprocal action of these various sides on one another"); and even if changes at one level are subject to a time-lag at the other levels ("the entire immense superstructure is *more or less rapidly* transformed"). The "matter which is displayed as a whole" is thought in terms of a broad determination; changes in the economic structure of society will, "more or less rapidly," produce consequent and determinate changes in the legal and political superstructures and in the "ideological forms in which men become conscious of this conflict and fight it out" that is, also, at the ideological level.

Louis Althusser would argue that, here, the social totality is conceptualised, essentially, as an "expressive totality"; in which, despite its apparent levels and differentiations, contradictions in the "base" appear to unroll, evenly, and to be reflected sooner or later through corresponding modifications in the superstructures and the ideological forms. This, then, is still an "essentialist" conceptualisation of a social formation. It is also "historicist," in Althusser's view, because it makes little if any separation between "theoretical productions" and "ideological forms"; it makes the theoretical level appear also as a "correspondence" or a reflection of the material base.

We shall return to the weight and force of this critique of the "historicist" Marx, at a later point. But, in the work of Althusser, *The German Ideology* is presented as the work of a "break" and "transitional" period in Marx's work;[5] to be superseded, in *Capital*, by a transformed dialectic, which produces an altogether different manner of conceptualising a social formation. It is therefore worth noting *where* and *how* this earlier formulation (which, appearing as it does in the 1859 "Preface," comes relatively very late in the so-called epistemological rupture between the early and middle Marx, and the "late") reappears again in Marx's mature work.

In a passage in *Capital* III, Marx offers an interesting and important gloss, which is, however, different, from *The German Ideology*, above all in the tightness of its formulation:

> The specific economic form in which unpaid surplus labour is pumped out of the direct producers determines the relation of domination and servitude, as it emerges directly out of production itself and in its turn reacts upon production. Upon this basis, however, is founded the entire structure of the economic community, which grows up out of the conditions of production itself, and consequently its specific political form. It is always the direct relation between the masters of the conditions of production and the direct producers which reveals the innermost secret, the hidden foundation of the entire social edifice, and therefore also of the political form of the relation between sovereignty and dependence, in short, of the particular form of the State.

Here it is the relations of "domination and servitude," defined far more specifically in terms of the way surplus value is extracted *in* capitalist production, which "reveals the innermost secret, the hidden foundations of the entire social edifice"; hence, its political forms; and thus the forms of the state itself. In another, more significant, passage, Marx quotes his own words from the 1859 "Preface" in a long and important footnote in the chapter "Commodities" in *Capital* I. He quotes it without modification—and clearly with approval. The context and development is, however, also significant. A German critic had quoted Marx's 1859 "Preface," and, while acknowledging the primacy of "the economic" in the capitalist epoch, denied its determining role for the feudal period or for classical antiquity, "where politics reigned supreme." Marx's reply restates the basic premise: it is "the economic structure" which is "the real basis." (We must remember, however, that whereas this "structure" is treated in a very reduced and simple form in the original formulation, it is now recalled in the context of a work which is devoted to an extremely comprehensive and elaborate consideration of just what the forms and relations of this "structure" are.) The Middle Ages, he continues, could not live on Catholicism nor Ancient Rome on politics.

However, he adds, "it is the mode in which they gained a livelihood which explains why here politics and there Catholicism played the chief part."[6] Thus, while the mode of production plays a determining role in all epochs, its role appears here as that of assigning to some *other* level of practice (politics, religion—i.e., ideology) the "chief role" (the *dominant* role, as it has come to be designated). This is a new way of formulating the problem of "determination by the economic" and one which, incidentally, gives far greater effectivity to the "superstructures" (which can now, in some epochs, be dominant). The argument is already anticipated in the 1857 "Introduction," where Marx argues that "in all forms of society there is one specific kind of production which predominates over the rest whose relations thus assign rank and influence to the others.... It is a particular ether which determines the specific gravity of every being which has materialised within it."[7]

These are, of course, two of the principal sources for the Althusserian distinction between "determining" and "dominant" instances: and thus for the thesis that, in his later work, Marx ceased to think a social formation as a simple expressive totality. We will return to this important turn in the argument later.

The crucial formulations of the base/superstructure problem first occur, and are given at least one decisive, and quite consistent form, in the period between the consignment of *The German Ideology* to the "gnawing criticism of the mice" and the replacement of the 1857 "Introduction" by the 1859 "Preface." Whether later superseded and transformed or not, these formulations give a radical impetus to the whole body of Marxist thought on the question of how to conceptualise a social formation and how to "explore" the nature of its unity. Let us sum it up.

The texts here are reformulated in the problematic of a broad epochal historical sweep. In this sweep, mode of production is given, first, its initial definition; secondly, its position of determination over the whole social edifice and structure. Mode of production is already conceptualised as consisting, neither of economic relations *per se*, nor of anything so vulgarly material as "level of technology": but as a combination of relations—productive forces, social relations of production. These, in each epoch, form the determining matrix, in which social life and material existence is produced and reproduced. And the structures raised on this foundation, which embody and articulate the social relations stemming from the productive matrix, correspond to it. Indeed, in the "double relationship," both—material and social reproduction—are simultaneously founded. As men, through the division of labour, progressively combine to intervene, by means of the developing forces of production in Nature to reproduce their material life, so they in the same moment reproduce the structure of their social relations and reproduce themselves as social individuals. The two cannot be separated, even if, in the last instance, it is the former which determines the form of the latter. Indeed, this "double relation" is conceptualised as *asymptotic*: since, in production, the social relations themselves progressively become "a productive force." As these social relations, rooted in and governed by production, develop, they achieve a distinct articulation: they are embodied in political and legal relations. They give rise to determinate forms of the state ("The existing relations of production must necessarily express themselves also as political legal relations"). They define the character of civil society ("Only in the eighteenth century, in 'civil society,' do the various forms of social connectedness confront the individual as mere means towards his private purposes, as external necessity").[8] They produce their corresponding theoretical fields and discourses (religion, ethics, philosophy, etc.) and "determinate forms of social consciousness" ("That these concepts are accepted as mysterious powers is a necessary consequence of the independent existence assumed by the real relations whose expression they are"). This is, indeed, the point towards which the whole trajectory of *The German Ideology* tended—the setting of the feet of German idealist speculation in the soil of man's "profane history."

No simple or reductive reflexivity of the superstructure is assumed here, though the *thrust* behind the many reformulations is consistent and unmistakable. And perhaps it is worth stressing that, if Marx's thought on the subject subsequently developed, what changed is *how* he came to understand determinacy by a mode of production, not whether it determined or not. When we leave the terrain of "determinations," we desert, not just this or that stage in Marx's thought, but his whole problematic. It is also worth noting that, though the determinacy of "the economic" over the superstructures is the prevailing form in which this is expressed here, it is sometimes overlaid by a second template: the tendency to reduce determination, not to "the economic" but to History itself—to *praxis*: to an undifferentiated *praxis* which rolls throughout the whole social formation, as its essential ground. Some passages of *The German Ideology* are not all that far from the more humanist-historicist assertion of *The Holy Family* that "history is nothing but the activity of men." Succinct as are its formulations, then, *The German Ideology* remains, at one and the same time, a key early text of historical materialism, *and* a text haunted or shadowed by the trace of more than one conceptual problematic.

Engels's Letters on Historical Materialism

One of the best ways of seeing what the problems were for Marxism of the "German Ideology" way of conceptualising the base/superstructure question, is to watch Engels wrestle with its consequences in his lengthy correspondence with a number of Marxist veterans of his and the next generation, in the two decades after Marx's death.[9] In addition to editing and bringing together Marx's vast unpublished work, Engels found himself both the guardian of his and Marx's joint legacy, and its most privileged interpreter: this was a key moment, and role, for it "marked the transition, so to speak, from Marx to Marxism and provided the formative moment of all the leading Marxist interpreters of the Second International and most of the leaders of the Third."[10] Marx had laid the foundations, above all in his work on the capitalist mode of production. But he left "no comparable *political* theory of the structures of the bourgeois State, or of the strategy and tactics of revolutionary socialist struggle by a working-class party for its overthrow." Nor did he provide any systematic general statement of historical materialism as a "world view." Engels attempted to repair both omissions—a task which gives the general sense "of a completion, more than a development, of Marx's heritage."[11]

Marx had established that the economy is determinant in the last instant, but that the superstructures had their own "effectivity" which could not be simply reduced to their base. But "the precise structural mechanism connecting the two is always left unclear by Marx."[12] The clarification of this problem was one of Engels's most urgent and important tasks: the more so since Marxism was fast becoming absorbed into the dominant field of "positive science," which reduced it to a simple economic determinism in which the superstructures were a pale and automatic reflex of the base—a tendency which was destined to be disastrously installed as the official version in the Second International. Engels struggled vainly to combat this reductionism. But he struggled to do so on the ground, essentially, of his and Marx's formulations of *The German Ideology* period: and the development and clarification he undertook were sustained by precisely those conceptual tools and instruments which had produced the formulation in this form in the first place. That is, *essentially* as an inversion of the idealist premises left intact in Left Hegelianism—by setting the Hegelian dialectic right-side-up, and working from its "revolutionary" aspect. In the letters, Engels wrestles with this inheritance valiantly, courageously and often elegantly. But the conceptual chickens are fast coming home to roost.

The German Ideology proposed a general historical scheme: but now that this threatened to harden into a rigid and abstract orthodoxy, Engels was obliged to insist that "all history must be studied afresh" and that Marx's materialism is "not a lever for construction à la Hegelianism."[13] Face to face with "determination by the economic," Engels has to win some space for the "interaction of all these elements," and for the "endless host of accidents" through which "the economic movement finally asserts itself as necessary."[14] He accepts some blame ("Marx and I are ourselves partly to blame . . .") for the tendency to reduce everything to the economic, and to disregard the effect of the superstructures and the ideological forms in "exercising their influence upon the course of the historical struggles." The play between contingency and necessity, the "infinite series of parallelograms of forces which give rise to one resultant," the intersection of many individual wills into "a collective mean, a common resultant" are bold and provocative attempts to circumvent some of the problems implicit in the original problematic.[15] There are some useful and provocative advances made in Engels's long, detailed letter to Conrad Schmidt (27 October 1876), which deal specifically with the superstructural instances of the law and the state, which are worth pursuing in a later context.

But we cannot depart far from Althusser's judgement on this correspondence, in the lucid Appendix to his "Contradiction and Overdetermination" essay,[16] which suggests that, despite their many strengths, Engels's attempts to find a theoretical solution in the correspondence principally have the result of declaring that a solution is not yet to hand, and of reminding us how difficult it is to find. The problem, Althusser suggests, is: how to think the specific relations between the relations of production and the political, juridical and ideological forms in such a way as to grasp, simultaneously, the "determination by the economic in the last instance" and the "relative autonomy" or effectivity of the superstructures. Engels knows what the question is: but he does not produce a satisfactory solution to it.

We have traced the "after-life" of *The German Ideology* formulations beyond Marx's death, partly as a way of registering the continuing theoretical power and resonance which they still—and in a sense, must—carry within the Marxist tradition. But the fact is that they were beginning to be superseded and transformed, implicitly if not explicitly, and in terms of the bringing into use of the elements of an alternative paradigm, even if not "fully theorised," within Marx's own lifetime and within the scope of his later work. We can identify three ways or directions in which this modification is taking place.

The first is to be found in the political writings—above all, *The Eighteenth Brumaire, The Class Struggles in France* and the more incidental notes on Britain—which Marx wrote after it became clear that the revolutions of 1848 were not destined to produce a swift resolution to the emerging proletarian struggles.[17] In these writings Marx is not only dealing with concrete social formations at a specific historical moment, but his attention is focused on one level of the superstructure—the *political* instance. Hence, though these writings contain no general theoretical reformulations, they contain essential insights into how, in detail, Marx thought of the "effectivity of the superstructures."

Second, there are Marx's cryptic notes at the end of the 1857 "Introduction," tantalisingly headed "Forms of the State and Forms of Consciousness in Relation to Relations of Production and Circulation. Legal Relations. Family Relations." These are too epigrammatic and condensed to help us much. But they point to Marx's recognition of the difficulty; and they contain the crucial, if cryptic, identification of the "law of uneven development."

Third, there is, of course, the whole monumental theoretical edifice of *Capital* itself. There is no extensive passage, as we have said, in *Capital* in which the "laws of motion of the capitalist mode of production" are extended into the other levels of a social formation. But there are absolutely pivotal indications and traces of how this might be done, on the basis of Marx's decipherment of capital's secret. These do not add up to a thorough reworking of the base/superstructure problem. But they do, in sum, constitute an important, if incomplete, reflexive theoretical clarification.

The Eighteenth Brumaire

Before briefly looking at each of these moments, in turn, we can usefully sum up here the direction in which this incomplete clarification points. Crudely put, the relation of base to superstructure is thought, in *The German Ideology*, as some kind of fairly direct or immediate correspondence—i.e., within the framework of an *identity* theory. Marx progressively criticises and departs from identity theory. Essentially, two things provoke this "break." Historically, the antagonisms multiplying at the economic level fail, in the revolutions of 1848, to produce their "corresponding" political resolutions. Marx is therefore forced, not only to abandon the perspective of "immediate catastrophe" which had been ringingly tolled out in *The Communist Manifesto*, but to look again at the much more complex inter-play between the political and the economic; and to consider the ways in which "solutions" could be found, at the political level, which thwarted, modified or even displaced the contradictions accumulating at the economic level—taking them forward, in their contradictory form, to a higher level of development.

The Eighteenth Brumaire is the classic instance of such an analysis of the "effectivity" and specificity of the political instance in relation to the economic. "Here Marx began, for the first time, to develop a systematic set of concepts for coming to grips with the phenomena of a politics which is certainly that of class struggle—the struggle of groups whose existence and interests are defined by the relations of production—but which is nevertheless *politics*, practised in the field of ideology and coercion that gives it its specific character."[18] This is the direct result of a longer and more complex perspective, born in the failed denouement of 1848. Gwyn Williams has recently brilliantly expounded, from an *internal* reading of *The Eighteenth Brumaire*, precisely how and where this historical "break" registers as an analytic "break" inside Marx's text.[19] Engels subsequently remarked that in 1848, he and Marx had mistaken the *birth-pangs* of capitalism for its *death-throes*.

But the break is also provoked theoretically. For the more Marx examined in depth the capitalist mode of production, the more he observed the internal complexities of its laws and relations: and the less he thought this complex whole could be expounded in terms of the immediate correspondence between one of its circuits and another, let alone one of its levels and all the others. This major revision is of course practically exemplified in the conceptual structure of *Capital* itself. But it is also stated, as a matter of theory and method, in the 1857 "Introduction," which contains a thorough critique of "identity theory" and begins to sketch out a Marxist alternative—a theory of *articulations* between relations which are in no sense immediately corresponding. We cannot examine this here, but it provides, so to speak, the pivotal transitional point between *The German Ideology* and *Capital* itself.[20]

Thus, in this period, Marx's "clarification" turns our attention in a new direction. He is concerned, now, with the *necessary complexity* of the social formations of advancing capitalism and of the relations between its different levels. He is concerned with the "unevenness," the non-immediate correspondences, between these levels which remain, nevertheless, connected. He is concerned with the functions which, specifically, the superstructures "perform" in relation either to the maintenance and reproduction, or the retardation of the development, of capitalist social relations: and with the fact that these functions not only appear in ever-more complex forms, but that, at a certain stage of their development, they may actually *require* the non-immediacy—the "relative autonomy"—they exhibit. This is a different problematic from that of *The German Ideology* period. It is also different from Engels's attempts to extend the chain of reflexivity between base and superstructures, in a simple, linear way.[21]

Before looking, briefly, at *The Eighteenth Brumaire*, his most "worked" example, we can pinpoint from a number of sources the problems which constitute the field of Marx's new problematic.

When Marx examined British politics in the series of articles for the *New York Daily Tribune* which he commenced in 1852, he had to confront the stubborn fact that, though the capitalist mode of production was fast developing, and with it an emergent industrial bourgeoisie, the latter appeared to "rule" either through a Tory party, representing the large landed proprietors, or through the Whig party, consisting of "the oldest, richest, and most arrogant portion of English landed property . . . the aristocratic representatives . . . of the industrial and commercial middle class." To them, apparently, the bourgeoisie had abandoned the "monopoly of government and the exclusive possession of office." How capital advanced through this complex political configuration—giving rise to a distinction between an "economically ruling class" and, at the level of the political superstructures, a "politically governing caste"—was a fundamental problem; for the dynamic of British politics (and the politics of the working class, which remained tied to the tail of the Whig-Radical alliance) was constantly mediated—deflected through its structure. In fact, as Fernbach notes, Marx understood Britain politically far less well than France. He never grasped the deep compromise on which, after the settlement, British political life was stabilised; and he believed that ultimately, the industrial bourgeoisie would transform everything in its wake and assume power directly, "battering Old England to pieces." In fact, "the industrial bourgeoisie managed to integrate itself politically and culturally into the old ruling bloc and the aristocratic 'mask' was to remain for at least a further half-century to camouflage and mystify the rule of capital."[22] But, if Marx mistook the line of development, he was not wrong in locating the issue: an issue, essentially, of non-identity between the classes in dominance at the economic level and the class factions in power, at the level of politics and the state.[23]

Take another superstructural domain. In his *Critique of Hegel's Philosophy of Right*, Marx noted that the law served "to perpetuate a particular mode of production"; yet insisted that "the influence exercised by laws on the preservation of existing conditions of distribution, and the effect they thereby exert on production, has to be examined *separately*." Engels echoed this sentiment when, in *Ludwig Feuerbach and the End of Classical German Philosophy*,[24] in a long and interesting section on the state, law and ideology, he shows how England retained the forms of the old feudal law, whilst giving them a bourgeois content; how Roman law provided the foundation for the evolution of bourgeois legal relations elsewhere; how this "working up into a special code of law" proved to be a poor basis for the development of Prussia, but—transformed into the *Code Civil*—an extremely favourable one for France. Thus, though "bourgeois legal rules merely express" the economic life conditions of society in legal form, they can do so well or ill according to circumstances. In the same passage, Engels notes how, to achieve articulation as a sphere of the superstructure, economic facts must "assume the form of juristic motives," thereby leading on to the formation of a fully-fledged juridical sphere, a set of complex legal ideologies, with an efficacy of their own. "It is indeed among professional politicians, theorists of public law and jurists of private law that the connection with the economic facts gets really lost." It is, then, not surprising that it is in relation to legal relations that Marx states his "law of uneven development" in the *Grundrisse*: "But the really difficult point to discuss here is how relations of production develop *unevenly* as legal relations. Thus, e.g., the relation of Roman private law ... to modern production." There seems little doubt that, had this point been expanded by Marx at the length of, say, Book One of *Capital*, the one thing it would *not* have exhibited is a simple law of correspondence between the material base and the forms of the superstructure.

The Eighteenth Brumaire is, then, relatively simple to set in this context of problems—though its argument is not simple either to follow or resume. It concerns, essentially, the relation of the politics of the 1851 crisis in France, the forms of political regime and of the state which emerge, the nature of the Bonapartist "solution," and, more incidentally, the basis of ideology—"Napoleon's ideas"—in the accumulating contradictions generated by the development of an industrial capitalist mode of production. The latter is, however, here refracted through the former: it is the political instance which is in the foreground, just as, in 1851, it was politics which "took command." The French mode of production is beginning to develop, throwing up its antagonisms: the class fractions related to this development are already, politically, on stage: but so are those fractions which represent continuing, if declining modes of production still coexisting with industrial capital in the French social formation (the fact that the political complexity of the moment of 1851 is related to the coexistence of modes of production, with no single mode as yet in full dominance, is a crucial step in the argument). In one sense, then, the political crisis of 1851 is *given* at the level of mode of production. It may even be seen that, in a long-term sense, the stage of development (i.e., underdevelopment) of the capitalist mode of production is what prescribes or determines, in an epochal sense—the *range* of "solutions" to the crisis possible at this stage of development (i.e., no clear resolutions, one way or another). What it certainly does *not* do is to prescribe, in detail, either the content or forms of the political conjuncture. The December crisis runs through a succession of different regimes, each representing a shifting coalition of class fractions. Daily, the political content of the Napoleonic state shifted—formed and dissolved. Each coalition temporarily gave rise to a succession of forms of regime: social republic, democratic republic, parliamentary republic. It is only as each exhausts its possibilities of hegemony, and is dissolved, since none can rule the whole social formation on its own, that the Bonapartist "solution" is prepared: the *coup d'état*. This is a regressive moment, from the point of view of capital, arresting its development. France "seems to have escaped the despotism of a class only to fall back beneath the despotism of one individual."[25] The falling of France on its face before the rifle butt of Louis-Napoleon's troops corresponds to the "backwardness" of the French mode of production—and ensures that backwardness for a period. The lack of resolution—the situation of almost perfect equilibrium between the various contending fractions, leaving room for none definitively to prevail—provides the conditions in which the state itself appears, as a neutral structure "above the contending classes," and enormously expands its range and "autonomy": finally, Louis-Napoleon's regime—which appears in the form of a single despotism—in fact is seated on the back of a particular class interest: that of the "most numerous" class in France at that moment, though one destined to decline—the small-holding peasantry. This class fraction cannot rule in its own name: it rules *through* Napoleon and through his ideas. It is this class which temporarily gives content to the expanding state—for the state is not "suspended in mid-air": but Louis-Napoleon, revivifying spirits, names, battle cries and costumes from the past (the past of another and greater Napoleon), is the *conductor* of the power of this class to the political level. Capital settles for a "postponement." "Bonapartism" is its name and form.

Without examining this argument in any further detail, it should be sufficient to see from this and the related essays of this period, that the domain of the political/juridical superstructures and the forms of the state itself are no longer thought by Marx as in any simple reflexive or expressive sense corresponding to their base. In the development of a Marxist theory of the superstructures, this essay must occupy a *pivotal position* (as it did for Gramsci, one of the major contributors to such a theory).

Re-reading *Capital*

We have suggested that, properly understood, there are hints in the structure of the argument in *Capital* about how this new problematic of base and superstructure can be developed, as well, of course, as a major exposition of the necessary conceptual ground on which this theoretical development should be undertaken. There is no space to take this very far here. One way is to take the law and tendencies of "the self-expansion of capital," not as specifying in detail the content and forms of the superstructures and thereby "determining," but as providing the governing movements (including the contradictions and crises in that self-expansion, and the "solutions" which permit capital to continue to accumulate while reproducing its antagonisms at a more advanced level of composition), dictating the tempo and rhythms of development in the other parts of the social formation: setting limits, as it were, to what can or cannot be a solution adaptable to capital's self-expanding needs, and thus as determining through the *repertoire* of solutions (political, social, ideological) likely to be drawn on in any particular historical moment or conjuncture.

This involves a "reading'"—some would say *another* "reading"—of *Capital*, treating it neither as the theoretical analysis of a "pure" mode of production (whatever that is), nor as a history of British capitalism in the nineteenth century, which seem at this point in time to be the two prevailing alternatives on offer. We would have to try, instead, to understand, for example, as Marx does, the shift from the extraction of absolute to the extraction of *relative* surplus value as one of the key dynamics of the developing capitalist mode of production; as not merely a theoretical distinction but one which can be made concrete and historically specific in, say, the capitalist mode in England after the factory legislation of the mid-century. We can then see this shift as providing the baseline of solutions to the contradictions to which capitalism, as a fully established mode of production, is progressively exposed. If we then attempt to think all that is involved—politically, socially, ideologically, in terms of the state, of politics, of the reproduction of skills, of the degree of labour and the application of science as a "productive force," as a consequence of the uneven development towards this second "moment" in the unfolding of capitalist accumulation (i.e., as the inner spark which prompts many of the transformations in capitalism which we now sum up as the "transition from laissez-faire to monopoly")—then, we begin to see how *Capital* provides a foundation for the development of a Marxist theory of the superstructures within the framework of "determination in the last instance"; without falling back into the identity-correspondence position outlined in *The German Ideology*.

That is, so to speak, re-examining the base/superstructure problem from the perspective of "the base." But it is also possible, within the framework of *Capital*, to reconstruct certain key mechanisms and tendencies of the superstructures from distinctions Marx is always drawing between the "base" levels of production and exchange. And this helps us to understand how it can be possible to insist that, within Marxism, the superstructures are at one and the same moment "determined" and yet absolutely, fundamentally necessary and required: not empty ideological forms and illusions. This relates to what is now sometimes called the theory of *Darstellung* or "representation" in Marx.[26] Without taking on a complex account of this theory here, we may try to approach it more easily through Marx's notion or concept of *appearances* (and thus to the theory of "fetishism" as outlined in *Capital* I, Part 1; though there is considerable argument as to whether the theories of *Darstellung* and the theory of "fetishism" are in fact the same).

Often, though by no means exclusively, the question of appearances or of "real relations"/ "phenomenal forms" is linked, in *Capital*, with the distinction between production and exchange. In the 1857 "Introduction" and throughout *Capital*, Marx insists on the necessary relation between the circuits of exchange (where value is realised) and the conditions pertaining to it, and the circuits of capital through production and the conditions pertaining to that. These, he says, must not be thought of as "identical." They are complementary but different; articulated with each other, but each still requiring its own conditions to be sustained. Hence the "unity" which these processes exhibit is not a unity of identity, but "unity of the diverse"—the "concentration of many determinations." Now, though these processes remain linked in their differences, and each is necessary for the "self-expansion and realisation of value," production is the determining level: "Consumption appears as a moment of production." The sphere of exchange is, however, what *appears* to dominate, to provide the "real" level of social relations under capitalism: it is also the sphere in which the myriad everyday "exchanges" of capitalist market relations take place, dictated only by the hidden but miraculous hand of the market. It is thus the sphere of capitalism's "common sense"—that is, where our spontaneous and everyday common-sense perceptions and experiences of the system arises: and it is also the starting point of bourgeois theory—both vulgar political economy and, after that, marginal economics deal principally with the domain of circulation.

Now, all the relations of the sphere of exchange really exist—they are not figments of anyone's imagination. Value could not be realised without them. There is a labour market, where labour power is bought and sold the form of the contract being the wage. There are markets in which commodities exchange against money—the form of the contract being prices. This sphere of "free exchange," where labour appears to exchange against its "due price" (a "fair wage") and where goods appear to exchange at their equivalences (real prices) is the domain of private egoistic exchanges which political economy named "civil society." To put it briefly, and in a very simplified form, Marx argues two things about this sphere of capitalist society. Looking—to use a spatial metaphor—"downwards," this sphere conceals the real, but highly unequal and exploitative relations of production. The concentration on, indeed *the fetishisation* of, the sphere of exchange *masks* what founds it and makes it possible: the generation and extraction of the surplus in the sphere of capitalist production. Thus, at the level of exchange, the agents of the process appear as one individual confronting another: whereas, of course, this epoch of egoistic individuals "which produces this standpoint, that of the isolated individual, is also precisely that of the hitherto most developed *social ... relations.*"[27] Thus, when the production relations of capitalism *appear as* (and are treated, conceptually as consisting of nothing except) exchange relations, the effect of this re-presentation is to mask and occlude what the "real relations" of capitalism are. This is the theory of representation, and it is also part of the theory of "fetishism." It indicates why Marx is so insistent throughout *Capital* on the difference between "real relations" and their "phenomenal forms"—without his entertaining for a moment the idea that the "phenomenal forms" are imaginary or do not exist.

However, looking—to use the spatial metaphor again—"upwards," Marx then notes that it is these phenomenal relations which constitute the basis of civil society and the politico-juridical relations: that is, the superstructures. And from that level, also, arise the various forms of ideological consciousness. "*On the surface* of bourgeois society," Marx writes, "the wage of the labourer *appears as* the price of labour, a certain quantity of money that is paid for a certain quantity of labour." ... "This phenomenal form which makes the actual relation invisible and indeed shows the direct opposite of that relation forms the basis of all the *juridical notions* of both labourer and capitalist, of all the mystifications of the capitalist mode of production, of all its illusions as to *liberty*, of all the apologetic shifts of the *vulgar economists*." ... "The exchange between capital and labour at first *presents itself to* the mind in the same guise as the buying and selling of all other commodities," he adds a little further on. Finally, he concludes, "The former [the 'phenomenal forms'] appear directly and spontaneously *as current modes of thought*; the latter [the real relations] must first be discovered by science."[28] Thus, he says elsewhere, in a famous passage at the end of Part II of the first volume of *Capital*, "we ... take leave for a time of this noisy sphere where everything takes place on the surface and in view of all men, and follow them ... to the hidden abode of production.... This sphere that we are deserting, within whose boundaries the sale and purchase of labour-power goes on, is in fact a very Eden of the innate rights of man. There alone rule Freedom, Equality, Property and Bentham. Freedom, because both buyer and seller of a commodity, say, labour power, are constrained only by their free will. They contract as free agents, and the agreement they come to is but the form in which they give legal expression to their common will." Those who would like to found a theory of the superstructures, and the ideological discourses and spontaneous common-sense notions which fill out and help to organise the terrain of the superstructures, and who wish nevertheless to know how *and why* these emerge, in determinate forms, from the level of a mode of production, have, it seems to me, little or no alternative but to begin to work outwards from this essential starting point at the heart of the argument in the mature Marx in *Capital* itself.[29]

Gramsci

The problem of base/superstructure has been the subject of considerable further development and theorising, especially within "Western Marxism"—though it must be said that few appear to try to work *outwards* from the terrain of the mature Marx in the way tentatively formulated above. Most attempts have preferred to go back to the less adequate formulations of the *German Ideology* period. What is more, many of these attempts have been concerned with the specifically *ideological* dimensions of the superstructures. We have neglected this aspect here, not only because it has been much written about, and because it constitutes a difficult area of theorising in itself, but also because the concentration on the problems of ideology has, until recently, obscured the fact that when Marx refers to the superstructures, he is discussing the forms, relations and apparatuses of the state and civil society, *as well as* the ideological forms and forms of social consciousness corresponding to them. Since Lenin and Gramsci—until Nicos Poulantzas and Althusser placed the problem once more squarely on the agenda—the superstructures in the true Marxian sense, including the absolutely critical question of the nature of the capitalist state, have been woefully neglected.

In the space left at our disposal, only two positions can, even cursorily, be considered. They constitute, however, in our view, the really significant contribution, post–Marx, Engels and Lenin, to the development of a Marxist "theory of the superstructures" and of the base/superstructure relation.

The first contributor here is Gramsci. Gramsci's work was undertaken first in the very centre of the great upsurge of proletarian struggle in Italy in the immediately post–First World War period, and then continued, under the most difficult circumstances of imprisonment. Gramsci was forced to ponder long and hard the difficult question of how Marxism could inform revolutionary political practice. He was also forced, by the "exceptional" nature of the Italian state, to consider deeply the question of the nature of the capitalist state in both its "normal" and its exceptional forms (it was one of those exceptions, after all—the fascist state of Mussolini—which put him behind bars). He was also, as a result of his Crocean early training, peculiarly alerted to the enlarging or (as Croce put it) "ethical" functions of the state, and what this concept would mean when translated into Marxist terms. And he was involved, as one of the leading militants in the international communist movement, directly with the same problems which had precipitated Lenin's fundamental text, *State and Revolution*.

It is not possible to recapitulate Gramsci's formulations about the state and the superstructures here. All that we can do is to indicate the *direction* of Gramsci's thinking in this domain. Much of Gramsci's work is directed in polemic against economic reductive theories of the superstructures. Hence, he argued that the proper posing of the relation between base and superstructures was the seminal issue in a Marxist theory of politics.[30] Fundamental class relations always, under conditions of developing capitalist relations, extend themselves in and through the "complex spheres of the superstructures"; for only thus could the reproduction of the social relations of capitalism be carried through in such a way as, progressively, to draw civil, social, political and cultural life into a larger conformity with capital and its needs. In developed capitalist social formations, this *enlargement* of capital's sway throughout the social formation as a whole depended, precisely, on the development of the state and of civil society. Here, Gramsci paid close attention to the "ethical" function of the state, by which he meant the "work" which the state performs on behalf of capital in establishing a new level of civilisation, creating a new kind of social individual appropriate to the new levels of material existence accomplished by the development of capitalism's base. It was through the state, through its work in and with the family, the law, education, the multiplicity of private associations, the cultural apparatus, the church, the formation of new strata of the intelligentsia, the formation of political parties and the development of public opinion—in short, in the complex sphere of the superstructures—that capitalism ceased to be simply a system of production and became a whole form of social life, conforming everything else to its own movement. This expansion of the conception of what it is the superstructures "do" for capital is Gramsci's first contribution.

The second is the manner in which he generates those critical intermediary concepts which enable us to think the *specificity* of a superstructural level. Here we have in mind Gramsci's development of the political instance, and the critical (if often provisional and cryptic) concepts he elaborates there of "relations of force," hegemony, historical bloc, corporate and subaltern classes, class fractions, Caesarism, Bonapartism, etc. Once again, in Gramsci's concept of "hegemony," for example, we discover the beginnings of a way of conceptualising how classes, constituted at the fundamental level of production relations, come to provide the basis of the social authority, the political sway and cultural domination of a "class alliance on behalf of capital," without reducing the idea to what Marx once called the "dirty Jewish" question of class interest, narrowly conceived. This latter form of economic reductionism, Gramsci argues, conceives of history as "a continuous *marche de dupes*, a competition in conjuring and sleight of hand. 'Critical' activity [i.e., Marxism] is reduced to the exposure of swindles, to creating scandals, and to prying into the pockets of public figures."[31] Which of us cannot quickly recall *that* brand of Marxism of exposure?

Gramsci's third contribution in this area is the attention he paid to the nature, specifically, of the *capitalist* state, its role in the generation of ideological consent, and thus to how class power secured itself in its "decisive passage from the structure to the sphere of the complex superstructures," whilst at the same time providing, at the level of the superstructures and of ideologies, that "cement" which welded the social formation together under the hegemonic sway of an alliance founded on the fundamental class of capital.

> In reality, the State must be conceived of as an "educator," in as much as it tends precisely to create a new type or level of civilisation. Because one is acting essentially on economic forces reorganising and developing the apparatus of economic production, creating a new structure, the conclusion must not be drawn that the superstructural factors should be left to themselves to develop spontaneously, to a haphazard and sporadic germination. The State, in this field too, is an instrument of rationalisation, of acceleration and of Taylorisation. It operates according to a plan, urges, incites, solicits, "punishes"; for, once the conditions are created in which a certain way of life is "possible," then "criminal action or omission" must have a punitive sanction, with moral implications, and not merely be judged generically as "dangerous." The Law is the repressive and negative aspect of the entire, positive, civilising activity undertaken by the State.[32]

A Marxist grasp of the nature of the state and its functions and processes under capitalism, especially in its classical "liberal" or laissez-faire form, and the complementary discussion of "consent" and "coercion," of the role of ideology and common sense, etc., which fill out Gramsci's subtle and perceptive thought on this question, has rarely if ever been surpassed. Gramsci's work remains, of course, theoretically underdeveloped: the concepts are often in what Althusserians would call their "practical" state: they are hardly ever "pure"— never thoroughly or radically dismembered from their location within specific conjunctures. But if Lenin was correct to argue that what a Marxist analysis pointed to as its proper conclusion was the "concrete analysis of a concrete situation"—in other words, precisely, the analysis of conjunctures—then it is Lenin himself, first, and Gramsci immediately behind who—in so far as such an analysis embraces the superstructures—lead the way.

Gramsci is the one "historicist" whose work continues to haunt and can never be expunged from the starting points which the structuralists, like Althusser and Poulantzas, the other major contributors to a Marxist theory of base and superstructure, adopt. Both Althusser and Poulantzas criticise Gramsci's starting position within a "philosophy of praxis."[33] Both are massively indebted to Gramsci, in seminal not just in marginal or incidental ways. Poulantzas's work on the political instance and on the state is conceptually impossible without Gramsci. And, as Althusser has revised his more "theoreticist" earlier positions and moved towards a more substantive, less epistemological approach to the object of Marxist analysis (as for example in his seminal and extremely influential essay, "Ideology and Ideological State Apparatuses"),[34] so his debt to Gramsci, already handsomely acknowledged, becomes both more explicit and more pronounced. The concept of "ideological state apparatus," which has become a generative idea in the post-Althusserian analysis of the capitalist state, is a direct reworking of a few seminal passages on apparatuses of consent and coercion in Gramsci's "State and Civil Society" essay; though, of course, translated—with effect—into a more structuralist Marxist language.

Althusser

The contribution of Althusser and his followers, especially Poulantzas, in elaborating a Marxist theory of base/superstructure, is too complicated a matter to undertake here. We can only note three significant aspects which, taking up in his customarily rigorous fashion, Althusser has deeply transformed; thereby making a contribution of considerable theoretical significance to the problem of base and superstructure.

First, let us note that, in the manner in which a social formation is "thought" by Althusser—beginning with the formative and classic essay, "Contradiction and Overdetermination," in *For Marx*, and developed in *Reading Capital*—there is more than a hint that the topographical metaphor of "base/superstructure" ought to be superseded altogether. For Althusser conceives a social formation as composed of different practices—essentially the economic, political and ideological (with, perhaps, a fourth: theoretical practice?)—each of which is required for the production and reproduction of the relations of the capitalist mode: and each of which has its own inner constitution, its own specificity, its own dynamic and "relative autonomy" from the others. Some of Althusser's most effective polemical passages are indeed reserved for taking the base/superstructure metaphor *literally*: and thus showing the absurdity of waiting for a historical moment when the determining level—His Majesty, the Economy—could detach itself from its more incidental and epiphenomenal superstructural forms, and exert its "determination" over a social formation on its own! Neither in time nor history can "determination in the last instance by the economic" be so read as to suggest that the level of economic practice could stand free and appear denuded of political and ideological practices.

This theory of the necessity, as well as of the "relative autonomy," of the practices formerly consigned to the "superstructures"—as we have already seen—constitutes one end of the double chain of a Marxist theory of a social formation. But then, what of the other end of the chain? How, then, is determinacy to be understood?

It is not, in Althusser's view, to be understood in terms of what produces a particular conjuncture, especially a revolutionary conjuncture. Such moments of fundamental rupture are no more exclusively produced by the single determinacy of "the economic" than any other moment. Such moments are constituted, rather, by the accumulation of the different contradictions, peculiar to each of the levels or practices, in one space or moment: hence, such conjunctures are, like Freud's symptoms (from whom, indeed, the metaphor is adopted), not determined, but "overdetermined." Determinacy, then, for Althusser, is thought principally in terms of the economic level (determining) having, as one of its effects, the deciding which of the levels of the social formation—economic, political or ideological—will be "dominant."

Each level or practice is, thus, conceived, not as autonomous but as part of a "complex, structured whole, structured in dominance." Determinacy consists in the combination or articulation (the *Darstellung*) of instances and effects in and through this complex structure. "The fact that each of these times and each of these histories is *relatively autonomous* does not make them so many domains which are *independent* of the whole; the specificity of each of these times and each of these histories—in other words, their relative autonomy and independence—is based on a certain type of *dependence* with respect to the whole."[35] This is a conception of "determination" rigorously reinterpreted in the form of what Althusser calls a "structural" rather than a sequential causality. The whole point of *Reading Capital* is indeed to establish, via a "symptomatic reading" of Marx's work, that this is indeed the form of "causality" which the mature Marx employed.

The theoreticism, the "straightening out" of Marx in the interests of proving his structuralist lineage, which is characteristic especially of Althusser's work in the period of *Reading Capital*, has been widely criticised; not least by some of his former collaborators (e.g., Rancière), and by Althusser himself.[36] But this should not detract from the seminal advance which the base-superstructure problem has undergone in his hands. This is brought forcefully forwards in the now-famous "Ideological State Apparatuses" essay, in which Althusser puts forwards some "Notes" on the nature of ideology and the state, and restores some of the problems he had previously addressed to the more classical terrain of the "class struggle" (actually, both here and in Poulantzas, more often invoked than present, as a concept performing the work of knowledge, in their respective texts. Again, the "ISAs" essay cannot be resumed here. It requires careful and critical reading. It falls very much into two parts; and the first—which examines the locating of ideology in the apparatuses and structures of the state—is far more convincing than the second, which, following the sinuous path of a Lacanian revision of Freud, enters, it seems to us, another problematic which, however important, is as yet hardly within hailing distance of any which can be attributed to Marx without straining credibility.

What is most significant from our point of view here, however, is the manner in which the "effectivity" of the superstructures is posed in this essay. Althusser recapitulates the central position in Marxism occupied by the base/superstructure metaphor. It is, he suggests, a metaphor: a "metaphor of topography." It "makes something visible"—namely "that the upper floors could not 'stay up' alone, if they did not rest precisely on their base." Despite Althusser's probing irony here at the expense of this topographical depiction, he acknowledges that it has a function: "The great theoretical advantage of the Marxist topography . . . is simultaneously that it reveals that questions of determination (or of index of effectivity) are crucial: that it reveals that it is the base which in the last instance determines the whole edifice; and that, as a consequence, it obliges us to pose the theoretical problem of the type of 'derivatory' effectivity peculiar to the superstructures and the reciprocal action of the superstructure on the base." Thus, while retaining the classical metaphor, Althusser proposes to go beyond its purely descriptive limitations, and rethink the problem "on the basis of reproduction." What he means, broadly, by this is that the specific "effectivity" of the superstructures is to be understood in terms of their role in the *reproduction of the social relations of production*; or what has come to be termed, on the basis of the problematic of "social reproduction."

Althusser makes, at best, a tentative start in this essay with this concept. The idea of regarding the superstructures in terms of social reproduction has, however, already proved innovative and productive conceptually, not least in those areas of Marxist theory (for example, in relation to the family, the sexual division of labour and the role of so-called "unproductive labour") which have hitherto hardly survived the reductive thrust of the originating topographical metaphor. It is true that the notion of "social reproduction" tends to produce in its wake its own distortions: that of an endlessly successfully, functionally unfolding reproduction of capitalist social relations without either end, contradiction, crisis or break. But then, the one question which Althusserians, in their own peremptory haste to dismantle empirical and historicist-humanism forever ("Marxism is not a Humanism," "Marxism is not Historicism"), have not deeply enough considered is whether, in declaring that Marxism is a "structuralism," they have sufficiently satisfied themselves—or us—that Marxism *is not a functionalism*. However, while bearing this crucial but difficult theoretical issue in view, it must be said that the attempt to reconceptualise the base/superstructure problem in terms of "social reproduction," and thus in much closer conceptual touch with the starting point of Marx's mature work (production, reproduction), has done a great deal to revivify theoretical work on the problem, and to set work on it moving in what may well prove to be a fruitful direction.

To take this conceptual opening further—both to modify and extend it, critically—is at the same time, to advance Marxism as a critical science and as a theoretically informed revolutionary practice. Only when we can grasp and comprehend the dense, opaque integument of capitalist societies—their base and their complex superstructures—through the former are we likely to be able to develop a sufficiently informed practice to transform them.

NOTES

This essay, with a slightly different title, "Re-thinking the 'Base-and-Superstructure' Metaphor," first appeared in *Class, Hegemony and Party*, ed. Jon Bloomfield (London: Lawrence and Wishart, 1977), 43–72.

1. Preface to the French edition of *Capital*, 1872, in Karl Marx, *Capital* I (Moscow: Foreign Languages Publishing House, 1961).
2. "Afterword" to the second German edition of *Capital* I (Moscow: Foreign Languages Publishing House, 1961).
3. Karl Marx, *The Poverty of Philosophy*, in Marx and Engels, *Collected Works* (*MECW*), vol. 6 (London: Lawrence and Wishart, 1976).
4. Karl Marx, Preface to *A Contribution to the Critique of Political Economy* (London: Lawrence and Wishart, 1971).
5. Louis Althusser, *For Marx* (London: Allen Lane, 1969).
6. Marx, *Capital* I, 82.
7. Karl Marx, "Introduction," in *Grundrisse* (Harmondsworth, UK: Pelican, 1973), 106–7.
8. Marx, "Introduction," *Grundrisse*, 84.
9. See the "Correspondence," in Karl Marx and Frederick Engels, *Selected Works* (*MESW*), vol. 2 (London: Lawrence and Wishart, 1951).
10. Gareth Stedman Jones, "Engels and the End of Classical German Philosophy," *New Left Review* I/79 (1973).
11. Perry Anderson, *Considerations on Western Marxism* (London: New Left Books, 1976).
12. Stedman Jones, "Engels."
13. Engels, letter to Conrad Schmidt, 5 August 1890, *MESW*, vol. 2.
14. Engels, letter to Joseph Bloch, 21–22 September 1890, *MESW*, vol. 2.
15. Engels, letter to Bloch, *MESW*, vol. 2.
16. Louis Althusser, "Contradiction and Overdetermination," in *For Marx*.
17. See Karl Marx, *Surveys from Exile*, and David Fernbach's excellent "Introduction" (Harmondsworth, UK: Pelican/New Left Review, 1973).
18. Fernbach, "Introduction."
19. Gwyn A. Williams, "The Revolution of 1848," Course A321, Unit 7, *France, 1848–51* (Milton Keynes, UK: Open University, 1976).
20. See Stuart Hall, "Marx's Notes on Method" [chap. 1, this volume].
21. In the "Correspondence" especially: elsewhere, as we shall suggest, Engels contributes some useful insights for Marx's new problematic.
22. Fernbach, "Introduction."
23. See, on this problem, the extended controversy between Perry Anderson, Tom Nairn and E. P. Thompson on the "peculiarities of the English," which ran through *New Left Review* in the early 1960s.
24. In Karl Marx and Frederick Engels, *Selected Works in One Volume* (London: Lawrence and Wishart, 1968).
25. Karl Marx, *The Eighteenth Brumaire of Louis Bonaparte*, in Marx and Engels, *Selected Works in One Volume*.
26. See Louis Althusser and Étienne Balibar, *Reading Capital* (London: New Left Books, 1970); Norman Geras, "Fetishism in Marx's *Capital*," *New Left Review* I/65 (1971); John Mepham, "The Theory of Ideology in *Capital*," *Working Papers in*

Cultural Studies, no. 6 (1974); André Glucksmann, "The Althusserian Theatre," *New Left Review* I/72 (1972); Alex Callinicos, *Althusser's Marxism* (London: Pluto Press, 1976).

27 Marx, "Introduction," in *Grundrisse*, 84.
28 All these quotes are from chapter 19, "Wages," in *Capital* I. Our italics. The formulations are recapitulated again and again through that volume.
29 For an elaboration of this starting point, see Geras, "Fetishism"; Mepham, "The Theory of Ideology in *Capital*"; and Hall, "Marx's Notes on Method" [chap. 1, this volume].
30 See Antonio Gramsci, "The Modern Prince," in *Selections from the Prison Notebooks* (London: Lawrence and Wishart, 1971), 164–68, 177–82.
31 Gramsci, *Prison Notebooks*, 164.
32 Gramsci, "State and Civil Society," in *Prison Notebooks*, 247.
33 See Althusser, "Marxism Is Not a Historicism," in Althusser and Balibar, *Reading Capital*; and Nicos Poulantzas, "The Capitalist State and Ideologies," in *Political Power and Social Classes* (London: New Left Books, 1973).
34 In Louis Althusser, *Lenin and Philosophy and Other Essays* (London: New Left Books, 1971).
35 Louis Althusser, "The Errors of Classical Economics: An Outline for a Concept of Historical Time," in Althusser and Balibar, *Reading Capital*, 100.
36 Louis Althusser, *Essays in Self-Criticism* (London: New Left Books, 1976).

CHAPTER 3

The "Political" and the "Economic" in Marx's Theory of Classes

The limits on this paper will be immediately obvious. It is not possible, here, to present anything like a comprehensive or systematic "survey" of Marx's theory of classes. First, classes, class relations and class struggle are concepts central to everything which Marx wrote—including, of course, the major work of *Capital* on the "laws of motion" of the capitalist mode of production, where the discussion of classes is postponed to the very end, and was in fact tantalisingly incomplete. A comprehensive account of "Marx on class" would thus amount to a reconstruction of his entire work. Second, there is no such homogeneous entity or object as a "theory of class," in the singular, to be exposited. Marx wrote about class and class struggle at each of the major moments of his work. As we know, these texts have different degrees of status and purposes—a matter which crucially affects the level, the aspect, the degree of abstraction, etc., through which the question is approached. The polemic against the Left Hegelians in *The German Ideology*, the organisational purpose and rhetorical simplifications of *The Communist Manifesto*, the conjunctural political analyses of *The Class Struggles in France*, the theoretical labour of the *Grundrisse* and *Capital*—each, because of the difference in its aim and address, *inflects* the problem of classes differently.

We know from his comments and correspondence—for example, concerning the differences in the manner of exposition as between the "working notebooks" of the *Grundrisse* and *Capital*—that Marx took this question of mode of presentation very seriously. For example, in his letter of 1 February 1859, he writes to Joseph Weydemeyer about the intended order of publication of the first four sections of Book I of *Capital*: "You understand the *political* reasons which have moved me to hold back the third Chapter on 'Capital' until I have established myself again . . ."[1] Third, we know that these different texts are also to some degree bound and governed by the problematics within which Marx was thinking and writing at the time. These changed and altered as Marx's thinking developed. Althusser is correct in his argument that Marx's "discoveries" are in some critical sense bound up with the "breaks" between one problematic and another. Without necessarily accepting the severe and finalist manner in which Althusser has "periodised" Marx's work, with the aid of the powerful instrument of the "epistemological rupture"—an operation from which, in any case, Althusser has subsequently taken his necessary distance[2]—his intervention *does* prevent us from ever reading Marx again in such a way as to constitute, by a prospective-retrospective sleight-of-hand, a single, homogeneous "Marxism," always on its preordained way, from the *1844 Manuscripts* to *The Civil War in France*, towards its given, teleological end. It prevents an "essentialist," and therefore closed, reading of Marx such as would suggest that all that is really discovered in *Capital* is already "present," in embryo, in the *1844 Manuscripts*—that all the texts can be taken together, as a linear progression, and read transparently for their inevitable tendency, for what they incipiently lead to. Such a reading not only does an injustice to Marx, it also establishes a false and misleading picture of how theoretical work has to be done and obscures the retreats and detours by which it advances and develops. It incites in us a "lazy" Marxism, suggesting that there is no critical work left for us to do in really grappling with the differences and the developments in Marx's own work—and that all we have to do is rest on the "obviousness" of the "Marxism" always latent in Marx's texts. This kind of Marxist "common sense" has done profound damage to Marxism as a living and developing practice—including the necessary practice of struggle *in* theory itself. Such a linear transparency in Marx must be constantly and vigorously challenged.

In part, what is involved, then, is a particular practice of reading—one which tries to hold together the logic of the argument and exposition of a text, within the matrix of propositions and concepts which makes its discourse possible, which generates it. In the limited passages and texts discussed in this paper, much depends on the project to develop a mode of theoretical work of this kind. It involves ceasing to take a text at its face value, as a closed object. This applies both where the text is resoundingly "obvious," and where it is obviously complex, even obscure. The question of the class struggle is manifestly *present* in every line and paragraph of *The Communist Manifesto*. Yet the concept of classes which generates that text is, as we hope to show, not immediately graspable from its luminous surface. *Capital* is precisely the reverse—a complex, theoretical text, which has centrally as its object the capitalist mode of production; and which appears, for long stretches to have "postponed" the class struggle to another level, another moment. One of the most difficult exercises is to "read" the *Manifesto* for the concept of the relation between classes and modes of production which lies at its heart; and to "read" the laws and motion of capital in *Capital* in terms of the class struggle. In the latter instance, Marx gives us a beautiful insight—again, in a letter he wrote to Engels (30 April 1868)—into how the two relate. He is resuming the argument, essentially, of *Capital* III. He goes over some of the most complex—and technical—of concepts: the constitution of an "average rate of profit"; the relation between the different branches of production; the problem of the transformation "of value into price of production"; the tendency of the rate of profit to fall. Then he returns, at the end, to what constitutes the "starting point" for the vulgar economist: the famous Trinitarian Formula (the dismantling of which, *in extenso*, in *Capital* III is one of the richest and most devastating theoretical passages of that work). This is the "formula" which appeared to "explain" the distribution of profit in terms of the harmonious return of each proportionate part to its appointed factor in capitalist production: "rent originating from the land, profit (interest) from capital, wages from labour." In revealing the "real" movement behind this distribution, he has dismantled its "apparent form"; but this is no mere "theoretical" demystification. "Finally, since these three (wages, rent, profit [interest]) constitute the respective sources of income of the three classes of landowners, capitalists and wage labourers, we have, in conclusion the *class struggle* into which the movement and the analysis of the whole business [*Scheisse*, "shit," in the original] resolves itself."[3]

Althusser has given us a protocol for "reading" theoretical texts in this way—the method of a "symptomatic reading." My own remarks above stop some way short of proposing the full "symptomatic reading" of Marx's work. The idea has its source, of course, in Freud's theory of the formation of "symptoms" in the discourse of the patient, in his important work *The Interpretation of Dreams*. The difficulty with the full-blown theory of a "symptomatic reading" when applied to a theoretical text arises in terms of what are the controls on it. It is one thing to read a complex text with one eye always on the matrix of conceptual premises and propositions which generates it, gives it what theoretical coherence it possesses—and also helps us to identify its "silences," its absences. "Reading for absence" is certainly one of the principal foundations of a critical theoretical practice. But it is quite another thing to operate a "symptomatic reading" like a theoretical guillotine, beheading any concept which has the temerity to stray from its appointed path. The line between the two is unfortunately not very well defined.

It is not always easy to differentiate between a "symptomatic reading" which enables us to read with effect the theoretical structure of a Marx text out of those surface formulations where concepts appear in what is sometimes dubiously called their "practical state"; and a "symptomatic reading" which really provides the cover for so translating these "practical concepts" into their "pure" theoretical state that a text can be made to be "really" saying whatever it is that the reader has already determined to find there. *Reading Capital*, which operates this method in its most rigorous and extreme form, on the one hand prevents us from an "innocent" reading of Marx: but is often also guilty itself of so *transforming* "what Marx really said" that it—of course—produces what it first set out to discover. To put it bluntly, if Marx's "practical concepts" are systematically raised to a more theoretical level with the aid of structuralist instruments and concepts then it is not difficult, in this way, to produce at the end a "structuralist Marx." The question—the extremely important question posed at the opening of *Reading Capital*—as to what sort of "structuralist" the mature Marx really was, cannot be answered in this circular manner. Althusser himself knows this, since it is *he* who clearly demonstrated (in *For Marx*) the necessarily closed circularity of a "reading" which has its "answers" already premised in the form of the questions it poses. He called this circularity—ideological.[4]

In what follows I shall attempt to avoid *both* the "innocence" of a reading which sticks fast to the surface form of an argument; and the particular form of "guilt" attached to producing an interpretation which simply fits my preconceptions. I am aiming at a certain kind of *interrogation* of some critical passages in Marx on the question of classes and class struggle. I link the two together—classes and class struggle—because it is this articulation which concerns me most in this paper, and which has dictated the passages I have chosen to examine. The extremely difficult and complex matter of the theoretical designation of the anatomy of classes *as such* is handled at much greater length in other papers in this symposium, and is left to a brief passage at the end of this paper. I shall be particularly concerned to demonstrate how and why Marx's ideas on classes and class struggle differ, at different periods of his work; and of how they advance. I want, if possible, to reconsider some of the earlier and "transitional" texts again—many of them having been too swiftly assigned to the conceptual scrap-heap. But I shall certainly want to examine them from the viewpoint of Marx's mature and developed theory: I shall try to look at them, not "innocently," but *in the light of Capital*. Much of what I shall say ought therefore to be judged, by the reader, in terms of this declared line of departure.

I.

The Communist Manifesto was drafted by Marx and Engels for the Communist League "to make plain to all the true nature of the 'spectre' that was supposed to be haunting Europe." It was published on the eve of the great revolutionary upsurge of 1848—by the time it appeared, Marx was already in Paris at the invitation of the liberal-radical government which had overthrown Louis-Philippe. It was explicitly designed as a revolutionary tocsin; many, if not all, of its simplifications must be understood in that light. By the summer of 1848, the counterrevolution had begun to unroll; Marx and Engels were forced to admit that they had misread the birth-pangs of bourgeois society as its death-knell. Marx changed his mind—about many more things than the speed at which the revolutionary showdown would be enacted. Gwyn Williams has brilliantly demonstrated how this "break" in perspective—a *political* break—registers inside the *theoretical structure* of one of Marx's most critical texts, *The Eighteenth Brumaire of Louis Bonaparte*.[5] Indeed, without simplifying the connection, we could say that the historical collapse of the 1848 Revolutions produced a theoretical advance of the first order in Marx's understanding of the complex question of classes and their relation to political struggle. One way of assessing the distance he travelled and the discoveries he made can be measured in terms of the *differences*—and convergences—between the way he writes about classes in the *Manifesto* (1847) and the essays on *The Eighteenth Brumaire* and *The Class Struggles in France*, drafted between 1850 and 1852.

> The history of all hitherto existing society is the history of class struggles. Freeman and slave, patrician and plebeian, lord and serf, guild-master and journeyman, in a word, oppressor and oppressed, stood in constant opposition to one another, carried on an uninterrupted, now hidden, now

open fight, a fight that each time ended in a revolutionary reconstruction of society at large, or in the common ruin of the contending classes.

... With the development of industry the proletariat not only increases in number; it becomes concentrated in greater masses, its strength grows and it feels that strength more. The various interests are more and more equalised, in proportion as machinery obliterates all distinctions of labour, and nearly everywhere reduces wages to the same low level. The growing competition among the bourgeois... makes their livelihood more and more precarious; the collision between individual workmen and individual bourgeois takes more and more the character of the collision between two classes. Thereupon the workers begin to form combinations (trade unions) against the bourgeois.... This organisation of the proletarians into a class, and consequently into a political party, is continually being upset by the competition between the workers themselves. But it ever rises up again, stronger, firmer and mightier. It compels legislative recognition of particular interests of workers, by taking advantage of divisions among the bourgeoisie itself. Thus the Ten Hours Bill in England.[6]

What is so fatally seductive about this text is its simplifying revolutionary sweep: its *elan*, coupled with the optimistic sureness of its grasp on the unrolling, unstoppable tide of revolutionary struggle and proletarian victory; above all, its unmodified sense of historical inevitability. That note sits uneasily with our much-refined sense of the revolution's infinitely "long delay"—and of how much more complex, how less inevitable, its dénouement has proved to be. And this is connected with a rejection of one of the central propositions which appears to power and sustain this unrolling-through-revolution: the progressive simplification of class antagonisms, articulated along a linear path of historical time, into *basically* two hostile camps—bourgeoisie and proletarians, facing one another in a "process of dissolution of... a violent and glaring character." The whole logic of this part of the text is overdetermined by the historical conjuncture in which it was drafted. Undoubtedly, classes are constructed in the text historically, in the simple sense: the dissolution of feudalism; the revolutionary role of the emergent bourgeoisie; "free competition" and "free labour"—Marx's two preconditions for the installation of a capitalist mode of production on an expanded scale; the gigantic development of capital's productive capacities; then, industrial and commercial crises; progressive immiseration, class polarisation, revolutionary rupture and overthrow.

This *linearity*, this undisguised historical evolutionism, is interrupted or displaced by the play of, essentially, only *a* single antagonism: between the developing forces of production, and the "fettering" relations of production in which the former are embedded. It is this fundamental contradiction which provides the basic punctuation of the class struggle in the capitalist mode. Its course is subject, of course, to delays; but its essential tendency is forwards towards "collision." This is because the two levels are directly harnessed—the class struggle "matures" as capitalism "develops." Indeed, the latter develops and matures the former: capitalism is its own gravedigger. Capitalism thus produces its own "negation"—the oppressed classes whose rising struggles propel that phase to its conclusion, and drive society forwards to the next stage of its development. Since bourgeois versus proletarians is the most "universal" of the class struggles to date—the proletariat is the last class to be emancipated; that which "has nothing to lose but its chains"—the proletarian revolution entails the emancipation of all classes, or the abolition of class society *as such*.

The basic problematic of the *Manifesto* is hardly in doubt. Its presence is luminously rendered in the transparency of the writing—a transparency of style which recapitulates the way the relations and connections dealt with in the text are grasped and driven forwards. It treats classes as "whole" subjects—collective subjects or actors. It deals with the transposition of the class struggle from the economic to the political level unproblematically. They are interchangeable: the one leads, inexorably, to the other. They are connected by means of what Althusser has called a "transitive causality." It treats history as an unfolding sequence of struggles—arranged into epochs, punctuated by *the* class struggle, which is its motor. It conceives a capitalist social formation as, essentially, a simple structure—a structure whose immediate forms may be complex, but whose dynamic and articulation is simple and essentialist: its articulation is basically "given" by the terms of a single contradiction (forces/relations of production) which unrolls unproblematically from the economic "base," evenly throughout all its different levels, "indifferently." A break at one level therefore gives rise, sooner or later, to a parallel break at the other levels. This has been defined as a "historicist" conception because it deals with a social formation as what Althusser calls an "expressive totality."[7] There is even, behind this "historicism," the trace of an earlier problematic: that which conceives of the proletarian revolution as the liberation of all humanity, the "moment" of the installation of the rule of Reason in History—one which recalls the humanist thrust of, say, the section "On Communism" of the *1844*

Manuscripts, with its undisguised Feuerbachian and Hegelian overtones. It is a heroic, humanist vision. But it is flawed, both in its substantive predictions and in its mode of conceptualisation.[8]

The most decisive and definitive dismantling of this whole problematic is certainly to be found in Althusser's seminal essay, "Contradiction and Overdetermination," in *For Marx*. The *Manifesto* must now be read in the light of that intervention. Briefly, in it, Althusser argues that in the concrete analysis of any specific historical moment, although the principal contradiction of the capitalist mode of production—that between the forces of production and the "fettering" relations of production—provides the "final" determinacy, the terms of this contradiction, alone, are not sufficient for analysing the way *different levels of class struggle* lead to a revolutionary rupture. Because the levels of a social formation are not neatly aligned in the way the *Manifesto* suggests, contradictions do not immediately and unmediatedly unroll from the economic base, producing a rupture or break at all the different levels simultaneously. Indeed, as Lenin indicated with respect to 1917, the crucial question is rather how "absolutely dissimilar currents, absolutely heterogeneous class interests, absolutely contrary political and social strivings have merged . . . in a strikingly 'harmonious' manner" as the result of an "extremely unique historical situation." These dissimilar currents cannot, then, be reduced to the determinacy of the "laws" of the economic base. "The Capital-Labour contradiction is never simple, but always specified by the historically concrete forms and circumstances in which it is exercised. It is specified by the forms of the superstructure . . . by the internal and external historical situation . . . many of these phenomena deriving from the 'law of uneven development' in the Leninist sense."[9]

This requires us to conceive of different contradictions, each with its own specificity, its own tempo of development, internal history, and its own conditions of existence—at once "determined and determining": in short, it poses the question of the relative autonomy and the specific effectivity of the different levels of a social formation. If this is to be combined with the cardinal principle of Marxism—that without which it is theoretically indistinguishable from any other "sociology"—namely, "determination in the last instance by the (economic) mode of production," then a decisive turn in the relations of forces in a social formation cannot be adequately "thought" in terms of a *reduction* of all the secondary contradictions to the terms of the principal contradiction. In short, Marxism requires a form of determinacy which is *not* equivalent to an economic reductionism. The "merging" of these "heterogeneous currents," Althusser suggests, is better "thought," not as a reduction but as *a complex effect*—an accumulation of all the instances and effects, a merger, a rupture—an "overdetermination." It follows from this argument that a social formation is not a "totality" of the essentialist type, in which there is a simple "identity" between its different levels, with the superstructural levels the mere "epiphenomena" of the objective laws governing "the economic base." It is, rather, a unity of a necessarily complex type—an "ensemble" which is always the result of many determinations: a unity, moreover which is characterised by its *unevenness*.

In his 1857 "Introduction" to the *Grundrisse* Marx argued that, though Capital, in its prolonged circuit, requires both production, distribution and exchange, these must not be thought as "equivalents," but as different "moments" of a circuit, *articulated into* a "unity"—a unity which does not efface their necessary differences but must be "thought" rather "in terms of their differences." And though "production" does exert a final determinacy over the circuit as a whole, each "moment" has its own determinateness, plays its necessary, non-reducible role in the self-expanding value of capital, obeying its own conditions of existence.[10] The relation, specifically, of the economic to the political must, similarly, be conceptualised as articulated into a unity, through their necessary differences and displacements. There is therefore *no necessary immediate correspondence* between the "economic" and the "political" constitution of classes. The terms in which their "complex unity" could be thought, of course, remained to be developed. But there can be little doubt that these developments decisively mark out as radically different the terrain of Marx's subsequent work from that so lucidly prescribed in the *Manifesto*.

Important as it is to mark the line which separates the phase of Marx's thought which finds a definitive statement in the *Manifesto* from his subsequent development, it is also necessary to remind ourselves of what cannot be left behind—of what has already been gained, what is irreducible in it. This becomes clearer provided we detach the *Manifesto* a little from its immediate location, and reconsider its "advances," as I have tried to phrase it, "in the light of *Capital*." The declaration that "the history of all hitherto existing society is the history of class struggles," for example, is as fundamental to Marxism as it was to appear a "startling premise" when first enunciated. Marxism is unthinkable without it. The emphasis on "classes" there is almost as fundamental as the emphasis on "struggles." The brief articulation of this proposition which immediately follows—freeman and slave, lord and serf, bourgeois and proletarian—though in no sense an *adequate* account of the complex class structures of the modes of production to which they refer (and therefore the site of a continuing difficulty)—is an absolutely necessary starting point. The idea that "men" first appear as biological individuals, or as the "bare individuals" of market society, and only then are coalesced into classes—class as, so to speak, a secondary formation—is not a reading supportable from this text or anything in Marx which follows it. This premise therefore foreshadows the many later passages in which Marx dethrones the apparently natural and obvious reference back to "individuals" as the basis for a theory of classes.

From the standpoint of Marxism, "men" are always pre-constituted by the antagonistic class relations into which they are cast. Historically, they are always articulated, not in their profound and unique individuality, but *by* "the ensemble of social relations"—that is, as the supports for class relations. It is this prior constitution which produces, under specific conditions, as its *results*, a specific type of individuality: the possessive individual of bourgeois political theory, the needy individual of market society, the contracting individual of the society of "free labour." Outside these relations, the individual—this "Robinson Crusoe" of classical political economy, self-sufficient in a world surveyed only from the standpoint of "his" needs and wants—which has formed the natural, de-historicised point of origin of bourgeois society and theory, is not a possible theoretical starting point at all. It is only the "product of many determinations." The history of its production, Marx once remarked "is written in the annals of mankind in letters of blood and fire."[11] As he subsequently argued:

> Society is not merely an aggregate of individuals; it is the sum of relations in which individuals stand to one another. It is as though someone were to say that, from the point of view of society, slaves and citizens do not exist; they are all men. In fact, this is rather what they are outside society. Being a slave or a citizen is a socially determined relation between individual A and individual B. Individual A is not as such a slave. He is only a slave in and through society.[12]

> Like all its predecessors, the capitalist process of production proceeds under definite material conditions which are, however, simultaneously the bearers of definite social relations entered into by individuals in the process of reproducing their life. Those conditions, like these relations, are on the one hand, prerequisites, on the other hand results . . . of the capitalist process of production; they are produced and reproduced by it.[13]

Almost everything which passes for a sort of sociological "common sense" about social classes is contradicted and forbidden by those formulations: and their essential point is already implicit in the *Manifesto*.

Second, there is the premise which Marx himself noted as the nub of his own contribution[14] and which is reaffirmed again by Marx and Engels in their joint Preface to the 1872 German edition of the *Manifesto*: the premise that "the existence of classes is only bound up with particular phases in the development of production." It is the conditions and relations of production, made specific to different phases in the contradictory development of capital, which provides the basic and essential framework for a Marxist theory of classes. It is this premise which divides Marxism as a "scientific" theory from all previous and subsequent forms of Utopian Socialism. Henceforth the class struggle was no longer a moral assertion about the inhumanity of the capitalist system, nor was capitalism's destruction projected on to the system from the outside by an exercise of will or hope.

Capitalism, in this sense, produces and reproduces itself *as* an antagonistic structure of class relations: it remorselessly divides the "population," again and again into its antagonistic classes. Note, at the same time, that it is the phases in the development of the *mode of production* which provides the necessary, though not the sufficient, condition for a Marxist theory of classes: it is not "the economic" in some more obvious sense, which "determines." Marx is absolutely consistent about this, from the first formulations of the question in *The German Ideology*, through to the end. But so powerful is the grasp of bourgeois common-sense, and so persistently does it return to exert its influence even at the heart of Marxist theory itself, that it is worth repeating. It is the material and social relations within which men produce and reproduce their material conditions of existence which "determines"—*how* remains to be elucidated. The unequal distribution of economic wealth, goods and power, which forms the basis for a "socio-economic" conception of "social classes," is, for Marx, not the basis but the *result* of the *prior* distribution of the agents of capitalist production into classes and class relations, and the prior distribution of the means of production as between its "possessors" and its "dispossessed."

The simplification of classes, which appears to be a fundamental thesis of the *Manifesto*, is also not as simple an argument as it at first appears. In arguing that under capitalism bourgeois versus proletarians is the fundamental form of the class struggle, the *Manifesto* does not—as is sometimes supposed—neglect the presence of other classes and class fractions. Indeed, it contains a summary judgement on the revolutionary potential of *inter alia* "the lower middle classes, the small manufacturer, the shopkeeper, the artisan, the peasant" as well as "the dangerous class, the social scum," from which Marx never departed. What it argues is that "of all the classes that stand face to face with the bourgeoisie today, the proletariat alone is the really revolutionary class." This is a difficult point, requiring further examination.

Marx comes to the assertion on the basis of the objective position which the proletariat has in a mode of production, based on the latter's expropriation from the means of production and the exploitation of its labour power. In *this* sense the proposition stands—the revolutionary *position* of the proletariat being, in this sense, "given" (specified) by its location in a specific mode. This does, however, tend to treat the proletariat as an unfractured and undifferentiated "class subject"—a subject with a role *in* history but no internal, contradictory history of its own, at least within the capitalist epoch. This is a premise which Marx subsequently modified and which we must reject. But the passage could also be read as if it asserted that, *because* the proletariat has an objectively revolutionary *position* in the economic structure of capitalist production, *therefore* it also and always must exhibit empirically a revolutionary political consciousness and form of political organisation. It is just this further "move" which Lukács makes in *History and Class Consciousness*; and when he is obliged to recognise that this proletariat does not "empirically" always live up to its appointed form of consciousness, he treats it "abstractly" as if this is its ascribed destiny—its "potential consciousness"—from which its actual, concrete historical divergences are but temporary lapses. The enormous historical problem, for Marxism, of the "economism" of trade union consciousness, and of the containment of the Western European working-class movements within the confines of social democratic reformism, cannot be systematically elucidated from this position. We come back, then, to one of the critical weaknesses—it recurs in one form or another throughout the text—of the *Manifesto*: a weakness which can now be summarily stated.

The *Manifesto* is correct in its (obviously and necessarily schematic) discussion of the economic constitution of classes in terms of the phases of development of the mode of production. But it is fatally flawed in treating, systematically, the relation between the economic and the political. To this question the *Manifesto* either returns an unsatisfactory answer (i.e., they are more or less aligned, more or less "corresponding"); or it leaves a *space*, a gap, through which the abstract error of a Lukácsian historicism constantly escapes. In short, all that is necessary to think the specificity of the political class struggle and its relation to the economic level—on which our ability to expound "the ensemble" as a whole depends—is not yet present as usable concepts in Marx's thought. These further concepts are, indeed, *forced into discovery* by the historical and political conjuncture they were required to explain: the collapse of the 1848 revolutions. Thus, precisely, their clearest and most substantial formulation occurs in the essays and studies which immediately follow—the writings on France, especially, more fleetingly (and less satisfactorily) the asides on Britain: texts which, so to speak, appear in the light of theoretical reflection and clarification cast by a moment of revolutionary defeat. Here we are on the terrain of real discoveries, of a theoretically revolutionary *break-through*. This breakthrough occurs "in thought," certainly: but it can hardly be adequately understood as "epistemological."

Still, we have not fully plumbed the depth of that brilliantly surfaced text, the *Manifesto*. Why and how did Marx and Engels envisage the "simplification" of classes (with its profound consequences for deciphering the rhythm of the class struggle) to be *implicit* in the unfolding of capitalist development?

II.

It is the increasing size and scale of capitalist production which precipitates this "simplification." The circumstances which, first, produce the proletariat, then develop it, then drive all the intermediary class strata into its growing ranks are worth briefly detailing: (a) the formation of a class, expropriated from the ownership of the means of production, with only its labour power to sell, exposed to the "vicissitudes of competition and all the fluctuations of the market"; (b) the division of labour consequent on the extensive use of machinery which "deskills" the worker, reducing him to an appendage of the machine; (c) the growing exploitation of labour power "whether by prolongation of the working day in a given time or by increased speed of the machinery, *etc.*"; (d) the organisation of labour into an "industrial army" in factory conditions under the command of capital's "officers and sergeants"; (e) the *dilution* of labour through the lowering of the value of labour power—the employment, at lower wages, of women and children; (f) the exposure of the class to exploitation in the market for subsistence goods—by the landlord, the shop-keeper, the pawn-broker. In this context arises (g) the thesis that the lower strata of the middle class "sink gradually into the proletariat"—partly through their losing battle with (h) large-scale, concentrated "big" capital. The intermediary strata are what Gramsci would call "subaltern" fractions of the middle classes. They are intrinsically conservative, reactionary in outlook—trying to "roll back the wheel of history." They are or become "revolutionary" only face to face with their "impending transfer into the proletariat"—their "proletarianisation."

The attentive reader will recognise at once that all of these sketchy ideas reappear, and are subject to a major development, above all in Marx's seminal Chapter XV, "Machinery and Modern Industry," in *Capital* I. The formation, historically, of a class of "free labour," with nothing to sell but its labour-power, out of the matrix of feudal relations, is constantly returned to in *Capital* as its "historic basis." The progressive reduction of the worker to an "appendage of the machine" is central to Marx's description of the capitalist labour process, and to his qualitative distinction between the phase of "machinery" and the phase of "modern industry." The growing exploitation of labour power foreshadows the critical distinction in *Capital* between Absolute (the prolongation of the working day) and Relative (the increase of the ratio of "dead" to "living" labour) surplus value. The growing hierarchisation and "despotism" of capital's command leads on to Marx's distinction between the "formal" and the "real" subsumption of labour. The "dilution" of skilled labour and the formation of a "reserve army" are two of the critical "counter-acting tendencies" to the tendency of the rate of profit to fall, discussed both in *Capital* I (for example, Chapter XXV) and again in *Capital* III, where the processes leading to the growing concentration and centralisation of capitals are more fully described. In this context, also there arises the description of the emergence of the modern "collective worker" and the first hints at the *expansion* of the *new* intermediary classes, consequent on a developing division of labour, as the older petty-bourgeoisie and its material basis in "small" and trading capital is eroded. In the context of this major theoretical development, the sketchy outline of the *Manifesto*, which contains little but an *indication* of how the organisation of capitalist production provides the basis for this *formation* and *re-composition* of classes, is both expanded and transformed. Again, both continuities and the breaks necessary for their theoretical development must be observed.

When in *Capital* Marx sets out to resume, in a condensed form, the general overall tendency of this whole development, the terms he employs are *strikingly similar* to those he employed in the *Manifesto*. One has only to turn to the summary review contained in the brief Chapter XXXII of *Capital* I to hear again the familiar phrases:

At a certain stage of development it brings forth the material agencies of its own dissolution. From that moment new forces and new passions spring up in the bosom of society: but the old organisation fetters them and keeps them down.... As soon as this process of transformation has sufficiently decomposed the old society from top to bottom, as soon as the labourers are turned into proletarians, their means of labour into capital, then the further socialisation of labour . . . takes a new form. . . . This expropriation is accomplished by the action of immanent laws of capitalist production itself, by the centralisation of capital. . . . Hand in hand with this centralisation, or this expropriation of many capitals by few, develop on an ever-extending scale, the cooperative form of the labour process, the conscious technical application of science, the methodological cultivation of the soil, the transformation of the instruments of labour into instruments of labour only usable in common, the economising of all means of production by their use as the means of production of combined, socialised labour, the entanglement of all the working-class, a class always increasing in numbers, and disciplined, united, organised by the very mechanism of the process of capitalist production itself.[15]

This is the echo, the "voice" of the *Manifesto* inside *Capital*.

But side by side with this résumé, we must set the detail, but more significantly the *method*, by which the simple sketch of the *Manifesto* is transformed into the terms and concepts of *Capital*'s investigation. It is impossible within the scope of this paper to provide the "reading" which would substantiate in detail the nature of this theoretical transformation. But some examples can be taken in order to demonstrate how the sketch of the process in the *Manifesto*—structured largely on a linear development, punctuated by the rising tempo of class struggle—is *thoroughly transformed*, in its reworking in *Capital*, by really setting to work the concept of *contradiction* and the notion of dialectical development.

Two examples will have to suffice. In the opening section of Chapter XV, Marx established the technical difference between the nature of the instruments of production (and the consequent division of labour in the labour process itself) which characterises the *first* phase of capitalist development—the era of Machinery—and that further qualitative development—"machinery organised into a system," where the machine "uses" the worker rather than the reverse—which marks out the period of "Modern Industry." In the section "The Factory" Marx then explores the complex and contradictory effects of this transformation of capitalism's material basis. He comments, *inter alia*, on the decomposition of the traditional skills of the class, as these skills are increasingly "passing over" into the machine itself: here, he notes, the *tendency* towards the equalisation and reduction of skills "to one and the same level of every kind of work." But this has consequences, at once, for the *social* organisation of production: it brings in its train the re-composition of the elements of production into "the head workman" and his "mere attendants"; and, alongside this, the new "superior class of workmen, some of them scientifically educated" who look after the whole of the machinery itself and repair it.

As the machine begins to dictate the organisation of the labour process, it brings further contradictory developments with it: the greater ease of substituting one labour force for another; the introduction of continuous production and the shift system (the "relay system"); the dilution of labour and the erosion of traditional skills born of an earlier division of labour—"traditional habits" now "systematically remoulded." In the annexation of worker to the machine, the systematic "pumping dry" of living labour by dead labour proceeds at an enormous pace—the "special skills of each individual factory operator vanishes as an infinitesimal quantity before the science, the gigantic physical forces and the mass of labour that are embodied in the factory mechanism." But this has further consequences, too, for the nature of factory discipline, hierarchy and command—re-dividing workers into "operatives and overlookers" (the "private soldiers and sergeants of an industrial army")—and for the administration of a more detailed and coercive labour regime. Dr Andrew Ure, the "poet" of Modern Industry, himself saw how the revolution in the means of production both *required* and *made possible* the withdrawal of any process requiring particular skill and dexterity from the "cunning workman . . . prone to irregularities" to the "self-regulating mechanism" which even the child can superintend. Thus the "technical" revolution in the means of production produces an unlooked-for effect in the regulation of labour and the repression of the strikes and other "periodic revolts" of the working class against its conditions of life. Again, as Marx, quoting Ure, observes: when "capital enlists science into her service, the refractory hand of labour will always be taught docility."

In this section alone we see how what, in the *Manifesto*, appears to be organised around a simple antagonism, is articulated into a complex and contradictory one: the necessary terms are *effects*, not intended, which nevertheless have contradictory outcomes: effects at *levels* where no result was calculated: *tendencies*, immediately cross-cut by their opposite: advances which produce, elsewhere, regressive results. Above all, what was in the earlier text represented as an essentially homogeneous force—the proletariat—is now itself constantly and ceaselessly acted upon, redefined, recomposed, "remoulded" by the operation of capital's contradictory law. Already in the *Manifesto* Marx had foreseen how the growing cohesion of the proletariat, in the conditions of factory labour, was constantly interrupted by the tendency towards "competition between workers." But it is only when the process of development which lays the foundation for that growing cohesion is investigated in depth that we can see *why* it is that capital produces, of necessity, *both* the massification and the "simplification" of labour, as one of its tendencies; but also, equally "necessarily," the internal divisions between skilled and the unskilled, the distribution of skills into different branches of production, as "Modern Industry" seizes on them and transforms them *unevenly*: how the "dilution" of the traditional work-force by the employment on a large scale of women and children (a development made possible only by the revolution in the nature of the labour process itself) sets one group of workers against another, introducing as a further contradiction "the natural differences of age and sex"—i.e., the sexual division of labour into its social division; and how capital comes to be in a position to exploit these new elements in the division of labour (or the parallel one between supervisors, the "superior class of workmen" and the machine-minders) to its political advantage. In short how the production of two, opposite *tendencies* in capital's contradictory development decisively *intervenes* between any simple notion of the "inevitable cohesion of the proletariat" and its actual realisation under the new conditions of capital's historic organisation.

Something absolutely central about the form and character of the class struggle under modern conditions of production is already present in the deceptively simple remark, by Marx, that

> so far as division of labour reappears in the factory it is primarily a distribution of the workmen among the specialised machines; and of masses of workmen, not however organised into groups, among the various departments of the factory, in each of which they work at a number of similar machines placed together; their cooperation therefore is only simple. The organised group, peculiar to manufacture, is replaced by the connexion between the head workman and his few assistants.[16]

This tendency does not obliterate the earlier one: it represents both the expanding base for the "socialisation of labour" and the technical interdependence of the various branches of capitalist production: as well as the social basis for the formation of a modern proletariat. The development of capitalism reproduces *both* tendencies at once: in short, in driving itself forward through one of its "technical" limits, in overcoming one of the material barriers to its revolutionising self-expansion, capital produces new contradictions at a higher level of development. Its advance—quite contrary to the dominant impression of the *Manifesto*—is, in the *full* sense, dialectical.

We can see this at work in another instance, where also there are apparently straight "echoes" of the *Manifesto*. Marx noted in that text the two "paths" open to capital—prolongation of the working day, and the "increase of the work exacted in a given time ... the increased speed of machinery, *etc.*" He also noted, but in another context, the growing political strength of the proletariat—"it ever rises up again, stronger firmer, mightier"—compelling a recognition of the "particular interests of the workers"; in this latter context he cites the "Ten Hour bill." Again, it is striking to observe how deeply and thoroughly these ideas are transformed as they reappear in *Capital*. The enlarged application of machinery has the effect of increasing the productivity of labour—"shortening the working-time required in the production of a commodity." But it also has the effect of reducing the resistance of the workers to the prolongation of the working day. Here, at once, is a contradiction, "since of the two factors of the surplus-value created by a given amount of capital, one, the rate of surplus-value, cannot be increased except by diminishing the other, the number of workmen." The effects are, therefore, as contradictory as they are "unconscious."[17] If it extends the working day, "changes the method of labour, as also the character of the social working organism, in such a manner as to break down all opposition to this tendency," it also "produces, partly by opening out to the capitalist new strata of the working class ... partly by setting free the labourers it supplants, a surplus working population." It is this unfettered exploitation of labour power which provokes "a reaction" on the part of a section of the ruling class—a reaction leading to "divisions among the bourgeoisie itself" which the workers' struggle takes advantage of, forcing through the Factory legislation, with its statutory limits to the working day. Marx subsequently notes that the capitalists oppose this limit, politically, vigorously: they declare production to be "impossible" under such conditions. Yet it is precisely the imposition of this limit—which "the surging revolt of the working class compelled [on] Parliament"—which *drives* capital forward to "raising the productive power of the workman, so as to enable him to produce more in a given time with the same expenditure of labour." This is the enormous—the uneven and unplanned—threshold which capital crosses, from the epoch of Absolute to that of Relative surplus value.

Its effects are immense: the rise in the organic composition of capital; the lowering of the value component of every commodity; the intensification of the labour process; the "filling up of the pores of the working day"; the "increasing tension of labour power"; the speed-up of the production process; the great stimulus to technical advance and the application of science as a material force; and the gain in the administration of a regime of "regularity, uniformity, order, continuity" in labour—these are only *some* of the consequences Marx outlines. By 1858, Marx notes, the Factory Inspector is reporting that "the great improvements made in machines of every kind have raised their productive power very much. . . . Without any doubt, the shortening of the hours of labour . . . gave the impulse to these improvements." Towards the end of Chapter XV, Marx returns again to the complex outcome of the mid-century Factory legislation, dealing now more fully both with its technical and its social (education, children, the family) consequences. Thus what appears in the *Manifesto* as a simple disconnection between the levels of the mode of production and of political struggle, is brought together into a contradictory "unity": a unity which shows how, while the law of value obtains, capital advances, blindly, unconsciously—as Brecht would say, "from its bad side": how it is impelled to advance itself by contravening the very limits and barriers it establishes for itself: how its "political" consciousness is often at variance with its inner drive and necessities. It illustrates vividly capital's powers of *recuperation*: how it constantly is forced to weave together its own contradictory impulses into forms of social and economic organisation which it can bend and force to advance its own "logic." It shows how, in order to master the divisions of interest within its own ranks, and above all to master and contain within its framework those "particular" advances which the working class is able to force upon it, capital develops a different *repertoire*: it discovers new "solutions." Any idea that the "logic of capital" is a simple and straightforward functional "unfolding," or that its logic is one which can be separated from the logic of class struggle—two disconnected threads—is definitively disposed of in this chapter.

Out of this historical-analytic exposition Marx detaches the seminal theoretical argument, which is then presented (in the following chapter) in its "purer" theoretical form: the concepts of "The Production of Absolute and of Relative Surplus Value." The whole tendential direction is thus concisely summarised: the "general extension of factory legislation to all trades for the purpose of protecting the working class"—the outcome of an immediate political struggle—also "hastens on the general conversion of numerous isolated small industries into a few combined industries.... It therefore accelerates the concentration of capital and the exclusive predominance of the factory system." It "destroys ancient and transitional forms behind which the domination of capital is still in part concealed, and replaces them by the direct and open sway of capital; but thereby it also generalises the direct opposition to this sway." It enforces uniformity, regularity, order and economy, and provides the spur to technical improvement, the intensity of labour and the "competition of machinery with the worker." It destroys the material basis of petty and domestic production. "By maturing the material conditions and the combination on a social scale of the processes of production, it matures the contradictions and antagonisms of the capitalist form of production." If this appears to make a last-hour return to the terrain of the *Manifesto*, it is only in so far as the contradictory double-thrust of capitalist development and its intrinsically antagonistic nature lies at the heart of both conceptions. From the vantage point of *Capital*, the so-called "simplification of classes and the class struggle"—or what we must now call the *complex simplification* of classes and the logic of class struggle within the "logic" of capital's historic development—has been thoroughly and irreversibly transformed. In terms of the Marxist "theory of classes," we have entered quite new territory.

III.

As we have seen, one of the critical points left in an unsatisfactory state by the *Manifesto* is the relations between the economic and the political aspects of class struggle. Marx does pose the question of "this organisation of the proletarians into a class ... and consequently into a party": as if the political aspects were simply a more advanced form of the "economic," requiring no alteration of terms or extension of conceptual framework. In *The German Ideology*, Marx says of the capitalist class that "the separate individuals form a class in so far as they have to carry on a common battle against another class; otherwise they are on hostile terms with one another as competitors."[18] In *The Poverty of Philosophy* Marx speaks of Utopian Socialism as typical of a period in which "the proletariat is not sufficiently developed to constitute itself into a class" and consequently, "the very struggle of the proletariat with the bourgeoisie has not yet assumed a political character."[19] He calls the proletariat "this mass" which is already a class in opposition to capital but not yet a "class for itself." In *The Eighteenth Brumaire*, Marx writes:

> Insofar as millions of families live under economic conditions of existence that separate their mode of life, their interests and their culture from those of other classes and put them in hostile opposition to the latter, they form a class. In so far as there is merely a local interconnection among these small-holding peasants and the identity of their interests begets no community, no national bond, no political organisation amongst them, they do not form a class. They are consequently incapable of enforcing their class interests in their own name.

In 1871, in the Letter to Friedrich Bolte, which touches again on the Factory legislation discussed above, Marx writes:

> The ultimate object of the political movement of the working class is, of course, the conquest of political power for this class, and this naturally requires that the organisation of the working class, and the organisation which arises from its economic struggles should previously reach a certain level of development. On the other hand, however, every movement in which the working class as a class confronts the ruling classes and tries to constrain them by pressure from without is a political movement. For instance the attempt by strikes, etc., in a particular factory or even in a particular trade to compel individual capitalists to reduce the working day, is a purely economic movement. On the other hand, the movement to force through an eight hour, etc., law is a political movement. And in this way, out of the separate economic movements of the workers there grows up everywhere a political movement, that is to say, a class movement, with the object of enforcing its interests in a general form, in a form possessing general, socially coercive force. While these movements presuppose a certain degree of previous organisation, they are in turn equally a means of developing this organisation.[20]

Marx was writing here to clarify certain theses of the General Council of the International whose Rules he had formulated. A few days later Engels was to write in very similar terms for a very similar purpose to the Turin newspaper, *Il Proletario Italiano*:

> The economical emancipation of the working classes is ... the great end to which every political movement ought to be subordinated as a

means.... In the struggle of the working class its economic movement and its political action are indissolubly united.[21]

Here we find Marx and Engels rethinking precisely what is too simply proposed and glossed in the *Manifesto*: the necessary displacements as well as the conjunctures in the relation between the political and economic forms of the class struggle. The span of time is a lengthy one—from *The Poverty of Philosophy* to the Paris Commune; and in that period Marx's thought on this critical topic underwent what has been called "further fluctuations."[22] These "fluctuations" need to be treated with care.

The distinction drawn in *The Poverty of Philosophy* passage between class "in itself" and class "for itself" has, subsequently, hardened into a sort of pat formula. It appears to pose the economic/political relation in an incorrect manner. It suggests that there comes a moment when the proletariat as a whole develops the form of revolutionary class consciousness ascribed for it in its given, objective economic determination; and that only then does the class exist *at all* at the level of political struggle. We have indicated earlier the weakness which lies behind this too-neat bifurcation: which seems exclusively to reserve for such a moment of fulfilled consciousness the ascription "political class struggle"; which derives it too neatly from the economic determinations of class; which makes the achievement of an "autonomous" form of consciousness the only test of the political existence of a class; and which treats classes as unified historical subjects.

The "in itself / for itself" distinction *is* useful as a way of defining different moments and forms of class consciousness, and perhaps even as a very rough way of marking the development out of a "corporate" form of class struggle. But this would in fact require us to develop Marx's passing observation in a manner which is at odds with where it is pointing in this passage: for the distinction between "corporate" and what Marx later calls a struggle which possesses "general, socially coercive force" is *not* a distinction between the presence/absence of political struggle and its "appropriate" forms of class consciousness, but precisely the opposite: a distinction between *two different forms* of the class struggle, two modes of class consciousness, each with its own determinate conditions in the material circumstances of the classes under capitalism. As both Marx and Engels observed, and as Lenin remarked even more extensively, working class reformism and "trade union consciousness"—or what Lenin in *What Is to Be Done?* calls specifically "working class bourgeois politics"[23]—has its own conditions of existence, its own material base in the economic conditions of the working class under capitalism: far from being a level or form of class struggle, so to speak "below" the horizon of politics, it could be said to be the natural (or as Lenin called it, the "spontaneous") form of working class struggle, in conditions where the means of raising that struggle to its more "general" form are absent. But what those conditions might be, through which the forms of economic and political struggle can be heightened to their "general" form, is not given in the in itself / for itself distinction.

The Letter to Bolte, on the other hand, has quite a different purchase. The phrase "the conquest of political power for this class" has behind it the force of Marx's observations about the necessity of breaking the political power of the state erected by the bourgeoisie; and his stress on the "dictatorship of the proletariat," which arose from his analysis of the Paris Commune, was embodied in *The Civil War in France*. More interestingly, the terms "economic" and "political" appear to be used, here, to designate *where*, in any specific conjuncture, the class struggle appears to have pertinent effects. The organisation by the proletariat within production to constrain capital's efforts to intensify the exploitation of labour by prolongation of the working day is defined as an "economic movement" which attempts to modify the law governing the limitation of the working day (whose object must therefore be the bourgeois state itself) and constitutes a "political movement." Here, everything is translated to the level of the concrete conjuncture of a specific historical moment in which the class struggle "takes effect." Every trace of automatism in the movements between these two levels has been obliterated. What all the passages quoted put on the agenda, however, is the question of what the further conditions are, and what are the forms, by means of which the antagonistic relations of production of the capitalist mode can appear at, and have such pertinent effects in, the "theatre" of politics. It is above all in *The Class Struggles in France* and in *The Eighteenth Brumaire* that the concepts begin to emerge which enable us to grasp the sources and the mechanisms of the "relative autonomy" of the political level of the class struggle from the economic.

The first sections of *The Class Struggles in France* were composed in the immediate aftermath of 1848. Though already convinced that the proletariat was still too "immature" to carry the day, this part of Marx's analysis is concentrated by the way the bourgeois political forces are driven by their own internal contradictions to destroy the basis of their own "mature" political rule—universal suffrage—and consequently come gradually to confront the stark alternatives: retreat under the protection of Napoleon's bayonets, or proletarian revolution. The final section was, however, drafted and published later: and there is a major and irreversible "break" between the two perspectives. Fernbach has called it "perhaps the most important [break] during his entire political work as a communist." The nature of that break is resumed by Gwyn Williams:

> In the summer of 1850 Marx returned to his economic studies which were to immerse him in the British Museum for so many years. He came to the conclusion that the 1848 cycle of revolution had been set in train by a particular crisis in the new capitalist society . . . that the return of prosperity made a new wave of revolutions exceedingly unlikely and, more important, that no proletarian revolution was possible on the continent until capitalist economy and capitalist relations of production had been much more fully developed. . . . His new perspective was grounded in a much fuller and more structural analysis, the analysis which was in fact to reach its climax in *Capital* seventeen years later.[24]

The difference—most profoundly, then, registered in the analysis Marx offers in *The Eighteenth Brumaire*—does *not* differ from the schemas of the *Manifesto* in the sense of emphasising "politics" at the expense of the "objective conditions" constituted by the level of development of the forces and relations of capitalism. Quite the reverse. The objective determinations and the limits on what solutions were and were not "possible" at the political level are, in the later work, if anything *more* rigorously formulated, more structurally conceived and more systematically enforced than in the earlier texts. The elaboration of the "practical concepts" of the political, for which *The Eighteenth Brumaire* is justly famous, is structured, through and through, by this unrelenting application of the "determinations" which objective conditions place over the political resolutions. What Marx breaks with is any lingering assumption that the two levels exactly correspond: that the terms and contents of the one are fully given in the conditions and limits of the other. What he does, in the detailed and provocative tracing out of the forms which the class struggle assumes in what Gramsci calls "'its passage to the level of the complex superstructure,'"[25] is to put into place, for the first time, those concepts which alone enable us to "think" *the specificity of the political*.

Briefly, then, in its overall tendency and trajectory, the crisis of 1851 is fundamentally and decisively overdetermined by the objective development of French capitalism. It is this which establishes the outer limits, the determinations, the horizon within which the forms of the political arise and appear. Relatively, the French social formation is still at an early stage of its capitalist development. The proletariat, with its slogans and demands, is already "on stage"; but it cannot as yet play the decisive role, and, above all, it cannot play an autonomous role. The bourgeoisie is already fully formed, articulated in politics through its major fractions, each fraction playing now one, now another of the political parties and factions, trying now one, now another of the available solutions. But *its* historic role is not anywhere near completion: above all, it has by no means as yet "netted" those classes which arose in earlier modes of production within its hegemonic sway. The bourgeoisie is therefore not yet in a position where it can, on its own feet and in its own terms, lay hold of French society and "conform" its civil and political structures to the needs of the developing capitalist mode. The Republic thus totters from one unstable coalition to another; it runs through the entire repertoire of republican and democratic forms—constitutional assembly, parliamentary democracy, bourgeois-republican, republican-socialist. Each "form" represents the attempt by a fraction—always in a temporary *alliance*—to secure political hegemony. As each alliance is exhausted or defeated, the social base to a possible solution narrows: in each the proletariat is either a pertinent but subordinate partner, or—as the end approaches—the force which is isolated. Finally, when all the possible solutions are exhausted, the unstable equilibrium of political forces on stage falls into the keeping of Napoleon Bonaparte, who "would like to appear as the patriarchal benefactor of all classes" but only because he has already *broken them*: "Above all things, France requires tranquillity."

We must restrict ourselves here to only two aspects of this demonstration: the question of the classes and their political "forms of appearance," and the problem of the "determination in the last instance" of the economic mode of production over the forms and outcomes of the political struggle.

The first thing to notice is that, though the entire exposition is framed with the structural analysis of the fundamental classes of the capitalist mode constantly in mind as its *analytic framework*—it is this which provides the whole, dazzling, dramatic narrative with its mastering logic—there are no "whole classes" on stage here. The proletariat is the class which is most frequently treated as a "*bloc*"—and even here the designation of a specific and critical role to the "lumpen-proletariat" intersects the tendency to present the proletariat in the clash of positions as an "integral" force. For capital, Marx always distinguishes its dominant *fractions*—"big landed property"; "high finance, large-scale industry, large-scale trade"; capital's "two great interests," "financial aristocracy," "industrial bourgeoisie," etc. The petty-bourgeoisie—"a transitional class in which the interests of the two classes meet and become blurred"—is given, in fact, a pivotal role and position. When Marx comes finally to the class characterisation of Napoleon, he signals the presence of a class which was in fact a declining historical force and differentiates its key fraction: the "small peasant proprietors."

The second thing is to note that none of these fractions ever functions on the political stage in isolation. The key concept which connects the particular class fractions with the political and constitutional forms is the term—or, rather, the shifting and constantly reconstituted terms of the alliance or class bloc. The first constitutional form of the "crisis" is that of the *bourgeois republic*. The republic is hoisted to power by the June insurrection of the Paris proletariat: but though this is the class which bears the brunt of the struggle, it is a *subordinate* party to the alliance. Temporarily, the *leading fractions* in the alliance are the republican elements of the financial aristocracy and the industrial bourgeoisie, with the support of the petty-bourgeoisie.

There are other critical forces on the political stage—political forces to which no clear class designation corresponds, though their role and support is pivotal: the army, the press, the intellectual celebrities, the priests, the rural population. Occasionally, Marx hints at the class content of these supporting strata and coteries—for example, he calls the Mobile Guard "the organised lumpen-proletariat." This is the last moment when the Paris proletariat appears as a decisive actor; thereafter, the matter is settled "behind the back of society." But already it is in an alliance whose dominant fraction lies elsewhere. The republic thus reveals "only the unrestricted despotism of one class over other classes." This unstable political form then has, nevertheless, a structural and historical function: it is the classic "political form for the revolutionising of bourgeois society." Its "history" in this moment is the short-lived "history of the domination and dissolution of the republican fraction of the bourgeoisie." Opposed to it is the "Party of Order" rallied behind the ancient slogans: property, family, religion, order. This alliance, in the conjuncture, appears in its double royalist disguise—Bourbon Legitimists and Orleanists. But this unstable bloc has its class composition too: behind the "different shades of royalism" cluster "big landed property," with *its* coterie and forces (priests and lackeys), and "high finance, large-scale industry, large-scale trade, i.e., *capital*, with its retinue of advocates, professors and fine speech-makers." Here, too, the struggle for predominance is masked by the need for unity in the face of the Party of Anarchy. What essentially divides them—driving each to "restore its own supremacy and the subordination of the other interest"—is *not exclusively* their material conditions of existence ("two distinct sorts of property") but also the ideological traditions in which each has been formed. This is one of the many places where Marx demonstrates the pertinent, and the specific, effectivity of the *ideological* dimension of the class struggle upon the political, adding yet a further level of complexity: "A whole superstructure of different and specifically formed interests and feelings, illusions, modes of thought and views of life arises on the basis of the different forms of property, of the social conditions of existence." One must make, Marx adds, a sharp distinction "between the phrases and fantasies of the parties and their real organisation and real interests, between their conceptions of themselves and what they really are." In the conjuncture of May, what these fractions "thought" of themselves, though referrable in the last instance to the material basis of their existence, had real and pertinent effects—as *The Eighteenth Brumaire* dramatically demonstrates. Marx performs the same kind of analysis—the formation of complex alliances, based on class fractions, their internal contradictions, the "necessity" of the political positions, temporary programmes and ideological forms in which those "interests" appear—for each "moment" of the conjuncture of *Brumaire*.

The third point to note is the question of how these political fractions and strata achieve *political representation* in the course of the struggle. The two major fractions of the big bourgeoisie appear on the political stage in their respective royalist liveries: but the restoration of their respective ruling dynasties is not the objective "work" which this alliance performs. Their union into and representation through the Party of Order brings on the question of the rule of the class "as a whole," rather than the predominance of one fraction over another. Objectively, it is this temporary and unholy union which makes them the "representatives of the bourgeois world order." Time and again Marx returns to this central question of "class content" and its *means of political representation*. It is not simply that the representation of class interests through political alliances and "parties" is never a straightforward matter. It is also that the political interests of one class fraction can be represented through the role which another fraction plays on the political or the ideological stage. One excellent example is where Marx discusses the coalition of the proletariat and the petty-bourgeoisie into the "so-called social democratic party." This "party" has its immediate determinations: it advances, temporarily, the interests of those left aside by the forceful regrouping of bourgeois forces. It has its contradictory internal structure: through their subordination within it the proletariat lose "their revolutionary point" and gain "a democratic twist." Social democracy also has its objective *political* content: "weakening the antagonism between capital and wage labour and transforming it into a harmony."[26] It is "democratic" reform within the limits of bourgeois society.

It is in this precise context that Marx warns us about a too *reductive* conception of political representation. This temporary "solution" is not pettybourgeois because it advances the narrow interests of that transitional class. Its "representatives" cannot be analysed in terms of the reduction to the narrow terms of their class designation—they are not all "shopkeepers." The *position* of this alliance is "petty-bourgeois" in character because, temporarily, the *general* resolution to the crisis it proposes and endorses corresponds to the objective limits of the *particular* material interests and social situation of the petty bourgeois as a class. The political representatives, whoever they are and whatever their particular material designation, assume for the moment a pettybourgeois political *position*, play a petty-bourgeois political role, propose a petty-bourgeois political resolution. It is the convergence, from different starting points, around these objective limits which—Marx argues—provides the basis for deciphering the "general relationship between the political and literary representatives of a class and the class they represent."[27] Thus, though the social and material limits and the objective class content set the terms and provide the horizon within which a "petty-bourgeois" resolution to the crisis can appear, at a specific conjuncture, everything turns on the means and conditions which permit such a solution to surface and take a concrete shape as a *political force* in the theatre of the crisis.

It is this concept—of the *re-presentation* of the objective class content of the forces arrayed and the means and conditions of the political struggle, a struggle with its own forms of appearance, its own specific effectivity—which allows Marx to propose a dazzling solution to the central question which shadows *The Eighteenth Brumaire*. What does Napoleon, who does this exceptional suspension of the struggle through the execution of the *coup d'état, represent*? We know the solution for which Marx settled: he "represents" the small-holding peasant—the conservative not the revolutionary peasant, the peasant who wants to consolidate, not the one who wants to strike out beyond the *status quo*.

We can only summarise in the barest outline how this "solution" is constructed. It entails, first, an analysis of the specific mode of peasant production—based on the small holding—and of the form of social life which arises from it: the peasantry's isolation from mutual intercourse, its enforced self-sufficiency, the structure of village communities, its lack of diversity in development or wealth of social relationships. It traces the crucial transformation in the peasantry's economic role from semi-serfdom into free landed proprietors—accomplished under the aegis of the first Napoleon. It relates the immediate consequences of this uneven transformation: the fragmentation of peasant property, the penetration of free competition and the market, the role in this backward and traditional sector of the money lender, the mortgage and debt. Here the ravages of the disorganisation of peasant society by the capitalist invasion of the countryside is detailed. It is this which provides the basis of the developing antagonism between the peasantry and the bourgeoisie—an antagonism which gives Napoleon his "independence." Not only are the small-holding peasantry plunged into indebtedness; but the hidden burden of taxation fatally connects their immiseration with the swollen arms of the government and the executive apparatus of the state.

To this Marx adds a brilliant exposition of how the *ideological* outlook of the peasantry now finds, not a correspondence so much as a resonant *complementarity*, with the ideology of Louis Napoleon—"Napoleon's ideas." Napoleon's ideas are, in their objective content, nothing but "the ideas of the undeveloped small holding in its heyday." There is a "homology of forms" between them. Does this mean that the Napoleonic solution has, after all, no correspondence with France's developing mode of production, no lifeline to the bourgeoisie? It remains the fact, Marx suggests, that Napoleon can no longer directly represent any particular section of the bourgeoisie, for he has come to power only as the result of the successive defeat or retreat of each of its major fractions. This progressive liquidation founds the *coup d'état* on insecure and contradictory foundations. It is this which drives Napoleon to rest his political claims, finally, on a class which "cannot represent themselves, they must be represented. Their representative must appear simultaneously as their master, as an authority over them, an unrestricted governmental power that protects them from the other classes and sends them rain and sunshine from above."[28] But it is just here—where a whole class fraction appears politically only through the exceptional political form of a one-man dictatorship—that Marx executes the final ironic twist. For this makes the small-holding peasantry dependent, through Napoleon, directly on the executive—on *the state*.

It is in the maturing of state power, the creation of a swollen but "independent" state machine, perfected through Napoleon's regime, and resting on the contradictory basis of his "independence," that Bonaparte comes finally to do some service, not for this or that fraction of the bourgeoisie, but for the maturing of capitalist relations in France. "The material interest of the French bourgeoisie is most intimately imbricated precisely with the maintenance of that extensive and highly ramified state machine. It is that machine which provides its surplus population with jobs, and makes up through state salaries for what it cannot pocket in the form of profit, interest, rent and fees. Its *political* interests equally compelled it daily to increase the repression, and therefore to increase the resources and personnel of state power.... The French bourgeoisie was thus compelled by its class position both to liquidate the conditions of existence of all parliamentary power, including its own, and to make its opponent, the executive, irresistible." This is the long term "work" which, through its reversals and detours, its advances and retreats, the "crisis" of 1851 perfects and matures on behalf of the developing capitalist forces of French society. This is the objective labour which the revolution performs "on its journey through purgatory."[29]

The level of the political class struggle, then, has its own efficacy, its own forms, its specific conditions of existence, its own momentum, tempo and direction, its own contradictions internal to it, its "peculiar" outcomes and results. If everything is, here, governed in the last instance by the stage of development of the material and social relations through which the prevailing mode of production (and the subordinate or surviving modes of production which appear combined with it in any concrete society) reproduces itself, very little of the actual shifts in the political relations of class forces can be deciphered by reducing them back to the abstract terms of the "principal contradiction." The political *is* articulated with the level of the economic; and *both* (to make the distinction absolutely clear) are in a critical sense overdetermined (constituted fundamentally by, and limited in the possible variants or outcomes) by the forces and relations combined with the "mode of production."

To suggest that they are not articulated, that there is no "correspondence" of any kind, is to forfeit the first principle of historical materialism: the principle of social formations as a "complex unity," as an "ensemble of relations." But that articulation is accomplished only through a series of displacements and disarticulations. Between the classes constituted in the economic relations of production, either in their "pure" form (when the mode of production functions as an analytic framework) or in their concrete historical form (where they appear in complex forms, together with the formations of earlier modes) there intervenes a set of forms, processes, conditions and terms, graspable by a distinctive set of concepts—non-reducible concepts—which "fill out" the level of the political in a social formation. The re-presentation of the "economic" at the level of "the political" must pass through these representational forms and processes. This is a process, a complex set of practices—the practices of the political class struggle: without them there would be no "political" level at all. And once the class struggle is subject to the process of "representation" in the theatre of political class struggle, that articulation is permanent: it obeys, as well as the determinations upon it, its own internal dynamic; it respects its own, distinctive and specific conditions of existence. It cannot be reversed. It is this transformation which produces and sustains the necessary level of appearance of the political. Once the class forces appear as political class forces, they have consequent political results; they generate "solutions"—results, outcomes, consequences—which cannot be *translated back* into their original terms.

It is, of course, the "raw materials" of the social relations of production—at the mode of production level—which provide the political class struggle with its elements. And the political results and conclusions "won" or secured at the level of the political not only serve to articulate "the political" as a permanent practice in any social formation—one which can *never* thereafter be an "empty space"—they also have consequences for the manner in which the forces and relations of the material conditions of existence themselves develop. That is, they react, retrospectively, upon that which constitutes them—they have pertinent effects. The precise political form in which the "compromise" of the 1851 *coup d'état* was struck is important both for the pace and for the character of capitalist development in France. It affects both the political and the economic life of French society. That "reciprocal action"—if you like, of the political-ideological superstructures on the "base"—does not operate in a "free space." Yet the precise direction and tendency of that reaction is not given exclusively by the forces and relations of the base: it is *also* given by the forces and relations of the political and the ideological struggle, and by all that is specific—relatively autonomous—to them. The superstructural results can "react" upon the base by either favouring or hindering its development. Althusser noted that "an overdetermined contradiction may be either overdetermined in the direction of a historical inhibition, a real block . . . or in the direction of a revolutionary rupture, but in neither condition is it ever found in the 'pure' state."[30]

Engels, in his famous Letter to Schmidt, in which he dealt with this very question, suggested that the retroaction of the state power upon economic development can be one of three kinds: it can proceed in the same direction, and then things move more rapidly; it can move in the opposite direction... or it can prevent the economic development from proceeding along certain lines, and prescribe other lines.[31]

This, Althusser comments, "well suggests the character of the two limit positions."[32] (It is important to note that this concept of "determination" differs from the full-blown but more "formal" notion of determination through "structural causality" which Althusser and Balibar adopted for the exposition of *Reading Capital*. Its absence from the more formalist conception was one of the principal sources of the latter's "theoreticist deviation.")

Marx noted in the "Introduction" to the *Grundrisse* that, once we cease to think the relation between the different "moments" of a process as *identical*, we are of necessity into the terrain of *articulation*. Articulation marks the forms of the relationship through which two processes, which remain distinct—obeying their own conditions of existence—are drawn together to form a "complex unity." This unity is therefore the result of "many determinations," where the conditions of existence of the one does not coincide exactly with that of the other (politics to economic, circulation to production) *even if* the former is the "determinate effect" of the latter; and that is because the former also have their own internal "determinations."

The concepts which Marx begins to elaborate and operate in *The Eighteenth Brumaire*—alliances, *blocs*, constitutional forms, regime, political representatives, political ideologies or "ideas," fractions, factions, etc.—are the concepts which enable us to "think" the complexity of this double determination. Since these political forms and relations are themselves constituted by the antagonistic class relations of the capitalist mode in which they appear, they are the concrete objects of the practices of class struggle—the class struggle in "the theatre of politics." The very term "theatre" and the sustained dramaturgical nature of Marx's style of exposition in *The Eighteenth Brumaire* underlines the *representational* aspect of this relation. This level is always present—it is always "filled out" in one way or another—in any developed social formation. It performs a "function" for the social formation as a whole, in that, at this instance there appears the forms and relations of the political through which the various fractions of capital and its political allies can contend, both among themselves and with the subordinate classes, so as to dominate the class struggle and to draw civil society, politics, ideology and the State into conformity with the broad underlying "needs" of the developing mode or production. But those "needs" never appear in their "pure state." Indeed, as Marx was obliged to observe in relation to Britain, the fundamental classes of capital never emerge full-blown and united and "take charge of the social formation" in their own name and persona, "for capital." The distinction between the "economically dominant class" and the "politically leading or ruling caste," in Marx and Engels's writing on Britain, recapitulates in miniature the distinctions, drawn *in extenso*, in *The Eighteenth Brumaire*, and provided the key to deciphering the class struggle in Britain: "The governing caste... is by no means identical with the ruling class."[33] The political level therefore also provides the necessary space of representation where those bargains, coalitions, "unstable equilibria," are struck and dissolved which, *alone*, allow the "laws of capital" to have pertinent effects.

It is consequently also in this "space"—but also through its specific forms and relations—that the working class can struggle to contain the sway of capital in the form of its political representatives and forces, and, under a favourable conjuncture, to transform the *economic* structure of society by taking as its object the point where that structure is *condensed*: in the form of bourgeois state—i.e., *political* power. It follows that we cannot conceive of "the class struggle" as if classes were simply and homogeneously constituted at the level of the economic, and only then fractured at the level of the political. The political level is "dependent"—determinate—because its "raw materials" are given by the mode of production *as a whole*: a process of "representation" must have something to represent. But classes are *complexly constituted* at each of the levels of the social formation—the economic, the political and the ideological. To grasp the "state of play" in the relations of class forces in a concrete historical formation at a particular conjuncture *is* to grasp the necessary complexity and displacements of this "unity." It is only in the very exceptional conditions of a revolutionary rupture that the instances of these different levels will ever correspond. Thus to grasp the "unity" of the class struggle, so constituted, is of necessity to grasp the question of classes *in its contradictory form*.

IV.

Twenty years separate *The Eighteenth Brumaire* from *The Civil War in France*, in which Marx most directly extends some of the concepts elaborated in the former. It is a text whose conceptual developments are worked through directly in relation to a revolutionary political conjuncture requiring serious analysis (the Paris Commune), and is considerably influenced by Marx's and Engels's renewed political work in the context of the International (including the struggle against Bakunin and the Anarchists). Only three significant points can be indicated here from a body of political writing which is far too little studied and reflected upon in the Marxist movement.

The first concerns the indispensable necessity for the working class to constitute itself "into a party"; its aim being the "conquest of the political power," its object, the rupture of the state and state power, "the national power of capital over labour . . . a public force organised for social enslavement . . . an engine of class despotism." In the Preface to the reissue of the *Manifesto* which Marx and Engels published in 1872, this "lesson" was vividly enshrined: "One thing especially was proved by the Commune, viz. that 'the working class cannot simply lay hold of the ready-made state machinery and wield it for its own purpose.'" The detailed analysis of the Commune not only constitutes Marx's most extended writing on the forms of proletarian political power, but contains the critical argument for what, in the *Critique of the Gotha Programme*, he calls "a revolutionary dictatorship of the proletariat" as the only and necessary form in which the working class will "have to pass through long struggles, through a series of historic processes, transforming circumstances and men."[34]

It is in this context that Marx returns to the question, already posed in *The Eighteenth Brumaire*, as to what class forces the figure and formation of the Napoleonic state represents, and the relation of the Napoleonic "solution" to the economic development of capitalism in France. Here in *The Civil War in France*,[35] Marx considerably elaborates on the growing autonomization of the "centralised power of the state"; he résumés the constitutional forms of the 1851 crisis through which this state power is matured and developed—the "objective work" of the revolution; and the political work of domination over the under-developed fractions which they allowed Napoleon to accomplish. Here lies the basis for that theory of the state as a "class state," of the state as the "résumé of man's practical conflicts," the state as the relation of *political condensation*, which Lenin was subsequently to bring to a high order of importance (through his commentary on the fragmentary insights on this question of Marx and Engels in *State and Revolution*). One consequence of this emergent theory for our understanding of the relation between the political and economic aspects of the class struggle we will take up in a moment.

But first, Marx returns to the question of "representation." Napoleon, he now argues, "professed to rest upon the peasantry, the large mass of producers not directly involved in the struggle of capital and labour."[36] This class interest, apparently outside the direct play between the fundamental classes, served to substantiate the apparent "autonomy" of Napoleon from the immediate terms of the struggle—it secured for his *coup* the appearance of autonomy. It thus enabled him to project his political intervention—a classic ideological function of the state—as incarnating the "general interest," the "representative" of all the classes (because it represented none), of "the nation." "It professed to unite all classes by reviving for all the chimera of national glory."[37]

Marx suggests how and why this form of political resolution related to the immediate relations of forces in the central arena of struggle—related to it, but *indirectly*, as a representation, *as a postponement of it*. "In reality, it was the only form of government possible at a time when the bourgeoisie had already lost, and the working class had not yet acquired the faculty of ruling the nation" (ibid.). The "postponement" of a political resolution—appearing in the political domain as the temporary but displaced "rule" of an *absent* class—a class which could not appear in its own name—was a *form* which corresponded (but in no sense "immediately") to the precise state of under-development of the class relations of capitalist production in France. But this "unstable equilibrium" is also the condition which provides precisely the space through which the state drifts "apparently soaring high above society"—incarnating but also at the same time *masking* the class struggle. And it is in this form—the form of "the national power of capital over labour" (ibid.)—that capitalism in France develops—develops, of course, with its contradictory effects. Those effects are still to be seen in the peculiar form of "*étatisme*" which capitalist development manifests in the French social formation. The demonstration could hardly be clearer of how powerful are the consequences of the political *for* the economic. Just as it could hardly be more evident that the political and the economic are *coupled* but not as an *identity relation*.

In this context, it is noteworthy that Marx returns to a passage in the *Manifesto* which we have previously discussed, and offers a clarification which is (in the light of *The Eighteenth Brumaire*) a necessary correction. In the *Critique of the Gotha Programme* Marx takes up Lassalle's misinterpretation of his assertion that, face to face with the working class, "all other classes are a single reactionary mass" (i.e., the theses of the "simplification of the classes" in political struggle). He makes two points of clarification. First, he reiterates that what made the bourgeoisie *the* revolutionary class *vis-à-vis* the feudal classes was its historic role as "the bringer of large-scale industry." It is this objective condition which also gives to the proletariat its revolutionary position. But this does not mean *collapsing* the other classes into a single mass. The remnants of feudal classes may play an objectively reactionary role, but "these do not form a single reactionary mass together with the bourgeoisie."[38] In short, the political analysis is now definitively identified as *requiring* a theory of the complex formation of class fractions in class alliances. These—not some indistinguishable fusion of whole classes—constitute the terms of the political class struggle.

Time and again, especially in the subsidiary writings of this period, both Marx and Engels return, on the basis of the theses of the International, to reaffirm the necessity of "the political movement" as the means to the "economical emancipation of the working class."[39] The more the theory of the state and the centrality of state power to the expansion of capitalism is developed, the more central becomes the role of political struggle at the forefront of "the social revolution." It is true, as Fernbach observes, that Marx and Engels never work their way through to a fully developed theory of the corporate forms of working-class economic and political struggle: and he is right to attribute their failure, on the whole, to grasp the nature of the working class movement in Britain to this theoretical lacuna.[40] One has to turn to Lenin's polemic against Martynov and the "economists" for an adequate theorisation of this tendency. This debate cannot be presented here; but the whole chapter "Trade Union Politics and Social-Democratic Politics" in Lenin's *What Is to Be Done?* needs to be read in the context of this question: for the confusions which Lenin confronts there remain to plague us, with greatly augmented force, today.[41] The view that, because the economic relations and foundations determine, in the last instance, the forms and outcomes of the class struggle, therefore the struggle waged at the level of the economic is (as Martynov declared) "the most widely applicable method" of struggle, is dismantled by Lenin with all the cogency of his polemical force. He calls the proposition "the quintessence of Economism"; and this designation leads him into an analysis of the corporate character of a struggle limited to the battle "for better terms in the sale of their labour power, for better conditions of life and labour," which take us, in turn, directly to the heart of social-democratic reformism and "economism"—to "the soundly scientific (and 'soundly' opportunist) Mr and Mrs Webb and . . . the British

Trade unions."[42] What Lenin's intervention (and its subsequent development in the setting of his theory of imperialism) brings out far more sharply than Marx does, is the *damage* which has been wrought by the use, by Marx and by Marxists after him, of the same *term*—the "economic"—to designate *two* quite different things: the relations and forces of the mode of production and the site of those practices and forms of struggle which have economic relations (e.g., conditions of work, or wages) as their specific object.

V.

We can conclude by attempting very briefly to say how we begin to understand these terms and their effect for the constitution of classes and the class struggle. The "master concept" is that of mode of production. "Mode of production" is, in the first instance, the conceptual or analytic matrix which allows us to think, systematically, the fundamental structures of relations by means of which men, under determinant historical conditions, produce and reproduce the material conditions of their life. It consists of "forces" and "relations"—but this is only a summary formulation. Grasped within these apparently simple terms are sets of relations: relations both between agents and instruments, and agents and agents of production: the technical and the social division of labour under developing capitalist conditions—in which Marx gives priority of position to the "social" over the "technical." But even the "social" relations are not simple: they relate both to ownership of the means, organisation of the actual labour process and the power to set men and means, in certain combinations, to work.

The brief résumé we have offered of the "Machinery and Modern Industry" chapter from *Capital* should be enough to suggest how different sets of relations, in combination, are indexed by the ready formula of "forces and relations." To this we would have to add the "corresponding relations" of circulation and exchange—which are necessary to complete the long circuit of capital's realisation. When we say that the term "mode of production" is, first, an analytic matrix, we mean simply that it gives us a concept of the terms and the relations—the places and the conditions which must be filled—for what we can recognise as "production under capitalist conditions" to take place. It designates the fundamental places and spaces into which agents and means of production must be distributed, and where they are combined for capitalist production to proceed. It fundamentally designates the *site* of *class* relations in the economic structure of capitalism, since each of those positions entails antagonistic relations—antagonisms which Marx constantly invokes in his analysis in *Capital* through the "personifications," capitalist and wage-labourer. The site of classes does not designate "whole" classes as integral empirical groups of men and women; rather it indicates functions. As any sophisticated analysis of the anatomy of classes under the different phases of capitalist development clearly indicates, classes can shift at least some of their positions in relation to these functions: or they can perform "functions" on, so to speak, either side of the line of class antagonism.

This analysis is of particular importance in the designation of, for example, the new middle classes, which perform some (but not all) of the functions of *both* "global capital" *and* "the collective worker."[43] Thus in the actual concrete functioning of a particular mode of production, at any particular phase of its development, in a concrete historical society or social formation, the constitution of classes at this "economic" level is *already* complex and, in certain critical respects, contradictory. The idea that, somehow, by employing the terms of "mode of production" we can produce empirically constituted "whole classes" at the level of the economic, is an untenable proposition.

There are two, additional, reasons why this must be so. First, in actual concrete, historic, social formations, modes of production do not appear in their "pure" state, on their own. They are always combined with, and stand in a complex articulation to, other, previous or subordinate, modes of production—and their corresponding political and ideological relations—which cross-cut and over-determine any tendency of "pure" mode to produce a series of "pure" classes.

The second reason has already been anticipated. Social formations do not consist of an articulation of modes of production alone, but always sustain superstructural relations—the political, the juridical, the ideological. And, because these are not the mere efflorescences of the "base," they have pertinent effects: they have an effect of further complexifying the constitution of classes. Indeed, they exert an overdetermining effect in two, different ways. First, the political, juridical and ideological have effects *within* what we have broadly designated as "the economic." In certain phases of capitalist development, the real and the juridical ownership of the means of production coincides. But in, for example, monopoly capitalist conditions, the two functions do *not* coincide. Corporate property may be partly "owned" juridically by social groups who do not possess the "real" power to set the instruments of that property to work in production. But the political, juridical and the ideological also have *their own* effects, just as they have their own, determinate, conditions of existence, not reducible to "the economic." And since, as we have tried to demonstrate, these are related but "relatively autonomous" practices, and thus the sites of distinct forms of class struggle, with their own objects of struggle, and exhibiting a relatively independent retroactive effect on "the base," the forms in which classes, class interests and class forces *appear*, at each of these levels, will by no means necessarily fall in the same place, or indeed correspond in their form with that of another level. The example of the peasantry, Napoleon, the stalemate between the fundamental classes, the expansion of the state and capital, in *The Eighteenth Brumaire* should be enough to convince us of the non-immediacy, the non-transferability between these levels. The "general" concept of classes and of the class struggle, in its different aspects, will consist of our ability to grasp the *global* effect of these complex, contradictory effects. This implies a non-homogeneous conception of classes—including, for example, the non-homogeneity of capital, shorthand for the different kinds of capital, whose internal composition and differences of position in the circuit ensures that it has no singular, unproblematic "interest," even at the level of the economic. Hence it is most unlikely to appear as an integral force on the political stage, not to speak of the impossibility of conceiving it as appearing at the level of the ideological having, so to speak, "made up *its* mind."

In the foregoing sections we have been trying to explore just how Marx arrived at, and then how conceptually he filled out, the terms of this "non-homogeneity." Just to make the point a practical one, we need to think only of the significance of the moments in recent European history when "capital" has appeared to exert its compelling force ideologically, putting on the mask or draping itself in the robes (to use two metaphors from *The Eighteenth Brumaire*) of the petty-bourgeoisie (the class which, to coin a phrase, has nothing to lose but its moral rectitude).

These ideological displacements and disguisings are by no means confined to the past. One could read the economic and political situation in Britain since the early 1960s as a deepening crisis of the economic structure which assumes its most "natural" expression, at the political level, in the form of a Labour government—a paradoxical situation, where, in crisis, the party most favoured by capital is the "representative party of the working class." But this may have a great deal to do with what that party does when in power: living up, almost to the letter, to the description, offered in *The Eighteenth Brumaire*, of one of the historic roles of Social Democracy—"as a means not of doing away with two extremes, capital and wage-labour, but as weakening their antagonism and transforming it into harmony."[44] When Social Democracy attempts both to serve capital and represent the working class, it frequently does this by raising the index of its power to that of the "general interest": an interest which then, ideologically, appears in the rhetoric of Social Democracy in the ideological personification of "the consumer." On the other side of the parliamentary scene, we can observe the Thatcher leadership preparing for power and constructing an authoritarian popular consensus, in part by attempting to "represent" capital (anachronistically, but no less effectively) in the "venerable disguise and borrowed language," the "names, slogans and costumes" of a disappearing class fraction—the small shopkeeper! There could hardly be a more compelling argument—to anyone seeking to unravel the thread of class struggle which unites these discrepant appearances—for a theory of class struggle *as* a theory of the "unity" of these contradictory and displaced representations of class relations at a series of different sites or instances—the economic; the political; the ideological. In short, the need for a Marxist theory of representation, of *Darstellung*.

In the context of the debate about ideology, this concept of "representation" has been recently much criticised by Paul Hirst as being no more than a complex version of a "reflection" theory, with a tendency to return to the "givenness of the classes as social forces in the structure of the economic" (ultimately economistic) and a reliance on what he calls the "base-superstructure contestation," which he defines as tending "towards vulgar materialism." This argument is conducted against, especially, Althusser's theory of ideology, as developed in the article on "ideological state apparatuses,"[45] and therefore poses problems of an order outside the immediate framework of this essay. However, Hirst goes on to criticise the very concept of "representation," suggesting that if "representation" is used in its strong form, then the means by which relations are represented absolutely transform them; hence those means determine the form of "representation," which can then never be re-examined in terms of what is "represented." "It is not too much to argue that once any autonomy is conceded to these means of representation, it follows necessarily that the means of representation determine the represented. This obliterates the classic problem of 'representation.'"[46]

This argument appears to take the thesis concerning the non-transferability, the non-homogeneity, of the economic and political levels of class struggle (which we have been trying to establish in terms of its reference points in Marx's own work) to its *opposite extreme*, in the effort to banish every last strain of reductionism from the Marxist schema. From this position there follows what Hirst has been bold enough to name "the necessary non-correspondence" of the levels—a concept very different in fact from that of "*no necessary correspondence*." The difference between the two seems to me to be, precisely, the difference between *autonomy* and *relative autonomy*. And whereas "relative autonomy" appears, from the texts we have been examining, to catch exactly the way Marx sets out to think the *complex unity* of a social formation (both *complexity* and *unity* having equal importance), autonomy, or a "necessary non-correspondence" appears to fall outside the limits of Marxism as an identifiable theoretical terrain. It seems clear, from the passages I have examined, that Marx *does* advance to a concept of non-correspondence, not in any simple, reductionist or homogenous sense: he develops the concepts which enable us to think, in relation to specific historical conjunctures, just *how* and why these displacements have effects; what forms and relations sustain them in their "relative" independence; and what effects and consequences the non-reducibility of the structure of a social formation to its "base" has for the understanding and the continuation of class struggle as a complex practice. It seems equally clear that Marx *does*—as Althusser has now openly recognised[47]—continue to think the economic structure as in some sense other than a reductionist one, "determining"; that this does require the—quite new and original—problem of grasping a "unity" which is *not* a simple or reductionist one; that it is precisely this double movement which constitutes *The Eighteenth Brumaire* as the most remarkable of Marx's non-reductionist materialist analyses of politics; and that this conception does, finally, require the Marxist "topography" of base and superstructure. Indeed, what the base-superstructure topography "does" for Marxism, and why it provides a defining conceptual threshold and boundary-limit *for* Marxism (without which it becomes another thing, another kind of theory—a theory of the absolute autonomy of everything from everything else) is most eloquently expressed in Althusser's *Essays in Self-Criticism*: all the more pertinent in this case since it was his acknowledged "theoreticist deviation" which prompted, in the name of Marxism, a rigorous and often highly principled tendency to depart from its terrain. In the light of this continuing debate, therefore, it seemed worthwhile undertaking an investigation of how Marx himself made the theoretical departure from the terrain of essentialism and simplicity, and how, in detail, the concepts were forced into discovery which enabled him—and us, after him—to grasp the radical and necessary complexity of the practice of class struggle.

NOTES

This essay first appeared in *Class and Class Structure*, ed. Alan Hunt (London: Lawrence and Wishart, 1977), 15–60.

1. Karl Marx and Frederick Engels, *Selected Correspondence* (Moscow: Progress, 1975), 105.
2. See the major "revisions" in Louis Althusser, *Essays in Self-Criticism* (London: New Left Books, 1976).
3. Marx and Engels, *Selected Correspondence*.
4. Louis Althusser, *For Marx* (London: Allen Lane, 1969); Louis Althusser and Étienne Balibar, *Reading Capital* (London: New Left Books, 1970).
5. Gwyn A. Williams, *France 1848–1851*, in Course A321, *The Revolutions of 1848* (Milton Keynes, UK: Open University, 1976).
6. Karl Marx and Frederick Engels, *Manifesto of the Communist Party*, in Marx and Engels, *Selected Works in One Volume* (London: Lawrence and Wishart, 1968).
7. Althusser, *For Marx*.
8. Karl Marx, *Economic and Philosophic Manuscripts of 1844* (London: Lawrence and Wishart, 1964).
9. Althusser, "Contradiction and Overdetermination," in *For Marx*.
10. Karl Marx, *Grundrisse* (Harmondsworth, UK: Penguin, 1973).
11. Karl Marx, *Capital* I (London: Lawrence and Wishart, 1974), 669.
12. Marx, *Grundrisse*, 265.
13. Karl Marx, *Capital* III (London: Lawrence and Wishart, 1972), 818–19.
14. Karl Marx to Joseph Weydemeyer, 5 March 1852, in Marx and Engels, *Selected Correspondence*.
15. Marx, *Capital* I, 714–15.
16. Marx, *Capital* I, 396.
17. Marx, *Capital* I, 503.
18. Karl Marx and Frederick Engels, *The German Ideology* (London: Lawrence and Wishart, 1965), 69.
19. Karl Marx, *The Poverty of Philosophy*, in Karl Marx and Frederick Engels, *Collected Works* (London: Lawrence and Wishart, 1976), 6:177.
20. 23 November 1871 in Marx and Engels, *Selected Correspondence*, 254–55.
21. 29 November 1871 in Marx and Engels, *Selected Correspondence*, 255.
22. Nicos Poulantzas, *Political Power and Social Classes* (London: New Left Books, 1973), 58.
23. V. I. Lenin, *Collected Works* (Moscow: Progress, 1975), 5:437.
24. Williams, *France 1848–1851*, 112.
25. Antonio Gramsci, *Selections from the Prison Notebooks*, ed. and trans. Quintin Hoare and Geoffrey Nowell Smith (London: Lawrence and Wishart, 1971).
26. Karl Marx, *The Eighteenth Brumaire of Louis Bonaparte*, in Marx and Engels, *Selected Works* (Moscow: Progress, 1969), 1:423–24.
27. Marx and Engels, *Selected Works*, 1:424.
28. Marx and Engels, *Selected Works*, 1:479.

29. Marx and Engels, *Selected Works*, 1:476.
30. Althusser, *For Marx*, 106.
31. 27 October 1890 in Marx and Engels, *Selected Correspondence*, 399.
32. Althusser, *For Marx*, 106n23.
33. Karl Marx, "Parties and Cliques," in *Surveys from Exile*, ed. David Fernbach (Harmondsworth, UK: Penguin, 1973), 279.
34. Marx and Engels, *Selected Works in One Volume*, 327.
35. Marx and Engels, *Selected Works in One Volume*, 285–86.
36. Marx and Engels, *Selected Works*, 2:219.
37. Marx and Engels, *Selected Works*, 2:219.
38. Marx and Engels, *Selected Works*, 3:20.
39. Karl Marx, "Speech on the Anniversary of the International," in *The First International and After*, ed. David Fernbach (Harmondsworth, UK: Penguin, 1973–74), 271.
40. Marx, *Surveys from Exile*, 22–24.
41. Lenin, *Collected Works*, 5:397–440.
42. Lenin, *Collected Works*, 5:404.
43. To use Guglielmo Carchedi's terms. See "On the Economic Identification of the New Middle Class," *Economy and Society* 4, no. 1 (1975).
44. Marx, *The Eighteenth Brumaire*, 423–24.
45. Louis Althusser, "Ideology and Ideological State Apparatuses," in *Lenin and Philosophy and Other Essays* (London: New Left Books, 1971).
46. Paul Q. Hirst, "Althusser and the Theory of Ideology," *Economy and Society* 5, no. 4 (1976): 395.
47. Althusser, *Essays in Self-Criticism*.

CHAPTER 4

The Problem of Ideology:
Marxism without Guarantees

In the past two or three decades, Marxist theory has been going through a remarkable, but lop-sided and uneven revival. On the one hand, it has come once again to provide the principal pole of opposition to "bourgeois" social thought. On the other hand, many young intellectuals have passed *through* the revival and, after a heady and rapid apprenticeship, gone right out the other side again. They have "settled their accounts" with Marxism and moved on to fresh intellectual fields and pastures: but not quite. Post-Marxism remains one of our largest and most flourishing contemporary theoretical schools. The Post-Marxists use Marxist concepts while constantly demonstrating their inadequacy. They seem, in fact, to continue to stand on the shoulders of the very theories they have just definitely destroyed. Had Marxism not existed, "Post-Marxism" would have had to invent it, so that "deconstructing" it once more would give the "deconstructionists" something further to do. All this gives Marxism a curious life-after-death quality. It is constantly being "transcended" *and* "preserved." There is no more instructive site from which to observe this process than that of ideology itself.

I do not intend to trace through once again the precise twists and turns of these recent disputes, nor to try to follow the intricate theorising which has attended them. Instead, I want to place the debates about ideology in the wider context of Marxist theory as a whole. I also want to pose it as a general *problem*—a problem of theory, because it is also a problem of politics and strategy. I want to identify the most telling weaknesses and limitations in the classical Marxist formulations about ideology; and to assess what has been gained, what deserves to be lost, and what needs to be retained—and perhaps rethought—in the light of the critiques.

But first, why has the problem of ideology occupied so prominent a place within Marxist debate in recent years? Perry Anderson, in his magisterial sweep of the Western European Marxist intellectual scene,[1] noted the intense preoccupation in these quarters with problems relating to philosophy, epistemology, ideology and the superstructures. He clearly regarded this as a deformation in the development of Marxist thought. The privileging of *these* questions in Marxism, he argued, reflected the general isolation of Western European Marxist intellectuals from the imperatives of mass political struggle and organisation; their divorce from the "controlling tensions of a direct or active relationship to a proletarian audience"; their distance from "popular practice" and their continuing subjection to the dominance of bourgeois thought. This had resulted, he argued, in a general disengagement from the classical themes and problems of the mature Marx and of Marxism. The over-preoccupation with the ideological could be taken as an eloquent sign of this.

There is much to this argument—as those who have survived the theoreticist deluge in "Western Marxism" in recent years will testify. The emphases of "Western Marxism" may well account for *the way* the problem of ideology was constructed, how the debate has been conducted and *the degree* to which it has been abstracted into the high realms of speculative theory. But I think we must reject any implication that, but for the distortions produced by "Western Marxism," Marxist theory could have comfortably proceeded on its appointed path, following the established agenda: leaving the problem of ideology to its subordinate, second-order place. The rise to visibility of the problem of ideology has a more objective basis. First, the real developments which have taken place in the means by which mass consciousness is shaped and transformed— the massive growth of the "cultural industries." Second, the troubling questions of the "consent" of the mass of the working class to the system in advanced capitalist societies in Europe and thus their partial stabilisation, against all expectations. Of course, "consent" is *not* maintained through the mechanisms of ideology alone. But the two cannot be divorced. It also reflects certain real theoretical weaknesses in the original Marxist formulations about ideology. And it throws light on some of the most critical issues in political strategy and the politics of the socialist movement in advanced capitalist societies.

In briefly reviewing some of these questions, I want to foreground, not so much the theory as the *problem* of ideology. The *problem* of ideology is to give an account, within a materialist theory, of how social ideas arise. We need to understand what their role is in a particular social formation, so as to inform the struggle to change society and open the road towards a socialist transformation of society. By ideology I mean the mental frameworks—the languages, the concepts, categories, imagery of thought, and the systems of representation—which different classes and social groups deploy in order to make sense of, define, figure out and render intelligible the way society works.

The problem of ideology, therefore, concerns the ways in which ideas of different kinds grip the minds of masses, and thereby become a "material force." In this, more politicised, perspective, the theory of ideology helps us to analyze how a particular set of ideas comes to dominate the social thinking of a historical bloc, in Gramsci's sense; and, thus, helps to unite such a *bloc* from the inside, and maintain its dominance and leadership over society as a whole. It has especially to do with the concepts and the languages of practical thought which stabilise a particular form of power and domination; or which reconcile and accommodate the mass of the people to their subordinate place in the social formation. It has also to do with the processes by which new forms of consciousness, new conceptions of the world, arise, which move the masses of the people into historical action against the prevailing system. These questions are at *stake* in a range of social struggles. It is to explain them, in order that we may better comprehend and master the terrain of ideological struggle, that we need not only a theory but a theory adequate to the complexities of what we are trying to explain.

No such theory exists, fully prepackaged, in Marx's and Engels's works. Marx developed no general explanation of how social ideas worked, comparable to his historico-theoretical work on the economic forms and relations of the capitalist mode of production. His remarks in this area were never intended to have a "law-like" status. And, mistaking them for statements of that more fully theorised kind may well be where the problem of ideology for Marxism first began. In fact, his theorising on this subject was much more *ad hoc*. There are consequently severe fluctuations in Marx's usage of the term. In our time—as you will see in the definition I offered above—the term "ideology" has come to have a wider, more descriptive, less systematic reference than it did in the classical Marxist texts. We *now* use it to refer to *all* organised forms of social thinking. This leaves open the degree and nature of its "distortions." It certainly refers to the domain of practical thinking and reasoning (the form, after all, in which most ideas are likely to grip the minds of the masses and draw them into action), rather than simply to well-elaborated and internally consistent "systems of thought." We mean the practical as well as the theoretical knowledges which enable people to "figure out" society, and within whose categories and discourses we "live out" and "experience" our objective positioning in social relations.

Marx did, on many occasions, use the term "ideology," practically, in this way. So its usage with this meaning *is* in fact sanctioned by his work.

Thus, for example, he spoke in a famous passage of the "ideological forms in which men become conscious of . . . conflict and fight it out."[2] In *Capital* he frequently, in asides, addresses the "everyday consciousness" of the capitalist entrepreneur; or the "common sense of capitalism." By this he means the forms of spontaneous thought within which the capitalist represents to himself the workings of the capitalist system and "lives out" (i.e., genuinely experiences) his practical relations to it. Indeed, there are already clues there to the subsequent uses of the term which many, I suspect, do not believe could be warranted from Marx's own work. For example, the spontaneous forms of "practical bourgeois consciousness" are real, but they cannot be *adequate* forms of thought, since there are aspects of the capitalist system—the generation of surplus value, for example—which simply cannot be "thought" or explained, using those vulgar categories. On the other hand, they can't be *false* in any simple sense either, since these practical bourgeois men seem capable enough of making profit, working the system, sustaining its relations, exploiting labour, without benefit of a more sophisticated or "truer" understanding of what they are involved in. To take another example, it is a fair deduction from what Marx said, that the *same* sets of relations—the capitalist circuit—can be represented in several *different ways* or (as the modern school would say) *represented within different systems of discourse*.

To name but three—there is the discourse of "bourgeois common sense"; the sophisticated theories of the classical political economists, like Ricardo, from whom Marx learned so much; and, of course, Marx's own theoretical discourse—the discourse of *Capital* itself.

As soon as we divorce ourselves from a religious and doctrinal reading of Marx, therefore, the openings between many of the classical uses of the term, and its more recent elaborations, are not as closed as current theoreticist polemics would lead us to believe.

Nevertheless, the fact is that Marx most often used "ideology" to refer specifically to the manifestations of bourgeois thought; and above all to its negative and distorted features. Also, he tended to employ it—in, for example, *The German Ideology*, the joint work of Marx and Engels—in contestation against what he thought were incorrect ideas: often, of a well-informed and systematic kind (what we would *now* call theoretical ideologies, or, following Gramsci, "philosophies"; as opposed to the categories of practical consciousness, or what Gramsci called "common sense"). Marx used the term as a critical weapon against the speculative mysteries of Hegelianism; against religion and the critique of religion; against idealist philosophy, and political economy of the vulgar and degenerated varieties. In *The German Ideology* and *The Poverty of Philosophy* Marx and Engels were combatting bourgeois ideas. They were contesting the anti-materialist philosophy which underpinned the dominance of those ideas. In order to make their polemical point, they simplified many of their formulations. Our subsequent problems have arisen, in part, from treating these polemical inversions as the basis for a labour of *positive* general theorising.

Within that broad framework of usage, Marx advances certain more fully elaborated theses, which have come to form the theoretical basis of the theory in its so-called classical form. First, the materialist premise: ideas arise from and reflect the material conditions and circumstances in which they are generated. They express social relations and their contradictions in thought. The notion that ideas provide the motor of history, or proceed independent of material relations and generate their own autonomous effects, is, specifically, what is declared as speculative and illusory about bourgeois ideology. Second, the thesis of determinateness: ideas are only the dependent effects of the ultimately determining level in the social formation—the economic in the last instance. So that transformations in the latter will show up, sooner or later, as corresponding modifications in the former. Thirdly, the fixed correspondences between dominance in the socio-economic sphere and the ideological: "ruling ideas" are the ideas of the "ruling class"—the class position of the latter providing the coupling and the guarantee of correspondence with the former.

The critique of the classical theory has been addressed precisely to these propositions. To say that ideas are "mere reflexes" establishes their materialism but leaves them without specific effects; a realm of pure dependency. To say that ideas are determined "in the last instance" by the economic is to set out along the economic reductionist road. Ultimately, ideas can be reduced to the essence of their truth—their economic content. The only stopping point before this ultimate reductionism arises through the attempt to delay it a little and preserve some space for manoeuvre by increasing the number of "mediations." To say that the "ruling-ness" of a class is the guarantee of the dominance of certain ideas is to ascribe them as the exclusive property of that class, and to define particular forms of consciousness as class-specific.

It should be noted that, though these criticisms are directly addressed to formulations concerning the problem of ideology, they in effect recapitulate the substance of the more general and wide-ranging criticisms advanced against classical Marxism itself: its rigid structural determinacy, its reductionism of two varieties—class and economic; its way of conceptualising the social formation itself. Marx's model of ideology has been criticised because it did not conceptualise the social formation as a determinate complex formation, composed of different practices, but as a *simple* (or, as Althusser called it in *For Marx* and *Reading Capital*, an "expressive") structure.[3] By this Althusser meant that one practice—"the economic"—determines in a direct manner all others, and each effect is simply and simultaneously reproduced correspondingly (i.e., "expressed") on all the other levels.

Those who know the literature and the debates will easily identify the main lines of the more specific revisions advanced, from different sides, against these positions. They begin with the denial that any such correspondences exist, or that the "superstructures" are totally devoid of their own specific effects, in Engels's gloss on "what Marx thought" (especially in the later correspondence). The glosses by Engels are immensely fruitful, suggestive and generative. They provide, not the solution to the problem of ideology but the starting point of all serious reflection on the problem. The simplifications developed, he argued, because Marx was in contestation with the speculative idealism of his day. They were one-sided distortions, the necessary exaggerations of polemic. The criticism leads on through the richly tapestried efforts of Marxist theorists like Lukács to hold, polemically, to the strict orthodoxy of a particular "Hegelian" reading of Marx, while in practice introducing a whole range of "mediating and intermediary factors" which soften and displace the drive towards reductionism and economism implicit in some of Marx's original formulations. They include Gramsci— but from another direction—whose contribution will be discussed at a later place in the argument. They culminate in the highly sophisticated theoretical interventions of Althusser and the Althusserians: their contestation of economic and class reductionism and of the "expressive totality" approach.

Althusser's revisions (in *For Marx* and especially in the "Ideology and Ideological State Apparatuses" chapter of *Lenin and Philosophy and Other Essays*)[4] sponsored a decisive move away from the "distorted ideas" and "false consciousness" approach to ideology. It opened the gate to a more linguistic or "discursive" conception of ideology. It put on the agenda the whole neglected issue of how ideology becomes internalised, how we come to speak "spontaneously," within the limits of the categories of thought which exist outside us and which can more accurately be said to think us. (This is the so-called problem of the interpellation of subjects at the centre of ideological discourse. It led to the subsequent bringing into Marxism of the psychoanalytic interpretations of how individuals enter into the ideological categories of language at all.) In insisting (e.g., in "Ideological State Apparatuses") on the *function* of ideology in the reproduction of social relations of production and (in *Essays in Self-Criticism*)[5] on the metaphorical utility of the base-superstructure metaphor, Althusser attempted some last-hour regrouping on the classical Marxist terrain.

But his first revision was too "functionalist." If the function of ideology is to "reproduce" capitalist social relations according to the "requirements" of the system, how does one account for subversive ideas or for ideological struggle? And the second was too "orthodox." It was Althusser who had displaced so thoroughly the "base/superstructure" metaphor! In fact, the doors he opened provided precisely the exit points through which many abandoned the problematic of the classical Marxist theory of ideology altogether. They gave up, not only Marx's particular way in *The German Ideology* of coupling "ruling class and ruling ideas," but the very preoccupations with the class structuring of ideology, and its role in the generation and maintenance of hegemony.

Discourse and psychoanalytic theories, originally conceived as theoretical supports to the critical work of theory revision and development, provided instead categories which substituted for those of the earlier paradigm. Thus, the very real gaps and lacunae in the "objective" thrust of the Marxist theory, around the modalities of consciousness and the "subjectification" of ideologies, which Althusser's use of the terms "interpellation" (borrowed from Freud) and "positioning" (borrowed from Lacan) were intended to address, became themselves the exclusive object of the exercise. The *only* problem about ideology was the problem of how ideological subjects were formed through the psychoanalytic processes. The theoretical tensions were then untied. This is the long descent of "revisionist" work on ideology, which leads ultimately (in Foucault) to the abolition of the category of "ideology" altogether. Yet its highly sophisticated theorists, for reasons quite obscure, continue to insist that their theories are "really" materialist, political, historical, and so on: as if haunted by Marx's ghost still rattling around in the theoretical machine.

I have recapitulated this story in an immensely abbreviated form because I do not intend to engage in detail with its conjectures and refutations. Instead, I want to pick up their thread, acknowledging their force and cogency at least in modifying substantially the classical propositions about ideology, and, in the light of them, to re-examine some of the earlier formulations by Marx, and consider whether they can be refashioned and developed in the positive light of the criticisms advanced—as most good theories ought to be capable of— without losing some of the essential qualities and insights (what used to be called the "rational core") which they originally possessed. Crudely speaking, that is because—as I hope to show—I acknowledge the immense force of many of the criticisms advanced. But I am not convinced that they wholly and entirely abolish every useful insight, every essential starting point, in a materialist theory of ideology. If, according to the fashionable canon, all that is left, in the light of the devastatingly advanced, clever and cogent critiques, is the labour of perpetual "deconstruction," this essay is devoted to a little modest work of "reconstruction"—without, I hope, being too defeated by ritual orthodoxy.

Take, for example, the extremely tricky ground of the "distortions" of ideology, and the question of "false consciousness." Now it is not difficult to see why these kinds of formulations have brought Marx's critics bearing down on him. "Distortions" opens immediately the question as to why some people—those living their relation to their conditions of existence through the categories of a distorted ideology—cannot recognise that it is distorted, while we, with our superior wisdom, or armed with properly formed concepts, can. Are the "distortions" simply falsehoods? Are they deliberately sponsored falsifications? If so, by whom? Does ideology really function like conscious class propaganda? And if ideology is the product or function of "the structure" rather than of a group of conspirators, how *does* an economic *structure* generate a guaranteed set of ideological effects? The terms are, clearly, unhelpful as they stand. They make both the masses and the capitalists look like judgemental dopes. They also entail a peculiar view of the formation of alternative forms of consciousness. Presumably, they arise as scales fall from people's eyes or as they wake up, as if from a dream, and, all at once, see the light, glance directly through the transparency of things immediately to their essential truth, their concealed structural processes. This is an account of the development of working-class consciousness founded on the rather surprising model of St Paul and the Damascus Road.

Let us undertake a little excavation work of our own. Marx did not assume that, because Hegel was the summit of speculative bourgeois thought, and because the "Hegelians" vulgarised and etherealised his thought, Hegel was therefore not a thinker to be reckoned with, a figure worth learning from. More so with classical political economy, from Smith to Ricardo, where again the distinctions between different levels of an ideological formation are important. There is classical political economy which Marx calls "scientific"; its vulgarisers engaged in "mere apologetics"; and the "everyday consciousness" in which practical bourgeois entrepreneurs calculate their odds informed by, but utterly unconscious (until Thatcherism appeared) of, Ricardo's or Adam Smith's advanced thoughts on the subject. Even more instructive is Marx's insistence that (a) classical political economy *was* a powerful, substantial scientific body of work, which (b) *nevertheless* contained an essential ideological limit, a distortion. This distortion was not, according to Marx, anything directly to do with technical errors or absences in their argument, but with a broader prohibition. Specifically, the distorted or ideological features arose from the fact that they *assumed* the categories of bourgeois political economy as the foundations of all economic calculation, refusing to see the historical determinacy of their starting-points and premises; and, at the other end, from the assumption that, with capitalist production, economic development had achieved, not simply its highest point to date (Marx agreed with that), but its final conclusion and apogee. There could be no new forms of economic relations after it. Its forms and relations would go on forever. The distortions, to be precise, within bourgeois theoretical ideology at its more "scientific" were, nevertheless, real and substantial. They did not destroy many aspects of its scientific validity—hence it was not "false" simply because it was confined within the limits and horizon of bourgeois thought. On the other hand, the distortions limited its scientific validity, its capacity to advance beyond certain points, its ability to resolve its own internal contradictions, its power to think outside the skin of the social relations reflected in it.

Now this relation between Marx and the classical political economists represents a far more complex way of posing the relation between "truth" and "falsehood" *inside* a so-called scientific mode of thought, than many of Marx's critics have assumed. Indeed, critical theorists, in their search for greater theoretical vigour, an absolute divide between "science" and "ideology" and a clean epistemological break between "bourgeois" and "non-bourgeois" ideas, have done much themselves to simplify the relations which Marx, not so much argued, as established in practice (i.e., in terms of how he actually used classical political economy as both a support and adversary). We can rename the specific "distortions," of which Marx accused political economy, to remind us later of their general applicability. Marx called them the *eternalisation* of relations which are in fact historically specific; and the *naturalisation* effect—treating what are the products of a specific historical development as if universally valid, and arising, not through historical processes but, as it were, from Nature itself.

We can consider one of the most contested points—the "falseness" or distortions of ideology, from another standpoint. It is well known that Marx attributed the spontaneous categories of vulgar bourgeois thought to its grounding in the "surface forms" of the capitalist circuit. Specifically, Marx identified the importance of the market and market exchange, where things were sold and profits made. This approach, as Marx argued, left aside the critical domain—the "hidden abode"—of capitalist production itself. Some of his most important formulations flow from this argument.

In summary, the argument is as follows. Market exchange is what appears to govern and regulate economic processes under capitalism. Market relations are sustained by a number of elements and these appear (are represented) in every discourse which tries to explain the capitalist circuit from this standpoint. The market brings together, under conditions of equal exchange, consumers and producers who do not—and need not, given the market's "hidden hand"—know one another. Similarly, the *labour* market brings together those who have something to sell (labour power) and those who have something to buy with (wages): a "fair price" is struck. Since the market works, as it were, by magic, harmonising needs and their satisfaction "blindly," there is no compulsion about it. We can "choose" to buy and sell, or not (and presumably take the consequences: though this part is *not* so well represented in the discourses of the market, which are more elaborated on the *positive* side of market-choice than they are on its *negative* consequences). Buyer or seller need not be driven by goodwill, or love of his neighbour or fellow feeling to succeed in the market game. In fact, the market works best if each party to the transaction consults only his or her self-interest directly. It is a system driven by the real and practical imperatives of self-interest. Yet it achieves satisfaction of a kind, all round. The capitalist hires his labour and makes his profit; the landlord lets his property and gets a rent; the worker gets her wages and thus can buy the goods she needs.

Now market-exchange also "appears" in a rather different sense. It is the part of the capitalist circuit which everyone can plainly *see*, the bit we all experience daily. Without buying and selling, in a money economy, we would all physically and socially come to a halt very quickly. Unless we are deeply involved in other aspects of the capitalist process, we would not necessarily know much about the other parts of the circuit which are necessary if capital is to be valorised and if the whole process is to reproduce itself and expand. And yet, unless commodities are produced there is nothing to sell; and—Marx argued, at any rate—it is first in production itself that labour is exploited. Whereas the kind of "exploitation" which a market-ideology is best able to see and grasp is "profiteering"—taking too big a rake-off on the market price. So the market is the part of the system which is universally encountered and experienced. It is the obvious, the visible part: the part which constantly *appears*.

Now, if you extrapolate from this generative set of categories, based on market exchange, it is possible to extend it to other spheres of social life, and to see them, as, also, constituted on a similar model. And this is precisely what Marx, in a justly famous passage, suggests happens:

> This sphere that we are deserting, within whose boundaries the sale and purchase power of labour-power goes on, is in fact a very Eden of the innate rights of man. There alone rule Freedom, Equality, Property and Bentham. Freedom, because both buyer and seller of a commodity, say of labour-power, are constrained only by their own free will. They contract as free agents, and the agreement they come to, is but the form in which they give legal expression to their common will. Equality, because each enters into relation with the other, as with a simple owner of commodities, and they exchange equivalent for equivalent. Property, because each disposes only of what is his own. And Bentham, because each looks only to himself. The only force that brings them together and puts them in relation with each other, is the selfishness, the gain and the private interests of each.[6]

In short, our ideas of "Freedom," "Equality," "Property" and "Bentham" (i.e., "Individualism")—the ruling ideological principles of the bourgeois lexicon, and the key political themes which, in our time, have made a powerful and compelling return to the ideological stage under the auspices of Mrs. Thatcher and neoliberalism—may derive from the categories we use in our practical, common sense thinking about the market economy. This is how there arises, out of daily, mundane experience, the powerful categories of bourgeois legal, political, social and philosophical thought.

This is a critical *locus classicus* of the debate; from this Marx extrapolated several of the theses which have come to form the contested territory of the theory of ideology. First, he establishes as a *source* of "ideas" a particular point or moment of the economic circuit of capital. Second, he demonstrates how the translation from the economic to ideological categories can be effected; from the "market exchange of equivalents" to the bourgeois notions of "Freedom" and "Equality"; from the fact that each must possess the means of exchange to the legal categories of property rights. Third, he defines in a more precise manner what he means by "distortion." For this "taking off" from the exchange point of the recircuit of capital is an ideological process. It "obscures, hides, conceals"—the terms are all in the text— another set of relations: the relations, which do *not* appear on the surface but are concealed in the "hidden abode" of production (where property, ownership, the exploitation of waged labour and the expropriation of surplus value all take place). The ideological categories "hide" this underlying reality, and *substitute* for all that the "truth" of market relations. In many ways, then, the passage contains all the so-called cardinal sins of the classical Marxist theory of ideology rolled into one: economic reductionism, a too simple correspondence between the economic and the political ideological; the true v. false, real v. distortion, "true" consciousness v. false consciousness distinctions.

However, it also seems to me possible to "re-read" the passage from the standpoint of many contemporary critiques in such a way as (a) to retain many of the profound insights of the original, while (b) expanding it, using some of the theories of ideology developed in more recent times. Capitalist production is defined in Marx's terms as a circuit. This circuit explains not only production and consumption, but *re*production—the ways in which the conditions for keeping the circuit moving are sustained. Each moment is vital to the generation and realisation of value. Each establishes certain determinate conditions for the other—that is, each is dependent on or determinate for the other. Thus, if some part of what is realised through sale is not paid as wages to labour, labour cannot reproduce itself, physically and socially, to work and buy again another day. Thus "production," too, is dependent on "consumption"; even though in the analysis Marx tends to insist on the prior analytic value to be accorded to the relations of *production*. (This in itself has had serious consequences, since it has led Marxists not only to prioritise "production" but to argue as if the moments of "consumption and exchange" are of no value or importance to the theory—a fatal, one-side productivist reading.)

Now this circuit can be construed, ideologically, in different ways. This is something which modern theorists of ideology insist on, as against the vulgar conception of ideology as arising from a fixed and unalterable relation between the economic relation and how it is "expressed" or represented in ideas. Modern theorists have tended to arrive at this break with a simple notion of economic determinacy over ideology through their borrowing from recent work on the nature of language and discourse. Language is the medium *par excellence* through which things are "represented" in thought and thus the medium in which ideology is generated and transformed. But in language, the same social relation can be *differently* represented and construed. And this is so, they would argue, because language by its nature is *not fixed in* a one-to-one relation to its referent but is "multi-referential": it can construct different meanings around what is apparently the same social relation or phenomenon.

It may or may not be the case, that, in the passage under discussion, Marx is using a fixed, determinate and unalterable relationship between market exchange and how it is appropriated in thought. But you will see from what I have said that I do not believe this to be so. As I understand it, "the market" means one thing in bourgeois political economy and the spontaneous consciousness of practical bourgeois men, and quite another thing in Marxist economic analysis. So my argument would be that, implicitly, Marx is saying that, in a world where markets exist and market economy dominates economic life, it would be distinctly odd if there were no category allowing us to think, speak and act in relation to it. In *that* sense, all economic categories—bourgeois or Marxist—express existing social relations. But I think it *also* follows from the argument that market relations are not always represented by the same categories of thought.

There is no fixed and unalterable relation between what the market is and how it is construed within an ideological or explanatory framework. We could even say that one of the purposes of *Capital* is precisely to *displace* the discourse of bourgeois political economy—the discourse in which the market is most usually and obviously understood—and to replace it with another discourse, that of the market as it fits into the Marxist schema. If the point is not pressed too literally, therefore, the two kinds of approaches to the understanding of ideology are not totally contradictory.

What, then, about the "distortions" of bourgeois political economy as an ideology? One way of reading this is to think that since Marx calls bourgeois political economy "distorted," it must be *false*. Thus those who live their relation to economic life exclusively within its categories of thought and experience are, by definition, in "false consciousness." Again, we must be on our guard here about arguments too easily won. For one thing, Marx makes an important distinction between "vulgar" versions of political economy and more advanced versions, like that of Ricardo, which, he says clearly, "has scientific value." But, still, what can he mean by "false" and "distorted" in this context?

He cannot mean that "the market" does not exist. In fact, it is *all too real*. It is the very life blood of capitalism, from one viewpoint. Without it capitalism would never have broken through the framework of feudalism; and without its ceaseless continuation, the circuits of capital would come to a sudden and disastrous halt. I think we can only make sense of these terms if we think of giving an account of an economic circuit, which consists of several interconnected moments, from the vantage point of *one* of those moments alone. If, in our explanation, we privilege one moment only, and do not take account of the differentiated whole or "ensemble" of which it is a part; or if we use categories of thought, appropriate to one such moment alone, to explain the whole process; then we are in danger of giving what Marx would have called (after Hegel) a "one-sided" account.

One-sided explanations are always a distortion. Not in the sense that they are a lie about the system, but in the sense that a "half-truth" cannot be the whole truth about anything. With those ideas, you will always represent a part of the whole. You will thereby produce an explanation which is only *partially* adequate—and, in that sense, "false." Also, if you use only "market categories and concepts" to understand the capitalist circuit as a whole, there are literally many aspects of it which you cannot see. In that sense, the categories of market exchange obscure and mystify our understanding of the capitalist process: that is, they do not enable us to see or formulate questions about them, for they render other aspects invisible.

Is the worker who lives his or her relation to the circuits of capitalist production exclusively through the categories of a "fair price" and a "fair wage" in "false consciousness"? Yes, if by that we mean there is something about her situation which she cannot grasp with the categories she is using; something about the process as a whole which is systematically hidden because the available concepts only give her a grasp of one of its many-sided moments. No, if by that we mean that she is utterly deluded about what goes on under capitalism.

The falseness therefore arises, not from the fact that the market is an illusion, a trick, a sleight-of-hand, but only in the sense that it is an *inadequate* explanation of a process. It has also substituted one part of the process for the whole—a procedure which, in linguistics, is known as "metonymy" and in anthropology, psychoanalysis and (with special meaning) in Marx's work, as *fetishism*. The other "lost" moments of the circuit are, however, unconscious, not in the Freudian sense, because they have been repressed from consciousness, but in the sense of being invisible, given the concepts and categories we are using.

This also helps us to explain the otherwise extremely confusing terminology in *Capital*, concerning what "appears on the surface" (which is sometimes said to be "merely phenomenal": i.e., not very important, not the real thing); and what lies "hidden beneath," and is embedded in the structure, not lying about the surface. It is crucial to see, however—as the market exchange/production example makes clear—that "surface" and "phenomenal" do not mean false or illusory, in the ordinary sense of the words. The market is no more or less "real" than other aspects—production, for example. In Marx's terms production is only where, analytically, we ought to start the analysis of the circuit: "the act through which the whole process again runs its course."[7] But production is not independent of the circuit, since profits made and labour hired in the market must flow back into production. So, "real" expresses only some theoretical primacy which Marxist analysis gives to production. In any other sense, market exchange is as much a real process materially, and an absolutely "real" requirement of the system, as any other part: they are all "moments of one process."[8]

There is also a problem about "appearance" and "surface" as terms. Appearances may connote something which is "false": surface forms do not seem to run as deep as "deep structures." These linguistic connotations have the unfortunate effect of making us rank the different moments in terms of their being more/less real, more/less important. But from another viewpoint, what is on the surface, what constantly appears, is what we are always seeing, what we encounter daily, what we come to take for granted as the obvious and manifest form of the process. It is not surprising, then, that we come spontaneously to *think* of the capitalist system in terms of the bits of it which constantly engage us, and which so manifestly announce their presence. What chance does the extraction of "surplus labour" have, as a concept, as against the hard fact of wages in the pocket, savings in the bank, pennies in the slot, money in the till? Even the nineteenth-century economist, Nassau Senior, couldn't actually put his hand on the hour in the day when the worker worked for the surplus and not to replace his or her own subsistence.

In a world saturated by money exchange, and everywhere mediated by money, the "market" experience is *the* most immediate, daily and universal experience of the economic system for everyone. It is therefore not surprising that we take the market for granted, do not question what makes it possible, what it is founded or premised on. It should not surprise us if the mass of working people don't possess the concepts with which to cut into the process at another point, frame another set of questions, and bring to the surface or reveal what the overwhelming facticity of the market constantly renders invisible. It is clear why we should generate, out of these fundamental categories for which we have found everyday words, phrases and idiomatic expressions in practical consciousness, the *model* of other social and political relations. After all, they too belong to the same system and appear to work according to its protocols. Thus we see, in the "free choice" of the market, the material symbol of the more abstract freedoms; or in the self-interest and intrinsic competitiveness of market advantage the "representation" of something natural, normal and universal about human nature itself.

Let me now draw some tentative conclusions from the "re-reading" I have offered about the meaning of Marx's passage in light of more recent critiques and the new theories advanced.

The analysis is no longer organised around the distinction between the "real" and the "false." The obscuring or mystifying effects of ideology are no longer seen as the product of a trick or magical illusion. Nor are they simply attributed to false consciousness, in which our poor, benighted, untheoretical proletarians are forever immured. The relations in which people exist are the "real relations" which the categories and concepts they use help them to grasp and articulate in thought. But—and here we may be on a route contrary to emphasis from that with which "materialism" is usually associated—the economic relations themselves cannot prescribe a single, fixed and unalterable way of conceptualising it. It can be "expressed" within different ideological discourses. What's more, these discourses can employ the conceptual model and transpose it into other, more strictly "ideological," domains. For example, it can develop a discourse—e.g., latter-day monetarism—which deduces the grand value of "Freedom" from the freedom from compulsion which brings men and women, once again, every working day, into the labour market. We have also by-passed the distinction "true" and "false," replacing them with other, more accurate terms: like "partial" and "adequate," or "one-sided" and "in its differentiated totality." To say that a theoretical discourse allows us to grasp a concrete relation "in thought" adequately means that the discourse provides us with a more complete grasp of all the different relations of which that relation is composed, and of the many determinations which form its conditions of existence. It means that our grasp is concrete and whole, rather than a thin, one-sided abstraction. One-sided explanations, which are partial, part-for-the-whole, types of explanation, and which allow us only to abstract one element out (the market, for example) and explain that are inadequate *precisely on those grounds*. For that reason alone, they may be considered "false." Though, strictly speaking, the term is misleading if what we have in mind is some simple, all-or-nothing distinction between the True and the False, or between Science and Ideology. Fortunately or unfortunately, social explanations rarely fall into such neat pigeonholes.

In our "re-reading," we have also attempted to take on board a number of secondary propositions, derived from the more recent theorising about "ideology" in an effort to see how incompatible they are with Marx's formulation. As we have seen, the explanation relates to concepts, ideas, terminology, categories, perhaps also images and symbols (money; the wage packet freedom) which allow us to grasp some aspect of a social process *in thought*. These enable us to represent to ourselves and to others how the system works, why it functions as it does.

The same process—capitalist production and exchange—can be expressed within a different ideological framework, by the use of different "systems of representation." There is the discourse of "the market," the discourse of "production," the discourse of "the circuits": each produces a different definition of the system. Each also locates us differently—as worker, capitalist, wage worker, wage slave, producer, consumer, etc. Each thus *situates us* as social actors or as a member of a social group in a particular relation to the process and prescribes certain social identities for us. The ideological categories in use, in other words, *position us* in relation to the account of the process as depicted in the discourse. The worker who relates to his or her condition of existence in the capitalist process as "consumer"—who enters the system, so to speak, through that gateway—participates in the process by way of a different practice from those who are inscribed in the system as "skilled labourer"—or not inscribed in it at all, as "housewife." All these inscriptions have effects which are real. They make a material difference, since how we act in certain situations depends on what our definitions of the situation are.

I believe that a similar kind of "re-reading" can be made in relation to another set of propositions about ideology which has in recent years been vigorously contested: namely, the class-determination of ideas and the direct correspondences between "ruling ideas" and "ruling classes." Ernesto Laclau has demonstrated definitively (in *Politics and Ideology in Marxist Theory*) the untenable nature of the proposition that classes, as such, are the subjects of fixed and ascribed class ideologies.[9] He has also dismantled the proposition that particular ideas and concepts "belong" exclusively to one particular class. He demonstrates, with considerable effect, the failure of any social formation to correspond to this picture of ascribed class ideologies. He argues cogently why the notion of particular ideas being fixed permanently to a particular class is antithetical to what we now know about the very nature of language and discourse. Ideas, and concepts do not occur, in language or thought, in that single, isolated, way with their content and reference irremovably fixed. Language in its widest sense is the vehicle of practical reasoning, calculation and consciousness, because of the ways by which certain meanings and references have been historically secured. But its cogency depends on the "logics" which connect one proposition to another in a chain of connected meanings; where the social connotations and historical meaning are condensed and reverberate off one another. Moreover, these chains are never permanently secured, either in their internal systems of meanings, or in terms of the social classes and groups to which they "belong." Otherwise, the notion of ideological struggle and the transformations of consciousness—questions central to the politics of any Marxist project—would be an empty sham, the dance of dead rhetorical figures.

It is precisely because language, the medium of thought and ideological calculation, is "multi-accentual," as V. N. Volosinov put it, that the field of the ideological is always a field of "intersecting accents" and the "intersecting of differently oriented social interests":

> Thus various different classes will use one and the same language. As a result differently orientated accents intersect in every ideological sign. Sign becomes the arena of the class struggle.... A sign that has been withdrawn from the pressures of the social struggle—which, so to speak, crosses beyond the pale of class struggle, inevitably loses force, degenerating into allegory and becoming the object not of live social intelligibility but of philological comprehension.[10]

This approach replaces the notion of fixed ideological meanings and class-ascribed ideologies with the concepts of ideological terrains of struggle and the task of ideological transformation. It is the general movement in this direction, away from an abstract general theory of ideology, and towards the more concrete analysis of how, in particular historical situations, ideas "organize human masses, and create the terrain on which men move, acquire consciousness of their position, struggle, *etc.*,"[11] which makes the work of Gramsci (from whom that quotation is taken) a figure of seminal importance in the development of Marxist thinking in the domain of the ideological.

One of the consequences of this kind of revisionist work has often been to destroy altogether the *problem* of the class structuring of ideology and the ways in which ideology intervenes in social struggles. Often this approach replaces the inadequate notions of ideologies ascribed in blocks to classes with an equally unsatisfactory "discursive" notion which implies total free-floatingness of all ideological elements and discourses. The image of great, immovable class battalions heaving their ascribed ideological luggage about the field of struggle, with their ideological number-plates on their backs, as Nicos Poulantzas once put it, is replaced here by the infinity of subtle variations through which the elements of a discourse appears spontaneously to combine and recombine with each other, without material constraints of any kind other than that provided by the discursive operations themselves.

Now it is perfectly correct to suggest that the concept "democracy" does not have a totally fixed meaning, which can be ascribed to the discourse of bourgeois forms of political representation. "Democracy" in the discourse of the "Free West" does not carry the same meaning as it does when we speak of "popular-democratic" struggle or of deepening the democratic content of political life. We cannot allow the term to be wholly expropriated into the discourse of the Right. Instead, we need to develop a strategic contestation around the concept itself. Of course, this is no mere "discursive" operation. Powerful symbols and slogans of that kind, with a powerfully positive political charge, do not swing about from side to side in language or ideological representation alone. The expropriation of the concept has to be contested through the development of a series of polemics, through the conduct of particular forms of ideological struggle: to detach one meaning of the concept from the domain of public consciousness and supplant it within the logic of another political discourse. Gramsci argued precisely that ideological struggle does not take place by displacing one whole, integral, class-mode of thought with another wholly formed system of ideas:

> What matters is the criticism to which such an ideological complex is subjected by the first representatives of the new historical phases. This criticism makes possible a process of differentiation and change in the relative weight that the elements of the old ideological used to possess. What was previously secondary and subordinate, or even incidental, is now taken to be primary—becomes the nucleus of a new ideological and theoretical complex. The old collective will dissolves into its contradictory elements since the subordinate ones develop socially, *etc.*[12]

In short, his is a "war of position" conception of ideological struggle. It also means articulating the different conceptions of "democracy" within a whole chain of associated ideas. And it means articulating this process of ideological de-construction and re-construction to a set of organised political positions, and to a particular set of social forces. Ideologies do not become effective as a material force because they emanate from the needs of fully formed social classes. But the reverse is also true—though it puts the relationship between ideas and social forces the opposite way round. No ideological conception can ever become materially effective unless and until it *can be* articulated to the field of political and social forces and to the struggles between different forces at stake.

Certainly, it is not necessarily a form of vulgar materialism to say that, though we cannot ascribe ideas to class position in certain fixed combinations, ideas *do* arise from and *may* reflect the material conditions in which social groups and classes exist. In that sense—i.e., historically—there may well be certain *tendential alignments*—between, say, those who stand in a "corner shop" relation to the processes of modern capitalist development, and the fact that they may therefore be predisposed to imagine that the whole advanced economy of capitalism can be conceptualised in this "corner shop" way. I think this is what Marx meant in *The Eighteenth Brumaire* when he said that it was not necessary for people actually to make their living as members of the older petty bourgeoisie for them to be attracted to petty bourgeois ideas. Nevertheless, there was, he suggested, some relationship, or tendency, between the objective position of that class fraction, and the limits and horizons of thought to which they would be "spontaneously" attracted. This was a judgement about the "characteristic forms of thought" appropriate as an ideal type to certain positions in the social structure. It was definitely not a simple equation in actual historical reality between class position and ideas. The point about "tendential historical relations" is that there is nothing inevitable, necessary or fixed forever about them. The tendential lines of forces define only the *givenness* of the historical terrain.

They indicate how the terrain has been structured, historically. Thus it is perfectly possible for the idea of "the nation" to be given a progressive meaning and connotation embodying a national-popular collective will, as Gramsci argued. Nevertheless, in a society like Britain, the idea of "nation" has been consistently articulated towards the right. Ideas of "national identity" and "national greatness" are intimately bound up with imperial supremacy, tinged with racist connotations and underpinned by a four-century-long history of colonisation, world market supremacy, imperial expansion and global destiny over native peoples. It is therefore much more difficult to give the notion of "Britain" a socially radical or democratic reference. These associations are not given for all time. But they are difficult to break because the ideological terrain of this particular social formation has been so powerfully structured in that way by its previous history. These historical connections define the ways in which the ideological terrain of a particular society has been mapped out. They are the "traces" which Gramsci mentioned: the "stratified deposits in popular philosophy,"[13] which no longer have an inventory, but which establish and define the fields along which ideological struggle is *likely* to move.

That terrain, Gramsci suggested, was above all the terrain of what he called "common sense": a historical, not a natural or universal or spontaneous form of popular thinking, necessarily "fragmentary, disjointed and episodic." The "subject" of common sense is composed of very contradictory ideological formations—"it contains Stone Age elements and principles of a more advanced science, prejudices from all past phases of history at the local level and intuitions of a future philosophy which will be that of a human race united the world over."[14] And yet, because this network of pre-existing traces and common sense elements constitutes the realm of practical thinking for the masses of the people, Gramsci insisted that it was precisely on this terrain that ideological struggle most frequently took place. "Common sense" became one of the stakes over which ideological struggle is conducted. Ultimately, "the relation between common sense and the upper level of philosophy is assured by 'politics.'"[15]

Ideas only become effective if they do, in the end, *connect* with a particular constellation of social forces. In that sense, ideological struggle is a part of the general social struggle for mastery and leadership—in short for hegemony. But "hegemony" in Gramsci's sense requires, not the simple escalation of a whole class to power, with its fully formed "philosophy," but the *process* by which a historical bloc of social forces is constructed and the ascendancy of that bloc secured. So the way we conceptualise the relationship between "ruling ideas" and "ruling classes" is best thought in terms of the processes of "hegemonic domination."

On the other hand, to abandon the question or problem of "rule"—of hegemony, domination and authority—because the ways in which it was originally posed are unsatisfactory is to cast the baby out with the bath water. Ruling ideas are not guaranteed their dominance by their already given coupling with ruling classes. Rather, the effective coupling of dominant ideas *to* the historical bloc which has acquired hegemonic power in a particular period is what the process of ideological struggle is *intended to secure*. It is the object of the exercise—not the playing out of an already written and concluded script.

It will be clear that, although the argument has been conducted in connection with the problem of ideology, it has much wider ramifications for the development of Marxist theory as a whole. The general question at issue is a particular conception of "theory": theory as the working out of a set of guarantees. What is also at issue is a particular definition of "determination." It is clear from the "reading" I offered earlier that the economic aspect of capitalist production processes has real limiting and constraining effects (i.e., determinacy), for the categories in which the circuits of production are *thought*, ideologically, and vice versa. The economic provides the repertoire of categories which will be used, in thought. What the economic cannot do is (a) to provide the *contents* of the particular thoughts of particular social classes or groups at any specific time; (b) to fix or guarantee for all time which ideas will be made use of by which classes. The determinacy of the economic for the ideological can, therefore, be only in terms of the former setting the limits for defining the terrain of operations, establishing the "raw materials," of thought. Material circumstances are the net of constraints, the "conditions of existence" for practical thought and calculation about society.

This is a different concept of "determinacy" from that which is entailed by the normal sense of "economic determinism," or by the expressive totality way of conceiving the relations between the different practices in a social formation. The relations between these different levels is, indeed, *determinate*: i.e., mutually determining. The structure of social practices—the ensemble—is therefore neither free floating or immaterial. But nor is it a transitive structure, in which its intelligibility lies exclusively in the one-way transmission of effects from base upwards. The economic *cannot* effect a final closure on the domain of ideology, in the strict sense of always guaranteeing a result. It cannot always secure a particular set of correspondences or always deliver particular modes of reasoning to particular classes according to their place within its system. This is precisely because (a) ideological categories are developed, generated and transformed according to their own laws of development and evolution; though of course, they are generated *out* of given materials. It is also because (b) of the necessary "openness" of historical development to practice and struggle. We have to acknowledge the real indeterminacy of the political—the level which condenses all the other levels of practice and secures their functioning in a particular system of power.

This relative openness or relative indeterminacy is necessary to Marxism itself as a theory. What is "scientific" about the Marxist theory of politics is that it seeks to understand the limits to political action given by the terrain on which it operates. This terrain is defined, not by forces we can predict with the certainty of natural science, but by the existing balance of social forces, the specific nature of the concrete conjuncture. It is "scientific" because it understands itself as determinate; and because it seeks to develop a practice which is theoretically informed. But it is *not* "scientific" in the sense that political outcomes and the consequences of the conduct of political struggles are foreordained in the economic stars.

Understanding "determinacy" in terms of setting of limits, the establishment of parameters, the defining of the space of operations, the concrete conditions of existence, the "givenness" of social practices, rather than in terms of the absolute predictability of particular outcomes, is the only basis of a "Marxism without final guarantees." It establishes the *open horizon* of Marxist theorising—determinacy without guaranteed closures. The paradigm of perfectly closed, perfectly predictable systems of thought is religion or astrology, not science. It would be preferable, from this perspective, to think of the "materialism" of Marxist theory in terms of "determination by the economic in the *first* instance," since Marxism is surely correct, against all idealisms, to insist that no social practice or set of relations floats free of the determinate effects of the concrete relations in which they are located. However, "determination in the last instance" has long been the repository of the lost dream or illusion of theoretical *certainty*. And this has been bought at considerable cost, since certainty stimulates orthodoxy, the frozen rituals and intonation of already witnessed truth, and all the other attributes of a theory that is incapable of fresh insights. It represents the end of the *process of theorising*, of the development and refinement of new concepts and explanations which, alone, is the sign of a living body of thought, capable still of engaging and grasping something of the truth about new historical realities.

NOTES

This essay first appeared in *Marx: A Hundred Years On*, ed. Betty Matthews (London: Lawrence and Wishart, 1983), 57–85.

1 Perry Anderson, *Considerations on Western Marxism* (London: New Left Books, 1976).
2 Karl Marx, "Preface," in *A Contribution to the Critique of Political Economy* (London: Lawrence and Wishart, 1982), 21.

3 Louis Althusser, *For Marx* (London: Allen Lane, 1969); Louis Althusser and Étienne Balibar, *Reading Capital* (London: New Left Books, 1970).
4 Louis Althusser, "Ideology and Ideological State Apparatuses," in *Lenin and Philosophy and Other Essays* (London: New Left Books, 1971).
5 Louis Althusser, *Essays in Self-Criticism* (London: New Left Books, 1976).
6 Karl Marx, *Capital* I (London: Lawrence and Wishart, 1974), 172.
7 Karl Marx, "Introduction," in *Grundrisse: Foundations of the Critique of Political Economy (Rough Draft)*, ed. and with a foreword by Martin Nicolaus (Harmondsworth, UK: Pelican, 1973), 94.
8 Marx, "Introduction," 94.
9 Ernesto Laclau, *Politics and Ideology in Marxist Theory* (London: New Left Books, 1977).
10 V. N. Volosinov, *Marxism and the Philosophy of Language* (New York: Seminar Press, 1973), 23.
11 Antonio Gramsci, *Selections from the Prison Notebooks* (London: Lawrence and Wishart, 1971), 337.
12 Gramsci, *Prison Notebooks*, 195. Quoted in Chantal Mouffe, "Hegemony and Ideology in Gramsci," in *Gramsci and Marxist Theory*, ed. Mouffe (London: Routledge and Kegan Paul, 1979), 191.
13 Gramsci, *Prison Notebooks*, 324.
14 Gramsci, *Prison Notebooks*, 324.
15 Gramsci, *Prison Notebooks*, 321.

EDITOR'S DISCUSSION OF THE PART I WRITINGS

Marxism: Prepackaged versus Reconstructed

The four writings collected in this part, when stacked together in this arrangement, underline the fact that for many of his prime-time years, Stuart Hall's absorbing intellectual concerns were located decisively *inside* the terms and norms of contemporary Marxist thought. In these papers Hall, like most other regular Marxists, positions *Capital* as the fulcrum of Marx's achievement, in relation to which his other writings should be weighed. Thus, the "earlier and transitional" texts, Hall announces in chapter 3, must be reread "from the viewpoint of Marx's mature and developed theory," which is to say, "in the light of *Capital*." This is interesting, because there is an understandable tendency to think of Hall as decidedly more concerned with conjunctural analysis than with the high level of abstraction at which Marx rolled out his delineation of the basic underlying mechanisms of capitalism. And that is perfectly correct—but only if not taken disjunctively. Hall's uptake of "conjuncture" closely tracked Louis Althusser's and Antonio Gramsci's usages, neither of whom equated that concept with the now, with whatever political situation stands immediately and urgently before us. For Gramsci, organic movements ("relatively permanent") should be distinguished from conjunctural movements—which "*appear as* occasional, immediate, almost accidental" (emphasis added)—but it is the correct relation between the two that matters, their mutuality in a "dialectical nexus." Gramsci recognized that getting the right balance is difficult, with the twin "errors" of "economism," on the one hand, and "ideologism," on the other, lying in wait. "Socio-historical criticism," Gramsci asserted, must constantly connect the day-to-day operation of public figures and "top leaders" to the "wider social groupings" and "structural contradictions" that necessarily shape their context.[1]

Following that template, in both "Base and Superstructure" and "Classes," Hall takes us through Marx's anatomy, in *The Eighteenth Brumaire*, of the various factions and figures on the French political scene at that historical juncture. Marx does acknowledge the specific coloration and effectiveness of ideological currents and personalities: Hall shows that "there are no 'whole classes' on stage here"; indeed, he notes that in Marx's panorama, and in very short order, the supposed interests of even the dominant class fractions, of which there are several, get variously misaligned, blurred, and deferred. And the bizarre outcome is the victory of the "mountebank" Louis Napoleon, his rise to dictatorial power secured only through the beliefs and interests of the (subordinate) class fraction that, ironically, is the one most "destined to decline," namely, the smallholding peasantry. So while crediting the specificity of ideology and politics in this shifting kaleidoscope of events and agents, Marx persists in superimposing on it a longer-term rationale, pitched in terms of the historical success and continuous self-transformation of capital (and, hovering in the distance, as the subterranean workings of the "old mole," the transition to socialism itself). Hall brings to our attention not only the indispensability of both aspects of Marx's procedure, forming a continuous problem field, but also the presence of a difficult *dilemma*. On the one hand, even if the long-term causes and consequences of the political are difficult to perceive at the level of the action itself, the true significance of the latter cannot be gauged without reference to those shaping forces. On the other hand, "very little of the actual shifts in the political relations of class forces," the happenstance forms of their *representation*, can be deciphered just in terms of the principal economic contradictions of the epoch. The nature and role of the state is something Hall wants us to understand as particularly difficult to explain in terms of class representativeness, yet equally we must avoid being entranced by the state's form (and typical self-image) as standing above, and arbitrating among, class and other social forces.[2]

What Hall draws out of the conjunctural-organic dialectic as operated by Marx is an understanding of the work of determination—by class interests, by the mode of production—as the setting of *limits* to the play of politics and ideology. Within those limits, there can never be any simple coincidence between basic and superstructural factors or forces. Indeed, drawing again on Althusser, Hall insists that the necessary complexity of any social formation means that there is always a lack of fit between its different levels and elements. Hall resists any supposition that such necessary friction and unevenness contradicts the thinking behind *Capital* itself. Yes, Marx is schematizing the systemic logic of capital, such that actors and social positions must be conceived for that purpose as "personifications" of socioeconomic categories. But this does not mean that we are only dealing, even in this rarefied atmosphere, with self-sustaining, unidirectional "laws of motion," far less purely economic ones, operating over and above the fabric of ideational forms and political contestations. Hence, for several closely worked pages toward the end of Hall's reading of Marx's 1857 "Introduction," he breaks away from the detail of that work to *Capital* itself, to find what he needs to counter what he sees as Maurice Godelier's (and by extension Althusser's) structural-functionalist understanding of the workings of "the system." And in "Base and Superstructure," while accepting that *Capital* provides the grounding analytical delineation of the mechanisms of capitalism, Hall interprets this in terms of setting out a broad "determining matrix," governing the available "repertoire of solutions" within which social forms and antagonisms adapt, variously, to "capital's self-expanding needs."[3]

As I pointed out in my introduction, Hall is also supporting and defending Marx in these writings. Some ostensibly admiring but in fact far from sympathetic commentators, such as Jon Elster, brusquely disqualify Marx's efforts in texts like *The Eighteenth Brumaire* to deliver the class analysis of politics. Taking up a kind of "external" standpoint of fair assessment, Elster sees Marx's thinking in that regard as rhetorically contorted, lacking in evidence, and overloaded by teleological wishful thinking.[4] Hall was aware of the latter flaw, just as he could similarly hear the "echo" of the *Manifesto* in *Capital*. But he chooses to stick it out with Marx, habitually giving him the benefit of the doubt, perhaps partly because the method of "reading" invites what we might call "inside-out" appreciation. At any rate, Hall does not often stop to pose sharp questions to Marx concerning adequacy in general. In the same way, Hall sought after a consistent neo-Marxist pattern of understanding, settling firmly on the resident triumvirate that steers so many of his surveys and arguments:[5] the best Marx, the Althusser of *For Marx*, and highlighted segments of Gramsci's *Prison Notebooks*. We can see this pattern of analysis starting to take hold, and at length, in the series of papers Hall produced in 1971–73 on communications, television, the media, and deviance, some of which are collected in the volume on the media in Duke's Stuart Hall: Selected Writings series.[6] That approach is strongly consolidated in our collection.

With that level of consistency, it is not plausible to think that Hall was choosing only strategically to occupy the radical discourse of the day (Marxism) in order to develop his own perspective, or that of cultural studies as such. These things may not have been identical, but nor were they separable. As neatly phrased in "Literature/Society: Mapping the Field," Hall took Marxism to be "absolutely central" to the literature-and-society problem, just as that problem was "absolutely central to the development of historical materialism as a science."[7] And in "The Hinterland of Science," Hall describes his task as scouring through the sociology of knowledge traditions for "whatever insights can be rescued for a Marxist theory of ideology."[8] In "Base and Superstructure," he talks of Althusser's expression of ideology in terms of social reproduction as notably advancing "Marxism as a critical science and as a theoretically informed revolutionary practice." The issue was not whether but how determination by the mode of production was best conceived (because there was no question of deserting the problematic of determination, as such). Thus, in "Classes," Hall criticizes Paul Hirst's Manichaean switch from "relative autonomy" to "necessary non-correspondence" as falling "outside the limits of Marxism as an identifiable theoretical terrain."[9]

Such dutiful declarations of allegiance might appear surprising, given Hall's tendency to portray dogmatic Marxism as the latter's dominant current. And certainly, in the period of the formation of "the 'first' New Left,"[10] Hall found it impossible to identify in any way with Communist orthodoxy, regarding the prevailing Marxist approach to culture from the 1930s to the early 1960s as "extremely bad and simplistic!"[11] Yet by the 1970s, notwithstanding the persistence of a degree of fundamentalism (of different political stripes, it should be said), much had changed. Thus, in the revisionist atmosphere of the Communist University of London (CUL) summer school, Hall was in his element when delivering the scintillating 1976 talk that was later written up as "Base and Superstructure." All four of the other CUL contributions selected for the book in which that piece appeared were also couched as embodying the sort of Marxism that would give politics, ideology, and social relations their full due.[12] Arguably, by this stage the notion of a "dominant" dogmatic and economistic Marxism had become little more than an obligatory foil. Indeed, the opposite danger of excessive revisionism and pluralism loomed up, heading out of Marxism altogether. Thus, Hall's meticulous presentation at the outstanding 1976 event debating Nicos Poulantzas's thinking on class (with Poulantzas present) was geared as much to countering *that* move as to probing the vulnerabilities of Marxian class theory. Always the mediator, no one could better orchestrate the *continuity* of, as well as the differences within, the spectrum of Marxism and critical thought. Coherent and assured expressions of Hall's subtle Marxism, "Classes" and "Base and Superstructure," helped situate Hall within the front rank of general Marxist debate in the United Kingdom, along with his reputation as a tremendous speaker.

Chapter 4 is a model of problem-posing. It contains plenty of references to the classic texts of Marx, and Hall seeks to wrestle them out of the grasp of old-style understandings; but he also wants to indicate that aspects of current conceptions of "ideology" are beginning to outrun *all* previous Marxist theorizations. No longer referring only to reality-screening, power-reinforcing systems of thought, ideology today is taken to encompass all the varied and half-formed social ideas and frameworks that help people "figure out . . . the way society works," bringing out the malleable texture of common sense and the realities of situated experience. For Hall, this means that "fully prepackaged" Marxist accounts of ideologies as reflexes of socioeconomic positions and interests, or as expressions of false consciousness, must once and for all be jettisoned. Hall does not greatly like the term "post-Marxism," but he is sympathetic to some of the new ways of deconstructing assumed truths, including the truths of Marx himself. Thus, the emphases on linguistic, psychoanalytic, and subjective aspects of ideology cannot be answered by exercises in "ritual orthodoxy." Yet he proceeds to embark on "a little modest work of reconstruction" on behalf of Marxism, pivoting around Gramsci's concept of hegemony. This reference point—*of course*—continues to require relating ideologies to class and power factors, but is more fully attuned to the vital, contested role of "educative" moral discourses throughout social life.[13]

Hall's gift as a mediator invariably meant angling his lines of thought to audiences and contexts, often brilliantly. Whether his constructions of problem-and-solution were always entirely successful is a matter for discussion, and "The Problem of Ideology" provides an interesting case in point. It was written for a Communist Party publishing house volume marking the centenary of Marx's death, and the book's other contributors represented both relatively traditionalist and highly revisionist inclinations.[14] In that setting, Hall clearly decided to hold nothing back in his presentation of the kind of Marxism with which he was taking issue. Thus, he talks of scientific Marxism's "perfectly closed, perfectly predictable" paradigm; its worldview according to which "political outcomes . . . are foreordained in the economic stars." However, even nonfatalistic Marxists might find that characterization stilted, especially running alongside Hall's acknowledgment of the "immense force" of post-Marxist critical inroads. Against that backdrop, Hall's "work of reconstruction" on behalf of Marxism could only be presented as "modest," because the brunt of it was taken by hugely qualified formulations, along the lines of Hall not being completely convinced that the "post" critiques "*wholly and entirely* abolish *every* useful insight, every essential *starting point*" in a materialist theory of ideology (my italics).[15] For some, this phrasing will be taken as wittily ironical, directed toward the *post*-Marxist section of the audience. This is because what follows, occupying no less than two-thirds of the essay, is a major "re-reading" (Hall's term) of the problem of ideology, in which, step by step, he persuades us that on no account should Marx's understanding of the "distortions," "falsity," and "class determinacy" of ideological conceptions be taken at face value. This would be to miss all that was intellectually subtle, and explanatorily powerful, in Marx. Others, however, might conclude that the very drive of the "re-reading," which satisfyingly expresses Hall's baseline allegiance to Marxism, is compromised by those awkwardly hesitant, unnecessarily minimalist prefatory remarks.

Unpacking Hall's "Reading"

Just as the 1857 "Introduction" was regarded by Hall as nuclear to Marx's thinking, despite being highly condensed and even enigmatic, so his reading of that work sits among the most pivotal and intriguing of Hall's own writings. With references to its foundational status scattered through his subsequent work, the reading is crucial for figuring out where Hall stood within the range of Marxist interpretation. Relatedly, the text has also been central to discussions about the degree to which Hall develops a distinctive approach of his own to matters of culture-and-society over and above— or, better, in and through—the reading's evidently Marxist bearings. Hall's "prefatory note" is alluring in that regard, suggesting that Marx provides major "points of departure" for a wider space of thinking about the "methodological problems that beset our field of study," though Hall quickly adds that he has not established that connection in the paper. Accordingly, it is presented chiefly as a work of exposition and explication, although it is also felt, "inevitably," to reflect his own "problematic." In digging into the nature of that problematic, we should bear in mind the context of its production.

David McLellan had produced a short book of extracts from the *Grundrisse* in 1971 (including the 1857 "Introduction"), with which Hall was familiar, having convened a conference at CCCS in the same year—titled Situating Marx, which later became a book—at which McLellan spoke.[16] McLellan argued that the *Grundrisse* was the single most important work by Marx, the one that bridged the early and the late works, thereby fueling further the fiery debates of the time about Karl the humanist versus Karl the structuralist, with McLellan favoring the former. Hall, too, was fast developing an interest in adjudicating that polarity, but he would not take it down the same track: McLellan was not a Marxist, and his selection gave only a limited flavor of the large bulk of the *Grundrisse* (plus his translation sources were queried by other experts). But when the authoritative Pelican *Grundrisse*, translated by Martin Nicolaus, appeared in mid-1973,[17] Hall's full attention was switched on; he densely covered the pages of his copy with comments and questions. One mixed effect of the splash made by Nicolaus's edition, for all its differences from McLellan's, was the inclination for debaters to treat the *Grundrisse* as a single work, indeed a "book," although in reality it was sixteen hundred pages of separate, diverse, and unevenly scripted "Notebooks" that were decidedly *not* intended for publication in that form. Other Marxists frowned on the elevated perch allotted to the *Grundrisse*, arguing that its mass of ongoing inquiries was neither internally consistent nor anything like Marx's considered word.[18] The 1857 "Introduction" itself was not in fact the introduction to something called the *Grundrisse*; rather, it was the prelude to certain parts of the "Notebooks" that were updated and trimmed later as *Contribution to the Critique of Political Economy*, itself superseded by the larger enterprise of *Capital*, the whole three volumes of which represented only the first layers of Marx's envisaged six-plus phased program, in the "Notebooks," of economic critique and political-cultural analysis. Necessarily, then, decisive points of detail and status surrounding the "Introduction" were bound to remain uncertain. But Hall was drawn to thinkers in their exploratory, unfinished middle phases, so this was just the Marx for him.

It seems that Marx took barely three weeks to write the "Introduction," but Hall's own process of engagement with it was also speedy, only a few months elapsing from the publication of the Pelican *Grundrisse* to the appearance, in November/December 1973, of the first, longer version of Hall's reading of the "Introduction," taking the form of a CCCS Stencilled Paper following presentations by Hall at CCCS seminars a little earlier. The basic content of Hall's interpretation was therefore in place by September 1973.

Around a fifth of the length of the Stencilled Paper was cut for the more polished *Working Papers in Cultural Studies* (*WPCS*) version, dated autumn 1974, with little new material added.[19] We get a sense of how close to the wire Hall absorbed relevant writings and fed them into his own positioning by marking that Pierre Vilar's article on Althusser, drawn on by Hall for "materialist" support, surfaced only in the July–August 1973 issue of the *New Left Review*. Hall also adjusted smartly to Lucio Colletti's *Marxism and Hegel*, published in the same year, this "Kantian" Marxist analysis assisting Hall to steer clear of the Hegelian Marx without thereby falling into Althusser's hands.[20] Such points of timing and influence are relevant in ascertaining Hall's problematic in his reading of Marx, and I will touch on others.

The Idea of Articulation

Not infrequently in the cultural studies literature, Hall's problematic is distilled in terms of the concept (or theory, or method) of "articulation." This refers to his sense that (1) the components or levels making up an economy, culture, or society are fundamentally *different* from one another—they can be reduced neither to one another nor to the essence of the overall structure which they help constitute; yet also (2) those different components derive their causal rationale and symbolic meaning from being part of a structured, unifying totality. The elements/levels thus stand in a relation of articulation with one another, and the parts-whole relationship is also one of complex articulation. A further aspect of the term concerns the theoretical discourse that brings out such socially interconnected relationships, because this is also an articulation, in two senses. First, theorizing articulates (voices, elucidates) the logic and dynamic of the differentiated social totality under examination. Second, while theorizing's characteristic mode is abstraction, this, too, is a situated human-social *practice*, necessarily articulated with other parts and practices of the social totality.

Flagging up articulation in this way registers Hall's sharp sense of the importance of the concept, and it serves well as a theme to steer us through the density of his interpretation of the 1857 "Introduction." But we should be careful not to overstate its reach or the degree to which articulation is a specifically Hall-Ian contribution. As he recounted with great clarity in "Race, Articulation and Societies Structured in Dominance,"[21] "articulation" was everywhere in Marxist theoretical analysis in the early to mid-1970s: articulation of the forces and relations of production within the mode of production; articulation of different modes of production within a given social formation; articulation of the social formation and its political and ideological conditions of existence; articulation of base and superstructure in a complex social totality. Hall also accepted that the emphasis on articulation as complex societal structuration was due principally to Althusser and Étienne Balibar, who were the first fully to rope Marx's 1857 "Introduction" into this terminology. Moreover, articulation talk was adopted by many who, like Hall, had serious reservations about those thinkers.[22] All in all, it is misleading to think that in his own reading of Marx Hall was breaking new ground with articulation. What he was doing was spelling it out in more detail in relation to the 1857 "Introduction" and in a much more flexible register than that of the Althusserians. It is therefore hazardous to derive an overarching methodological principle out of Hall's dealings with the concept, for example by presenting it as "a way of thinking the structures of what we know as a play of correspondences, non-correspondences and contradictions, as fragments in the constitution of what we take to be unities."[23] Paradoxically, when the specifically Marxist provenance and resonance of articulation is screened out in favor of this sort of generalized formula, it runs against the strong *contextualism* that is also said to be at the heart of Hall's theoretical endeavor.[24]

The section of Hall's reading of the "Introduction" where the social dimension of articulation is best brought out is his commentary on Marx's discussion of the different elements that constitute the capitalist economy: production, consumption, distribution, and exchange. It is important to remember that these are the categories of political economy itself, and Marx, more than anywhere else in his work, is seeking here to unpick their logical form. Thus, Hall takes us through how Marx establishes three types of relationship between these mutually implicated moments in the total economic process: (1) *immediate identity* (production is a species of consumption, consumption is a species of production, etc.); (2) *mutual dependence* or mediation (each moment is a prerequisite and medium for the realization of the others); and (3) *internal connection*, a dialectically superior involvement, taking us from the definitional meanings of the terms to a more substantive and dynamic way of grasping relationships. As Hall explains: "Here, in contrast with relation (2), production not only proceeds to its own completion, but is *itself reproduced again* through consumption."

Hall is typically generous to Marx's rather convoluted reflections in these passages, noting only in a polite footnote that "the distinctions between the three types of relation are not as clearly sustained as one could wish." What Hall is mainly concerned to endorse is Marx's treatment of inner connection as the type of relation that goes beyond conceptual formality, entailing definite substantive content. This is, he argues, what decisively takes Marx beyond Hegel. Thus, the mutual entailments of the economic categories making up the production-consumption chain need to be fleshed out by reference to the real social needs, practices, and struggles that are its conditions of realization. Overall, Hall is lending his support to Althusser's claim that Marx is presenting us here, if only in embryo, with a model of the social formation as a whole, the levels or moments of which are simultaneously both differentiated out and conjointly constitutive. However, *against* the Althusserian tilt toward a structural-functionalist conception of the totality, Hall highlights Marx's stress on the historical movement of, and tensions among, all structural relations.

What about the more discursive or epistemological dimension of articulation? The part of the "Introduction" that most gets to grips with this is the section elucidating "the method of political economy." Its gist is that the cycle of adequate understanding begins from "simple concrete" phenomena or ideas about them—"population" is the exemplar—which are then broken down by analysis into their constituent elements, still separately and statically imagined. For Marx, this procedure of analysis is valid enough in its way—indeed, it is inescapable and necessary. But the "scientifically correct" method comes fully into play only through synthesis, that is, thoroughly interconnecting and thereby transcending the purely stipulative elements by way of further theoretical elaboration and substantive investigation. This is the move back from—counterintuitively, Marx phrases it as "rising from"— the abstract to the concrete. But this time the concrete is not a simple empirical or uncritical theoretical datum (which were the initial points of departure); rather, it is a "rich totality of many determinations and relations." As Hall often puts it: necessarily, the *concrete* is the *complex*.

In his treatment of the abstract-concrete relationship, Hall acknowledges that the process and conceptual tools of theorizing are relatively autonomous; that our sense of the real and the historical is necessarily framed through theoretical categories, such that "no reflective or copy theory of truth is now adequate." He therefore stresses that the concrete and the empirically given are not one and the same thing, because the determinations constituting the real-concrete are necessarily reconstructed in thought. So far, so Althusserian. However, Hall is determined to demonstrate that Marx did *not* share Althusser's intensely theory-dominated understanding of science, which establishes an "impassable threshold" between thought and its object, resulting in the full autonomy and indeed the apparent *primacy* of the work of abstraction in relation to "the real." Hall counters in two ways. First, he pitches theory in historical materialist terms as the working up of concepts out of observation and praxis, socially situated human activities whose products inevitably express their time and place, even in the form of science. Second, he affirms Marx's default instinct that philosophical materialism is a nonnegotiable *presupposition* of inquiry, not its intellectual result. According to this rather basic "realism," even if we get at reality only indirectly, the real world exists and continues outside the thinking head, and the latter forms part of the former, never the reverse.

It is appropriate, once again, to note that Hall's arguments here were widely shared at the time, as was the sense of scandal caused by Althusser's seemingly blatant philosophical idealism. Certainly, there were some convinced Althusserians on the British scene—the journals *Theoretical Practice* and the early *Economy and Society* formed the hub of this current. But Hall took the majority view, though it came in varieties that made for much secondary disputation. For example, CCCS member Robin Rusher's critique of Althusser, in the same *WPCS* issue as Hall's reading of the "Introduction," made surprisingly little reference to it, though the Stencilled Paper version had been around for a year. Instead, Rusher gave prominence to the root-and-branch demolition of Althusser by André Glucksmann.[25] Hall, we may assume, would not have wholly agreed with Glucksmann's presentation of Althusser as little more than an intellectual fraud and political conservative. He preferred Norman Geras's incisive but less wholly condemnatory "Althusser's Marxism: An Account and Assessment."[26] Hall quoted Geras extensively in a formative 1972 seminar typescript, "Gramsci and Althusser: Ideology and Hegemony," noting in another foundational manuscript of the time titled "Settling Accounts with Althusser" that he found Geras's assessment "far and away the most accomplished and satisfactory." Even so, Hall proceeded according to his own methodological instincts, entering into a more "differentiated," albeit "laborious," process of scrutiny in which all the relevant Althusser and Marx texts, including the 1857 "Introduction," were given the closest possible attention.[27]

Though radically streamlining both the gargantuan "Settling Accounts" and the bulky Stencilled Paper, Hall's final published reading of the 1857 "Introduction" remains long and painstaking. Yet it brings out more clearly than those ur-papers that as Marxist mediator, Hall had found his métier. He wants to get Marx right, though he knows there is room for dispute, and through his reading of Marx, Hall is working to prevent any easy polarization of the strands of culturalism and structuralism, historicism and theoreticism, materialism and idealism, rationalism and empiricism in contemporary Marxist discourse. He fully knows that while these interpretative contrasts have their own criteria of adjudication,[28] they are shot through with practical political postures and consequences. And Hall's distinctive characteristic in that regard is a complete lack of sectarianism, so he strives to find an appropriate place for all valid emphases—not whole *positions*—in the repertoire of Marxist ideas. What I am proposing as Hall's mediational Marxism in that sense can productively be described in other ways too. Along with John Clarke, for example, I have often thought that what Hall is providing in this mode is not so much a theory of articulation as an embodied *practice* of articulation. And Larry Grossberg helpfully depicts Hall as concerned always, in theory and practice, to produce "new relationalities, unities in difference, articulated unities."[29]

The Question of Hegel: Toward a Regulative Marxist Method

Hall probably accepted that this mode of mediation—practice of articulation, concern with relationality—sometimes comes at a scholarly price, or at least a sense of the point at which further points of contention must be left hanging. His reading of Marx in 1857 presents us with a fascinating example of this, regarding the relationship between Hegel and Marx. Hall acknowledges that Marx makes more use of Hegel's dialectic in the "Introduction" than elsewhere. At the same time, Marx strenuously muscles Hegel aside, just as he always did, on account of the latter's unacceptable philosophical idealism, a stance couched by both Marx and Hall in terms of Hegel's conviction that reality/history is ultimately constituted by mind or spirit. This standard interpretation prompts Hall regularly to underline Marx's decisive differences from Hegel. Thus, in his account of the production-consumption-exchange-distribution nexus, the inferior relation of immediate identity, which holds true largely by conceptual definition or by dint of merely "syllogistic" reasoning, is designated as definitively Hegelian. The trouble is, however, that these are exactly the criticisms that Hegel himself makes both of formal logic and of the monistic metaphysics—the "expressive totality"—that he associated with Baruch Spinoza. Indeed, the very labels for Marx's superior categories, through which immediate identity is given substance first by way of "mutual dependence/mediation" then (decisively) by "differentiated unity" and "inner connection," are those of Hegel himself, in the *Science of Logic*. The same applies to the presentation of the movement from simple abstract through analytical elaboration and substantive development back, synthetically, to the real-concrete, this time as a "rich totality of many determinations and relations," for this is largely Hegel's own vocabulary.[30]

Does this matter? It does, because the placing of Hegel is central to how Hall develops his reading of Marx, and it shows him prepared to take Marx at his word beyond what might be accurate. (Unlike Hall, Marx never acknowledged the extent of his intellectual debts.) It also opens up areas of debate that remain contentious today, chiefly on the epistemological side of the articulation idea. Most crucially, the two key concepts in the section on method are "concrete" and "determination," both of which are Hegelian terms, intended by Hegel to illuminate and exemplify how conceptual notion-hood and substantive realities (in the empirical-historical world) are indissolubly coexistent. Thus, while we take the real-concrete as actually existing—as did Hegel, though this is often ignored—and existing moreover in the form that deep analysis takes it to possess, its characteristics and tendencies are "determined" (brought into view, specified, sifted out, interrelated) through the process of many-sided abstraction. Determination thus refers both to theoretical *specification* (we determine the nature of the case) *and* to the relations that are thought to hold between different sets of real-world factors (all phenomena are complexly determined by other things). Without the determinative work of dialectical abstraction, in the Hegelian view, whatever exists can only be imagined in an inadequate ("Kantian") sense as a dumb "thing in itself," devoid of intrinsic determinations and therefore lying forever beyond the grasp of true knowledge.

In passing, we can note that this "Hegelian" set of problems is close to Ernesto Laclau's theorization of the discursive dimension of articulation, which Hall inched closer to as the years went by. Laclau's first step in this direction was heavily influenced by Althusser, who in this respect stood nearer to Hegel than he liked to admit.[31]

Be that as it may, one problem Marx faced was that adopting the logic of inner connection does not by itself tell us *which* factors—which determinations and relations—are decisive, including the determinations set by production itself. The method section of the "Introduction" provides no fresh or convincing further argument for the substantive priority of relations of production, because for Marx the latter's overall organization of the complex totality was doctrinal, something he took for granted. And epistemologically, Marx only shakes Hegel off by resorting to another presuppositional commitment, a nononsense brand of materialism: the real is the material, could never be the conceptual, and that is that. But this then represents a kind of *external* resolution to the dialectic of complexity and mutuality, leading us to wonder why the whole discourse of abstraction-concretion was embarked upon at all, at least in the way that Marx took it over from Hegel. (By the time of *Capital*, Marx had dropped that terminology as the key to his scientific method.) On that basis, some Marxist philosophers around the time Hall was writing decided that what was needed was a (sophisticated) defense of good old "reflectionist" materialism, while others turned to a resolutely empiricist account of Marx's historical practice and methodological guidelines. Another important contribution explained why Marx, though an uncompromising materialist, failed fully to realize that the dialectical method cannot be "clearly separated from Hegel's vision of the way the world is," that is, his metaphysics, which was simultaneously organicist (aspects of which Marx shared) and idealist (which Marx opposed).[32] But in developing any of these views, we should note, the "Introduction" had to be downgraded or problematized, and Hall was reluctant to accept this. Nor was he prepared to conclude—as his colleague Richard Johnson did, in a later essay building on Hall's interpretation—that Marx's 1857 statement may simply have been trying to achieve too many things, becoming blurred and even self-contradictory as a result.[33] Instead, Hall persisted in holding on to elements of *all* the possibilities: the complex process of abstraction, dialectical entailment, "historical epistemology," the empirical working up of concepts, the relative autonomy of theory, and the straightforward materialism that came from Engels via Vilar.

As detailed, in the WPCS version of Hall's exegesis there is a strong contrast between Marx and Hegel. However, the earlier Stencilled Paper shows that Hall was more exercised by Hegel-Marx than the final publication reveals. Most of the four-thousand-plus words that were cut from the Stencilled Paper are taken up with further reflections on that very relationship. And in those segments, Hall considers that Marx might *not* have made such a clean break from the Hegelian identities; that the question of how to establish the relation between the complexity of the thought-concrete and that of the real-concrete raises the "thorniest problems"; that, following Hegel, Marx was clear that the concrete was not to be confused with empirical particularity; that Althusser's reading of these issues is insightful; that resort to simple materialism is not the answer; and that it is even a moot point whether in the "Introduction" Marx did actually establish *why* (rather than how) production ultimately determines the economic (and social) circuit. Overall, Hall's Stencilled Paper conveys a greater sense of unresolved difficulty (and genuine curiosity) concerning Hegel than comes across in the WPCS edition.

Intriguingly, in one of only two new footnotes appearing in the WPCS version, Hall refers us to G. L. Kline for further information on Hegel's and Marx's usage of "concrete." This turns out to be incongruous, because what Kline tells us, in just a couple of crisp pages, is that Marx's version of the abstract-concrete connection is casual and confusing, mixing up very different meanings of the term—Hegelian, empiricist, and commonsensical.[34] Hall makes no comment on the source he is recommending, but why cite it at all if it cut across the reading he was developing?[35]

Hall, I want to suggest, found such questions of intellectual history and theory compelling, even if he did not manage to clear a fully convincing path through them—partly because Marx himself was thoroughly entangled. But we should ask once more: Did this *really* matter for Hall's primary purpose, if that purpose was essentially mediational? He could see very well that the epistemological-ontological level of debate could not lightly be dismissed, whether in philistine materialist or overtly political fashion. Yet he also sensed that philosophical questions about the relationship between knowledge and reality, between what we take to be actual history and the categories we use to construct a meaningful past from the point of view of the present, could readily become intractable. And this could hardly be suited to a Marxist approach to intellectual life, summarized in the eleventh of Marx's *Theses on Feuerbach*: the philosophers had only interpreted the world, the point was (also) to change it. Accordingly, for good measure, Hall sprinkles into the mix a third take on Marx's perspective, namely that knowledge is essentially a *practical* and not a contemplative business, a matter of ongoing social praxis.[36] However, Hall knew that Marxism-as-pragmatism generates problems of its own: either the thesis of the primacy of practice derives from a dangerous, if understandable, anti-intellectualism; or it operates at the same (abstract) level of reflection and research as alternative philosophical/anthropological stances.

So, what I want to emphasize in conclusion is a further interpretative strand of Hall's, representing a different sort of mediation between epistemological and instrumental approaches to methodology. This was what we might call the *regulative* approach, in which indispensable "rules of method" are formulated, but in advisory mode rather than as a seamless logical or epistemological package. Thus, without ever being wholly explicit that this is principally what he is doing, in his reading Hall digs out of Marx's "Introduction" three main "premises" of inquiry: the materialist premise, the historical premise, and the structural premise. Hall indicates that Marx may not always have developed these modes completely or consistently, but all three are productively at work in his best thinking, whereas many later Marxists neglected or underemphasized one or more of those equally essential dimensions. In Althusser's case, the structural premise is valuably underscored in relation to culturalist and historicist/empiricist positions (including those tendencies as they arise in Marx himself), but only at the cost of demoting the historical premise, which Hall persuades us was entirely central for Marx. Furthermore, a key proposition in Hall's paper is that regulative methodological reflexivity is especially important in what is surely the primary register of Marx's (and Marxist) theory, namely, *critique*. On that terrain, the point cannot be to achieve a cognitively complete theoretical understanding—the very aspiration again contravenes the historical premise, which includes the idea that knowledge itself constantly changes. Rather, the compound task—which remains philosophically demanding—is to identify influential forms of abstraction that can be shown to be variously one-sided, simplistic, static, chaotic, forced, ahistorical, apologetic ... and to attribute their deficits, to whatever degree is appropriate, to the operation of definite socioeconomic and political interests.[37]

NOTES

1 Antonio Gramsci, *Selections from the Prison Notebooks*, ed. and trans. Quintin Hoare and Geoffrey Nowell Smith (London: Lawrence and Wishart, 1971), 177–78.
2 Quotations in this paragraph are from this volume, p. 77–78, 115, 120.
3 This volume, p. 70, 78.
4 Jon Elster, *Making Sense of Marx* (Cambridge: Cambridge University Press, 1985), 384–90, 416–18.
5 On "neo-Marxism," see note 19 in this book's introduction.
6 Stuart Hall, *Writings on Media: History of the Present*, edited by Charlotte Brunsdon (Durham, NC: Duke University Press, 2021).
7 "Literature/Society: Mapping the Field," *Working Papers in Cultural Studies*, no. 4 (Birmingham: Centre for Contemporary Cultural Studies, University of Birmingham, 1973), 31–32. In an endnote to this paper, explaining how it was collectively developed, mention is made of the "major organizing of the material by Stuart

Hall." Since the passages from which the quote is taken contain characteristic formulations of his, it is reasonable to attribute the sentiments to Hall.
8 Stuart Hall, *Essential Essays*, vol. 1, *Foundations of Cultural Studies*, ed. David Morley (Durham, NC: Duke University Press, 2019), 127.
9 This volume, p. 131.
10 See the essay of that title in Stuart Hall, *Selected Political Writings*, ed. Sally Davison, David Featherstone, Michael Rustin, and Bill Schwarz (Durham, NC: Duke University Press, 2017), 117–41.
11 Stuart Hall, *Cultural Studies 1983: A Theoretical History*, ed. Jennifer Daryl Slack and Lawrence Grossberg (Durham, NC: Duke University Press, 2016), 20.
12 Jon Bloomfield, ed., *Class, Hegemony and Party* (London: Lawrence and Wishart, 1977).
13 This volume, p. 136, 141.
14 Betty Matthews, ed., *Marx: A Hundred Years On* (London: Lawrence and Wishart, 1983).
15 This volume, p. 141, 156.
16 David McLellan, *Marx's "Grundrisse"* (London: Macmillan, 1971); Paul Walton and Stuart Hall, eds., *Situating Marx: Evaluations and Departures* (London: Human Context Books, 1972).
17 Karl Marx, *Grundrisse: Foundations of the Critique of Political Economy (Rough Draft)*, ed. and with a foreword by Martin Nicolaus (Harmondsworth, UK: Pelican, 1973). Hall considered that foreword "excellent," and his interpretation of the text is aligned with Nicolaus's, though on the question of Hegel (see my later discussion of this) Nicolaus's analysis is in fact rather ambiguous.
18 For example, see Keith Tribe, "Remarks on the Theoretical Significance of Marx's *Grundrisse*," *Economy and Society* 3, no. 2 (1974): 180–210.
19 The text of the original Stencilled Paper is available at on the University of Birmingham's "Staff Research in History" page, https://www.birmingham.ac.uk/schools/historycultures/departments/history/research/projects/cccs/publications/stencilled-occasional-papers.aspx. The sense of uncertainty surrounding the relationship between the two different versions was compounded rather than clarified when Hall's reading of the 1857 "Introduction" was included in the blockbuster *CCCS Selected Working Papers*, vol. 1, ed. Ann Gray, Jan Campbell, Mark Erikson, Stuart Hanson, and Helen Wood (Abingdon, UK: Routledge, 2007). The impression given by the editors is that the reproduced text was the Stencilled Paper of 1973, as indicated in its (not quite accurately rendered) title. But in fact, the main body of the piece was the 1974 WPCS version, as per our chapter 1.
20 Lucio Colletti, *Marxism and Hegel* (London: Verso, 1973).
21 Hall, *Essential Essays*, 1:196–201.
22 See Ted Benton, *The Rise and Fall of Structuralist Marxism: Althusser and His Influence* (London: Macmillan, 1984), chap. 6.
23 Jennifer Daryl Slack, "The Theory and Method of Articulation in Cultural Studies," in *Stuart Hall: Critical Dialogues in Cultural Studies*, ed. David Morley and Kuan-Hsing Chen (London: Routledge, 1996), 112–27, 112.

24 Perhaps the most elevated—but also overstated—account of articulation as both the "central theoretical problem" of cultural studies and its veritable "poetic" was given by Fredric Jameson, who construed articulation as a kind of "turning structure" or "ion-exchange." Jameson, "On 'Cultural Studies,'" *Social Text*, no. 34 (1993): 17–52, 31–33.

25 Robin Rusher, "What Is It He's Done? The Ideology of Althusser," in "Cultural Studies and Theory," *Working Papers in Cultural Studies*, no. 6 (Birmingham: Centre for Contemporary Cultural Studies, University of Birmingham, 1974), 70–97; André Glucksmann, "A Ventriloquist Structuralism," *New Left Review*, I/72 (1972): 68–92.

26 Norman Geras, "Althusser's Marxism: An Account and Assessment,'" *New Left Review*, I/71 (1972): 57–86.

27 The unpublished papers are deposited in the Hall/CCCS archives held in the Cadbury Research Library Special Collections at the University of Birmingham. Along with some others composed in 1972–73, they contain everything that appeared in both versions of Hall's reading of the 1857 "Introduction," and it seems that he envisaged that group of writings as forming a substantial book of his on Marxism and cultural studies—some of which later reemerges, revised, in *Cultural Studies 1983*. As testimony to Hall's methodology of scrupulous "reading," "Settling Accounts" is extraordinarily fine-grained, ground out over eighty tightly crammed pages, both typed and handwritten. Although there is no mention of the latter paper in the WPCS 6 version of Hall's Marx commentary, his Stencilled Paper version twice refers (and defers) to it.

28 In that regard, despite notable similarities between Hall's take on the 1857 "Introduction" and those of interpreters such as Galvano Della Volpe, *Logic as a Positive Science* (1969; repr., London: New Left Books, 1980), and Jindrich Zeleny, *The Logic of Marx* (1968; repr., Totowa, NJ: Rowman and Littlefield, 1980), Hall does not share their ambitions to articulate a new philosophy of science having Marx's style of inquiry at its heart.

29 John Clarke, "Stuart Hall and the Theory and Practice of Articulation," *Discourse: Studies in the Cultural Politics of Education* 36, no. 2 (2015): 275–86; Lawrence Grossberg, "Learning from Stuart Hall, Following the Path with Heart," *Cultural Studies* 29, no. 1 (2015): 3–11, 6.

30 For the most authoritative commentary on these and other aspects of Marx's 1857 "Introduction," see Terrell Carver, "A Commentary on the Text," in *Karl Marx: Texts on Method*, ed. Carver (Oxford: Basil Blackwell, 1975), 88–158. See also Hiroshi Uchida, *Marx's "Grundrisse" and Hegel's "Logic"* (London: Routledge, 1988).

31 Ernesto Laclau, "The Specificity of the Political," in *Politics and Ideology in Marxist Theory* (London: Verso, 1977), 51–79, 59–60.

32 For excellent examples of these different strategies, respectively, see David Hillel-Ruben, *Marxism and Materialism: A Study in Marxist Theory of Knowledge* (Brighton, UK: Harvester Press, 1977); Derek Sayer, *Marx's Method: Ideology, Science and Critique in "Capital"* (Brighton, UK: Harvester Press, 1979); and Allen W. Wood, *Karl Marx* (London: Routledge and Kegan Paul, 1981), chaps. 12–14. The quote is from Wood, *Karl Marx*, 215.

33 Richard Johnson, "Reading for the Best Marx: History-Writing and Historical Abstraction," in Centre for Contemporary Cultural Studies, *Making Histories: Studies in History-Writing and Politics* (London: Hutchinson, 1982), 153–201, 155.

34 George L. Kline, "Some Critical Comments on Marx's Philosophy," in *Marx and the Western World*, ed. Nicholas Lobkowicz (Notre Dame, IN: University of Notre Dame Press, 1967), 419–32, 431–32.

35 One obvious answer is that Hall never quite attains a satisfactory view of the Marx-Hegel (and therefore of the Marx-Hegel-Althusser) relationship. The WPCS and Stencilled Paper discussions, as I suggested, are not entirely congruent, and in a note from 1979 in his archived papers, Hall remarks that the final pages of *both* versions of the reading—which are partly about what is to be done with Hegel— "don't work," and may even be "whistling in the dark." Hall then nods to "Settling Accounts with Althusser" as though a clearer grip on the issue can be found there, but as I read it, the same conundrums arise, albeit couched in yet another set of interesting nuances.

36 In what may be the only sustained discussion of Hall's reading of the 1857 "Introduction" in the academic domain of social and political theory, Samuel A. Chambers argues that Hall was mistaken to take Althusser as giving an *epistemological* account of the relation between thought and object realms. Correspondingly, Chambers thinks Hall should have resisted making "realist" complaints about Althusser. This interesting account supposes Marx to be a militant pragmatist and seeks to recruit Althusser to later-Hall- or Laclau-style conclusions: that our theoretical problematics are primarily social and political *imaginaries* that entail a discursive-political construction of the "social formation" itself, thus altogether displacing "bourgeois" philosophical issues of realism versus idealism. The difficulty with this line, however, is that the stated primacy of imaginaries is both ontologically idealist and intrinsically open-ended politically, even if cast toward radical-sounding ends. Samuel A. Chambers, *Bearing Society in Mind: Theories and Politics of the Social Formation* (London: Rowman and Littlefield, 2014).

37 On adequate and inadequate forms of abstraction, see Johnson, "Reading for the Best Marx."

PART II THEMATIC OVERVIEWS

CHAPTER 5

Subcultures, Cultures and Class:
A Theoretical Overview

with John Clarke, Tony Jefferson, and Brian Roberts

Our subject in this volume is youth cultures: our object, to explain them as a phenomenon, and their appearance in the post-war period. The subject has, of course, been massively treated, above all in the mass media. Yet, many of these surveys and analyses seem mainly to have multiplied the confusions and extended the mythologies surrounding the topic. By treating it in terms of its spectacular features only, these surveys have become part of the very phenomenon we want to explain. First, then, we must clear the ground, try to get behind the myths and explanations which cover up, rather than clarify, the problem. We have to construct the topic first—partly by demolishing certain concepts which, at present, are taken as adequately defining it. Necessarily, this exercise of penetrating beneath a popular construction must be done with care, lest we discard the "rational kernel" along with its over-publicised husk.

The social and political meaning of "youth cultures" is not easy to assess, though their visibility has been consistently high. "Youth" appeared as an emergent category in post-war Britain, one of the most striking and visible manifestations of social change in the period. "Youth" provided the focus for official reports, pieces of legislation, official interventions. It was signified as a social problem by the moral guardians of the society—something we "ought to do something about." Above all, youth played an important role as a cornerstone in the construction of understandings, interpretations and quasi-explanations *about* the period. As the Rowntree study of the popular press and social change suggested:

> Youth was, in both papers [the *Daily Express* and the *Daily Mirror*] and perhaps in the whole press of the period, a powerful but concealed *metaphor* for social change: the compressed image of a society which had crucially changed, in terms of basic life-styles and values—changed, in ways calculated to upset the official political framework, but in ways *not yet calculable in traditional political terms*.[1]

It would be difficult to sustain the argument that a phenomenon as massively present and visible as youth culture, occupying a pivotal position in the history and consciousness of the period, was a pure construction of the media, a surface phenomenon only. However, Gramsci warned us that, "in studying a structure, it is necessary to distinguish organic movements (relatively permanent) from movements which may be termed 'conjunctural', and which appear as occasional, immediate, almost accidental." The aim must be to "find the correct relation between what is organic and what is conjunctural."[2] The "phenomenal form"—youth culture—provides a point of departure, only, for such an analysis. We cannot afford to be blind to such a development (as some "sceptical materialists" of the old left have been, with due respect to the recent debate in *Marxism Today*) any more than we can afford to be blinded by them (as some "visionary idealists" of the new left have at times been).

Some Definitions

We begin with some minimal definitions. The term "youth culture" directs us to the "cultural" aspects of youth. We understand the word "culture" to refer to that level at which social groups develop distinct patterns of life and give *expressive form* to their social and material life-experience. Culture is the way, the forms, in which groups "handle" the raw material of their social and material existence. "We must suppose the raw material of life experience to be at one pole, and all the infinitely complex human disciplines and systems, articulate and inarticulate, formalised in institutions or dispersed in the least formal ways, which 'handle', transmit or distort this raw material, to be at the other."[3] "Culture" is the practice which realises or *objectivates* group life in meaningful shape and form. "As individuals express their life, so they are. What they are, therefore, coincides with their production, both with *what* they produce and with *how* they produce."[4] The "culture" of a group or class is the peculiar and distinctive "way of life" of the group or class, the meanings, values and ideas embodied in institutions, in social relations, in systems of beliefs, in *mores* and customs, in the uses of objects and material life. Culture is the distinctive shapes in which this material and social organisation of life expresses itself. A culture includes the "maps of meaning" which make things intelligible to its members. These "maps of meaning" are not simply carried around in the head: they are objectivated in the patterns of social organisation and relationship through which the individual becomes a "social individual." Culture is the way the social relations of a group are structured and shaped: but it is also the way those shapes are experienced, understood and interpreted.

A social individual, born into a particular set of institutions and relations, is at the same moment born into a peculiar configuration of meanings, which give her access to and locate her within "a culture." The "law of society" and the "law of culture" (the symbolic ordering of social life) are one and the same. These structures—of social relationship and of meaning—shape the ongoing collective existence of groups. But they also limit, modify and *constrain* how groups live and reproduce their social existence. Men and women are, thus, formed, and form themselves through society, culture and history. So the existing cultural patterns form a sort of historical reservoir—a preconstituted "field of the possible"—which groups take up, transform, develop. Each group makes something of its starting conditions and through this "making," through this practice, culture is reproduced and transmitted. But this practice only takes place within the given field of possibilities and constraints.[5] "Men make their own history, but they do not make it just as they please; they do not make it under circumstances chosen by themselves, but under circumstances directly encountered, given and transmitted from the past."[6] Culture, then, embodies the trajectory of group life through history: always under conditions and with "raw materials" which cannot wholly be of its own making.

Groups which exist within the same society and share some of the same material and historical conditions no doubt also understand, and to a certain extent share each other's "culture." But just as different groups and classes are unequally ranked in relation to one another, in terms of their productive relations, wealth and power, so *cultures* are differently ranked, and stand in opposition to one another, in relations of domination and subordination, along the scale of "cultural power." The definitions of the world, the "maps of meaning" which express the life situation of those groups which hold the monopoly of power in society, command the greatest weight and influence, secrete the greatest legitimacy. The world tends to be classified out and ordered in terms and through structures which most directly express the power, the position, the *hegemony*, of the powerful interests in that society. Thus,

> The class which has the means of material production at its disposal, has control, at the same time, over the means of mental production, so that, thereby, generally speaking, the ideas of those who lack the means of mental production are subject to it. . . . Insofar as they rule as a class and determine the extent and compass of an epoch . . . they do this in its whole range, hence, among other things rule also as thinkers, as producers of ideas, and regulate the production and distribution of the ideas of their age: thus their ideas are the ruling ideas of the epoch.[7]

This does not mean that there is only *one* set of ideas or cultural forms in a society. There will be more than one tendency at work within the dominant ideas of a society. Groups or classes which do not stand at the apex of power nevertheless find ways of expressing and realising in their culture their subordinate position and experiences. In so far as there is more than one fundamental class in a society (and capitalism is essentially the bringing together, around production, of two fundamentally *different* classes—capital and labour) there will be more than one major cultural configuration in play at a particular historical moment. But the structures and meanings which most adequately reflect the position and interests of the most powerful class—however complex it is internally—will stand, in relation to all the others, as a *dominant* social-cultural order. The dominant culture represents itself as *the* culture. It tries to define and contain all other cultures within its inclusive range. *Its* views of the world, unless challenged, will stand as the most natural, all-embracing, universal culture. Other cultural configurations will not only be subordinate to this dominant order: they will enter into struggle with it, seek to modify, negotiate, resist or even overthrow its reign—its *hegemony*. The struggle between classes over material and social life thus always assumes the forms of a continuous struggle over the distribution of "cultural power." We might want, here, to make a distinction between "culture" and "ideology." Dominant and subordinate classes will each have distinct cultures. But when one culture gains ascendancy over the other, and when the subordinate culture *experiences* itself in terms prescribed by the dominant culture, then the dominant culture has also become the basis of a dominant ideology.

The dominant culture of a complex society is never a homogeneous structure. It is layered, reflecting different interests within the dominant class (e.g., an aristocratic versus a bourgeois outlook), containing different traces from the past (e.g., religious ideas within a largely secular culture), as well as emergent elements in the present. Subordinate cultures will not always be in open conflict with it. They may, for long periods, coexist with it, negotiate the spaces and gaps in it, make inroads into it, "warrening it from within."[8] However, though the nature of this struggle over culture can never be reduced to a simple opposition, it is crucial to replace the notion of "culture" with the more concrete, historical concept of "cultures": a redefinition which brings out more clearly the fact that cultures always stand in relations of domination—and subordination—to one another, are always, in some sense, in struggle with one another. The singular term, "culture," can only indicate, in the most general and abstract way, the large cultural configurations at play in a society at any historical moment. We must move at once to the determining relationships of domination and subordination in which these configurations stand; to the processes of incorporation and resistance which define the cultural dialectic between them; and to the institutions which transmit and reproduce "the culture" (i.e., the dominant culture) in its dominant or "hegemonic" form.

In modern societies, the most fundamental groups are the social classes, and the major cultural configurations will be, in a fundamental though often mediated way, "class cultures." Relative to these cultural-class configurations, *sub*cultures are subsets—smaller, more localised and differentiated structures, within one or other of the larger cultural networks. We must, first, see subcultures in terms of their relation to the wider class-cultural networks of which they form a distinctive part. When we examine this relationship between a subculture and the "culture" of which it is a part, we call the latter the "parent" culture. This must not be confused with the particular relationship between "youth" and their parents, of which much will be said below. What we mean is that a subculture, though differing in important ways—in its "focal concerns," its peculiar shapes and activities—from the culture from which it derives, will also share some things in common with that "parent" culture. The bohemian subculture of the *avant-garde* which has arisen from time to time in the modern city, is both distinct from its "parent" culture (the urban culture of the middle-class intelligentsia) and yet also a part of it (sharing with it a modernising outlook, standards of education, a privileged position vis-à-vis productive labour, and so on). In the same way, the "search for pleasure and excitement" which some analysts have noted as a marked feature of the "delinquent subculture of the gang" in the working class, also shares something basic and fundamental with it. Subcultures, then, must first be related to the "parent cultures" of which they are a subset. But subcultures must *also* be analysed in terms of their relation to the dominant culture—the overall disposition of cultural power in the society as a whole. Thus, we may distinguish the respectable, "rough," delinquent and criminal subcultures *within* working-class culture: but we may also say that, though they differ amongst themselves, they all derive in the first instance from a "working-class parent culture": hence, they are all subordinate subcultures, in relation to the dominant middle-class or bourgeois culture. (We believe this goes some way towards meeting Graham Murdock's call for a more "symmetrical" analysis of subcultures.)[9]

Subcultures must exhibit a distinctive enough shape and structure to make them identifiably different from their parent culture. They must be focused around certain activities, values, certain uses of material artefacts, territorial spaces etc. which significantly differentiate them from the wider culture. But, since they are subsets, there must also be significant things which bind and articulate them with the parent culture. The famous Kray twins, for example, belonged both to a highly differentiated "criminal subculture" in East London and to the "normal" life and culture of the East End working class (of which, indeed, the "criminal subculture" has always been a clearly identifiable part). The behaviour of the Krays in terms of the criminal fraternity marks the differentiating axis of that subculture: the relation of the Krays to their mother, family, home and local pub is the binding, the articulating axis.[10]

Subcultures, therefore, take shape around the distinctive activities and "focal concerns" of groups. They can be loosely or tightly bounded. Some subcultures are merely loosely defined strands or "milieux" within the parent culture: they possess no distinctive "world" of their own. Others develop a clear, coherent identity and structure. Generally, we deal *only* with subcultures (whether drawn from a middle- or working-class parent culture) which have reasonably tight boundaries, distinctive shapes, which have cohered around particular activities, focal concerns and territorial spaces. When these tightly defined groups are also distinguished by age and generation, we call them "youth subcultures."

Youth subcultures form up on the terrain of social and cultural life. Some youth subcultures are regular and persistent features of the parent class culture: the ill-famed "culture of delinquency" of the working-class adolescent male, for example. But some subcultures appear only at particular historical moments: they become visible, are identified and labelled (either by themselves or by others): they command the stage of public attention for a time: then they fade, disappear or are so widely diffused that they lose their distinctiveness. It is the *latter* kind of subcultural formation which primarily concerns us here. The peculiar dress, style, focal concerns, milieux, etc. of the

Teddy Boy, the Mod, the Rocker or the Skinhead set them off, as distinctive groupings, both from the broad patterns of working-class culture as a whole, and also from the more diffused patterns exhibited by "ordinary" working-class boys (and, to a more limited extent, girls). Yet, despite these differences, it is important to stress that, as subcultures, they continue to exist within, and coexist with, the more inclusive culture of the class from which they spring. Members of a subculture may walk, talk, act, look "different" from their parents and from some of their peers: but they belong to the same families, go to the same schools, work at much the same jobs, live down the same "mean streets" as their peers and parents. In certain crucial respects, they share the same position (vis-à-vis the dominant culture), the same fundamental and determining life experiences, as the parent culture from which they derive. Through dress, activities, leisure pursuits and lifestyle, they may project a different cultural response or "solution" to the problems posed for them by their material and social class position and experience. But the membership of a subculture cannot protect them from the determining matrix of experiences and conditions which shape the life of their class as a whole. They experience and respond to the *same basic problematic* as other members of their class who are not so differentiated and distinctive in a "subcultural" sense. Especially in relation to the *dominant* culture, their subculture remains like other elements in their class culture—subordinate and subordinated.

In what follows, we shall try to show why this *double articulation* of youth subcultures—first to their parent culture (e.g., working-class culture), second, to the dominant culture—is a necessary way of staging the analysis. For our purposes, subcultures represent a necessary, "relatively autonomous," but *intermediary* level of analysis. Any attempt to relate subcultures to the "socio-cultural formation as a whole" must grasp its complex unity by way of these necessary differentiations.

[...]

Dominant and Subordinate Cultures

[...]

To locate youth subculture in this kind of analysis, we must first situate youth in the dialectic between a "hegemonic" dominant culture and the subordinate working-class parent culture, of which youth is a fraction. These terms—"hegemonic/corporate," "dominant/subordinate"—are crucial for the analysis, but need further elaboration before the sub-cultural dimension can be introduced. Gramsci used the term "hegemony" to refer to the moment when a ruling class is able, not only to *coerce* a subordinate class to conform to its interests, but to exert a "hegemony" or "total social authority" over subordinate classes. This involves the exercise of a special kind of power—the power to frame alternatives and contain opportunities, *to win and shape consent*, so that the granting of legitimacy to the dominant classes appears not only "spontaneous" but natural and normal. Steven Lukes has recently defined this as the power to define the agenda, to shape preferences, to "prevent conflict from arising in the first place," or to contain conflict when it does arise by defining what sorts of resolution are "reasonable" and "realistic"—i.e., within the existing framework.[11] The terrain on which this hegemony is won or lost is the terrain of the superstructures; the institutions of civil society and the state—what Louis Althusser and Nicos Poulantzas, somewhat misleadingly, call "ideological state apparatuses."[12] Conflicts of interest arise, fundamentally, from the difference in the structural position of the classes in the productive realm: but they have their effect in social and political life. Politics, in the widest sense, frames the passage from the first level to the second. The terrain of civil and state institutions thus becomes essentially "the stake, but also the site of class struggle."[13] In part, these apparatuses work "by ideology." That is, the definitions of reality institutionalised within these apparatuses come to constitute a lived "reality as such" for the subordinate classes—that, at least, is what hegemony attempts and secures. Gramsci, using the example of the church, says that it preserves "the ideological unity of the entire social bloc which that ideology serves to cement and unify."[14] A hegemonic cultural order tries to *frame* all competing definitions of the world within *its* range. It provides the horizon of thought and action within which conflicts are fought through, appropriated (i.e., experienced), obscured (i.e., concealed as a "national interest" which should unite all conflicting parties) or contained (i.e., settled to the profit of the ruling class). A hegemonic order prescribes, not the specific content of ideas, but the *limits* within which ideas and conflicts move and are resolved. Hegemony always rests on force and coercion, but "the normal exercise of hegemony on the now classical terrain of the parliamentary regime is characterised by the combination of force and consent . . . without force predominating excessively over consent."[15] Hegemony thus provides the base line and the base structures of legitimation for ruling-class power.

Hegemony works through ideology, but it does not consist of false ideas, perceptions, definitions. It works *primarily* by inserting the subordinate class into the key institutions and structures which support the power and social authority of the dominant order. It is, above all, in these structures and relations that a subordinate class *lives its subordination*. Often, this subordination is secured only because the dominant order succeeds in weakening, destroying, displacing or incorporating alternative institutions of defence and resistance thrown up by the subordinate class. Gramsci insists, quite correctly, that "the thesis which asserts that men become conscious of fundamental conflicts on the level of ideology is not psychological or moralistic in character but *structural and epistemological*."[16]

Hegemony can rarely be sustained by one single class stratum. Almost always it requires an *alliance* of ruling-class fractions—a "historical bloc." The content of hegemony will be determined, in part, by precisely which class fractions compose such a "hegemonic bloc," and thus what interests have to be taken into account within it. Hegemony is not simple "class rule." It requires to some degree the "consent" of the subordinate class, which has, in turn, to be won and secured; thus, an ascendancy of social authority, not only in the state but in civil society as well, in culture and ideology. Hegemony prevails when ruling classes not only rule or "direct" but *lead*. The state is a major educative force in this process. It educates through its regulation of the life of the subordinate classes. These apparatuses reproduce class relations, and thus class subordination (the family, the school, the church and cultural institutions, as well as the law, the police and the army, the courts).

The struggle against class hegemony also takes place within these institutions, as well as outside them—they become the "site" of class struggle. But the apparatuses also depend on the operation of "a set of predominant values, beliefs, rituals and institutional procedures ('rules of the game') that operate systematically and consistently to the benefit of certain persons and groups."[17]

Gramsci believes that, in the Italian state, the dominant classes had frequently ruled without that "natural social authority" which would make them "hegemonic." So hegemony cannot be taken for granted—either by the state and the dominant classes, or, for that matter, by the analyst. The current use of the term, to suggest the unending and unproblematic exercise of class power by every ruling class, and its opposite—the permanent and finished incorporation of the subordinate class—is quite false to Gramsci's usage. It limits the historical specificity of the concept. To make that point concrete. we would argue that, though the dominant classes remained massively in command during the 1930s, it is difficult to define them as "hegemonic." Economic crisis and unemployment disciplined, rather than "led," the working classes into subordination in this period. The defeats suffered by the labour movement in the 1920s powerfully contributed to the coercive sway of the former over the latter. By contrast, the 1950s seem to us a period of true "hegemonic domination," it being precisely the role of "affluence," as an ideology, to dismantle working-class resistance and deliver the "spontaneous consent" of the class to the authority of the dominant classes. Increasingly, in the 1960s, and more openly in the 1970s, this "leadership" has again been undermined. The society has polarised, conflict has reappeared on many levels. The dominant classes retain power, but their "repertoire" of control is progressively challenged, weakened, exhausted. One of the most striking features of this later period is the shift in the exercise of control from the mechanisms of consent to those of coercion (e.g., the use of the law, the courts, the police and the army, of legal repression, conspiracy charges and of force to contain an escalating threat to the state and to "law and order"). This marks a *crisis* in the hegemony of the ruling class.

Hegemony, then, is not universal and "given" to the continuing rule of a particular class. It has to be *won*, worked for, reproduced, sustained. Hegemony is, as Gramsci said, a "moving equilibrium," containing "relations of forces favourable or unfavourable to this or that tendency." It is a matter of the nature of the balance struck between contending classes: the compromises made to sustain it; the relations of force; the solutions adopted. Its character and content can only be established by looking at concrete situations, at concrete historical moments. The idea of "permanent class hegemony" or of "permanent incorporation" must be ditched.

In relation to the hegemony of a ruling class, the working class is, by definition, a *subordinate* social and cultural formation. Capitalist production, Marx suggested, reproduces capital and labour in their ever-antagonistic forms. The role of hegemony is to ensure that, in the social relations between the classes, each class is continually *reproduced* in its existing dominant-or-subordinate form. Hegemony can never wholly and absolutely absorb the working class *into* the dominant order. Society may seem to be, but cannot actually ever be, in the capitalist mode of production, "one-dimensional." Of course, at times, hegemony is strong and cohesive, and the subordinate class is weak, vulnerable and exposed. But it cannot, by definition, disappear. It remains, as a subordinate structure, often separate and impermeable, yet still contained by the overall rule and domination of the ruling class. The subordinate class has developed its own corporate culture, its own forms of social relationship, its characteristic institutions, values, modes of life. Class conflict never disappears. English working-class culture is a peculiarly strong, densely impacted, cohesive and defensive structure of this corporate kind. Class conflict, then, is rooted and embodied in this culture: it cannot "disappear"—contrary to the ideology of affluence—until the productive relations which produce and sustain it disappear. But it can be more or less open, more or less formal, more or less institutionalised, more or less autonomous. The period between the 1880s and the present shows, not a single thrust towards incorporation, but a marked alternating rhythm. It is important to insist that, even when class conflict is most institutionalised, it remains as one of the fundamental base-rhythms of the society.

[...]

The Subcultural Response

We can return, now, to the question of "subcultures." Working-class subcultures, we suggested, take shape on the level of the social and cultural class relations of the subordinate classes. In themselves, they are not simply "ideological" constructs. They, too, *win space* for the young: cultural space in the neighbourhood and institutions, real time for leisure and recreation, actual room on the street or street-corner. They serve to mark out and appropriate "territory" in the localities. They focus around key occasions of social interaction: the weekend, the disco, the bank-holiday trip, the night out in the "centre," the "standing-about-doing-nothing" of the weekday evening, the Saturday match. They cluster around particular locations. They develop specific rhythms of interchange, structured relations between members: younger to older, experienced to novice, stylish to square. They explore "focal concerns" central to the inner life of the group: things "always done" or "never done," a set of social rituals which underpin their collective identity and define them as a "group" instead of a mere collection of individuals. They adopt and adapt material objects—goods and possessions—and reorganise them into distinctive "styles" which express the collectivity of their being-as-a-group. These concerns, activities, relationships, materials become embodied in rituals of relationship and occasion and movement. Sometimes, the world is marked out, linguistically, by names or an *argot* which classifies the social world exterior to them in terms meaningful only within their group perspective and maintains its boundaries. This also helps them to develop, ahead of immediate activities, a perspective on the immediate future—plans, projects, things to do to fill out time, exploits. They too are concrete, identifiable social formations constructed as a collective response to the material and situated experience of their class.

Though not "ideological," subcultures have an ideological dimension: and, in the problematic situation of the post-war period, this ideological component became more prominent. In addressing the "class problematic" of the particular strata from which they were drawn, the different subcultures provided for a section of working-class youth (mainly boys) *one* strategy for negotiating their collective existence. But their highly ritualised and stylised form suggests that they were also *attempts at a solution* to that problematic experience: a resolution which, because pitched largely at the symbolic level, was fated to fail. The problematic of a subordinate class experience can be "lived through," negotiated or resisted; but it cannot be *resolved* at that level or by those means. There is no "subcultural career" for the working-class lad, no "solution" in the subcultural milieu, for problems posed by the key structuring experiences of the class.

There is no "subcultural solution" to working-class youth unemployment, educational disadvantage, compulsory miseducation, dead-end jobs, the routinisation and specialisation of labour, low pay and the loss of skills. Subcultural strategies cannot match, meet or answer the structuring dimensions emerging in this period for the class as a whole. So, when the post-war subcultures address the problematics of their class experience, they often do so in ways which reproduce the gaps and discrepancies between real negotiations and symbolically displaced "resolutions." They "solve," but in an imaginary way, problems which at the concrete material level remain unresolved. Thus the "Teddy Boy" expropriation of an upper-class style of dress "covers" the gap between largely manual, unskilled, near-lumpen real careers and life-chances, and the "all-dressed-up-and-nowhere-to-go" experience of Saturday evening. Thus, in the expropriation and fetishisation of consumption and style itself, the "Mods" cover for the gap between the never-ending-weekend and Monday's resumption of boring, dead-end work. Thus, in the resurrection of an archetypal and "symbolic" (but, in fact, anachronistic) form of working-class dress, in the displaced focusing on the football match and the "occupation" of the football "ends," Skinheads reassert, but "imaginarily," the values of a class, the essence of a style, a kind of "fan-ship" to which few working-class adults any longer subscribe: they "re-present" a sense of territory and locality which the planners and speculators are rapidly destroying: they "declare" as alive and well a game which is being commercialised, professionalised and spectacularised. "Skins Rule, OK." OK? But "in ideology, men do indeed express, not the real relation between them and their conditions of existence, but the way they live the relation between them and the conditions of their existence; this presupposes both a real and an *'imaginary,' 'lived'* relation. Ideology then, is . . . the (overdetermined) unity of the real relation and the imaginary relation . . . that expresses a will . . . a hope, or a nostalgia, rather than describing a reality."[18]

Working-class subcultures are a response to a problematic which youth shares with other members of the parent class culture. But class structures the adolescent's experience of that problematic in distinctive ways. First, it locates the young, at a formative stage of their development, in a particular material and cultural milieu, in distinctive relations and experiences. These provide the essential cultural frameworks through which that problematic is made sense of by the youth. This socialisation of youth *into* a class identity and position operates particularly through two informal agencies: family and neighbourhood. Family and neighbourhood are the specific structures which *form*, as well as frame, youth's early passage into a class. For example, the sex-typing roles and responsibilities characteristic of a class are reproduced, not only through language and talk in the family, but through daily interaction and example. In the neighbourhood, patterns of community sociality are embedded partly through the structure of interactions between older and younger kids.[19] These intimate contexts also refer the young to the larger world outside. Thus it is largely through friends and relations that the distant but increasingly imminent worlds of work or of face-to-face authority (the rent man, council officials, social security, the police) are appropriated. Through these formative networks, relations, distances, interactions, orientations to the wider world and its social types are delineated and reproduced in the young.

Class also, broadly, structures the young individual's life chances. It determines, in terms of statistical class probabilities, the distribution of "achievement" and "failure." It establishes certain crucial orientations towards careers in education and work—it produces the notoriously "realistic" expectations of working-class kids about future opportunities. It teaches ways of relating to and negotiating authority. For example, the social distance, deference, anxiety and dressing-up of parents in meetings with schoolteachers may confirm or reinforce the experience of school as essentially part of an alien and external world.

These are only some of the many ways in which the way youth is inserted within the culture of a class also serves to reproduce, within the young, the problematics of that class. But, over and above these shared class situations, there remains something privileged about the specifically *generational experience* of the young. Fundamentally, this is due to the fact that youth encounters the problematic of its class culture in *different sets of institutions and experiences* from those of its parents; and when youth encounters the same structures, it encounters them at *crucially different points* in its biographical careers.

We can identify these aspects of "generational specificity" in relation to three main life areas: education, work and leisure. Between the ages of five and sixteen, education is the institutional sphere which has the most sustained and intensive impact on the lives of the young. It is the "paramount reality" imposing itself on experience, not least through the fact that it cannot (easily) be avoided. By contrast, the older members of the class encounter education in various *indirect* and distanced ways: through remembered experiences ("things have changed" nowadays); through special mediating occasions—parents' evenings, etc.; and through the interpretations the young give of their school experiences.

In the area of work, the difference is perhaps less obvious, in that both young and old alike are facing similar institutional arrangements, organisations and occupational situations. But within this, crucial differences remain. The young face the problem of choosing and entering jobs, of learning both the formal and informal cultures of work—the whole difficult transition from school to work. We have already observed how the changing occupational structures of some areas and industries may dislocate the traditionally evolved "family-work-career structure"—thus making the transition even more difficult. For the older members of the class, work has become a relatively routine aspect of life; they have learnt occupational identities and the cultures of work, involving strategies for coping with the problems that work poses—methods of "getting by."

In the broader context, the young are likely to be more vulnerable to the consequence of increasing unemployment than are older workers: in the unemployment statistics of the late 1960s, unskilled school leavers were twice as likely to be unemployed as were older, unskilled workers. In addition, the fact of unemployment is likely to be differentially *experienced* at different stages in the occupational "career."

Finally, leisure must be seen as a significant life-area for the class. As Marx observed,

> The worker therefore only feels himself outside his work, and in his work feels outside himself. He is at home when he is not working, and when he is working he is not at home. His labour is therefore not voluntary but coerced; it is forced labour. It is therefore not the satisfaction of a need; it is merely the means to satisfy needs external to it.[20]

In working-class leisure, we see many of the results of that "warrening" of society by the working-class discussed above. Leisure and recreation seem to have provided a more negotiable space than the tightly disciplined and controlled work situation. The working class has imprinted itself indelibly on many areas of mass leisure and recreation. These form an important part of the corporate culture and are central to the experience and cultural identity of the whole class. Nevertheless, there are major differences in the ways working-class adults and young people experience and regard leisure. This difference became intensified in the 1950s and 1960s, with the growth of the "teenage consumer" and the reorganisation of consumption and leisure provision (both commercial and non-commercial) in favour of a range of goods and services specifically designed to attract a youthful clientele. This widespread availability and high visibility of youth culture structured the leisure sphere in crucially different ways for the young. The equation of youth with consumption and leisure rearranged and *intensified* certain long-standing parent culture orientations; for example, towards the special and privileged meaning of "free time," and towards "youth" as a period for "having a good time while you can"—the "last fling." This reshaping of attitudes from within the class, in conjunction with pressures to rearrange and redistribute the patterns of leisure for the young from outside, served to highlight—indeed, to *fetishise*—the meaning of leisure for the young. Thus, not only did youth encounter leisure in different characteristic institutions from their parents (caffs, discos, youth clubs, "all-nighters," etc.): these institutions powerfully presented themselves to the young as different from the past, partly because they were so uncompromisingly youthful.

Here we begin to see how forces, working right across a class, but differentially experienced as between the generations, may have formed the basis for generating an outlook—a kind of consciousness—specific to age position: a *generational consciousness*. We can also see exactly why this "consciousness," though formed by class situation and the forces working in it, may nevertheless have taken the form of a consciousness apparently separate from, unrelated to, indeed, able to be set over against, its class content and context. Though we can see how and why this specific kind of "generational consciousness" might arise, the problem is not resolved by simply reading it once again out of existence—that is, by re-assigning to youth a clear and simple class-based identity and consciousness. This would be simply to overreact against "generational consciousness." We have suggested that, though a fully-blown "generational consciousness" served unwittingly to repress and obscure the class dimension, it did have a "rational core" in the very experience of the working-class young in the period; the specificity of the institutions in which post-war changes were encountered, and above all, in the way this sphere was reshaped by changes in the leisure market. It may also have been located in other, material experiences of the youth of the class in this period. A "generational consciousness" is likely to be strong among those sectors of youth which are upwardly and outwardly mobile from the working class—e.g., Hoggart's "scholarship boy." Occupational and educational change in this period led to an increase in these paths of limited mobility. The upward path, through education, leads to a special focusing on the *school and the education system* as the main mechanism of advancement: it is this which "makes the difference" between parents who stay where they were and children who move on and up. It involves the young person valuing the dominant culture positively and sacrificing the parent culture—even where this is accompanied by a distinct sense of cultural disorientation. His experience and self-identity will be based around mobility—something specific to his generation—rather than to the overdetermining power of class. One of the things which supports this taking over of a "generational consciousness" by the scholarship boy is, precisely, his cultural isolation—the fact that his career is different from the majority of his peers. The peer group is, of course, one of the real and continuing bases for collective identities organised around the focus of "generation." But a sense of generational distinctness may also flow from an individual's isolation from the typical involvement in kinds of peer-group activities which, though specific to youth, are clearly understood as forming a sort of cultural apprenticeship to the parent class culture. This kind of isolation may be the result of biographical factors, e.g., inability to enter the local football game where football is the primary activity of the peer group; or being a member of a relatively closed and tight family situation. A young person who, for whatever reasons, fails to go through this class-culture apprenticeship, may be more vulnerable to the vicarious peer-group experience provided by the highly visible and widely accessible commercially provided youth culture, where the audience as a whole substitutes for the real peer group as one, vast, symbolic "peer group": "our generation."

"Generational consciousness" thus has roots in the real experience of working-class youth as a whole. But it took a peculiarly intense form in the post-war subcultures which were sharply demarcated—amongst other factors—by age and generation. Youth felt and experienced itself as "different," especially when this difference was inscribed in activities and interests to which "age," principally, provided the passport. This does not necessarily mean that a "sense of class" was thereby obliterated. Skinheads, for example, are clearly both "generationally" and "class" conscious. As Phil Cohen suggested, "Subculture is . . . a compromise solution, between two contradictory needs: the need to create and express *autonomy and difference* from parents . . . and the need to maintain . . . the *parental identifications* which support them."[21]

[. . .]

Rise of the Counter Cultures

Up to this point, we have dealt exclusively with working-class youth subcultures. And there are some problems in deciding whether we can speak of *middle-class* subcultures in the same way and within the same sort of theoretical framework. Yet, not only has the period since the war witnessed the rise of quite distinctive kinds of "expressive movements" among middle-class youth, different from the school or "student" cultures of the prewar period, but, as we get closer to the 1970s, these have attracted, if anything, *more* public attention—and reaction—than their working-class counterparts. We point, of course, not simply to the growing involvement of middle-class youth with the commercialised popular culture and leisure associated with youth culture, but the appearance of quite distinct subcultural currents: the Hippie movement; the various "deviant" drug, drop-out and gay subcultures; the elements of cultural revolt in the student protest movements, etc. Most significant is the widespread cultural disaffiliation of broad sectors of middle-class youth—the phenomenon of the counter culture. This has, in turn, been linked with the general radicalisation and politicisation (and depoliticisation) of some middle-class youth strata.

We must note some clear structural differences in the response of the youth of the different classes. Working-class subcultures are clearly articulated, collective structures, often "near-" or "quasi-" gangs. Middle-class counter cultures are diffuse, less group-centred, more individualised. The latter precipitate, typically, not tight subcultures but a diffuse counter cultural *milieu*. Working-class subcultures reproduce a clear dichotomy between those aspects of group life still fully under the constraint of dominant or parent institutions (family, home, school, work), and those focused on non-work hours—leisure, peer-group association. Middle-class counter cultural *milieux* merge and blur the distinctions between "necessary" and "free" time and activities. Indeed, the latter are distinguished precisely by their attempt to explore "alternative institutions" to the central institutions of the dominant culture: new patterns of living, of family life, of work or even "un-careers." Middle-class youth remain longer than their working-class peers "in the transitional stage." Typically, working-class youth appropriate the existing environment, they construct distinct leisure time activities around the given working-class environment—street, neighbourhood, football ground, seaside town, dance hall, cinema, bomb site, pub, disco. Middle-class youth tend to construct enclaves within the interstices of the dominant culture. Where the former represent an appropriation of the "ghetto," the latter often make an exodus to the "ghetto." During the high point of the counter culture, in the 1960s, the middle-class counter cultures formed a whole embryo "alternative society," providing the counter culture with an underground, institutional base. Here, the youth of each class reproduces the position of the parent classes to which they belong. Middle-class culture affords the space and opportunity for sections of it to "drop out" of circulation. Working-class youth is persistently and consistently structured by the dominating alternative rhythm of Saturday Night and Monday Morning.

The objective oppositional content of working-class subcultures expresses itself socially. It is therefore often assimilated by the control culture to traditional forms of working-class "delinquency," defined as hooliganism or vandalism. The counter cultures take a more overtly ideological or political form. They make articulate their opposition to dominant values and institutions—even when, as has frequently occurred, this does not take the form of an *overtly* political response. Even when working-class subcultures are aggressively class conscious, this dimension tends to be repressed by the control culture, which treats them as "typical delinquents." Even when the middle-class counter cultures are explicitly anti-political, their objective tendency is treated as, potentially, political.

Middle-class counter cultures are a feature of the mid-1960s and after, rather than of the 1950s. Only a handful of the more intellectual youth was involved in the English counterpart to the "Beat Movement." The post-Beat, "on-the-road" style was prevalent in and around CND and the peace-movement in the late 1950s—the beatnik/peacenik period, associated with the folk revival and the music of Bob Dylan. The Hippies of the later 1960s were the most distinctive of the middle-class subcultures. Their cultural influence on this sector of youth was immense, and many counter cultural values must still be traced back to their Hippie roots. Hippies helped a whole quasi-bohemian subcultural *milieu* to come into existence, shaped styles, dress, attitudes, music and so on. The alternative institutions of the Underground emerged, basically, from this matrix. But Hippie culture quickly fragmented into different strands—heads, freaks, street people, etc. It fed both the "drop-out" and the drug subcultures of the period. It permeated student and ex-student culture. It was then crosscut by influences stemming from the more political elements among middle-class youth—the student protest movement, radical social work, community action groups, the growth of the left sects and so on. All these tendencies came to a partial fusion in the period between 1967 and 1970—the high point of the counter culture. This formation, too, has fragmented in several directions. The two most distinctive strands flow, one way, via drugs, mysticism, the "revolution in lifestyle" into a Utopian alternative culture; or, the other way, via community action, protest action and libertarian goals, into a more activist politics. What we have here, in short, is a host of variant strands, connections and divergencies within a broadly defined counter cultural *milieu*, rather than (with the exception of the drug and sexual subcultures) a sequence of tightly defined, middle-class subcultures.

Both working-class subcultures and middle-class counter cultures are seen, by moral guardians and the control culture, as marking a "crisis in authority." The "delinquency" of the one and the "disaffiliation" of the other index a weakening of the bonds of social attachment and of the formative institutions which manage how the former "mature" into hard-working, law-abiding, respectable working-class citizens, or the latter into sober, career-minded, "possessively individual" bourgeois citizens. This is a break in, if not a breakdown of, the reproduction of cultural class relations and identities, as well as a loss of deference to "betters and elders." The difference is that where the first was a weakening of control over the youth of a subordinate class, the second was a crisis among the youth of the dominant class. As Gramsci remarked, when a "crisis of authority" is spoken of, "this is precisely the crisis of hegemony or general crisis of the state."

[...]

NOTES

This essay first appeared in "Resistance through Rituals: Youth Subcultures in Post-war Britain," *Working Papers in Cultural Studies* 7–8 (Birmingham: Centre for Contemporary Cultural Studies, University of Birmingham, 1975), 9–74.
1 A. C. Smith, T. Blackwell, and E. Immirzi, *Paper Voices* (London: Chatto and Windus, 1975).
2 Antonio Gramsci, *Selections from the Prison Notebooks* (London: Lawrence and Wishart, 1971), 177.

3. E. P. Thompson, "The Long Revolution," *New Left Review*, I/9–10 (1961).
4. Karl Marx and Frederick Engels, *The German Ideology* (London: Lawrence and Wishart, 1970), 42.
5. See Jean-Paul Sartre, *The Problem of Method* (London: Methuen, 1963).
6. Karl Marx, *The Eighteenth Brumaire of Louis Bonaparte*, in *Marx and Engels Selected Works*, vol. 1 (London: Lawrence and Wishart, 1951), 225.
7. Marx and Engels, *The German Ideology*, 64.
8. E. P. Thompson, "The Peculiarities of the English," in *Socialist Register*, ed. Ralph Miliband and John Saville (London: Merlin, 1965).
9. Graham Murdock and Robin McCron, "Consciousness of Class and Consciousness of Generation," in "Resistance through Rituals," *Working Papers in Cultural Studies*, nos. 7–8 (Birmingham: Centre for Contemporary Cultural Studies, University of Birmingham, 1975).
10. Geoffrey Pearson, *The Deviant Imagination* (London: Macmillan, 1975); Dick Hebdige, "Aspects of Style in the Deviant Sub-cultures of the 1960s," CCCS Stencilled Papers Nos. 20, 21, 24, and 25 (1974).
11. Steven Lukes, *Power: A Radical View* (London: Macmillan, 1974), 23–24.
12. Louis Althusser, "Ideology and Ideological State Apparatuses," in *Lenin and Philosophy and Other Essays* (London: New Left Books, 1971); Nicos Poulantzas, *Political Power and Social Classes* (London: New Left Books, 1973).
13. Althusser, "Ideology and Ideological State Apparatuses."
14. Gramsci, *Prison Notebooks*, 328.
15. Gramsci, *Prison Notebooks*, 80.
16. Gramsci, *Prison Notebooks*, 164, our italics.
17. Peter Bachrach and Morton S. Baratz, "The Two Faces of Power," *American Political Science Review* 56, no. 4 (1962).
18. Louis Althusser, *For Marx* (London: Allen Lane, 1969), 233–34.
19. Howard Parker, *View from the Boys* (Newton Abbott, UK: David and Charles, 1974), has commented on the role of street football as a way in which younger kids "learn" a distinctive kind of class sociability.
20. Karl Marx, *Economic and Philosophic Manuscripts of 1844* (London: Lawrence and Wishart, 1964), 110–11.
21. Phil Cohen, "Sub-cultural Conflict and Working-class Community," *Working Papers in Cultural Studies*, no. 2 (Birmingham: Centre for Contemporary Cultural Studies, University of Birmingham, 1972), 26.

CHAPTER 6

Black Crime, Black Proletariat

with Chas Critcher, Tony Jefferson, John Clarke, and Brian Roberts

We must depart, at this point, from the immediate logic driving certain sections of black youth into "the mugging solution." To assess the viability of "crime" as a political strategy, we must re-examine the criminalised part of the black labour force in relation to the black working class as a whole, and the relations which govern and determine its position—above all, in terms of its fundamental position in the present stage of the capitalist mode of production, the social division of labour and its role in the appropriation and realisation of surplus labour. We must include these structural relations in our assessment of the relation of crime to political struggle in the present conjuncture.

In recent years social historians have given increasing attention to forms of social rebellion and political insurgency adopted by classes other than that of the classical proletariat of the developed industrial capitalist societies of Western Europe. This is the result, in part, of the long political containment of the working class in such societies, coupled with the fact of major historical transformations elsewhere which have been spearheaded by classes other than the proletariat—the role of the peasantry in the Chinese Revolution being only the most significant example. In addition, then, to the study of the present revolutions and questions of strategy arising from those societies (for example, Latin America) which contain both substantial peasant and developing industrial working-class sectors, there have also been studies of other forms of social rebellion—pre-industrial riot and rebellion, the city mobs, rural unrest, social banditry, etc. Despite this, the orthodox view seems to prevail that, where developed industrial societies are concerned, the "rebellions" of the poor and the lumpen classes, or the forms of quasi-political resistance inscribed in the activities of the criminal elements and "dangerous classes," cannot be of much long-term interest to those concerned with fundamental social movements. Eric Hobsbawm, who has himself made a major contribution to the studies referred to above (with his books on primitive rebels, insurrections amongst the landless proletariat and social banditry),[1] has stated the limits in admirably clear terms. Criminal underworlds, he argues, "are anti-social insofar as they deliberately set their values against the prevailing ones." But

> the underworld (as distinct from say, peasant bandits) rarely take part in wider social and revolutionary moments, at least in Western Europe.... There are obvious overlaps, especially in certain environments (slum quarters of big cities, concentrations of semi-proletarian poor, ghettoes of "outside" minorities, *etc.*) and non-social criminals may be a substitute for social protest or be idealised as such a substitute, but on the whole this type of criminality has only marginal interest for the historian of social and labour movements.[2]

This is because, in advanced industrial capitalist societies, the fundamental revolutionary class is the proletariat, which has not only been formed in and by capital, but whose struggle against capital is organised—made collective and "methodical"—because it is a class schooled by the discipline of the wage and by the conditions and relations of social labour. There is a phased or staged history of class conflict present here which makes the struggles of organised labour the historical agency with the most advanced form of struggle at the present stage of the development of capitalism:

> As a conscious social movement and especially as a labour movement develops, the role of "criminal" forms of social protest diminishes; except, of course, insofar as they involve "political crime." ... For the historian of labour movements, the study of "social criminality" is important during the prehistoric and formative periods of the movements of the labouring poor, in pre-industrial countries, and possibly during periods of great social effervescence, but otherwise he will only be very marginally concerned with it.[3]

Elsewhere, Hobsbawm has argued:

The underworld (as its name implies) is an anti-society, which exists by reversing the values of the "straight" world—it is, in its own phrase, "bent"—but it is otherwise parasitic on it. A revolutionary world is also a "straight" world.... The underworld enters the history of revolutions only insofar as the *classes dangereuses* are mixed up with the *classes labourieuses*, mainly in certain quarters of the city, and because rebels and insurgents are often treated by the authorities as criminals and outlaws; but in principles the distinction is clear.[4]

This argument poses questions of far-reaching importance.

Hobsbawm and others are pointing to the conditions which might seem to make the movements of the "criminal poor" what Gramsci called "conjunctural" rather than "organic." This entails three propositions. The criminal classes cannot play a fundamental role in such social movements, first, because their position is marginal to the productive life and relations of social formations of this kind; second, because historically, they have become marginal to the proletariat which has replaced them at the centre of the theatre of political struggle; third, because the form of consciousness traditionally developed by this stratum is not adequate to that required by a class which aims to supplant one mode of production by another. Thus, though the life and values of the "dangerous classes" represent an inversion of the bourgeois world, they remain ultimately enclosed by it—confined by it and thus in the end parasitic upon it. The effect of this orthodox interpretation on the development of a "Marxist theory of crime" has been noted. Alvin Gouldner, for example, once commented:

> Viewing criminals and deviants as *lumpenproletariat* that would play no decisive role in the class struggle, and indeed, as susceptible to use by reactionary forces, Marxists were not usually motivated to develop a systematic theory of crime and deviance. In short, being neither proletarian nor bourgeois, and standing off to the periphery of the central political struggle, criminals and deviants were at the best butlers and maids, the spear carriers, the colourful actors perhaps, but nameless, and worst of all, lacking in a historical "mission." They could be, indeed, *had* to be, ignored by those devoted to the study of the more "important" issues—power, political struggle and class conflict.[5]

Some Marxist writers would indeed argue that the very concepts required to "think" the problems of crime and deviance are foreign to Marx's conceptual field—to the problematic of historical materialism as a theory. Paul Hirst argues, on this basis, that there *cannot* by definition be a "Marxist theory of crime."[6] In his mature work, Hirst argues—the work, essentially, of *Capital*—Marx adopts a viewpoint on crime which breaks with moral critique and bases himself instead on the scientific propositions of a fully materialist viewpoint. Within this framework, crime (theft) is merely redistributive; unlike prostitution, gambling or racketeering, it is a form of "unproductive" rather than "productive" labour, and though it may be "illegal" with respect to the norms which govern normal capitalist relations, it is most often "capitalistic" in form (e.g., organised criminal enterprises)—i.e., adapted to the system on which it is parasitic. This analysis of the "marginal" position of crime may be extended by looking at the role and nature Marx ascribes to the "criminal classes." The centrality of the proletariat to any transformation of the capitalist mode of production lies in its role in production, as the source of surplus value. This position is ascribed to the proletariat by the mode of production. It is this *position*—rather than that process of coming to consciousness as a collective historical agent, of which Marx spoke in *The Poverty of Philosophy*[7] and elsewhere in the earlier works—which defines productive labour as the only class capable of carrying through the struggle to transform the capitalist mode into socialism. Now the proletariat and the bourgeoisie are, in this schema, the fundamental political forces. Other classes exist as a result of the combination within any social formation of more than one mode of production; but they cannot be the decisive forces in the political class struggle. Marx does suggest that, at certain moments of struggle, the proletariat will seek alliances with other subordinate classes; and these allies may include the petty bourgeoisie, the *lumpenproletariat* of the cities, the small peasants or agricultural labourers. But, Hirst concludes, Marx believed the *lumpenproletariat* to be unreliable class allies. Since, through theft, extortion, begging, prostitution and gambling, the *lumpenproletariat* tends to live parasitically off the working class, "their interests are diametrically opposed to those of the workers." Further, because of their precarious economic position, they are bribable by "the reactionary elements of the ruling classes and the state." Thus, the argument runs, individual acts of crime are the volitionless acts of victims of capitalism, "not in effect forms of political rebellion against the existing order but a more or less reactionary accommodation to them."[8] Even the more obviously "political" crimes, like the machine-breaking of the Luddites, represent immediate, spontaneous but ultimately inadequate forms of struggle since they are directed "not against the bourgeois conditions of production but against the conditions of production themselves." As the basis for a revolutionary struggle, such acts are useless; the only task is to "transform such forms and ideologies of struggle."[9]

How historically specific was Marx's analysis of the composition and nature of the *lumpenproletariat*? He and Engels seem clearly to have had the "dangerous classes" of mid-Victorian England and of Paris in mind as they wrote. One of the key passages is their analysis of their role in the crisis of 1851 which Marx offered in *The Eighteenth Brumaire*. The *lumpenproletariat* appears in that graphic passage as the criminal detritus of *all* classes—the *déclassés* at the bottom of the human pile:

> Alongside decayed *roués* with dubious means of subsistence and of dubious origins, alongside ruined and adventurous off-shoots of the bourgeoisie, were vagabonds, discharged soldiers, discharged jailbirds, escaped galley slaves, swindlers, mountebanks, *lazzaroni*, pickpockets, tricksters, gamblers, *maquereaus*, brothel-keepers, porters, *literati*, organ-grinders, ragpickers, knife grinders, tinkers, beggars—in short, the whole indefinite, disintegrated mass thrown hither and thither, which the French term *la bohème*.[10]

The list will be familiar from the pages of Engels's *Condition of the Working Class in England*,[11] or from Mayhew's account of life in East London.[12] It is open to question whether a class stratum with this precise social composition could so easily be identified under the conditions of monopoly capitalism. This is not simply a way of saying that Marx's historical and political predictions are out of date. The old petty bourgeoisie, about which Marx and Engels were occasionally more optimistic as allies of the proletariat, still survives, though greatly reduced in number. When they do appear on the political stage, they tend to play the reactionary role which Marx believed predictable from their positions—for example, in the various types of Poujadism in France, and in the rise of fascism in Germany in 1930s. But alongside this, stemming from the fundamental reorganisation of capitalist production consequent on the shift to monopoly forms, new strata have arisen—what is sometimes designated as the "new petty bourgeoisie." Its economic identification, and its political and ideological character, present real and complex problems for contemporary Marxist theory. Such internal shifts in the strata and composition of the classes is perfectly in line with Marx's mature reflections. He was about to plunge into its complexity where the manuscript of *Capital* breaks off. The question, then, of who and what corresponds to the *lumpenproletariat* in contemporary capitalist social formations is not an idle speculation. And the further question of whether all those involved in crime as a way of life belong, analytically, to the category of the "lumpen" is a matter requiring serious theoretical and definitional work, not a problem of simple empirical observation.

The relationship between classes constituted in the economic relations of capitalist production and the forms in which they appear as political forces in the theatre of political class struggle is no simple matter either, especially when considered from the standpoint of Marx's more mature theory. But the later work—the analysis of the economic forms and relations of capital accumulation conducted in *Capital*—differs from some of Marx's earlier writings, especially in the position of the working class with respect to the "laws of motion" of capitalist production. Whereas, earlier, Marx had tended to see the proletariat as the "oppressed" class in a political struggle with the oppressors, *Capital* thoroughly reconstitutes his argument on the terrain of capitalist production itself and the circuit of its self-expansion. It is in the exploitation of the labourer within production, the identification of labour-power as the "commodity" on which the whole process rests, which finds in surplus labour the source of surplus value which is realised as "capital": this provides the basis of Marx's "immense theoretical revolution" in *Capital*. Capital had at its disposal many ways of exploiting labour-power and extracting the surplus, first, by lengthening the working day, then by intensifying the exploitation of labour-power through augmenting the productive power of advanced machinery, in the form of constant capital, to which the labourer is increasingly directly subsumed. But, in whatever form, capital could not exist for a day without production; and production was not possible without the exploitation of productive labour in the class-structured relations of capitalist production. Marx then lodged the fundamental mechanism of capitalist societies in the contradictions which arose in this fundamental relation—that between the "forces" and "relations" of production. Many other forms were necessary, outside of the sphere of production proper, to ensure the "circuit of capital"—the relations of market, exchange and circulation; the spheres of the family, where, through wages, labour-power was renewed; the state which superintended the society in which this mode of production was installed; and so on. Ultimately, the whole circuit of capitalist production depended on these other unrelated spheres—what have come to be called the "spheres of reproduction"—and on the various classes and class strata exploited by them. But production relations dominated the whole complex circuit "in the last instance"; and other forms of exploitation, other social relations, had to be thought, ultimately, in terms of the essential contradictions of the productive level. Marx makes the point in several places in *Capital*:

> The specific economic form, in which unpaid surplus labour is pumped out of direct producers, determines the relationship of rulers and ruled, as it grows directly out of production itself and, in turn, reacts upon it as a determining element.... It is always the direct relationship of the owners of the conditions of production to the direct producers—a relation always naturally corresponding to a definite stage in the development of methods of labour and thereby its social productivity—which reveals the innermost secret, the hidden basis of the entire social structure, and with it the political form of the relation of sovereignty and dependence, in short, the corresponding specific form of the state. This does not prevent the same economic base—the same from the standpoint of its main conditions—due to innumerable different empirical circumstances, natural environment, racial relations, external historical influences, *etc.*, from showing infinite gradations and variations in appearance.[13]

From this perspective, it follows that, even if we depart from the strict implications of the earlier discussion of crime and the *lumpenproletariat* outlined above, a political struggle arising from a sector of a class living through crime cannot be, analytically, so central to the contradictions stemming from its relations of production; at the simplest level of analysis, it is simply not strategically placed with respect to capital's "laws of motion." This, however, omits the question of what the role of the criminalised part of a class is, structurally, *to the waged*, to the productive sectors of that class. And this returns us to the question of what the relation is between the "waged" and the "wage-less" sector of the black labour force in relation to capital in its present form. Marx had something critical to say about this in *Capital*, in terms of the relation of what he called the "reserve army of labour"—the different strata of the unemployed—to the fundamental rhythms of capital accumulation, and we will turn to this in a moment.

First, however, we must enter a brief caveat against treating Marx's theory of capital as, essentially, what has been called a form of *productivist* theory—as if nothing mattered, for capital, but that sector of the labouring masses involved *directly* in "productive labour." Marx did, following but differing in his definition from the classical political economists, use the distinction between "productive" and "unproductive" labour. Productive labour was that sector directly involved in the production of surplus value, exchanging directly against capital. Many other sectors of the work-force, though equally exploited by capital, did *not* directly produce surplus value, and exchanged not against capital, but against revenue: "Labour in the process of pure circulation does not produce use-values and therefore cannot add value or surplus-value. Alongside this group of unproductive labourers are all workers supported directly out of revenue, whether retainers or state employees."[14]

The theory of productive and unproductive labour is one of the most complex and contested areas of Marxist theory, and its ramifications do not directly concern us here. In the capitalism which Marx knew, "unproductive labour" was relatively underdeveloped, and often confined either to idlers, parasites on the labour of others, or to marginal producers. The same cannot be said of modern forms of capitalism, where the service and "unproductive" sectors of the work-force have been enormously expanded, performing what are clearly *key* functions for capital, and where the largest proportion of workers exchange against revenue (state employees, for example) and the proportion involved in the direct production of surplus value appears to be growing smaller. In these circumstances, the line—apparently relatively simple for Marx—between "productive" and "unproductive" labour has become increasingly difficult to draw with any clear result. The distinction may, nevertheless, be important for identifying the position and identity of the many new layers and strata in the modern working class. However, it seems clear that the argument has also been bedevilled by a clear misunderstanding of the distinction, even as Marx made it. "Unproductive" labour has sometimes been interpreted exclusively in Marx's pejorative and more frivolous sense—as economically and politically insignificant. This was clearly not his meaning, as a reading of Volume II of *Capital*, where Marx deals at length with circulation and reproduction, soon reveals. The whole argument in *Capital* demonstrates how vital and necessary to the realisation of capital, and to its expansion and reproduction, are those relations which are not directly tied to the surplus-value-producing sphere of capital. Capital could not, literally, complete its passage or circuit without "passing through" these related spheres. Further, he stated directly that it is not only the sector of the class which directly produces surplus value which is *exploited* by capital; many other class sectors are exploited by capital, even if the form of that exploitation is not the direct extraction of surplus value. Thus, even if we need to retain the terms "productive" and "unproductive" for purposes of analysis, relating to the identification of different strata of the working class, there is no warrant in Marx for treating the classes and strata exploited outside production proper as unnecessary or "superfluous" classes, beyond capital's contradictory dialectic:

> The aim of Marx in developing the concepts of productive and unproductive labour was not to divide the workers. Exactly the opposite.... With the aid of these concepts it proved possible for Marx to analyse how value is expanded in the direct process of production and how it is circulated in the reproduction process.[15]

The point is seminal for, and can be nicely illustrated from, the recent debate within Marxism and the feminist movement about the position of female domestic labour with respect to capital. In an early contribution to this debate, Wally Seccombe argued that "housework" must be judged, from a Marxist perspective, "unproductive," and seemed to imply that, for that reason, no decisive political struggle, capable of striking back against capital, could be organised from that base.[16] (Similarly, it could, by analogy, be argued that no fundamental political struggle which could affect capital could be mounted from a base constituted by black wage-less, black hustlers involved in the essentially redistributive activities of "crime," and black men and women largely confined to the service and "unproductive" sectors.) Many aspects of Seccombe's argument were challenged in the course of a lengthy and important theoretical debate.[17] In a subsequent contribution, Seccombe has clarified his position.[18] Housework may be strictly speaking "unproductive," but "the working-class housewife contributes to the production of a commodity—labour power... and through this process participates in social production."[19] Indeed, the reproduction of labour-power, through the family and the sexual division of labour, is, in Marx's strict terms, one of the fundamental conditions of existence of the capitalist mode of production, to which capital devotes a part of what it has extracted from the labourer—variable capital—and "advances" to him and his family, in the form of wages, so that this "reproduction" can be effected. Domestic labour may be "unproductive," but it produces value, Seccombe agrees. It is exploited by capital—indeed, doubly exploited, through the sexual division of labour; and is fundamental to the laws of motion of capital. It is through the sexual division of labour that capital is able to seize "not only the economic but every other sphere of society.... Value regulates labour conducted beyond the direct auspices of capital."[20]

Although not directly linked with our main argument, this digression on domestic labour has some significant pay-offs for our consideration.

The housewife appears to "do nothing" productively; she *labours* but does not appear to *work*. Her sphere—the home—is thus perceived as lying at, apparently, the opposite end of the spectrum to capital's productive heart: spare, marginal, useless. Yet, by her contribution to the reproduction of labour-power, and by her role as the agent of the family's consumption, the housewife sustains a necessary and pivotal relation to capitalist production. What is important is that this is hived off, segmented, segregated and compartmentalised from the production process proper. And what simultaneously connects and obscures this relation is the intermediation of the *sexual* division of labour as a structure within the *social* division of labour. *In this specific form*, capital extends, without appearing to do so, "its auspices." And, when women are drawn into work outside the home, they substantially appear in work which is not only at the unskilled, un-unionised and "unproductive" end of the occupational spectrum, but in kinds of work which are often similar in nature to, and are experienced like, "housework" or "women's work"—only done outside the home (service trades, textiles, catering, etc.). Harry Braverman argues that in the US economy women have become "the prime supplementary reservoir of labour," a movement essentially "to the poorly paid, menial and 'supplementary' occupations."[21] Seccombe points out that one of the crucial ways in which capital extends its sway over domestic labour is in regulating what proportion of it will be drawn into or thrown back out of "productive work." "It [capital] structures the relation of the working population to the industrial reserve army of which housewives are a latent and often active component."[22] Without attempting to draw the parallels too tightly, we may then point to the following: (1) the struggles of both women and blacks present acute problems of strategy in aligning *sectoral* struggle with a more general class struggle; (2) this may have something to do with the fact that both occupy a structurally segmentary position, or are related to capitalist exploitation through a "double structure"— the *sexual* division within class relations in the first case, the *racial* division within class relations in the second; (3) the key to unravelling the relation of both is not the question of whether each directly receives a wage or not, since a proportion of each is, at any time, in employment—i.e., "waged"— while the rest are "wage-less"; (4) the key lies in the reference to capital's control over the movement into and out of the *reserve army of labour*.

In the debate with Seccombe, the strongest case in favour of regarding housework as "productive" was advanced by Selma James and Mariarosa Dalla Costa, in *The Power of Women and the Subversion of the Community*.[23]

"Wages for housework" was, for them, a strategy of feminist mobilisation, with subversive potential, directly against capital. In Selma James's *Sex, Race and Class* this analysis is extended to black struggles.[24] The introduction to the earlier pamphlet put the nub of the argument clearly, highlighting the strategic value of the refusal to work:

> The family under capitalism is a centre ... essentially of *social production*. When previously so-called Marxists said that the capitalist family did not produce for capitalism, was not a part of social production, it followed that they repudiated women's potential *social power*. Or rather, presuming that women in the home could not have social power, they could not see that women in the home produced. If your production is vital for capitalism, refusing to produce, refusing to *work*, is a fundamental lever of social power.[25]

In *Sex, Race and Class*, Selma James also extended the argument into a novel interpretation of how the struggles undertaken by such groups as women and blacks relate to class struggle as a whole. It is based essentially on a reworking of the notions of *caste* and *class*. "Manufacture," Marx argued in *Capital*, "develops a hierarchy of labour powers, to which there corresponds a scale of wages."[26] The international division of labour, argues Selma James, leads to an accentuation in the "hierarchy of labour powers," which splits the working class along racial, sexual, national and generational lines, and confines each sector of the class to its position within this "caste," at the expense of its position in the class as a whole. "The individual labourers," Marx added, "are appropriated and annexed for life by a limited function.... The various operations of the hierarchy are parcelled out among the labourers according to both their natural and their acquired capabilities."[27] (Marx, of course, was writing here of an early phase of capitalist development. "Modern industry," he argued, involved a *different* division of labour. Selma James does not defend her extension of the "hierarchy of labour-powers" concept to this later phase of capitalist development.) This segmentation of the classes—hierarchy of labour-powers—represents a weakness in the face of capital. But at present, it is argued, no alternative "general" class strategy is possible. (The argument at this point closely follows that of C. L. R. James, perhaps the most seminal and influential Caribbean Marxist to date, in his insistence that no vanguard party of the Leninist mould can claim to "speak for" a class so internally divided.) The accent of struggle thus (in line with James's own stresses) falls on the autonomous self-activity of each sector of the class. *Each sector* must make its "autonomous power" felt first; and, by using "the specificity of its experience . . . redefine class and the class struggle itself. . . . In our view, identity—caste—is the very substance of class."[28] Only through autonomous struggle in each sector will the "power of the class" as a whole come to be felt. This line of argument, theoretically developed in *Race Today*,[29] has become the most powerful political tendency within active black groups in Britain. It is predicated on the autonomy and self-activity of black groups in struggle; and it identifies the most significant theme of this struggle as the growing "refusal to work" of the black unemployed. The high levels of youthful black unemployment are here reinterpreted as part of a conscious political "refusal to work." This refusal to work is crucial, since it strikes at capital. It means that this sector of the class refuses to enter competition with those already in productive work. Hence, it *refuses* the traditional role of the "reserve army of labour"—i.e., as an instrument which can be used to break or undermine the bargaining power of those still in work. Thus it "subverted Capital's plan for maximum surplus-value from the immigrant work force."[30] Police activity, which is principally directed against this "workless" stratum of the class, is defined as an attempt to bring the wage-less back into wage-labour. The "wage-less" are not to be equated with the traditional disorganised and undisciplined "*lumpenproletariat*." This false identification arises only because the black working class is understood exclusively in relation to British capital. But, in fact, black labour can only be adequately understood, historically, if it is also seen as a class which has already developed in the Caribbean—*vis-à-vis* "colonial" forms of capital—as a cohesive social force. In the colonial setting "wage-lessness" was one of its key strategies. It is not surprising that this wage-less sector has reconstructed in the metropolitan "colony" a supporting institutional network and culture. Finally, the entrance of young, second-generation blacks "into the class of unemployeds represents not only an increase in numbers but also a qualitative change in the composition of the class." This new generation now brings to the struggle through "wage-lessness" a new confidence and boldness.[31]

The position originally outlined in Selma James's *Sex, Race and Class* has been extended and developed in the Power of Women Collective's pamphlet, *All Work and No Pay*.[32] Here, the original argument about the "hierarchy of labour powers" is repeated, with an interesting and relevant addition. The wage-lessness of housework is now shown to be disguising its real character as capitalist commodity production; and the payment of the "family wage" to the male worker structures the dependency of the female labour force on the male. This is called the "patriarchy of the wage"—one product of which is sexism. On this analogy, the structurally differentiated position of black labour as a whole to the white working class may be similarly understood as a form of structured dependence, one product of which is racism—the "racism of the wage relation," to coin a phrase. (But see the penetrating critique by Barbara Taylor which questions whether an analysis of female and domestic labour can be so directly based on an assumed homogeneity or perfect homology between production and ideology, structure and superstructures.[33] This is also one of the main critiques of the *Race Today* position advanced by A. X. Cambridge and Cecil Gutzmore in *The Black Liberator*.)

It should be added that, though there is not as yet a fully theorised account of the present stage of metropolitan capitalist development in the *Race Today* position, some parts of their analysis of the position of blacks is quite close to that elaborated by a major current in contemporary Italian Marxist theory (what is sometimes called "the Italian school").[34] Very crudely, this tendency identifies the present phase of capitalist development as it was characterised by Marx in Volume III of *Capital* as "social capital." This involves the subsumption of "many capitals" into one capital, based on a vastly expanded reproduction process; the progressive abolition of capital as *private* property and the socialisation of the accumulation process; and the transformation of the whole of society into a sort of "social factory" for capital. In this phase, the state is progressively synonymous with social capital—its "thinking head"—and assumes the functions of integration, harmonisation, rationalisation and repression hitherto partly the responsibility of capital itself. This massive concentration of capital—on an international scale—is matched by the growing concentration (again, on an international scale) and massification of the proletariat. The higher the organic composition of capital, the greater the "proletarianisation" of the worker. The re-composition of capital along "social-capital" lines has been accomplished, principally, by three factors: the reorganisation of the labour process, through the application of "Fordist" techniques to production; the Keynesian revolution in economic management; and the "integration" of the organised institutions of the working class through social democracy and reformism. The re-composition of capital has therefore, in turn, "recomposed" the working class. The tendency, progressively, to deskill the working class and to subsume it into massified processes of production is tending to create the "mass worker." Although operating in advanced modes of production, the "mass worker" is not the old skilled worker of an earlier capitalism, but literally a worker who can be moved from one part of a fragmented and automated labour process to another, and from one country to another (the use of migrant labour in the more advanced capitalist countries of Europe is a key instance of this). This "productive" re-composition of the class also involves a political re-composition—the old reflexes and organisations of class struggle belonging to an earlier phase being dismantled, and class struggle tending to generate new forms of militant resistance directly against the exploitation of the new labour process, often directly at the "point of production." Hence, many of the forms of direct workers' resistance—of "organised spontaneity"—hitherto thought of as syndicalist in character, represent an advanced mode of struggle face to face with the new conditions of capitalist accumulation and production. This "mass worker" is a concrete embodiment of Marx's "abstract labourer." Without going into this argument further, it can be seen at once how this analysis can be extended to illuminate the specific position of black labour (and other migrant "labours") in the "advanced" sectors of modern British industry; but also how forms of "direct resistance"—like the refusal to work—can assume a quite different meaning and strategic position, as forms of class struggle, not of a marginal but of pivotal sections of the working class.

It is useful at this point to turn to the altogether different analysis of the position of black labour and the black wage-less advanced by the *Black Liberator* collective. Cambridge and Gutzmore are critical of the *Race Today* position, and the main arguments advanced against them are as follows. The refusal to work amongst black labour, and black youth especially, is a real phenomenon, but it represents an ideological not a political struggle. It does not "subvert capital" directly, since even if the whole working class, black and white, were employed, the rate of exploitation of labour by capital would not necessarily be intensified. Black workers are therefore conceived in more classical terms as a "reserve army of labour" (of a special, racially differentiated type). They are used, productively or unproductively, in relation to the needs and rhythms of capital. As such they constitute a black *sub-proletarian stratum* of the general working class. When productively employed, they are "super-exploited," in that a relatively higher level of surplus value is extracted from them. They are exploited and oppressed at two different levels: as black workers (super-exploitation) and as a racial minority (racism). The idea that the function of the police in relation to this sector is *directly* to regulate the conditions of class struggle and to tie the working class to wage-labour is undercut on the grounds (mentioned above) that it constitutes a false reduction of the level of the state (political) to the level of the economic. The position adopted here is directly and explicitly in line with Seccombe's argument on domestic labour,[35] and it shares *something* with the Hirst argument at least in seeing the "refusal to work" of this wage-less sector as, at best, a quasi-political rebellion, not as a fully formed class perspective.[36] There are critical differences of theoretical analysis between the two positions here, and both—necessarily—lead to very different political assessments of the correct strategy for the development of black political struggle. Whereas the *Race Today* position stresses the self-activating dynamic of a developing black struggle, with the black wage-less clearly providing this struggle with one of its key supports, Cambridge and Gutzmore, in *The Black Liberator*, while supporting the developing industrial and community struggles of blacks against exploitation and oppression, are obliged to define these as, inevitably at this point in time, "economist" or corporatist in form.[37] Both positions, however, agree in defining the various sectors of black labour as "super-exploited"; and both analyse blacks as constituting a racially distinct stratum of the class, different in character from the traditional notion of the *lumpenproletariat* as advanced, for example, by Paul Hirst.[38]

Marx, it will be recalled, called the lumpen "the social scum, the passively rotting mass thrown off by the lowest layers of the old society."[39] Engels characterised them thus:

> The lumpen proletariat, this scum of the depraved elements of all classes, which establishes its headquarters in the big cities, is the worst of all possible allies. This rabble is absolutely venal and absolutely brazen.... Every leader of the workers who uses these scoundrels as guards or relies on them for support proves himself by this action a traitor to the movement.[40]

This is a very different picture from that presented by Darcus Howe:

> And now I want to speak specifically of the unemployed. In the Caribbean it is not simply that you are unemployed and you drift in hunger and total demoralisation from day to day. That is absolutely untrue. I know how I first got the idea that people thought about that was from the White Left. When they talk about the unemployed, they talk about a miserable, downtrodden, beaten population that does not constitute itself as a section of the working class and in one way or another carry on struggles of their own, and so the unemployed I talk about in the Caribbean, that has not got a wage,

an official wage of any kind, no wealth, is a vibrant powerful section of the society. It has always been that. Culturally, steel band, Calypso, reggae come from that section of the population. What little there is of *National* culture in the Caribbean, came out of the vibrancy of that section of the population.[41]

This section of the class typically survives by "hustling"—which Howe describes as "eking out" a survival in a wage-less world, *not*, usually, by resorting to crime. The same sense of vibrancy emerges in the positive stress on avoiding the humiliation of work, and also, in the way the class can be *disciplined* by such activities:

> In my view the *minority* would be carrying on activities called criminal, in the sense of robbery and burglary and things like that. What normally happens in those days would be somehow your whole social personality develops skills by which you get portions of the wage. Either by using your physical strength as a gang leader, or your cunning—so that section of the working class is disciplined by that general term and form called "hustling." Ganja in Jamaica, anything like that—I do not think ganja is a crime in that sense. All different ways, you eke out, which does not involve, in my view, a kind of humiliation.[42]

Survival by these means produces a *political* awareness. Talking of the intervention of the Prime Minister of Trinidad and the Commissioner of Police to end one of the fiercest of local gang wars, and the need to do this by "winning over" the gangs, rather than by confrontation, Howe has this to say:

> They could not choose confrontation because by and large that section of the working class was the military arm of the Nationalist movement, of the African section of the Nationalist Movement. So that when the Indian had a tendency to attack the African political leaders with guns at meetings and things, we constituted the military arm of the African section. So that we always had to be courted. So the Prime Minister comes and negotiates with the gang leader and the police to terminate the war. At which point the class now begins to see itself as a section with formidable power, so we begin to raise the question of unemployment.[43]

The steady drift of youngsters with "O" levels into the ranks of the wage-less helped to transform the class; and this is, again, exemplified by the refusal of the Army (largely made up of the unemployed) to quell the mass demonstrations during the 1970 political crisis in Trinidad:

So that this section of the working class, although not disciplined, organised and unified by the very mechanism of capitalist production itself, were necessarily concentrated and socialised through hustling, in some kind of quasi-disciplinary way, to make an intervention in the society and break up the army, and leave the opening for the working class to come on the stage.[44]

This interpellated history of the Trinidadian wage-less has direct relevance, Howe maintains, for an understanding of the British situation, though he is aware of the dangers of suggesting such simple political parallels. Furthermore, he does not deny that this section of the class displays negative tendencies (that, for example, the criminal element supplies most of the police informers). But he insists that these tendencies exist in the class as a whole, and are not specific to the wage-less. This conception of the black wage-less is very different from that offered by the editors of *The Black Liberator*. For them, the *whole* of the black proletariat is best conceived of as a *sub-proletariat*: a stratum of the working class that is the object of two specific mechanisms—*super-exploitation* and *racial oppression*:

> The *interlacing* of these specific mechanisms operate such that they pervade the reproduction process of *surplus value extraction* where the *rate of exploitation*—i.e., super-exploitation—is high with the sub-proletariat; such that where unemployed, the Black Masses form a disproportionate section of the *reserve army of labour*; such that their class struggles combine forms, against *racial oppression* and *cultural-imperialism*, other than those specifically practised by the indigenous white working class.[45]

Although, as Cambridge goes on to say, "the mechanisms whereby surplus-value extraction is specified as peculiar to Black workers in the metropolitan economy is still to be worked out," the introduction of the notion of the *reserve army of labour* and of the black masses, where unemployed, forming a disproportionate section of this, marks a crucial departure from the "wage-less" argument of *Race Today*. Cambridge defines the reserve army this way:

> Along with the accumulation of capital, the life blood of *the capitalist mode of production* created by the surplus labour of the working class and vital for *expanded reproduction of the conditions of production* goes the reproduction not only of their means of exploitation (employment) but also of their own dispensability (unemployment). The reproduction of the *capitalist mode of production* depends on its constantly finding new markets and unproductive sectors of production must go. In this

connexion, capitalism has a two-fold need—on the one hand, for a mass of labour-power always ready for exploitation which allows for the possibility of throwing great masses of productive workers on the decisive point of production without upset to the scale of production, and on the other, to dispose of these workers when their exploitation is no longer profitable. Capitalist production depends, therefore, upon the constant transformation of a part of the labour force into an "*unemployed*" and "*under-employed*" disposable "industrial reserve army of labour." In the Imperialist dominated world economy, where unemployed, the *Black Masses* form a substantial section of this industrial reserve army of labour, increasingly unlikely to be used in production as the productivity of labour increases in the context of centralised capital.[46]

Some of the analytic difficulties now begin to emerge fully from the juxtaposition of these positions—all of them, it must be noted, posited within a Marxist framework. Marx and Engels clearly regard the *lumpenproletariat* and the "dangerous classes" as "scum"—the depraved element of all classes. Parasitic in their modes of economic existence, they are also outside the framework of productive labour which alone could hone and temper them into a cohesive class capable of revolutionary struggle at a point of insertion in the productive system which could limit and roll back the sway of capital. Darcus Howe regards this element, not as the dregs and deposit of all classes, but as an identifiable sector of the working class—that sector which, *both* in the West Indies and in Britain, has been consigned to a position of *wage-lessness* and which has developed, from such a base, an autonomous level of struggle capable, in economic and political terms, of inflicting, through the wage-less strategy, severe damage on capital and "subverting" its purposes. This is clearly not a description any longer of a *lumpenproletariat* in the classic Marxist sense. Cambridge and Gutzmore regard the whole of the black labour force as a *super-exploited stratum* of the proletariat. Its more-or-less permanent position, structurally, below the white working class makes it a *sub-proletariat*. Its exploitation is then "overdetermined" by racial exploitation and oppression. The wage-less part of this sub-proletariat does not have either the "lumpen" character ascribed by Marx and Engels, or the strategic political role predicted by *Race Today*. Classically, they are *that sector of the black sub-proletariat which at the present time capital cannot employ*. Thus they perform the classic function of a "reserve army of labour"—they can be used to undermine the position of the waged sectors, but their own wage-lessness, far from constituting a striking base on capital, is a token of their containment.

One of the main sources of the difference between these descriptions arises from the different historical periods and phases in the development of capitalism to which they refer. Marx and Engels were observing the transitional period from domestic to factory labour and the historic epoch of "classical" capitalist development. The decanting of rural populations into the centres of factory production, the development of the discipline of factory labour and the break-up of older systems of production created in their wake, at one end, the first industrial proletariat, at the other end, the casual poor and the destitute classes. In Hobsbawm and Rudé's studies,[47] the Wilkes, "King and Country" and city "mobs" and "crowds," which appear at the end of the eighteenth century, are the last occasion when the latter are seen—in combination with skilled artisans in declining trades and the petty-criminals—in a leading role on the political stage. After that, to be sure, this human detritus of the capitalist system—its massive casualty list—accumulates in the hovels and wens, often (as Hobsbawm argued) overlapping through their occupancy of certain slum areas of the cities with the "labouring classes," but already declining in historical importance. Both *Race Today* and *The Black Liberator* base their analyses on accounts of the *subsequent* phase of capitalism—that period of growing monopoly which, under the title of "imperialism," Lenin characterised as capitalism's "highest"—and hopefully its last—stage. The main outlines of Lenin's thesis are too well known to rehearse at length—the growing concentration of production; the replacement of competition by monopoly; the shift of power within the ruling fractions of capital from industrial to finance capital; the deepening of the crises of overproduction and underconsumption; leading to the sharpening competition for overseas markets and overseas outlets for profitable capital investment; and thus the period of "imperialist rivalries" and of world wars.[48] What is important for us is the impact which Lenin assumed this new phase in the development of capitalism would have on the *internal* structure and composition of the proletariat. He argued that the much higher profits obtainable through overseas investment and the exploitation of the hinterlands by a global capitalism would enable the ruling classes to bribe or buy off an "upper" stratum of the proletariat at home—incorporate it in the imperialist net and blunt its revolutionary edge. This would create *sharper* distinctions *within* the proletariat, between its "upper" and "lower" sectors. The term he coined for that stratum successfully bought off in this way was the "aristocracy of labour." Lenin also believed it would widen the gap between the British proletariat *as a whole* (upper and lower) and the "super-exploited" colonial proletariat at the other end of the imperialist chain. The concept of an "aristocracy of labour," as a way of accounting for the sectionalism and internal divisions of the proletariat, was not new. Hobsbawm notes that the phrase "seems to have been used from the middle of the nineteenth century at least to describe certain distinctive strata of the working class, better paid, better treated and generally regarded as more 'respectable' and politically moderate than the rest of the proletariat."[49] Lenin, in fact, had quoted with approval Engels's letter to Marx (7 October 1858), in which the former noted that "the English proletariat is actually becoming more and more bourgeois, so that the most bourgeois of all nations is apparently aiming ultimately at the possession of a bourgeois aristocracy and a bourgeois proletariat *alongside* the bourgeoisie. For a nation which exploits the whole world, this is of course to a certain extent justifiable."[50] Already contained within Engels's ironic exasperation is (i) the appearance of new internal stratifications within the metropolitan working class; and (ii) the germ of the idea that the proletariat of an imperialist power benefits economically (and so the ruling classes profit politically) from the super-exploitation of the colonial proletariat. Looked at from the underside, within the global framework of the capitalist system, the colonial proletariat which is excessively exploited so as to produce the super-profits with which to placate the proletariat at home is, structurally, *already* a *sub-proletariat* to the latter. It is hardly surprising, then, that when, at a later stage, sections of this colonial proletariat are attracted to work in the metropolis, they are inserted into the productive relations in a sectionally appropriate role—as an *internalised* sub-proletariat. The subordinate economic role which this black sub-class has always played, historically, to the white metropolitan working class is reproduced in the metropoles: in part, through ideological distinctions based on racism, the effects of which are to reproduce that subordination, ideologically, within the metropolitan economy, and to legitimate it as a "permanent"—or caste—division within the working class as a whole. But the picture is not complete until we look at those underside conditions in which, before emigration, the colonial proletariat was constituted. And here, of course, we find, as a constant and apparently *necessary condition* of its super-exploitation, the condition of "wage-lessness":

> One of the major features of the contemporary Third World is the explosive growth of urban populations composed of immigrants from the countryside and the smaller towns who are not established proletarians

either in terms of occupation—since they live in a chronic state of unemployment or underemployment—or of political culture, since they have not absorbed the lifestyle and mentality of established urban workers. Countries like India and China are indeed overwhelmingly peasant societies. But in Argentina, Chile, Venezuela and Uruguay, 40% and more of the population live in towns or cities with more than 200,000 inhabitants.... Every year thousands of new recruits flock to the favelas, barridas, bidonvilles, shanty-towns or whatever you like, in encampments made out of cardboard, flattened petrol tins and old packing cases. Whatever term we may use to describe this social category it is high time to abandon the highly insulting, inaccurate and analytically befogging Marxist term *lumpenproletariat* which is so commonly used. "Underclass" or "subproletariat" would seem much more apt characterisations of these victims of "urbanisation without industrialisation."[51]

Such an "underclass," as Peter Worsley describes in his important essay, may, in strict terms, be "unproductive," in that its members are not in regular productive employment. But in Third World societies, where shanty towns are a permanent and structural feature of life, they cannot be considered "marginal" in any other sense. They are large in number, and growing; their economic activities, however transient and precarious, are of crucial importance to the whole society; and their strength must be compared to what, in many cases, is a very small and sometimes non-existent urban proletariat in the classical sense. The Portuguese-African leader, Amilcar Cabral, who spoke of *two* categories within the "rootless"—"young folk come lately from the countryside," and "beggars, layabouts, prostitutes, *etc.*"—said, of the latter category, it "is easily identified and might easily be called our *lumpenproletariat*, if we had anything in Guinea we could properly call a proletariat."[52] And, so far as political role is concerned, it was, of course, just this group of urban dispossessed, in and out of work, chronically un- or under-employed, scraping a living by all means—straight, illegal, and in between—permanently on the border of survival, whom Fanon believed constituted "one of the most spontaneous and the most radically revolutionary forces of a colonised people."[53] They, with the peasantry, *were* the "wretched of the earth."

We have here two, apparently divergent ways of attempting to understand the nature and position of the black working class and of the types of political struggles and forms of political consciousness available to it. These divergent paths may be summed up in the following way. If we focus on *wage-lessness*, as a pertinent and growing condition for a greater and greater proportion of black labour, but limit our treatment of it to its British metropolitan context, then the wage-less appear as a sinking class fraction, expelled into poverty as superfluous to capital; then the temptation to assimilate it, analytically, to the classic *lumpenproletariat* of Marx and Engels's earlier descriptions is a strong one. *Race Today* breaks with this ascription, by redefining black labour in terms of two "histories." First, it is a sector of *Caribbean* labour, and, as such, central to the history of struggle and the peculiar conditions of the Caribbean working class from which it originates. Second, it tends to be inserted into metropolitan capitalist relations as the deskilled, super-exploited "mass worker." In redrawing the historical boundaries of black labour in this way, so to speak, the *Race Today* collective is able to redefine "wage-lessness"—in two different contexts—as a positive rather than as a passive form of struggle: as belonging to a majority rather than a "marginal" working-class experience, a position thoroughly *filled out* and amplified, culturally and ideologically, and therefore capable of providing the base of a viable class strategy. From this combination of Third, and "First" World perspectives, the black wage-less are very different indeed from the "passive and rotting scum" of the traditional lumpen. *The Black Liberator* is as concerned with Caribbean and "Third World" politics as is *Race Today*. But it analyses the position of black labour in Britain principally in relation to the present class relations of British capital, into which the migrant labour force has been directly subsumed; that is to say, not historically, in terms of the mechanisms of "colonial" capital in the past, but structurally, in terms of the mechanisms of British capital and in the present conjuncture. What matters is how black labour has been subsumed under the sway of capital in the metropolis—i.e., as a subproletariat—and how its relations to capital are governed—i.e., in terms, not of the cultural struggle expressed in strategy of "wage-lessness," but through the more classic mechanisms of the reserve army of labour.

Another way of examining the same terrain would be to distinguish more carefully between the determinacy over black labour of the level of the *economic*, and the *political and ideological* practices of struggle. We cannot push this argument too far at this point; but it is sufficient merely to sketch out the possibilities it entails.

What determines the size of the wage-less sector of the black working class at any point may be less the political strategy of a minority "not to take shit-work any longer," and more the fundamental economic rhythms which Marx analysed as structuring the size and character of the different strata of the "reserve army of labour." However, it is still possible for those so ascribed (economic class relations) to develop this into a more positive strategy of class struggle (political and ideological). The forms of *political* class struggle would then relate to previous modes of survival and resistance by that class, deriving, essentially, from its pre-metropolitan past. This latter position is not as constrained by a "history of origins" as it may at first appear. For there may be political factors *in the present* re-creating for black labour the possibilities of waging a political struggle of this kind from such a base. In the section which follows, we trace some of the factors which may have helped to determine the forms of political struggle face to face with metropolitan capital in the present conjuncture. On the other hand, this type of explanation remains open to the objection that it tends to be "historicist": it explains *present* forms of struggle in terms of traditions derived from the past. It is of critical importance at this point to remind ourselves of the economic mechanisms which do, indeed, appear to have the effect of fundamental determinate forces governing the size and position of the black wage-less today. This returns us to Marx's analysis of the "reserve army" of labour. For Marx, the industrial reserve army of labour (the "relative surplus population") becomes a permanent feature of capital accumulation only after the transition from manufacture to modern industry, when capital takes "real control." Modern industry requires "the constant formation, the greater or less absorption and the re-formation, of the industrial reserve army or surplus population." As capital advances into new areas of production, "there must be the possibility of throwing great masses of men suddenly on the decisive points without injury to the scale of production in other spheres."[54] Capitalism, thus, not only required a disposable reserve army, but attempted to govern its size and character—that is, the rate at which, in accordance with capital accumulation, sections were drawn into production or expelled into unemployment. Thus, for Marx, the question of the reserve army was centrally linked to the capitalist accumulation cycle. As the proportion of "dead" to "living" labour (machines to labourers) increased, so a section of the waged force was "set free" to be available elsewhere as and when capital required. The presence of the reserve army thus also helped to determine the conditions and wages of those in employment. When the reserve army was large, employed workers were obliged to accept lower wages since they could easily be replaced by their substitutes. The presence of a "permanent" reserve army therefore was considered to have a competitive effect on the employed, tending to lower the value of labour-power to capital. If the reserve army is small, workers are in a better position to demand higher wages. But the resulting fall in profits and capital accumulation leads to workers being thrown out of work and a consequent growth of the reserve army, and a fall or slower rise in wage levels.[55] In the different phases of this cycle, capital continually composes and recomposes the working class through its own dynamic movement: it generates a certain level of unemployment as a necessary feature of that movement, unless this tendency is counteracted in some other way. The "recomposition of the labour force" argument here is a critical one. For sections of the waged, thrown temporarily into the reserve army, may not necessarily be re-employed either in the same sectors of production, or at the same levels of skill. Both "deskilling" and substitution—replacing one sector of labour by a cheaper one—are therefore central aspects of the process of the formation and dissolution of the reserve army. This "then raises the question of the sources of labour which become part of the working class" when labour is being attracted into production from the reserve army, "while the tendency to repulsion raises the question of the destiny of the labourers, whether employed or unemployed (for example, the tendency towards the marginalisation of certain groups of workers)."[56]

Marx, in fact, distinguished several different layers or strata *within* the "reserve army": the *floating* strata were those repelled and drawn back into production in the heart of the productive sector; the *latent* strata were principally those in agricultural production displaced in the course of the capitalist advance into the rural economy; the *stagnant* were those "permanently" irregularly employed. All three were distinct from the *lumpenproletariat*—the "dangerous classes," and from *pauperism*—"the demoralised and ragged and those unable to work ... the victims of industry." Pauperism, he added, is the "hospital of the active labour-army and the dead weight of the industrial reserve army."[57] As we shall see, there is no intrinsic reason why these mechanisms should not operate at the marginal poles of capitalism as a global system—i.e., in the colonial hinterlands—as well as in the metropolis. Thus we must modify, now, the argument outlined a little earlier. The size and significance of the unemployed, the wage-less, the semi-employed and the "marginalised" sectors of the colonial proletariat may differ from that in the metropolitan society; but *vis-à-vis* colonial capital, too, its formation may well be governed by the kinds of rhythms outlined by Marx in this crucial argument in *Capital*.

The industrial reserve army of the unemployed is as fundamental to the laws of capitalist accumulation as the size of the productive "labour-army." But in the developed countries of Western Europe in the post-war period, it has proved increasingly difficult to sustain it in its classical form, at least until recently. As a result of a complex set of factors which cannot be rehearsed here—including the growing strength of the labour movement itself—capitalism, in order to survive, had to aim for continuous productive expansion and "full employment" for the native work force. This ran counter to the need for a "reserve army." A substitute "reserve army" was therefore needed: one neither costly nor politically unacceptable—as unemployment resulting from capitalism's cyclical movement then was. Modern capitalism has made use of two principal "reserve" sources: women and migrant labour. "The solution to these problems adopted by West European capitalism has been the employment of immigrant workers from under-developed areas of Southern Europe or from the Third World."[58] These had always played a part; but in post-war conditions they became a *permanent* feature of the economic structure of these societies (as, according to Braverman, Latin American and Oriental labour has become for the American post-war economy). Migrant workers now form *the permanent basis of the modern industrial reserve army*. In the period of productive expansion, labour was sucked into production from the Caribbean and Asian sub-continent. Gradually, as economic recession began to bite, a more restrictive practice was instituted—in effect, forcing a part of the "reserve army" to remain where it already was, in the Caribbean and Asian homelands. Now, in the depths of the economic crisis, we are in the alternate pole of the "reserve-army" cycle: the phase of control and expulsion. In the intervening period, both women and some southern European labour had already begun to "substitute" for the black reserve army. In the 1970s, the political assault on "full employment" has demolished the political barriers; and the reconstitution of the layers of the "reserve army" is proceeding full tilt. The black youths roaming the streets of British cities in search for work are its latest, and rawest, recruits.

[...]

NOTES

This essay first appeared in Stuart Hall, Chas Critcher, Tony Jefferson, John Clarke, and Brian Roberts, *Policing the Crisis: Mugging, the State, and Law and Order* (London: Macmillan, 1978), 362–81.

1 E. J. Hobsbawm, *Primitive Rebels* (Manchester: Manchester University Press, 1959); *Labouring Men* (London: Weidenfeld and Nicolson, 1964); *Bandits* (Harmondsworth, UK: Pelican, 1972).

2   Hobsbawm, "Conference Report," *Bulletin*, no. 25 (Autumn 1972).
3   Hobsbawm, "Conference Report."
4   Hobsbawm, *Bandits*, 98.
5   Alvin Gouldner, "Foreword," in Ian Taylor, Paul Walton, and Jock Young, *The New Criminology* (London: Routledge and Kegan Paul, 1973), xii.
6   Paul Q. Hirst, "Marx and Engels on Law, Crime and Morality," in *Critical Criminology*, ed. Ian Taylor, Paul Walton, and Jock Young (London: Routledge and Kegan Paul, 1975).
7   Karl Marx, *The Poverty of Philosophy*, in Karl Marx and Friedrich Engels, *Collected Works*, vol. 6 (London: Lawrence and Wishart, 1976).
8   Hirst, "Marx and Engels on Law, Crime and Morality," 218.
9   Hirst, "Marx and Engels on Law, Crime and Morality," 219.
10 Karl Marx, *The Eighteenth Brumaire of Louis Bonaparte*, in Karl Marx and Friedrich Engels, *Selected Works* (London: Lawrence and Wishart, 1951), 1:267.
11 Frederick Engels, *The Condition of the Working Class in England* (London: Panther, 1969).
12 Henry Mayhew, *London Labour and the London Poor*, vol. 4, *Those That Will Not Work, Comprising Prostitutes, Thieves, Swindlers and Beggars* (London: Constable/Dover, 1968).
13 Karl Marx, *Capital* I (London: Lawrence and Wishart, 1974), 791–92; for a relevant discussion, see Jean Gardiner, Susan Himmelweit, and Mary Mackintosh, "Women's Domestic Labour," *Bulletin of the Conference of Socialist Economists* 4, no. 2 (June 1975).
14 Ian Gough, "Productive and Unproductive Labour in Marx," *New Left Review*, I/76 (1972).
15 Peter Howell, "Once More on Productive and Unproductive Labour," *Revolutionary Communist*, nos. 3–4 (November 1975).
16 Wally Seccombe, "The Housewife and Her Labour under Capitalism," *New Left Review* I/83 (1973).
17 For example, M. Benston, "The Political Economy of Women's Liberation," *Monthly Review*, September 1969; P. Morton, "Women's Work Is Never Done," *Leviathan*, May 1970; Sheila Rowbotham, *Woman's Consciousness, Man's World* (Harmondsworth, UK: Penguin, 1970); Jean Harrison, "Political Economy of Housework," *Bulletin of the Conference of Socialist Economists* (Spring 1974); Caroline Freeman, "Introduction to 'Domestic Labour and Wage Labour,'" *Women and Socialism: Conference Paper 3*, Birmingham Woman's Liberation Group; Jean Gardiner, "Women's Domestic Labour," *New Left Review*, I/89 (1975); Margaret Coulson, Branka Magas, and Hilary Wainwright, "The Housewife and Her Labour under Capitalism—A Critique," *New Left Review*, I/89 (1975); and Gardiner, Himmelweit, and Mackintosh, "Women's Domestic Labour."
18 Wally Seccombe, "Domestic Labour: Reply to Critics," *New Left Review*, I/94 (1975).
19 Coulson, Magas, and Wainwright, "The Housewife and Her Labour under Capitalism."

20 Seccombe, "Domestic Labour."
21 Harry Braverman, *Labor and Monopoly Capital* (New York: Monthly Review Press, 1974).
22 Seccombe, "Domestic Labour."
23 Mariarosa Dalla Costa and Selma James, *The Power of Women and the Subversion of the Community* (Bristol: Falling Wall Press, 1972).
24 Selma James, *Sex, Race and Class* (Bristol: Falling Wall Press, 1975).
25 Dalla Costa and James, *The Power of Women*, 6.
26 Marx, *Capital* I.
27 Marx, *Capital* I.
28 James, *Sex, Race and Class*, 13.
29 For example, in Darcus Howe, "Fighting Back"; I. MacDonald, "The Creation of the British Police," *Race Today*, December 1973; and F. Dhondy, "The Black Explosion in Schools," *Race Today*, February 1974.
30 Howe, "Fighting Back."
31 Howe, "Fighting Back."
32 Power of Women Collective, *All Work and No Pay* (Bristol: Falling Wall Press, 1975).
33 Barbara Taylor, "Our Labour and Our Power," *Red Rag*, no. 10 (1976).
34 See Mario Tronti, "Social Capital," *Telos* (Autumn 1973); Tronti, "Workers and Capital," in Conference of Socialist Economists, *Labour Process and Class Strategies* (pamphlet, 1976); Sergio Bologna, "Class Composition and the Theory of the Party," in Conference of Socialist Economists, *Labour Process and Class Strategies*; Ferruccio Gambino, "Workers' Struggles and the Development of Ford in Britain," Red Notes pamphlet, London, 1976; Guido Boldi, "Theses on the Mass Worker and Social Capital," *Radical America*, May–June 1972.
35 See A. X. Cambridge, "Black Workers and the State: A Debate inside the Black Workers' Movement," *Black Liberator* 2, no. 2 (October–May 1973–74): 185n.
36 Hirst, "Marx and Engels on Law, Crime and Morality."
37 See A. X. Cambridge and Cecil Gutzmore, "Industrial Action of the Black Masses and the Class Struggle in Britain," *Black Liberator* 2, no. 3 (June–January 1974–75).
38 Hirst, "Marx and Engels on Law, Crime and Morality."
39 Marx, *The Eighteenth Brumaire*, 44.
40 Frederick Engels, "Preface" to *The Peasant War in Germany*, in Karl Marx and Friedrich Engels, *Selected Works* (London: Lawrence and Wishart, 1951), 2:646.
41 Darcus Howe, personal interview.
42 Howe, interview.
43 Howe, interview.
44 Howe, interview.
45 A. X. Cambridge, "Glossary," *Black Liberator* 2, no. 3 (June–January 1974–75): 280.
46 Cambridge, "Glossary," 279.
47 See George Rudé, *Paris and London in the Eighteenth Century* (London: Fontana, 1952); George Rudé, *The Crowd in the French Revolution* (Oxford: Oxford University Press, 1959); George Rudé, *Wilkes and Liberty* (New York: New York

University Press, 1965); George Rudé, *The Crowd in History* (London: John Wiley, 1964); and George Rudé and E. J. Hobsbawm, *Captain Swing* (London: Lawrence and Wishart, 1969).

48 V. I. Lenin, *Imperialism, the Highest Stage of Capitalism*, in Lenin, *Selected Works in One Volume* (London: Lawrence and Wishart, 1969); see also R. Owen and B. Sutcliffe, eds., *Studies in the Theory of Imperialism* (London: Longman, 1972).

49 Hobsbawm, *Labouring Men*, 272; see also John Foster, *Class Struggle and the Industrial Revolution* (London: Weidenfeld and Nicolson, 1975).

50 Quoted in Lenin, *Imperialism*, 247.

51 Peter Worsley, "Fanon and the 'Lumpenproletariat,'" in *Socialist Register*, ed. Ralph Miliband and John Saville (London: Merlin Press, 1972).

52 Quoted in Worsley, "Fanon and the 'Lumpenproletariat.'"

53 Franz Fanon, *The Wretched of the Earth* (New York: Grove Press, 1963).

54 Marx, *Capital* I, 633.

55 See Stephen Castles and Godula Kosack, *Immigrant Workers and Class Structure in Western Europe* (London: Oxford University Press/Institute of Race Relations, 1973), 4.

56 Veronica Beechey, "Female Wage Labour and the Capitalist Mode," unpublished ms., University of Warwick, 1976.

57 Marx, *Capital* I, 640–45.

58 Castles and Kosack, *Immigrant Workers and Class Structure in Western Europe*.

CHAPTER 7

Variants of Liberalism

[...]

The specific questions addressed in the chapter are as follows. What are the distinguishing "core concepts" of liberalism—how is its discursive field defined? How were liberal ideas shaped by the social and historical context in which they developed? This is a test, broadly, of what has come to be known as the materialistic theory about ideology. What is the link between liberal ideas and specific social classes and class interests? This question explores the Marxist thesis that ideologies "belong" to specific classes. Finally, how has liberalism reworked and reconstituted itself in different historical epochs?—a look at the process of ideological transformation.

The Core Conceptions of Liberalism

The first task is to identify the key propositions or core concepts of liberalism. These are the ideas which map out or define its distinctive discursive space as an ideology. Of course, liberal ideas are not static. Ideologies retain their relevance to changing historical circumstances only by constantly revising and updating their basic concepts. Nevertheless, if an ideology is to exhibit a degree of internal coherence over time, it must have a distinctive core of concepts and propositions, an internal reference system of themes and questions. We may call this matrix of core concepts, propositions and questions the *problematic* of an ideology.[1] The "core conceptions" summarised here really refer to *classic* liberalism—liberalism as it had cohered into a political ideology by the end of the eighteenth century. In philosophical terms, its twin pillars at this stage were the political theories of John Locke and the political economy of Adam Smith. In political terms, its main sources were the ideas of the English Civil War, the Glorious Settlement, which introduced parliamentary government to England, and the American and French Revolutions. I am focusing primarily on England throughout this discussion though that means leaving out the relevant history of liberalism in France, Germany, Italy and the US.

We cannot analyse these core conceptions in isolation. Ideas form a tradition. They "hang together." They mutually define and modify one another; they entail each other—they are inter-dependent. They tend to refer across, summoning up or echoing one another or, as Ernesto Laclau puts it, "connoting and condensing each other" within a discursive chain of meaning.[2] The concepts, working together, form a distinct discursive space of meanings, and sustain a particular "logic" of thought. Thus, for example, we cannot give a *liberal* definition of "liberty" without reference to the liberal conceptions of equality and the individual. Or, to take another example, references to "the individual" in classic liberal discourse always assume that a man's interests are identical to the interests of "his" wife and children. So in its early form, the liberal concept of the individual was implicitly *gendered*. Thus, when we analyse an ideology in terms of its "key concepts" we are really mapping the whole web of meanings, the discursive space, which these core ideas, working together, constitute as that ideology's "regime of truth"—to borrow Foucault's metaphor.

Liberalism "designates those progressive ideas which accompanied the gradual breakdown of traditional social hierarchies. Understood in this way, liberalism is the ideology most intimately connected with the birth and evolution of the modern capitalist world."[3] It is absolutely essential to "place" liberalism in this way, historically as a modernising ideology. Much is clarified by remembering that, from its inception, liberalism was *opposed* to something—the old order of feudal or traditional society—and *aligned with* something else—the new, emerging social order of bourgeois society. The opposition made liberalism, in its inception, a progressive social ideology. The alignment made it subsequently supportive of a new social establishment. This historic tension between its progressive and conservative tendencies is still to be observed at the very core of liberalism today.

Some of its key concepts can be directly derived from this historical placing. Born in opposition to a world dominated by monarchy, the aristocracy and the church, liberalism has subsequently tended to *oppose* the arbitrary power of absolute monarchs and the privileges and prescriptive right to rule of the nobility, based on birth or ascribed position in the social hierarchy. It has remained suspicious of the claims to authority of the Pope and established Church. It contested the whole traditional order of society characteristic of feudalism where individuals were permanently fixed in their appointed place in the "Great Chain of Being." It remains dubious of all traditional ideas claiming final authority. By contrast, liberalism has consistently *favoured* an "open" meritocratic society, where the energetic individual can rise to respectability and success, whatever his humble origins. (Given the gendered nature of liberal concepts, I have deliberately used the masculine forms of the pronoun, "him" and "his," when outlining liberal ideas.) Liberalism maintains a contractual and competitive rather than an ascriptive idea of social order. It favours free-thinking, rationalist and sceptical modes of thought, regarding religion as a matter of private conscience, not a matter for the state to legislate. In place of the acceptance of static social hierarchies characteristic of conservative social philosophies, liberalism has always displayed optimism about the results of change, dynamism, growth, mobility, accumulation and competition.

At the centre of its conception of the world in the seventeenth century was a novel way of conceptualising *individualism*. Now, people have always had some conception of what it is to be an individual. But individual*ism*—a whole conception of the world premised on the sovereign individual—was quite foreign to the social philosophies of feudal and Catholic Europe. It was the Reformation and Puritanism which loosened the individual from the institutional supports of the Church and set "him" in direct confrontation with God. This idea was then absorbed, in its more secular form, into the categories of the new social philosophy. This conception of the individual, stripped of status, position, relationship or place in the divine scheme of things was a highly atomistic and materialistic conception. Yet, it was also idealist and abstract—a category conceived as free of all constraints on action and endowed by Nature with certain inalienable rights. This stripped-down, atomistic version privileged Nature over society and destroyed the whole web of social and spiritual constraints in which, in the older philosophies, human beings were understood to be embedded.

This abstract individual was then ascribed with concrete characteristics and attributes said to be endowed by Nature and essential to its *human nature*. These explained what men naturally were, why they acted the way they did and what rights they had. Thus individuals were said to be "naturally" driven by the search for security, power and self-interest. Man was competitive and aggrandising "by nature." It was part of human nature to barter and truck, to compete, accumulate property unceasingly, to maximise one's advantages and struggle to rise in society. The state was essentially a set of external constraints on individual freedom, necessary for an ordered social existence, but arising outside of and artificially imposed on individuals.

The liberal concept of *society* is really the reverse side of this conception of the individual. The good society was that which guaranteed the liberty of the individual to maximise the self and its freedom of action. The purpose of the state was to create for individuals the conditions in which they could pursue their *private affairs* as equal members of society. Thomas Hobbes (1588–1679) had argued that competitive societies required a strong and sovereign power to impose constraints on individuals to prevent them from destroying one another in what he called the "war of all against all." On the other hand, classic liberals came to believe the state must interfere as little as possible with the individual's rights and freedom of movement. The only legitimate government was one to which individuals had freely ceded their inalienable rights and with which they had consented to make a contract—offering political loyalty, consent and obligation in return for good government, the protection of the individual's life, property and liberties. In short, classic liberalism had a strong but limited concept of the state and a contractual conception of the social bond.

The arena of individual interest and self-realisation was called *civil society*—the domain of private voluntary association, beyond the reach and regulation of the state. Civil society became, in liberal doctrine, *the* privileged domain of action. Our common-sense view often is that individual liberty of this kind has existed since time immemorial, only gradually being encroached on by the state. The fact is that liberalism as a doctrine and the forces that created liberal society *carved* this space of private rights, interest and action out of a much more corporate type of society. Civil society contained three major zones: the private domestic world of the family; the arena of free and contractual economic activity—the market; and the domain of voluntary social and political association. The raising of civil society over the state—hitherto, the realm of public duties and responsibilities—and the "privatising" of the whole conception of society represents a major *reversal* by liberalism of previous systems of social thought.

Natural rights, which now defined the individual's powers, were not thought of as arising from social intercourse, or from the struggles of groups to achieve certain collective powers, but "belong to individuals as individuals in the state of nature and (are) therefore prior to entry into society" (Locke). Liberalism later abandoned this theory of "natural rights": but this did not undermine the essentially individualist premises on which its theory was predicated. Thus only individuals could by their free consent abrogate their rights sufficiently to create society and government. Only this giving of consent made government legitimate.

This notion that individuals were already endowed with rights and liberties *outside* of society led to a very distinctive way of conceptualising the relationship *between* individuals and society. Many previous and later theories assume that individuals are at least in part formed by society. Liberalism maintains a strict logical separation between the individual and society, with what we might call "external relations only" between them. Liberalism thus played a role in constructing our prevailing common sense or "spontaneous" awareness of ourselves today as separate, isolable, and self-sufficient beings. This conception of individual rights is also the source of liberalism's particular claim to universality as a social doctrine. Its claims are "not for this group or this nation in this time, but for all human beings at all times in all places."[4]

The peculiarly liberal conception of *liberty* now falls into place. Liberty means freedom of the individual from constraint; freedom *for* the individual to exercise "his" natural egoistic drives and instincts. Liberty is defined essentially in a *negative* way—freedom *from* constraint. Equality is a subordinate value to this and means primarily that all individuals are equal because they are born with *the same* rights. None therefore should have prior status as a consequence of birth or inherited position. Everyone must have an *equal* chance to enter the competitive struggle—there must be no barriers to entry. Everyone must be *free* to compete. Whatever their real differences in power and wealth, the law recognises all individuals as equal "legal subjects." This is the "liberal" conception of equality.

Note that it does *not* mean that people must have equality *of condition* so that they can compete equally; or that those who start from a poorer position should be "positively advantaged" so that they can really, in fact, compete on equal terms; and certainly it does not mean that everyone should end up in roughly equal positions. Liberalism has always accepted that those who compete successfully must succeed. But since the fear of failure is the spur to competition, all cannot succeed. Hence, inevitably, many must lose in order for some to win. From its inception classic liberalism was identified with the "free market" and opposed any intervention by the state to remedy the unequal consequences of market competition or to distribute goods, resources and opportunities more equitably between the competing classes. This is an inherently inegalitarian position if we conceive liberty in a more *positive* sense. The tension around this point constitutes a recurring contradiction within liberal discourse.

This underlines the argument that no ideology is wholly consistent. Great, organic ideologies like liberalism survive because of their capacity to "bridge" the difficult transitions between contradictory ideas, their facility at "squaring the circle." Liberalism has subsequently shifted its position many times on this point but it has always come to rest firmly within the limits of what we might call an individualistic conception of equality. Liberty and equality are always articulated together in liberal discourse, but in ways which systematically privilege liberty *over* equality.

Liberalism's negative conception of liberty fits with its *legalistic* conception of equality. Liberalism has always placed considerable stress on equality before the law and the "rule of law" itself. Rich and poor alike must be treated as equals by the law. "The prince and the pauper are free in law to sleep beneath the bridges of Paris." F. A. Hayek, a modern neo-liberal, argues that this is "the fundamental principle of classic liberalism"—the limitation of government "to the passing of laws," meaning "general rules of just conduct applicable to all citizens."[5] Of course, the law has nothing to say about the deeply unequal *condition* of those who appear before it. The prince, after all, is "free" to go home to his palace; the beggar has nowhere else to go. But, for the purposes of legislation, all—rich and poor, who are manifestly *not* equal in fact—are treated as *formally* equal in the eyes of the law. This contrast between formal and substantive equality is another source of ambiguity in liberalism.

The law therefore appealed to liberals because it offered formal and systematic public criteria in place of the arbitrary power of earlier courts and judicial procedure. "The law must no longer vary with the length of a Lord Chancellor's foot," as they said during the Civil War. The law thus maintained fairness between competing contenders without questioning or interfering with the basic dispositions of wealth and power within society. Also, the law secured the contracts which individuals "freely" made with one another in civil society—and contract is a highly persuasive legalistic way of describing how sovereign individuals associate. The same liberal concern with submitting the state to the law also led liberals to be "constitutionalists"—whether in the written form of the American or the unwritten form of the British Constitution. Finally, the law protected the individual's rights, liberties and property. "The business of laws," John Locke once observed, "is not to provide for the truth of opinions but for the safety and security of the commonwealth and of every particular man's goods and person."

In terms of its *political* conceptions, then, liberals believed in good government: the state had to be strong but limited. Liberalism thus came to be associated with a range of mechanisms for weakening and dispersing the concentrated powers of government. For example, it affirmed the strict separation between the state and civil society; or, later, between political and economic power—so that concentrations of wealth are held to be separable from political equality. The difference in wealth and power between the millionaire and the beggar does not undermine, in liberalism, their equality as voting persons—one-person-one-vote. Another favoured feature of liberal constitutionalism was the separation of powers between executive, legislature and judiciary: between Presidential executive and Congress in the US system, or between Crown, Lords and Commons in the English "mixed" constitution.

In the feudal or traditional social order, political participation was limited exclusively to those estates at the apex of society. In liberalism only the consent of its citizens can confer legitimacy on government. Liberalism therefore favoured from the outset opening up the state to a wider political participation. One of liberalism's first historic tasks was to justify the entry into political society of those rising individuals hitherto excluded from the system of representation. However, as Dickinson has acutely observed, "By the term 'free man' the Whigs [who were the liberal heirs to the ideas of the Glorious Revolution] always meant a man of independent means."[6] Women, domestics, children and the labouring poor were not considered "free-born Englishmen," in the same sense. Liberalism is therefore identified with the idea of representative government, but *not* with universal democracy. Liberalism provided the justification for a widening of the franchise. But it did not lead the struggle for universal suffrage. The liberal commitment to individualism has always been hard to reconcile with the idea of a mass democracy. The latter was only grafted on to liberalism at a relatively late date, and C. B. Macpherson is right to suggest that one can still hear the grating sound which this grafting produced.[7] This is yet another tension in liberalism—between its universalistic claims on behalf of all citizens and its alignment with the interests of particular sections of society; between its commitment to representative government and its doubts about universal democracy.

The liberal conception of political rights (free association and participation in the political process) and of civil and legal rights (freedom from arbitrary arrest, freedom of thought, religion and opinion, the freedom to be tried by a jury of one's peers) were matched by an equally vigorous *economic* liberalism, predicated on a notion of the possessive individual—or "economic man." The individual's rights included the "right" to own and dispose of his own property, to buy and sell, to hire labour and make a profit. These were concretely rooted in the emerging economic relationships of commercial society which had begun to transform English society. This conception of the economy was materialist, because its operations no longer depended on moral ideas, fellow feelings, ethical idealism or good-will but on "an immediate and earthly recompense for labour."[8] It was utilitarian because it was grounded in the calculus of rationally pursued self-interest and the calculation of advantage. Its drives were held to be rooted in human nature—hence an economy built on these foundations was considered by most liberals to be a "natural" economy. Competition was its governing principle. This produced a *dynamic* conception of economic life—perhaps the first systematically dynamic economic theory in modern history. Hostile to the fixed and static economic relationships of feudalism, liberalism was articulated around the idea of an infinitely expanding, developing economy, propelled by productive labour, individual risk-taking and reward. Property was central to the definition of, and enhanced, the individual. It was the material expression of "his" powers. Its accumulation and disposal were the proper extension of "his" rights and liberties into the economic domain.

The market was thus the perfect instrument of such a system because, in market society, "central economic decisions ... result from the impersonal movement of prices reflecting the push and pull of forces of demand and supply which arise from a multitude of individual decisions and wills."[9] The market thus perfectly embodied the new economic individualism. Market relationships abolished the traditional restraints on the freedom to raise and invest capital, to fund loans and earn interest, sell property and realise a profit, hire and fire labour. They represented the "setting free" of the individual in the economic sphere, creating the conditions for the private speculation in land, capital and labour which, by the end of the eighteenth century, had transformed English society into the most dynamic capitalist economy on earth.

Liberalism's Historical Conditions of Existence

Having, for analytic purposes, treated liberalism's key ideas ahistorically, let us now situate them historically. Why these particular ideas *then*—at that particular historical moment? The claims of liberalism are universal. But what happens when these general conceptions are applied to specific societies, to particular historical circumstances and institutions? Does liberalism become imprinted with the interests of a particular class or group? Is it really the dominant ideology of a particular epoch or class?

You may recognise these as the kinds of question posed by the materialist theory of ideology, advanced by classical Marxism. Their most seminal formulation appeared in *The German Ideology*, the only sustained theoretical treatment of the topic by Marx and Engels. Jorge Larrain reminds us that probably few of the original generation of Marxists—Kautsky, Lenin, Gramsci, the young Lukacs—knew this text.[10] They relied on the abbreviated version of the theory contained in a summary passage in Marx's 1859 Preface to *The Critique of Political Economy*, a notably compressed and ambiguous text.

The broad "theses" Marx and Engels advanced can be summarised in the following propositions.[11]

1. Ideas arise from actual social relations. It is men, as "conditioned by the development of their productive forces and social intercourse," who produce conceptions, ideas, law, morality, religion, metaphysics etc. Consciousness is "a social product," and is always "interwoven with material reality." Social being determines consciousness, not—as we imagine—*vice versa*. Therefore, we should "explain the formation of ideas from material practice, consciousness from the contradictions of material life." This is the *materialist* proposition about ideology. It is important to remember that by "reality" Marx did not mean a reality "out there," which we could contemplate as fixed and already formed, but one constantly being produced and transformed by human practice. It was this social and material activity which produced ideas.
2. The second proposition concerns the social character or *class basis* of ideology. It is the proposition that ideologies arise from, express the interests of, and "belong" to particular classes, and they reflect in thought the position of those classes in the economic structure. "Ideas are the conscious expression—real or illusory—of the real relations and activities, of the production, of the intercourse, of the social and political conduct of particular classes."
3. The third thesis contains a proposition about the *power and domination* of particular ideas. "The ideas of the ruling class are in every

epoch . . . the ruling ideas." "The class which is the ruling material force of society is at the same time its ruling intellectual force." The class which monopolises material power also monopolises intellectual production and "regulates" the production and distribution of the ideas of its age.

These theses contain many challenging and problematic formulations. They have been extensively criticised on three main grounds. First, on the grounds of *reductionism*; they tend to reduce ideas to their "material basis" and therefore allow them little or no independent effectivity. Ideas become purely secondary factors—dependent variables—in history. Second, on grounds of *economism*; they are said to collapse ideas into the economy and make the latter the real content of ideas, which ideas merely mask or hide. Third, as *class essentialist*; they assume ideologies are only the expression of social classes and "belong" exclusively to them. Ideas flow from and are ascribed to the position of a class in the productive system. Critics have also drawn attention to the unfortunate implication of the proposition that ideology is "illusory." It is said to disguise the true material interests of those who subscribe to it and thereby produces a "false consciousness." Others have criticised the notion that ideas are mere "reflexes," "echoes," "sublimates" of material life, and therefore constitute a superstructure resting on, dependent on and determined by the economic "base." These criticisms have considerably weakened the specific form in which Marx and Engels first advanced their propositions and especially the "vulgar" form in which these have been transmitted by some schools within the Marxist tradition. The question is whether these criticisms have entirely disposed of the *broad* positions which the materialist theory advanced. In the following sections we will attempt to explore and test this question.

To do so we must turn again to the historical conditions of the emergence of classic liberalism. Liberalism is an ideology of the modern world. It appeared as the modern world emerged. For decades the idea of "modernity" was "thought" essentially, within its categories. A critical turning point in its evolution in England was the political, social and economic trends crystallised by the English Civil War of the 1640s. The founding arguments of liberalism were first rehearsed in these years and in direct relation to those epochal events. Hobbes's *Leviathan* (1651), a founding political text of liberalism which addressed the need of competitive society to have a strong and sovereign centre of power, was written in the wake of King Charles's execution of 1649. Thus its historical context was a period when Cromwell and Parliament were in command and debates about property, equality and the nature of political obligation and authority raged fiercely amongst the different Puritan sects who identified with the revolutionary cause. As D. D. Raphael observes about Hobbes, "To be a great philosopher it is not enough to have a great talent. The talent must also be faced with an important real-life problem."[12] Locke's *Two Treatises* (1689) were published around the time of the exclusion of James II from the throne and the Settlement of 1688, which consolidated a new political order based on a limited constitutional monarchy and representative government, religious toleration, a contractual theory of the state and a "natural rights" conception of the sovereign individual. Almost a century later, in 1776, Tom Paine produced his book, *Common Sense*, the basis for that essential liberal document, the American Declaration of Independence, and Adam Smith published the classic analysis of capitalist market society, *The Wealth of Nations*. These dates help to establish classic liberalism's "founding moment."[13]

Liberalism did not, however, suddenly appear. Many of its ideas have undergone a lengthy process of formulation, only gradually beginning to cohere into an organic conception of society. There are very few, if any, absolutely "new starts" in the history of ideology. But, looking back, we can see older conceptions of society beginning to disintegrate, losing their coherence, their purchase on common sense and yielding gradually to new conceptions of the world.

We can only sketchily suggest the historical preconditions of liberalism. The Reformation had challenged papal jurisdiction and authority. It posited the individual as the sovereign judge of all conduct and a direct interlocutor with God. It was therefore pivotal in setting in motion that conception of the individual as "captain of his destiny," without which liberalism could not have existed. The challenge to religious authority loosed upon the world the scandalous idea that men must follow the dictates of their own conscience guided by reason. It was the end of an absolutist notion of revealed truth.

Nature was no longer an order for men and women to contemplate but an external reality with which they must experiment, investigate, use the tools of science to explain, labour to transform and above all *master* (the masculine derivation was not fortuitous). Despite the religious impetus to these developments, their underlying thrust was inevitably secular. It committed men to free-thinking, rational, empirical and investigative modes of thought about the real and evident world. It liberated from the fetters of authority a new "scientific" attitude to reality. From this point onwards, as Andrew Gamble remarks, "Science appears as the essence of modernism" and becomes identified "as the natural ally of liberalism and democracy and 'open' societies."[14]

Harold Laski once suggested that this ideological revolution had three main components: the evolution of a new political doctrine—the state as a self-sufficient, secular entity; a new theology—undermining the hold of faith on men and women's minds; and a new cosmology—a new scientific attitude to nature.

In economic life, this revolution was not only underpinned by a "new spirit of enterprise," but appeared as a new "feverish activity," a "zest for innovation." In contrast with the static structures of feudal society there emerged a dynamic economy, throwing over the old barriers to expansion, revolutionising everything in its wake. Many of these "barriers" had been the very forms of property and production in familial and feudal society. Some of the "barriers" were also ideological: religious inhibitions on the pursuit of profit and on usury; the locking up of wealth and property in the fixed establishments of the Church; the dispersal of markets and legal authority under the fragmented feudal system of political, military, economic and ecclesiastical obligations. The Reformation not only sanctioned a new individualism, it transferred enormous wealth into secular hands. It unified the secular state. It freed men from the inhibition to trade, profit and expand which had been embodied in such notions as a "just price" and a "moral economy." The pursuit of gain, Max Weber noted in *The Protestant Ethic*,[15] is as old as recorded history. The systematic pursuit of profit through accumulation, however, was something new. When the individual seized this opportunity, the result was the whole material dynamic of commercial society. There was born the revolutionary idea of production without limit, of boundless accumulation. The unification of markets and territory under a single ruler created an entirely new economic and political framework—the secular sovereign state, whose boundaries are coterminous with a unified internal market under a single law and administrative regime. This is the point of origin of the nation-state and of modern ideas of sovereignty, which have dominated modern history from that time on. The promotion of free-thought, scepticism and religious toleration was followed by an expansion of the empire of reason. But this was matched by the material advances of the New Science—the microscope, the telescope, the advances in astronomy, mathematics, optics, hydro-mechanics, magnetism, electricity, medicine and botany. The period of exploration, navigation and discovery abroad paralleled the advances at home in agricultural production, engineering and mechanics. "In their search for wealth they required new power over nature, new instruments to develop that power. Their needs defined new horizons . . . out of which emerged a new picture of the universe and a new control of nature."[16]

It seems, then, even from this brief sketch, that liberalism was undoubtedly "of its time and place," profoundly shaped by its historical conditions of existence. Its forms of thought and consciousness were—as the first materialist proposition suggests—"a social product . . . interwoven with material life." We could not attempt to explain the formation of these ideas outside of material practice and changes in historical conditions. Of course, the genealogy of the ideas of liberalism is lengthy and exceedingly complicated. The ideas cannot be treated as simple "echoes" or "sublimates" of other processes. They have their own relatively independent history. Furthermore, the early forms which liberalism assumed owe their character to a revolution in thought and cosmology as much as to a revolution in material or technological conditions. The birth of liberalism, in short, had both material and ideological conditions of existence. In its "soft" form, then, the materialist proposition stands. But in its "harder" form—explaining ideas directly *from* material practice—it is more difficult to substantiate. It is clear that historical developments give rise to and shape particular ideas. However, it is not clear how precisely the causal links can be drawn which prove that material factors fully determine ideological outcomes. What seems to be validated, however, is the general proposition concerning the social and historical basis of ideas.

Liberalism's "Class Belongingness"

So far, we have briefly considered the historical preconditions which made liberalism possible as a distinctive body of ideas. It was formed in the series of "breaks" with the past which created modern society as we know it. However, the connections are too loose to serve as an adequate exploration of the materialist theory of ideology. Let us turn now to the period in the seventeenth and eighteenth centuries—liberalism's "founding historical moment"—to explore the second materialist proposition: the "class derivation or class belongingness" of liberal ideology.

Liberalism's historical emergence in England can be traced directly to the period of the English Revolution (1640–88). The Civil War itself—as later historians have shown—had complex and diverse causes. It came from the long accumulation of frustrations which the gentry and other men of property experienced as a result of the attempts of the Stuart monarchy to impose absolute rule and ecclesiastical authority on the populace and to re-establish in English government—with its long parliamentary tradition—the claims of divine right. The English Revolution was carried along on the complex tides of religious argument set in motion by the Reformation and the rise of Puritanism. The actual Civil War (1642–51) itself was triggered by a series of complicated, contingent events. The royalists and parliamentarians, both during and after the war, failed to resolve themselves into two, broad, simple opposing factions. It is impossible to identify factions which were coherent within themselves, opposed at every point to each other, which represented the major classes involved: the landed nobility standing for the monarchy, the Church and the traditional order and the rising gentry—the new bourgeois classes, to put it crudely—standing for the new forces of capital, property, commerce and trade. If we try to explain the social and ideological character of the English Revolution in these neatly blocked out terms—with each "class representative" carrying, so to speak, its appropriate ideology like a number plate on its back—we will be severely disappointed.[17] Whole classes are rarely ever unified in this way or neatly aligned behind their appropriate banners. Within the Parliamentary forces, there were a variety of political and social groupings; ranging from the highly respectable and substantial men of property (led by Cromwell and Ireton) through Lilburn (who stood for the small men of the city against the big men of commerce) to the Levellers (with their radical programme of popular democracy for the poorer sections of society) and Winstanley (who spoke a kind of agrarian communism on behalf of the new landless labourers). Yet they all belonged to the Parliamentary cause. They were all opposed to the absolutism of the Stuart monarchy. But they also diverged widely in terms of their social class origins and their economic interests. And they substantially differed amongst themselves, and debated passionately, about a number of critical political positions such as the question of to whom the rights of political representation under the new franchise should be extended. There is thus no neat correspondence between the economic, political and ideological positions.

In fact, when the air finally cleared, it was manifest that there had been, effectively, not one but *two* revolutions. The revolution which won civil, political and economic rights for the new men of property, which enshrined their rights, liberties and property as the proper object of good government, which curbed the powers of the state, monarch, church and nobility over them and enlarged their sphere of action, succeeded. It is this which was later consolidated under the settlement of the so-called "Glorious Revolution" of 1688. The second revolution, supported by the property-less and designed to eliminate the poverty and social injustice experienced by the mass of the poorer classes—the "poorest sort of us," as Lilburn put it—did not succeed.

Liberalism was, therefore, never in any simple sense *"the* ideology of *the* ruling class." The Civil War was not fought out as a simple class *versus* class issue of this kind. It had more of the character of a political struggle *within* the ruling classes about which section should become the ruling or "leading" class in society. Even so, it never became a straightforward duel between the landed nobility and the commercial bourgeoisie. The latter, if anything, were conspicuous by their relative absence in the actual ranks of the parliamentary leaders. The struggle assumed much more the character of a struggle between the declining and the emergent fractions of the propertied classes, to which the lower social ranks became, for a time, aligned. Liberalism was one discourse in which these different class fractions first fought out what they wanted, what their interests were, the justification for their actions. It was the framework of thought in which they came to consciousness. It was also an arena of struggle and contestation between different fractions *within* these emerging class formations.

Yet the Civil War did create the conditions in which capitalism developed and the bourgeois classes of society became the leading classes. And this historic outcome was inconceivable without the framework of classic liberal theory. Indeed, liberalism helped to *constitute* those ideas as a political tradition. It is here that we find invoked, as part of a concrete historical struggle, the liberal principle that a monarch who abuses the trust placed in him has broken a contract with society. It is here that we see advanced the claims to representation and political participation by the new classes rising to prominence in civil society. Here we find the case advanced that these rights arise not from society or the state but in nature itself. Here too is the argument that the only right to rule is that which flows from the consent of "the people" and that therefore they have a right to rebel against an arbitrary tyranny. This is the basic liberal lexicon of representative government and individual civil rights. So liberal ideology was *articulated* to the emergence to dominance of a rising class, though it was not the exclusive product or property of that class.

This complex relation of ideology and class is demonstrated in the flood of radical and popular thought circulating by way of pamphlets and debates among Cromwell's army, the radical Puritan sects and the poor, where we find the seeds of a *second* strand or "tradition" within liberalism. This represented a more radical line of thought, designed by and for the "little people," the people without property and power, who articulated liberal principles into a more thorough-going egalitarian democratic programme. They called, within the general demand for liberty, for social justice and freedom from want. They argued that if *all* men were born equal then they must be "free born Englishmen" too—a cry at once seized on and taken up, in an even more radical form, by the very first feminists among the Puritan sects, who used the natural rights argument to support their case.[18]

It would therefore be wrong to attempt to give this emerging liberalism a finished, unified or coherent character attached exclusively by origin to a single class—*the* dominant ideology of the ruling class. Liberalism actually emerged as a contested space already divided into its more conservative and its more radical tendencies—a tension which has been repeated again and again throughout its history. Depending on which tendency was the dominant one, liberalism could be articulated to the demands of different social strata. It was not entirely "class belonging" in its social basis. Both conservative and radical tendencies were premised on the fundamentally *liberal* concepts of individual liberties and rights and a conception of society as an association of free and rational persons bound by contract and consent. The quarrel between those who saw good government as the extension and preservation of *their* property and those who saw liberty as the end of "one rule for the rich and one for the poor" was a quarrel between different classes initially *within liberalism*.

It was John Locke (1632–1704) who consolidated the former tradition as the dominant one in liberalism by elaborating it philosophically. He defined the principles of classic liberalism for two centuries in ways which identified it with the more conservative tendency. Locke powerfully stated the case for constitutional and representative government. He regarded the state as the result of a contract between the citizen and society. Men could only be bound in the first place into political obligation by giving up some of their rights with free consent. These rights were inalienable because they were natural rights—the first of which was the right of property. "The reason why men enter society is the preservation of their property." Each man was the "sole proprietor" of his own person and capacities.

In the settlement of the Glorious Revolution, when Stuart claims to the throne were finally set aside and rule by constitutional monarchy and parliament installed, the Whig party (mainly representing the landed gentry who supported Parliament) set out to secure the gains which had been made by the Civil War, but at the same time to restore stability and continuity to the social order. The Glorious Revolution of 1688 was a "historic compromise." A limited monarchy, representative government and the consent of the people were moulded into "the English form of government." Research by Peter Laslett suggests that Locke's *Two Treatises on Government* were conceived and written before the year of the Glorious Revolution.[19] Nevertheless, as Laslett himself acknowledges, the book "did in actual fact justify the Revolution to posterity, as well as to contemporaries." In J. W. Gough's judgement, Locke "justified the constitutional principles of the Revolution Whigs ... by making them appear to be in accordance with the conclusions of pure reason." His discussion of the powers of government, however abstractly conceived, was "in effect a description of the régime approved of in current Whig political thought, which his argument represented as the logical conclusion of ordinary common sense, but in fact [embodied] his observation of the traditional assumptions of the English constitution."[20]

The subtle relationships between Locke's philosophy and Whig "common sense" does not mean that Locke was simply a vulgar apologist for the Whig solution or deliberately dressed up his arguments to plead a special case. The thesis about the relationship between class and ideology does not require us to *reduce* political ideas conspiratorially to mere class propaganda. Locke and the Whigs in their different ways clearly *did* genuinely understand themselves and their society by means of these new categories and concepts. And they *were* in their time subversive even though not in the end as subversive as they believed. (Locke did not acknowledge he was the author of the *Treatises* because its defence of rebellion against tyranny was widely understood to be potentially seditious.)[21]

The thesis about the relationship between class and ideology does *not* require us to reduce all ideas to a mere expression of class interest. But it *does* require an explanation of why certain liberal assumptions came to be so widely and commonly held; why they gradually became the dominant taken-for-granted conception of politics; why this way of conceptualising individuals, their rights, their relation to society and the state and their conceptions of property acquired, in this period, *both* the compulsory force of a natural attitude—obvious common sense—and the cogency of advanced philosophical Reason and sustained argument. It is the similarity or homology of structure between the new patterns which political thought assumed and the new patterns which political and economic relationships evolved, which establishes the basis of the connection.

The connection, provided it is not reductively treated, always enables us to provide a concrete reference for what is posed by ideology in an abstract or universal manner. Take for example the question of property. Locke gave, as we have seen, a central place to property in the "natural rights" of the individual. However, he had to explain how men acquired a *private* right over God's common heritage. He reached the revolutionary conclusion that it was mixing *labour* with material objects which gave man "his" right to the product of labour.[22] He argued that since labour gave man "an entitlement," property was something which men could also alienate or dispose of for money or a wage in the market. However, this argument did not make the labouring classes, in his view, a social interest like the propertied. Though in *abstract* terms, civil society was composed of a mass of free and equal individuals, in *concrete* terms it was implicitly acknowledged to be composed of the actual quite unequal classes of the propertied and the property-less. This is not because Locke wished deliberately to "do down" the poor or to disguise the class structure of his society. In this he merely reflected the common and widespread assumption that "free born Englishmen" with rights of representation *were* inevitably *propertied men*. And yet, by way of this unstated presupposition, the whole class and gender structure of market society, the new relationships of property and capital, the emerging social order of bourgeois society and the structure of sexual divisions were *premised* at the heart of his doctrine as the silent but salient, absent/present assumption on which its logic was founded. In theorising about it, he transferred these assumptions "into a supposed state of nature" and generalised "some attributes of seventeenth century society and man as attributes . . . of *man as such*."[23]

In fact, then, the link between ideology and class is forged, not because the former directly "expresses" the latter, but by way of a more complex process in which a specific disposition of class power is unconsciously transferred or displaced into the unstated premise of an argument, which then structures the whole of the logic apparently beyond the conscious awareness of the so-called author of the philosophy. Marx first drew attention to this mechanism in ideology in *The Germany Ideology* when he commented on the tendency of ideology to *universalise* the particular—giving what are in fact, concrete, particular interests the form of a general universal argument. Marx observed that "increasingly abstract ideas hold sway, i.e., ideas which increasingly take on the form of universality." He elaborated on the political *effect* this had on winning ascendancy for those ideas and winning support among *different* classes for those ideas. "For each new class which puts itself in the place of one ruling before it, is compelled, merely in order to carry through its aim, to represent its interests as the common interest of all the members of society, that is, expressed in ideal form; it has to give its ideas the form of universality, and represent them as the only rational, universally valid ones."[24] Marx also commented on the *naturalising* or *eternalising* effect of ideology: grounding what is historically specific in the apparently timeless and eternally changeless terrain of Nature. The problem is that these mechanisms or effects have usually been interpreted as deliberate and self-conscious conspiracy rather than as a result of the constitutive function of ideology. They are the mechanisms by which ideologies *construct* the world in definite ways, through certain distinct categories, which is the great positive role of an organic mode of thought.

[. . .]

NOTES

This essay first appeared in *Politics and Ideology*, ed. James Donald and Stuart Hall (Milton Keynes, UK: Open University Press, 1986), 34–69.

1 Louis Althusser, *For Marx* (London: Allen Lane, 1969).
2 Ernesto Laclau, "Class Interpellations and Popular-Democratic Interpellations," in *Politics and Ideology*, ed. James Donald and Stuart Hall (Milton Keynes, UK: Open University Press, 1986).
3 Robert Eccleshall, "Liberalism," in *Political Ideologies*, ed. Eccleshall (London: Hutchinson, 1984).
4 Andrew Gamble, *An Introduction to Modern Social and Political Thought* (London: Macmillan, 1981).
5 F. A. Hayek, *Economic Freedom and Representative Government* (London: Institute of Economic Affairs, 1973).
6 H. T. Dickinson, *Liberty and Property* (London: Weidenfeld and Nicolson, 1977).
7 C. B. Macpherson, *The Life and Times of Liberal Democracy* (Oxford: Oxford University Press).
8 Harold Laski, *The Rise of Modern Liberalism* (London: Allen and Unwin, 1936).
9 Gamble, *An Introduction to Modern Social and Political Thought*.
10 Jorge Larrain, *Marxism and Ideology* (London: Macmillan, 1983).
11 [Hall takes us through some of the central statements in the Marx and Engels manuscripts of 1846, later known as *The German Ideology*. Hall was using the version of part 1 (Feuerbach) together with selections from parts 2 and 3 edited and translated by C. J. Arthur (London: Lawrence and Wishart, 1970).—Ed.]
12 D. D. Raphael, *Hobbes* (London: Allen and Unwin, 1977).
13 John Locke, *Two Treatises of Government*, ed. Peter Laslett (Cambridge: Cambridge University Press, 1967 [1689]); Adam Smith, *The Wealth of Nations*,

books 1–3, ed. Andrew Skinner (Harmondsworth, UK: Penguin, 1982 [1776]); Tom Paine, *Common Sense*, ed. Isaac Kramnick (Harmondsworth, UK: Penguin, 1976 [1776]).
14 Gamble, *An Introduction to Modern Social and Political Thought*.
15 Max Weber, *The Protestant Ethic and the Spirit of Capitalism* (London: Allen and Unwin, 1930 [1905]).
16 Laski, *The Rise of Modern Liberalism*.
17 Nicos Poulantzas, *Political Power and Social Classes* (London: New Left Books, 1973).
18 See Juliet Mitchell, "Women and Equality," in *Politics and Ideology*, ed. James Donald and Stuart Hall (Milton Keynes, UK: Open University Press, 1986).
19 Peter Laslett, "Introduction," in *Locke's Two Treatises of Government*, ed. Laslett (Cambridge: Cambridge University Press, 1967).
20 J. W. Gough, *John Locke's Political Philosophy* (Oxford: Clarendon, 1968).
21 John Dunn, *Locke* (Oxford: Oxford University Press, 1984).
22 Dunn, *Locke*.
23 C. B. Macpherson, *The Political Theory of Possessive Individualism: Hobbes to Locke* (Oxford: Oxford University Press, 1962), our italics.
24 Marx and Engels, *The German Ideology*, ed. Arthur, 65–66.

EDITOR'S DISCUSSION OF THE PART II WRITINGS

Birmingham Centerpieces

Given the way I have organized the material, it may be tempting to think of the first four selections as being directly about and within Marxism—the best Marx, the best way of inhabiting contemporary Marxism, the central problems of Marxist social and cultural theory. Chapters 5 and 6 would then be figured as deploying Hall's neo-Marxist perspective, including his critique of economistic Marxism, in order to consolidate the problematic of cultural studies as it addresses more "applied" and empirical matters: youth subcultures and the politics of style, the work of the media in amplifying moral panics (e.g., about "mugging"), and the drift toward a racialized authoritarian state. Perhaps the coauthorship of chapters 5 and 6 could be taken to indicate further this shift in level and focus, representing a more project-based, collaborative genre of inquiry.

That kind of contrast provides a useful initial way of approaching the key texts; but our reading of them should have suggested that any "Marxism in theory, cultural studies in application" formula as a guide to Hall's work cannot be right. For one thing, Hall was thoroughly engaged in developing a "problematic" for cultural studies before he turned to ("Western") Marxist theory for resources in that pursuit. Second, it was the trademark rationale of the Marxist tradition itself to forbid, so to speak, any artificial separation between abstract theory and concrete understanding, between philosophizing and political activism. So, when cultural studies began to couch its intellectual goals in terms of making decisive *interventions* in the present conjuncture by way of close attention to urgent social realities, this was an already-existing vocabulary and posture, due in good part to Marxism. Moreover, the collaborative cast of some of the writings, together with the impression of purely solo effort in others, should not be overpitched. As explained in the discussion of part I, Hall's concerns represented common terrain in the Left thinking of the day, his ideas always adjusting to a constant stream of fresh contributions coming out of *New Left Review* and other radical arenas. His thinking in this period was self-consciously on the move. Hall's ideas were also hammered out at close quarters within the Centre for Contemporary Cultural Studies, in its theory seminars and working groups, and sifted through the more intangible questioning buzz of CCCS life generally. Correspondingly, the working-up into published form of the projects in which he was involved was, like the research process itself, intrinsically interactive. Indeed, his way of working exemplified his own politics of radical intellectual work, with collaboration as a touchstone. In other words, the relationships between the Marxism and the cultural studies, the theoretical and the concrete investigations, the academic and the political impulses, the collective and the individual contributions were *symbiotic* in character, if no doubt sometimes tensely so.

In this part, I have omitted a considerable amount from the original sources in order to make the volume manageable; but the gain is that the theoretical and specifically Marxist character of the discourse comes out clearly. The absent portions include further valuable perspectival contrasts and material of a more granular texture. Thus, in the sixty-five-page first chapter of *Resistance through Rituals*, there is more than we can glean from our extract on the topics of "youth as a metaphor for social change" in postwar British culture and politics; and on "group identity, situation and trajectory in a visible style" within subcultural life.[1] Similarly, at the point where we break away from the extensive final chapter of *Policing the Crisis*, the discussion soars off further into decidedly global contexts and the conceptual variants that go with them—notions of the Third World, Fanon on the wretched of the earth, the Black Panthers, Latin American and African interrogations of what is to be considered truly central and what marginal in the logics of the relevant mode of production in those mixed-mode contexts. The authors then swing back home, via Harlem, to Handsworth, Birmingham, the focal point of this extraordinary "case study." It is a gripping ride. Even so, our selected chunks of those lengthy and wide-ranging originals bring into lucid relief the theoretical spine that holds it all together.

Resistance and *Policing* were republished unrevised, respectively, in 2006 and 2013, with the addition of new prefaces. Apart from reminding us that those two major ventures need to be read as essentially continuous with one another, defenses are mounted against assorted reviewer complaints over the years: that there is a lack of ethnographic detail in the "subcultures" and "mugging" work; a relative lack of concern for subcultures in their own expressive terms; a relatively thin treatment of particular issues, actors, and actions in the institutional realms of crime, law, and state. Hall and his coauthors' response is that these criticisms, while reasonable enough in their way, mistake the level at which the CCCS studies primarily operate, which is not that of precise observational insight and experience-capture. Rather, the task is to grasp the nature of the social formation in its differentiated totality; the "structural configurations" and histories that are "taking place behind all our backs"; the way in which "generational disaffiliation" (regarding youth subcultures) becomes "a sign of broader social contradictions"; and the way that (regarding mugging) "varieties of sociology and media studies" had to be "framed by a Marxist approach to conjunctural analysis" in order to illuminate the underlying rationale of the move toward a law-and-order society.[2]

These are effective ripostes. However, the new prefaces also convey a fresh sense of equivocation about Marxism. The priority, in the subcultures restatement, seems to be to make the case for retaining a generally modernist approach in the face of the postmodernist emphasis on the sui generis singularity of actors' collective experience and meaning-making. Thus, the Birmingham team insists that subcultural particularities, for all their interest, must continually be situated within "wider social relations and formations," without whose determinations any exclusive concern for lived experience risks lapsing into unstable impressionism. Yet these clarifications are rather euphemistic, because it is not as though the Marxist take on structural realities was just one possible way of instantiating the necessary linking up of structure and agency in general. Rather, it was regarded as the *only* adequate approach, at least potentially, and this is evident from our extract. So when Hall and Jefferson concede in the 2006 preface that their definitive use of Gramsci and Althusser may have been—inevitably—"a product of its (theoretical) time,"[3] it looks as though something essential to the project is being too lightly traded away.

The authors then contest the accusation of class reductionism, and in familiar fashion: that kind of Marxism was never in favor at CCCS. This does not completely clear the damage, because it is not as though social stratifications *other* than class (in conjunction with generation) are given much attention in the Birmingham treatment of youth cultures. So, for non-Marxist critics, reformulating class-reductionism in the softer terms of class relationism will not relieve the basic problem, which is that, reductively or not, class almost entirely dominates the Birmingham investigative scenario. The 2006 retrospect accepts this objection up to a point, admitting that with hindsight the prominence given to class in the original study "may or may not be valid."[4] On the other hand, even if "class can no longer be predicated as primary in the production or explanation of stylistic 'solutions,'" does this mean that class has "disappeared as a meaningful category"? Has it ceased "to exert massive influence . . . in every sphere of life," including across the generations, or ceased to be profoundly "embedded in the social order"? "The answer has to be a resounding 'no.'"[5] The master mediator is hard at work here.

As for *Policing*, it is similarly acknowledged in the preface to its thirty-fifth anniversary edition that the book's last chapter especially—the one from which our chapter 6 is taken—is "ethnography lite"; and again this is justified on the basis that it is excavating the deeper level that alone can reveal the "structural position of, and political forms of struggle and consciousness among, black people." More generally, while "in their detail" the theoretical approaches adopted in that keynote chapter may "have since been superseded . . . the perspectives that inform them have not been fully exhausted."[6]

My sense is that the partial concessions are less compromising for Hall and his coauthors in relation to *Policing* than in the repositioning of *Resistance*. One reason for this might be that by 2013, Marxism had made something of a comeback, along with open talk about capitalism's madness and, on the Left, a return to no-nonsense readings of the way that the class interests and power of capital are shored up and rationalized by the rampant dominant ideology, *neoliberalism*. Whereas, even as late as 2006, that straight-Marxist way with ideology was still struggling for legitimacy in the face of sophisticated poststructuralist, feminist, and psychoanalytic thinking about subjectivity. It was therefore easier for Hall and others to be open about the fact that the literatures constituting the discussion in *Policing*'s final chapter were all largely "posited within a Marxist framework."[7]

Furthermore, the discussion in "Black Crime, Black Proletariat" represents an important extension and reformulation of Marxism's core concepts themselves. The originality and range of this part of *Policing* seems to me always to have flown under the radar, perhaps simply because it comes at the end of a long, densely layered work and sits somewhat removed from the study's more immediately conjunctural aspects. But this is the very crux with Hall's (and Marx's) Marxism: there are no easy shortcuts to the essential big picture, which necessarily includes the structural-historical considerations without which thinking about the conjuncture can become little more than gut-instinct politics. The cumulative way that the Birmingham team tracks through a series of substantial debates is in fact remarkable: historical imaginaries of the "lumpenproletariat"; productive and unproductive labor in Marxist economic theory; the contrasts and the overlaps between the *Race Today* and *Black Liberator* positions on the "reserve army" explanation of black wage-lessness; feminist contentions regarding the family and social reproduction, together with the controversial "wages for housework" thesis.[8] The interconnected way in which these domains are sequenced and adjudicated is not just a matter of giving each angle and position their due, nor even about encouraging the contending parties, despite their differences, to see that they share the same broad coordinates. A genuinely novel synthesis is being progressed, in which a complex Marxist grasp of the economic level itself—*phases* of the modes of production, different *types* of capital in different metropolitan and colonial contexts, the *recomposition* of labor within different forms of *labor process*—is brought into articulation with more directly political and ideological factors, moments, and motivations.

Accordingly, as part of being decidedly theoretical, much of this chapter progresses in rhetorically "appreciative" fashion, in line with the personalized practice of "reading" that I have emphasized as capturing a distinctive component of Hall's mediator mode. He is always seeking to listen to, to "hear," *think with*, alongside, and to that extent even in a sense even *promote*, the particular stresses of the contending parties to the problem-discourse. In this case, Darcus Howe's and A. X. Cambridge's positions are given detailed textual airing, without gratuitous comment or correction by Hall, not least because he knows that those writers in their different ways demonstrate that serious political activism is intimately bound up with thoroughgoing theoretical reflection.

The breadth and insight of the discussion in "Black Crime, Black Proletariat" mark it out as an impressive early exemplification of what is now known as "intersectionality"—thinking across, and inter-relating, different structural situations and subjective formations, with race, gender, and class still perhaps the most prominently featured dimensions. Difficult questions continue to arise in this vital arena of critical social thought and politics. It is sometimes taken for granted, for example, that Marxists are bound to remain insufficiently intersectional due to their theoretical focus on the dynamics of class and capitalism. Some versions of intersectionality, on the other hand, could be argued to conceive too separately in the first place the phenomena being connected up, while in others class divisions and identities play a notably subordinate role. It is not easy to resolve these matters, but chapter 6 takes us a long way. Its continuing relevance, not least to the context, politics, and analysis of the Black Lives Matter movements in the United States and elsewhere, is palpable.

Not a Marxist Center . . . At Least in Any Simple Sense

The fact that chapters 5 and 6 are coauthored, and that the projects represented are collective, prompts us to consider briefly the extent to which the Birmingham CCCS as a whole can be regarded as Marxist, at least in the 1970s. Something to contextualize here is the external perception that "for many people, Stuart Hall *was* CCCS."[9] Hall's preeminent role and presence within CCCS is acknowledged by all who attended and observed, and his thinking about most things, including his brand of Marxism, was accordingly not only widely admired but also to some degree closely followed. It should not be forgotten that the CCCS had only a tiny contingent of academic faculty: the vast majority of CCCS members were graduate students. In that atmosphere, being committed to thinking for oneself was quite compatible with being steered in various ways, especially by a figure like Hall, who was at once impressive and personable. But it is hard to tally the experiences of all CCCS members in that regard, given that many people came to the Birmingham Centre already politically preformed. There were also some who were simply *around* a lot, while others were not. In that setting, Hall's influence, even when welcomed, was never wholesale, notwithstanding the strong psychological pull toward activist internal consensus. As Hall put it in a late interview designed for, but never given at, the CCCS fiftieth anniversary conference, "We had a couple of Conservatives, we certainly had people from the Labour Left, we had Communists, we had Trotskyists, we had the Far left, *etc*."[10] And while this array of commitments was already sensitive to the cross-cutting issues of race and gender, the latter's concentrated uplift in significance and urgency in the latter part of the "Marxist" decade exploded further the possibility that *anyone's* presence, or word, or any kind of Marxism, including Hall's, could be taken to define the CCCS. Certainly, Hall's ideas and persona, including his brand of neo-Marxism, represented the center of gravity for much of the intellectual discourse; but he was also a kind of barometer, taking in and modulating the different modes and strengths of radical interpretation that were circulating.

Accordingly, it is not easy to gauge the full range of insider feelings about CCCS Marxism, and this is tricky even in terms of the view "from the top." Uncontroversially, just as CCCS was forever asking "What is cultural studies anyway?"—in the title phrase of a 1983 paper by Hall's successor as director, Richard Johnson—so it was always asking, as part of that, "What is Marxism anyway?" In that analysis, Johnson registered that his own position had shifted somewhat. Against the run even of his already notably reflexive 1979 review "Three Problematics: Elements of a Theory of Working-Class Culture," Johnson now preferred to think of CCCS as "Marx-influenced" rather than Marxist. He therefore urged that cultural studies should no longer be analyzed in terms of contrasting problematics at all (Marxist, non-Marxist, structuralist, culturalist, etc.); that its principal concern was the "subjective side of social relations"; and that even Gramsci had to be considered too "productivist" about culture.[11] But this change of tack was essentially prospective rather setting the record straight.

Both those Johnson contributions reappeared in the mammoth two-volume repackaging in 2007 of more than eighty CCCS working papers, for which Hall supplied the preface, settling on the formulation that cultural studies had never "in any simple sense" been a Marxist center—that its main feature had been "a long-running 'quarrel' with orthodox Marxism." So far, so predictably Hall, except that this gloss, coming from his own retrospective standpoint, is once again a little euphemistic. Constitutive of theoretical work in the CCCS, Hall stated, was the "relative autonomy of cultural forms and the relationship between 'the cultural' and other practices in a social formation."[12] But we might pause to query this, because it is not as though any and every set of other practices in the social formation was imagined as having significance. It was the relative autonomy of the cultural from *socioeconomic practices*, the mode of production, the economic base, the class structure, that was primarily at issue in the earlier period, both for Hall and for many others at CCCS.

Summaries by cultural studies scholars who were not themselves at the CCCS during the 1970s are a little more straightforward and for that reason may be preferable. Thus, Ann Gray, in her introduction to the selected working papers, regards the collection as showing that much CCCS work in those years "focussed on class; theoretically, conceptually and experientially within a Marxist framework."[13] The editorial team of the second volume added: "The Marxist conception of consciousness, although contested, served as a framework within which different forms of cultural expression could be subsumed, thus allowing 'superficial' differences to be reconciled into an overarching theoretical perspective."[14] And in his contribution to the 2016 retrospective, *Cultural Studies: 50 Years On*, Dennis Dworkin summarized that, from the time of its 1969–71 annual report, the CCCS "was united by both its opposition to the orthodox [Marxist] formulation of the relationship between base and superstructure and its insistence that the model was indispensable."[15]

These generalizations gain support from the way that several, though not all, of the various CCCS thematic "subgroups" operated in the 1970s, the organizing topics and regular discussion texts for which were, in the main, Marxist or *Marxisant*. Similarly, while the annual *Working Papers* volumes ranged over diverse subjects and reflected different inclinations, there is a persistent Marxism-related thread that ties together a great deal of the material. Lots of articles directly presented and assessed individual Marxist thinkers and concepts, and in at least one strategic chapter of most of the volumes following *Working Papers in Cultural Studies* (WPCS) 6—the one that featured Hall's reading of Marx's 1857 "Introduction"—encounters were staged with prominent scholars in the relevant field, whether it was subcultures, working-class culture, community studies, education, race, or historiography. And in these set pieces, the opposition figures—often sociologists—were considered defective essentially because they were insufficiently Marxist, or not Marxist at all.

Debate along these lines was sometimes more internally than externally focused, as in one heated exchange around the semiotics of working-class speech, in WPCS 9, *Culture and Domination*.[16] Yet despite serious divergence among them, all parties to that dispute framed their contribution as aiming to achieve a better kind of Marxist, or materialist, or dialectical understanding of structure and culture. The aims and discourse of the book that was also, in effect, WPCS 11, *Women Take Issue*, cannot adequately be described in that way, because the patriarchal character not only of standard Marxist discussion and concepts but also the very norms and practices of the Centre for Contemporary Cultural Studies itself, were being fundamentally questioned. Thereafter, there was no going back, on either front. That said, two extensive chapters in that volume built on the Women's Studies Group's previous "marxist-feminist analysis of women's subordination" in WPCS 9 to provide one of the most in-depth analyses ever conducted at CCCS of "the structured relations of production and reproduction." While it may not have been the group's primary intention, these sustained reflections represented an original contribution to neo-Marxist understanding.[17] Like Hall, then, but in various independent ways, CCCS groupings and individuals continually negotiated the balance of continuity and dislocation within the borderlands of Marxism's mediation.

Liberalism: A Test

As with the chapters taken from *Resistance* and *Policing*, I should be clear about what, in chapter 7, I have omitted from the original "Variants of Liberalism" essay—essentially, a little at the beginning, and much of the second half. The first few pages covered some definitions of liberalism that are adequately recaptured in the "core conceptions" section reproduced here; they also introduced Gramsci, who by now should be thoroughly familiar to us. Where our chapter text ends, Hall went into more detail, on two fronts: first, on the keynote liberal *thinkers*, some of whom are summarized in our extract (Locke, Smith, Paine), some not (Burke, the utilitarians); and second, on the *periodization* of liberalism's rise, fall, and partial reconstitution. In our version, the emergence and consolidation of liberalism is tracked through the English Civil War and the "Glorious Revolution," with only hints about its class-related heyday in the nineteenth century. The full essay goes on to fill out liberalism's high Victorian moment and gives a synopsis of the "strange death of liberal England" argument concerning the developing split between radical and conservative tendencies at the turn of the twentieth century. In those original sections, the basic pattern of our version is still followed: an outline of the details of part of the historical sequence, followed by a résumé of the theoretical challenges these pose for the (Marxist) theory of ideology. Drawing things to a conclusion, Hall briefly signaled forward to Thatcherism's amalgam, in his own time, of conservative organicist ideological elements and the new neoliberal gospel of "free market, strong state."

Chapter 7 illuminates three things about Stuart Hall, apart from his abiding interest in history and historiography. The first is not visible in the text itself but relates to its context of production. His Open University (OU) period represented a new avenue for Hall's commitment to collaborative work, following the intense CCCS phase. There was less direct coauthorship as such, but the norm was that course team members' drafts of their individual teaching units would be supportively scrutinized by the whole group, sometimes through two or three iterations. It was a solidaristic and demanding process, routinely commended as such by well-regarded external examiners. This made it relatively easy to brush aside insinuations that the highest standards of teaching and learning could not be attained by such a nonselective educational institution. Steadily, it also became recognized not only that the OU was a field leader in terms of pedagogical presentation but also that its teamwork principles and practices generated enviable new, shared ways of addressing central issues in the critical intellectual politics of the day, which in turn fed into the formation of novel research clusters. None of this went unchallenged; the alleged Marxist bias of OU social scientists often came under attack by liberal academics and right-wing think tanks. Such controversy preceded Hall's arrival at the OU in 1979, but he assisted with the OU response to the highest-level complaint, lodged in 1984–85 by Margaret Thatcher's secretary of state for education, Sir Keith Joseph. Certainly, most OU social science academics, and the courses they created, were of Left-critical persuasion, and Marxist ideas were sometimes clearly prominent. But given that contested consensus was a persistent teaching theme, faculty were also responsive to calls for intellectual pluralism. Just as at CCCS, the OU mix contained different kinds of Marxists, ex-Marxists, non-Marxists, and indeed "a couple of conservatives" too. There were many seriously bright and engaging people, some already having forged considerable reputations, others soon to acquire them. Across this vibrant array of external and internal factors, disciplinary and interdisciplinary investments, dedicated pedagogy and pushy politics, Hall's galvanizing presence stood out, around which many angles and talents could be appreciated and harnessed.

A second observation can be derived from our reading of chapter 7. This is the way that Hall's "voicing" of Marxism in such outward-facing OU texts is simultaneously a little more distant *and* a little more positive than when directed toward intra-Marxist debate, at least as the 1980s progressed. The "Liberalism" discussion was written around 1985, by which time, as I have indicated, some aspects of Hall's Marxism were starting to wear thin. Yet while this chapter is explicitly set up as a "test" of Marxism (a.k.a. "the materialistic theory about ideology"),[18] it was not exactly relevant, or pedagogically appropriate, to exaggerate the inadequacy of orthodox Marxist positions, as if addressing recalcitrant insiders. Thus, the three objections to traditional Marxist approaches to ideology that Hall sets out are couched in the "It could be said" and "It has been argued" manner, even though these are Hall's own reservations too. Yet—for me, anyway—this more provisional, teacherly tone works superbly: it leaves more space for the students to develop their own thoughts, and it appears to prompt yet another bout of self-reflection on the part of Hall himself. He seems driven to ask, once again: Are these "classical" Marxist positions on ideology *really* so very wrong; or is it rather a matter of nuance, phrasing, and emphasis? It is in that spirit that Hall ends the crucial framing section: "The question is whether these criticisms have entirely disposed of the *broad* positions which the materialist theory advanced."[19]

The third point follows on from the second, but still perhaps comes as a mild surprise: Marxism *does* pass the test. Needless to say, the philosophical liberal tradition from Thomas Hobbes to Friedrich Hayek does not directly reflect the social interests and imperatives of the dominant classes. Nor can the empirical, contested aspect of even key political conjunctures in liberalism's development be conceived as the product of the logic of capital, or class, or history. Still, in this underappreciated showcase of Hall's variation of timbre, his persistent investment in the historical *longue durée*, and in the theoretical big picture, a classical Marxist reasoning comes through:

> In fact, then, the link between ideology and class is forged, not because the former directly "expresses" the latter, but by way of a more complex process in which a specific disposition of class power is unconsciously transferred or displaced into the unstated premise of an argument, which then structures the whole of the logic apparently beyond the conscious awareness of the so-called author of the philosophy. Marx first drew attention to this mechanism in ideology in the *Germany Ideology* when he commented on the tendency of ideology to *universalize* the particular.[20]

NOTES

1 John Clarke, Stuart Hall, Tony Jefferson, and Brian Roberts, "Subcultures, Cultures and Class: A Theoretical Overview," in "Resistance through Rituals: Youth Subcultures in Post-war Britain," *Working Papers in Cultural Studies*, nos. 7–8 (Birmingham: Centre for Contemporary Cultural Studies, University of Birmingham, 1975), 9–74, 17–25, 56.

2 Stuart Hall and Tony Jefferson, "Once More around *Resistance through Rituals*," in *Resistance through Rituals: Youth Subcultures in Post-war Britain*, 2nd ed., ed. Hall and Jefferson (London: Routledge, 2006), vii–xxxii, viii–ix; Stuart Hall, Chas Critcher, Tony Jefferson, John Clarke, and Brian Roberts, "*Policing the Crisis*: Preface to the 35th Anniversary Edition," in Stuart Hall, *Essential Essays*, vol. 1,

    Foundations of Cultural Studies, ed. David Morley (Durham, NC: Duke University Press, 2019), 362–74, 364.
3 Hall and Jefferson, "Once More around *Resistance through Rituals*," ix.
4 Hall and Jefferson, "Once More around *Resistance through Rituals*," xv.
5 Hall and Jefferson, "Once More around *Resistance through Rituals*," xvi.
6 Hall et al., "*Policing the Crisis*: Preface to the 35th Anniversary Edition," 371–72.
7 This volume, p. 216.
8 The main self-critical note struck in the 2006 reissue of *Resistance* concerned the relative neglect of gender in the earlier subcultures analysis; here in chapter 6 feminist debates and concepts are directly engaged with and incorporated.
9 Michèle Barrett, "Stuart Hall," in *Key Sociological Thinkers*, ed. Rob Stones (Houndmills, UK: Macmillan, 1998), 266–78, 266.
10 Stuart Hall, "Interview," in *Cultural Studies: 50 Years On*, ed. Kieran Connell and Matthew Hilton (London: Rowman and Littlefield, 2016), 287–304, 294.
11 Richard Johnson, "What Is Cultural Studies Anyway?," in *CCCS Selected Working Papers*, vol. 1, ed. Ann Gray, Jan Campbell, Mark Erikson, Stuart Hanson, and Helen Wood (Abingdon, UK: Routledge, 2007), 655–93, 656. See also Johnson's "Three Problematics: Elements of a Theory of Working-Class Culture," in *Working Class Culture: Studies in Theory and History*, ed. John Clarke, Chas Critcher, and Richard Johnson (London: CCCS/Hutchinson, 1979), 201–37.
12 Stuart Hall, "Preface," in Gray et al., *CCCS Selected Working Papers*, 1:ix–xiv, 1:xiii.
13 Ann Gray, "Formations of Cultural Studies," in Gray et al., *CCCS Selected Working Papers*, 1:1–13, 1:9.
14 Ann Gray, Jan Campbell, Mark Erikson, Stuart Hanson, and Helen Wood, "Introduction," in *CCCS Selected Working Papers*, vol. 2, ed. Gray et al. (Abingdon, UK: Routledge, 2007), 1–12, 3.
15 Dennis Dworkin, "The Lost World of Cultural Studies, 1956–1971: An Intellectual History," in Connell and Hilton, *Cultural Studies: 50 Years On*, 3–24, 20.
16 "Culture and Domination," *Working Papers in Cultural Studies*, no. 9 (Birmingham: Centre for Contemporary Cultural Studies, University of Birmingham, 1976).
17 Lucy Bland, Charlotte Brunsdon, Dorothy Hobson, and Janice Winship, "Women 'Inside and Outside' the Relations of Production," in Women's Studies Group, *Women Take Issue* (London: CCCS/Hutchinson, 1978), 35–78; Lucy Bland, Rachel Harrison, Frank Mort, and Christine Weedon, "Relations of Reproduction: Approaches through Anthropology," in Women's Studies Group, *Women Take Issue*, 155–75. The quoted description of the earlier article published in *WPCS* 9 comes from the *Women Take Issue* Editorial Group's introductory chapter, "Women's Studies Group: Trying to Do Feminist Intellectual Work," 7–17, 13.
18 This volume, p. 227.
19 This volume, p. 236.
20 This volume, p. 244.

PART III | POINTS OF DEPARTURE

CHAPTER 8

Nicos Poulantzas:
State, Power, Socialism

The unexpected and tragic death of Nicos Poulantzas, in Paris, in October 1979 has robbed Marxist theory and the socialist movement of one of its most distinguished comrades. Though only forty-three at his death, he had already established for himself a just reputation as a theoretician of exceptional and original stature. He was also, to those privileged to know him, a person who commanded respect and affection, above all for the depth of his commitment to practical and theoretical struggle. Born in Greece, he was active in the Greek student movement in the 1950s, when he joined the Greek Democratic Alliance, a broad, legal form of the then proscribed Communist Party. After his law studies, he came to France, and at that time joined the Greek Communist Party. In 1968, after the internal split, in the wake of the Colonels' coup, he joined, and remained, a member of the Greek Communist Party of the Interior. In an interview which Alan Hunt and I conducted with him shortly before his death, he told us that it was virtually impossible in the early days even to acquire the classical texts of Marx and Engels, and he came to Marxism largely through French philosophy, especially Sartre.[1] His doctoral thesis in the philosophy of law attempted to develop a conception of Law drawing on Goldmann and Lukács. It was published in 1964: but he was already beginning to feel the limitations of this orientation within Marxism. He encountered and read Gramsci seriously for the first time then. An early article published in *Les Temps Modernes* attracted the attention of Louis Althusser, and he then became one of that remarkable company of young

Marxists—including Étienne Balibar, Pierre Macherey, Jacques Rancière, Régis Debray—which constituted the core of the "Althusser" group.

Between 1968 and 1979, in a series of major interventions which established his international reputation as a Marxist scholar, Poulantzas set his distinctive mark on some of the most advanced and intractable debates within Marxist theory: particularly those concerning social classes, the state and the analysis of "the political." Through the range of his treatment of these themes, and the analytic rigour of his thinking, he imposed himself, not only on debates within Marxism and between Marxists, but also on the more recalcitrant territory of "conventional" political science. The "Miliband/Poulantzas" debate, first initiated in these pages, has become an obligatory reference-point for all subsequent theorising on the modern capitalist state. Poulantzas made this topic—at once of the utmost political and theoretical resonance—his own. It is appropriate, then, that the most recent of his books to be translated into English is one which returns, centrally, to this topic; also, that it should be a book as striking for its opening up of new questions as it is for securing and developing well-established positions.

Deciphering the State

This is not the appropriate time or place for a comprehensive assessment of his work. But it is necessary, briefly, to set *State, Power, Socialism* (1978) in the context of that earlier work, partly to identify its distinctiveness, partly to situate the evolution and "turns" in his thinking which the new book represents. *Political Power and Social Classes* was his most studiously Althusserian text: *Reading Capital* is footnoted on the very first page of the Introduction.[2] This book situated itself firmly within the Althusserian schema, as a "regional" study of the political instance. In its opening chapter, it worked through a discussion of classes and the state within the strict framework of Althusser's theory of "instances" and of structuralist causality. It attempted to substantiate the definition of classes as the complex and overdetermined "effects of the unity of the levels of the structure."[3] At the same time, it attempted to give a primacy, within this framework, to the constitutive effect of "the class struggle." This was already a sort of correction for the hyper-structuralism of *Reading Capital* and the integral functionalism of some aspects of "Ideological State Apparatuses" (where the "class struggle," though constantly invoked, is not integrated into the structure of the argument, and thus remains largely gestural).[4] Many would argue that this set up a tension in Poulantzas's work, between "structure" and "practice," which was not resolved there, and which continued to haunt his later work. In *Political Power and Social Classes* there is a double-framework to every question—each element appearing *twice*, once as the "effect of the structure," once as the "effect of a practice." This tension may, in part, account for another aspect of that work—its tendency towards a *formalism* of exposition—from which his work as a whole cannot be exempted. This tendency is also present in his later book, *Classes in Contemporary Capitalism*, which starts from a very different point—the imperialist chain—but then attempts to work formally through from that global level to its intersecting effects on the dominant classes of particular social formations. The problem of "formalism" recurs in the more explicitly political book, *Crisis of the Dictatorships*, which is an application of the same schema to the particular conjunctural crises in Greece, Spain and Portugal which resulted in the overthrow of the dictatorships. Here, too, what is gained in clarity—for example, in explaining the fractioning of the Portuguese bourgeoisie from the level of the global "crisis of valorisation"—is lost when one approaches the more conjectural elements which played a decisive effect both in the generation of the "crisis of the dictatorships" and in the limited nature of the "settlements" which replaced them.[5]

Despite these weaknesses, both *Political Power and Social Classes* and *Classes in Contemporary Capitalism* were, in their different ways, major theoretical interventions. *Political Power and Social Classes* was especially innovatory. It is interesting that "the State" does not appear in its title, since it is now—rightly—thought of as making its most significant contribution in this area. The substantive sections on "Fundamental Characteristics" and "Relative Autonomy" of the state are the chapters most frequently referred to. Already, Poulantzas marked himself off from both an "instrumentalist" and a "technico-economic" conception of the state. He took his stand on a particular reading of what he called, ambiguously, "the Marxist scientific problematic."[6] In a series of challenging exegeses, he developed a conception of the capitalist state grounded in Marx, Engels, Lenin and Gramsci. In his arguments concerning the separation of the "economic" and the "political," the role of the state in organising the power bloc and disorganising the dominated classes, and in displacing the class struggle through the construction of a "general interest" and the isolation-effect (the constitution of the legal-individual citizen), Poulantzas clearly attempted to give Gramsci's concept of "hegemony" a more theoreticised and systematic formulation—though his manifest debt to Gramsci (handsomely acknowledged elsewhere) always awakens in him an extended ambiguity: Gramsci is nowhere praised without being, also, criticised. This signals a problem, concerning Poulantzas's search for consistency and "orthodoxy," and his retrospective construction of an impeccable Marxist lineage which reappears, in a different form, in the new book, and on which we comment more extensively below. "Exceptional" forms of the state then provided the basis for the volume on *Fascism and Dictatorship*, with its more detailed historical cases, and its delineation of the distinctions between "fascism," "Caesarism" and "Bonapartism."[7]

Both *Political Power and Social Classes* and *Fascism and Dictatorship* were criticised at the time for their tendency to "over-politicise" the state. Poulantzas sternly resisted this criticism at the time, though since then (and again in the book under review) he half-acknowledges its force. Whether or not he took the point, it is the case that his other major theoretical work, *Classes in Contemporary Capitalism* adopted a more decisively "economic" framework. It begins with the "imperialist chain." Though its middle sections did deal with the "State and the Bourgeoisie," it was within the framework of the inter-relationships he traced between contradictions at the "global" and the "nation-state" levels. The book is, perhaps, better known for its contribution to quite another—though related—issue: the vexed question of the delineation of class fractions within Marxist theory. Poulantzas's theses on the "new" and the "old" petty-bourgeoisie, and on productive and unproductive labour, have since provided a seminal point of reference for a continuing debate (to which Harry Braverman, Guglielmo Carchedi, André Gorz, Erik Olin Wright, Alan Hunt and others have also contributed). The complexities of these arguments need not detain us further.

What *is* significant is the way in which these highly theoretical and often abstract debates progressively become politicised. If one looks, for example, at the way Poulantzas returns to the discussion of the "new petty-bourgeoisie" three or four years later—in his contribution to *Class and Class Structure*—it is clear that the problem of "specifying the boundary of the working class" is "not simply a theoretical problem; it involves political questions of the greatest general importance concerning the role of the working class and of alliances in the transition to socialism."[8] This theme gives this latter piece a clarity of formulation and a thrust sometimes missing from his earlier work. From this point forwards, he begins to work on the theory/practice nexus in a more direct and pertinent way. In part, this marks his response to conjunctural developments—the break-up of the old dictatorships, the Chilean experience, the emergence of "Eurocommunist" currents in Europe, his closer involvement with the opening and the dilemmas of a "Common Programme" in France, the contradictory evolution of the Italian Communist Party's "historic compromise." Significantly, these also engage, in different ways, others of the original Althusser group—Althusser himself, Balibar, Rancière, Debray. But in Poulantzas's case (perhaps also in others) it must also be regarded as symptomatic of a deeper "turn" in his work. The crisis of the capitalist state becomes more pressing; simultaneously, openings to the left appear as real historical alternatives; there is, however, the shadow of Stalinism and the Gulag. Socialism returns to the agenda: correspondingly, so does the "crisis of socialism"/ "crisis of Marxism." The critical interview with Poulantzas by Henri Weber, which deals with the state and democracy in the context of "the transition to socialism," indicates a shift of perspective, a new agenda and strikes a new note of political urgency.[9] There is also a clear dissolution of some of the certainties which underpinned the "orthodoxy" of his previous work. This "openness" to new themes is sustained in the interview in *Marxism Today* referred to above. The capitalist state is defined, not only in terms of contradictions but of "crisis." But some of the fixed reference-points of his previous discourse—e.g., Leninism, the "dictatorship of the proletariat"—are put in question. The fulcrum of his theoretical universe shifts. *State, Power, Socialism* is now—alas—the most complete/uncompleted statement from this changing position we are likely to see. This constitutes the importance, the resonance—also, the poignancy—of the book, in the light of his untimely death.

Foucault and the Materiality of Power

"Openness" and "orthodoxy" are terms which require a little more elucidation. The first is a value which—in the context of the sectarian climate which disfigures Marxist intellectual culture in Britain—is hard to over-rate. But, if one takes theoretical issues seriously, as Poulantzas always did, it is not a self-evident or self-validating "good." At a time when anything and everything claims the fashionable mantle of "materialism," a touch of orthodoxy remarkably concentrates the mind. These are not minor matters: they bear directly on the formation and deformation of a Marxist culture and the politics of intellectual work. The different kinds of "openness" which *State, Power, Socialism* evidences are not difficult to specify, at a simple level. He takes on and engages with a whole series of new positions and arguments—of which Michel Foucault's contradictory appearance in the text is only the most significant example. Some of these new concepts begin to inflect his own discourse. He is open to reformulations of his earlier positions. He is "open" on some of the central issues in "the transition to socialism." The effect of giving way to these profound uncertainties about questions which the "older" Poulantzas would have regarded as settled, must have been, in itself, a profoundly unsettling experience, personally and intellectually. In sum, this leads, in *State, Power, Socialism*, on the one hand, to the opening up of a rich, new seam of concepts and ideas, not subject to his normal tendency to orthodox closure; on the other hand, it leads to certain fluctuations of tone and address, to a continuous discursive movement of advance and retreat, which gives the marked impression of—tragically—unfinished business.

The Introduction to *State, Power, Socialism* offers, in three brief sections, a resumé of the major themes to be examined. The first of these sections advances the argument that there can be "no general theory of the state to be found in the Marxist classics."[10] Paradoxically, given his previous tendency to invoke a consistent "classical" tradition, the propounding of what is described as "the Marxist-Leninist theory of the State" is now declared a "stupendous dogmatism." His distance from the "economism and structuralism" implicit in Balibar's contribution to *Reading Capital*, first signalled in a highly significant footnote to the opening page of *Classes in Contemporary Capitalism*, is now extended to include the "formalist-economistic position"; also the "topographical representation of 'base' and 'superstructure;'" and "the social totality . . . conceived in the form of instances or levels"; later still, to Balibar's sterling defence of the "dictatorship of the proletariat." Characteristically, this loosening of the bonds of "classical" Althusserianism, and the retrospective question-mark it must place over Poulantzas's earlier orthodoxies, are not fully confronted or their theoretical effects reckoned with. Poulantzas's reticence here is part of that fluctuation of address commented on above. Here, too, another "enemy" is engaged: the "New Philosophers," whose active presence on the French intellectual scene and threatened expropriation of Foucault haunts this text throughout (and they are not the only eloquent ghosts in the machine). The thesis is advanced (it is, surely, Poulantzas's latest attempt to deal with the problem of the relation of the "economic" and the "political" in his theory of the state) that, though the state is the site of the political condensation of struggle, it is not external to the relations of production, but penetrates them and, indeed, is constitutive for them. The second section challenges the notion that the state can be adequately conceptualised as "coercion plus consent." Here, Foucault's work makes the first of many pertinent and contradictory appearances. He is "present," both as a challenging theory to be criticised, *but also* as a major new influence within Poulantzas's own discourse: now, Poulantzas speaks, in his own voice, of "bourgeois discourses," of "discipline," the "bodily order" and "techniques of knowledge." Again, the theoretical effect of these "loans" is not directly confronted. The third section deals with the concept of "power," on which Poulantzas has written before. Here, almost exclusively, his preoccupation is with the "abstract diagram of power" in Foucault, and the latter's tendency to dilute and disperse power amongst a "pluralism of micropowers," which Poulantzas rightly sees as providing a cover for the "New Philosophers" in their vivid oscillation from a 1968-style libertarianism of the left, to a 1979-style, anti-the-Gulag-state "libertarianism of the right." Power as deriving from objective positions, rooted in the division of labour, is advanced as more adequate than Foucault's thesis of the dispersal of power, everywhere.

The main body of the text is then divided into three chapters, dealing with the processes of the capitalist state, the state and political struggles, the state and the economy. Each advances a challenging thesis. The first insists on the "institutional materiality" of the state as a complex of apparatuses. The second develops the proposition that, in relation to political struggles, the state must be conceived as a "condensation of the relations of [class] forces." This theme, already present in Poulantzas's work in a more muted form, here displaces his earlier conception of the state as the "cement" of a social formation. The third reviews the economic functions of the state, in the context of the argument that the state does not only reproduce the "general external conditions of production" (a phrase culled from Engels's *Anti-Dühring*) but enters into the constitution of the relations of production. Each of these, in a different way, represents a shift, either of emphasis or of tendency, from his earlier work.

The most instructive, in many ways, is the chapter on "institutional materiality": the interest, here, residing not only in the intrinsic novelty of the proposition (which requires fuller exploration), but in the way Poulantzas's arguments are constantly inflected, and frequently deflected and interrupted, by the running debate with Foucault. "Institutional materiality" is more than a filling-out of Althusser's earlier emphasis on *apparatuses*. The material processes of state action have here been transformed by Foucault's concepts. Thus, the way the state articulates the intellectual/manual division of labour is developed through Foucault's emphasis on the coupling of "knowledge" and "power." We hear, now, of its "practical supremacy of knowledge and discourse." At the same time, Foucault's abstract diagram of "power" is criticised for its failure to recognise the crystallisation of knowledge and power in the state's "organisational framework."

There are many arresting propositions and generative ideas in these pages. Nevertheless, the way they are handled and developed is not, ultimately, satisfactory. And here, theoretical fluctuations are most marked. Key terms, concepts and formulations have been "loaned" from Foucault. They add new dimensions to Poulantzas's thinking. However, their overall theoretical effect, in modifying not just the surface discourse but the problematic in which Poulantzas has been working, is nowhere adequately confronted. This is related to the fact that Foucault is not, after all, simply stringing together a set of new ideas. He is developing a different problematic—one, moreover, which is, at several key points, theoretically inconsistent with Poulantzas's framework of "classical Marxism." Foucault is not simply pointing, in particular instances, to the proliferation of discourses. He is advancing a theory of their *necessary heterogeneity*. Similarly, Foucault's "abstract diagram of power," present everywhere in the positive face of power, and in the microstructures of all types of social relations, is explicitly counterposed to the concept of power radiating from a complex centre. The capitalist state is largely missing from this schema, not by inadvertence but by design. Thus, it is not possible, theoretically, for Poulantzas to take these concepts on, only "correcting" them by reintegrating them into a more conventional conception of the state, state power and class relations. This has the effect, in Poulantzas's discourse, of returning to a set of more-inclusive "truths" which are simply asserted. Foucault is then awarded marks for his insights but ticked off and put in his place by a process of Marxist rectification. I am not advancing a dogmatic argument for the absolute incompatibility of theoretical paradigms: but it is to warn against a procedure of selective conflation. In part, this arises because, though Foucault's traces are everywhere, there is no integrated exposition-and-critique of his position—such, for example, as we find in Peter Dews's recent, lucid article "*Nouvelle Philosophie* and Foucault." It is true that part of Poulantzas's project appears to be to rescue the valid insights in Foucault's work from their misappropriation into the camp of the "New Philosophers." But the prior question must be whether—the real differences of political outlook notwithstanding—there isn't, after all, a consistent convergence here, which has to be unearthed at the level of its problematic, before particular concepts can be borrowed and transformed. Foucault *does* see knowledge-power (*savoir/pouvoir*) as implied in the very fact of institutionalisation. Every regulation is an exclusion, and every exclusion is an operation of power. No distinction is drawn, as Dews shows, between "a politically enforced silence and a silence of absence which is merely the reverse side of the positivity of a given cultural formation."[11] Power, for him, *is* an "abstract machine," whose action is everywhere, and which is assumed prior to its concretisation in any particular field.[12]

Since power is everywhere, resistance *is*, ultimately, a concept without a home: there is no theoretical reason why it should appear, no accounting for its appearances, and nothing to check its assignment as just another aspect of the "positivity" of power—"coextensive and contemporary" with it. It is acknowledged that side-stepping the question of the relationship between the shift in the modality of "discipline" which he traces in Foucault's *Discipline and Punish* and other relations which occur at the same time often leads Foucault into an abrupt descent into a "vulgar" economism on the side. But this is no mere forgetfulness. It is because Foucault remains explicitly agnostic about such convergences in order to retain his thesis of the necessary heterogeneity of instances. His "power" is dispersed precisely so that it cannot, theoretically, be traced back to any single organising instance, such as "the State." It voids the question of the economic precisely because it cannot, in his view, be crystallised into any set of global relations—e.g., class relations. Foucault's implicit "anarcho-libertarianism," with its characteristic oscillations—power/the body; power/resistance—is not, as Poulantzas sometimes claims, merely the effect of his "second-order epistemological discourse."[13] This does not mean that his ideas cannot be transposed into a different framework. But it does mean that Poulantzas's attempts at a synthesis are accomplished too fast, leaving certain glaring inconsistencies.

Another consequence of dealing with Foucault, so to speak, on the run, is that Poulantzas does not allow himself the space to develop his own new and positive insights. For example, the state's monopoly of knowledge might have usefully led to a more extended discussion of the role of "organic state intellectuals." The same is true when we turn to the chapter of the state and political struggle. The argument that the state must be conceived as the condensation in the relations of class forces, and that these contradictory relations are not external to the state but inscribed in its very materiality and in its functioning, is a welcome development from the rather all-encompassing picture of the state derivable from *Political Power and Social Classes*. These are some of the most arresting and innovatory passages in *State, Power, Socialism*.[14] They begin to break that knot in Marxist theory which has retarded the development of an adequate conception of the state for so long—best represented in terms of the opposed poles of the state as "functional to the needs/logic of capital" and the state as "nothing but the product of class struggle." We could have done with more on this theme, especially on the organisational role the state plays in Gramsci's "unstable equilibrium of compromises" and its articulation with popular struggles. The rather harder critique of Foucault offered here is welcome and apposite—but, given the intrinsic novelty of the thesis, something of an unwarranted detour.[15]

A Generative Openness

The chapter on the state and the economy is comprehensive, though less original. Both chapters are marked by a running engagement with a whole galaxy of enemies and errors—Balibar, the PCF's theses on "state monopoly capitalism," the logic-of-capital school, the Italians, Santiago Carrillo. The book picks up steam again in its final section, the first part of which deals with the "crisis" of the capitalist state, the second with the prospect for "a democratic Socialism." Poulantzas's characterisation of the "state in crisis" as the state of "authoritarian statism" is an important formulation, which nets certain critical features of Western European capitalist states in a period of crisis, and usefully distinguishes it from "fascism." My only reservation is that Poulantzas does not deal sufficiently with how this progress towards "authoritarian statism" has been secured at the base by a complementary shift in popular consent-to-authority—the product of a remarkable and intensive ideological struggle, of which "Thatcherism" is a symptomatic example. This has led me, elsewhere, to argue that the thesis of "authoritarian statism" needs to be complemented by a theory of "authoritarian populism," which has come to characterise the evolution towards a more directly disciplinary form of the state. Poulantzas also omits the specific contribution which the statism of social democracy in power in a period of capitalist crisis has made in providing "authoritarian populism" with the popular contradictions on which is it able to work. But the debate is well joined.

Readers may find even more of interest in the remarkably open discussion of the forms of the state and political organisation in the "transition to socialism," and the pertinence of democracy as an organising theme. The critique of some aspects of Leninism, and the abandonment of the "dictatorship of the proletariat" formula, is a mark of the distance which Poulantzas had travelled. The abandonment of "dual power" in favour of a "war of position" is effectively, if too summarily, announced. The affirmations that "a real permanence and continuity of the institutions of representative democracy" is "an essential condition of democratic socialism" will set hearts racing—and, no doubt, knives sharpening. The supporting arguments—against the fortress conception of the state, for Luxemburg against the Lenin of *What Is to Be Done?* and on how a strategy of "real breaks" is distinguished from reformism, are tantalisingly brief. Promises, promises ... Their elaboration is the legacy which, regrettably, *State, Power, Socialism* must now leave in other hands.

It should be clear, by now, that *State, Power, Socialism* is a profoundly unsettled, and therefore unsettling, book. Its incompleteness throws up far more than Poulantzas was ready to secure within the framework of a coherent and integrated argument. The book opens up a series of Pandora's boxes. Often, there is a too-swift attempt to secure their lids again, before their untameable genies can escape. This produces a real theoretical unevenness in the book. Yet, this very unevenness also constitutes, by its reverse side, the stimulus of the book, its generative openness. Poulantzas's earlier books gained much of their force precisely from their completeness and consistency: some would say from their straining after a consistency which contributes to a certain impression of premature closure, of dogmatism and orthodoxy. He leaves us with a book which is, in many ways, clearly coming apart at the seams; where no single consistent theoretical framework is wide enough to embrace its internal diversity. It is strikingly *unfinished*. It offers us a picture of one of the most able and fluent of "orthodox" Marxist-structuralist thinkers putting himself and his ideas at risk. This is Poulantzas adventuring ... The example it leaves to us—above all, in its determination, at the end, to address questions of the utmost and immediate political relevance—is, in a very special way, exemplary. The "perfectly complete and rigorous text" must wait for another moment. Given the way in which the search for correctness has systematically distorted Marxist intellectual work through its Althusserian, post-Althusserian, Lacanian and now its Foucauldian deluges, this infinite delay may be no bad thing.

NOTES

This essay first appeared in *New Left Review*, I/119 (1980): 60–69.
1 An edited version of this interview was published in *Marxism Today*, July 1979.
2 Nicos Poulantzas, *State, Power, Socialism* (London: Verso, 1978); Nicos Poulantzas, *Political Power and Social Classes* (London: New Left Books, 1973); Louis Althusser and Étienne Balibar, *Reading Capital* (London: New Left Books, 1970).
3 Poulantzas, *State, Power, Socialism*, 75.

4 Louis Althusser, "Ideology and Ideological State Apparatuses," in *Lenin and Philosophy and Other Essays* (London: New Left Books, 1971).
5 Nicos Poulantzas, *Classes in Contemporary Capitalism* (London: New Left Books, 1974), and *Crisis of the Dictatorships: Portugal, Greece, Spain* (London: New Left Books, 1976).
6 Poulantzas, *Political Power and Social Classes*, 127.
7 Nicos Poulantzas, *Fascism and Dictatorship: The Third International and the Problem of Fascism* (London: Verso, 1974).
8 Nicos Poulantzas, "The New Petty Bourgeoisie," in *Class and Class Structure*, ed. Alan Hunt (London: Lawrence and Wishart, 1977), 113.
9 First published in *Critique Communiste*, no. 16 (June 1977); English translation in *International* 4, no. 1 (Autumn 1977).
10 Poulantzas, *State, Power, Socialism*, 20.
11 Peter Dews, "The *Nouvelle Philosophie* and Foucault," *Economy and Society* 8, no. 2 (1979): 148.
12 Poulantzas, *State, Power, Socialism*, 68.
13 Poulantzas, *State, Power, Socialism*, 68.
14 Poulantzas, *State, Power, Socialism*, 127–39.
15 Poulantzas, *State, Power, Socialism*, 146–63.

CHAPTER 9

In Defence of Theory

Edward Thompson's *The Poverty of Theory* (1978) has proved to be a remarkable political and intellectual event. It has dominated intellectual debate on the left for more than a year. Part of its impact is undoubtedly due to Thompson's stature as an historian of the first rank. His *Making of the English Working Class* quickly and justly became a classic, inaugurating a new phase in social history and providing a source of political inspiration well outside the ranks of professional historians (History Workshop, for example, is unthinkable without it). Many of his qualities are to be seen to advantage in the essays reprinted in *The Poverty of Theory*—especially "The Peculiarities of the English," a brilliant sketch of English historical development first published, as a polemic against Perry Anderson, in *The Socialist Register*. But the greater immediate impact must be assigned to the name-essay, "The Poverty of Theory," which appears here for the first time. It is this essay which students are clutching to their hearts and which has raised the dust in intellectual circles. It develops the attack (first signalled at the end of *Whigs and Hunters*) into a sustained onslaught against Marxist Structuralism in general, and the influence of the dreaded Louis Althusser and British "Althusserians" in particular. For some time "Althusserianism" has been the leading tendency within British Marxist theory. Thompson regards it as an idealist deviation, a form of intellectual "Stalinism," which has exerted a baleful influence on political and theoretical work. *The Poverty of Theory* is dedicated, not simply to taking this tendency apart, intellectually, but to stopping "Althusserianism" dead in its tracks. It is this "taking of positions" within a current theoretical struggle for intellectual hegemony within the British left which has given the book its immediate political resonance—as well as its distinctive whiff of cordite.[1]

In fact, *The Poverty of Theory* appeared when Althusserianism, as a unified theoretical tendency, had already begun to fall apart, and theoreticism already exhausted. Althusser provided his own "self-criticism." But, before that, many of those who had been influenced by him had mounted a sustained critique—"from the inside," so to speak. Others, who regarded his work as important, but always refused to adopt a religious inclination before it, had sustained a critical engagement with many of his positions. More important, the climate of the times has proved increasingly inhospitable to the abstract, theoreticist tenor of his writing. In the face of Thatcherism, monetarism and the ascendancy of the right, many have turned to more concrete, historically informed kinds of analysis—a wholly welcome development. This return to more conjunctural and concrete kinds of writing has, of course, attempted to build on some of the theoretical insights of the preceding phase. One question, indeed, is whether *The Poverty of Theory* doesn't provide a warrant for a sort of mindless "anti-theory," taking us back behind positions laboriously won in the last few years. However this is assessed, the fact is that, though the book did not inaugurate the retreat from "theoreticism," it is certainly well placed—and aspires—to provide the *coup de grâce*.

Althusserianism—in the sense of gospel and doctrine—is a vulnerable tendency and Thompson scores a number of palpable hits. The highly formalist, logical and rationalist framework for analysing social formations, embodied in Althusser's theory of "structuralist causality," concealed an entrenched idealism, which Thompson rightly (but also Paul Hirst, Barry Hindess and indeed Althusser himself, and others, before Thompson) recognised as a self-generating theoreticist "machine." A similar excessive rationalism (and more than a due measure of intellectual elitism) disfigured his privileging of "Big" Theory, with a capital T, as the only judge and guarantor of Marxist intellectual and political practice. Especially when Theory only operated at the most rarefied levels of abstraction, and was represented as wholly autonomous of other practices. Much of this was exercised in the context of a series of attacks on various "theoretical errors"—also graced with grand capitals (Empiricism, Humanism, Lukácsianism, etc.), and wheeled about on the theoretical stage like heavy armoury. The conflation of the (genuine) problem of "empiricism" with an attack on any and every piece of empirical, concrete analysis (because it was empiricist) was wholly damaging. It led Althusserians of an orthodox hue into totally absurd positions about the necessarily empiricist character of all historical writing (coupled with the equally absurd argument that a theory could be "correct" even if all its propositions proved to be empirically unfounded) which fully deserved Thompson's scorn. It also licensed a species of intellectual terrorism—in which, despite claims of "scientific openness," the theoretical guillotine was wielded to despatch any concept which had the temerity to stray from its appointed epistemological path. I know of good graduate students unable to commit a single sentence to paper for fear of being impaled on one or other prong of the "either/or" theoretical scissors. This was "vulgar Althusserianism." It existed: and, while it did, it did much to disfigure and degrade Marxist intellectual debate. Its abject and supine dependency on anything, provided it was written in French, continues: it says much about the low temperature and failure of nerve of "English ideas." Thompson—social historian and socialist humanist—has been smarting for long from this irresponsible intellectual vandalism. Here, he offers the Althusserian *epigoni* their come-uppance.

Nevertheless, there is a question as to whether this is all that "the moment of Althusser" represents. Thompson's polemical caricature of it is an excellent basis for intellectual knock-about. It is less than adequate, either as an historical analysis of a complex intellectual phase, or for that definitive "placing" of it to which *The Poverty of Theory* aspires. I declare a personal interest here. I regard "the Althusserian moment" as a highly significant one. Certain positions—for example, precisely, a certain naive "humanism" to which I myself subscribed—were subject to a searching critique. He established the terms of a set of debates within and about Marxism, some of which are seriously inadequate or wrong, some of which are absolutely bang on target. His intervention thus provides one of the terms of reference—though by no means necessarily the correct solutions—to what he has, rightly, seen as the "crisis"/potential for fruitful development of Marxist theory. The debates do not have to take his positions: but they must register his starting points.

"Contradiction and Overdetermination" seems to me, by any standards, a seminal essay in Marxist theory on the critical issue of how to think the problem of determinacy in a non-reductionist way. *Reading Capital* I regarded, from the outset, as deeply flawed by its structuralism, formalism, etc. The influential "Ideological State Apparatuses" essay says important things, in a murky zone of Marxist theorising: but its functionalism stands out a mile; and its second half is a study in sustained ambiguity.[2] Since I am not religious, I have never regarded "working through" Althusser as a matter of belief, doubt or "conversion." I know that I am not alone in insisting, publicly, on a serious but critical engagement with these positions. Recent essays by my colleague, Richard Johnson, a social historian *formed* by Thompson's work, who has had to take the pressure of some parts of the structuralist critique, have been courageous enough to try to do this "thinking through" in public in a serious way—and been personally savaged for their pains. I cannot find any trace of recognition of this side of "Althusserianism" in Thompson's reductive caricatures.

This brings us to the strengths and limitations of the polemical mode, more generally. Thompson is indeed a master of polemic. But, as a mode, it has distinct weaknesses. In its search for the telling condensation, it woefully simplifies complex positions and arguments. It erects, against the Althusserian galaxy, its own equally composite hate-figures. This is to replace one form of intellectual brutalism with another. It does not provide that delicacy and sense of complexity which serious intellectual matters always require—something which Thompson, writing, say, about intellectual movements in the 1790s, would instantly acknowledge (indeed, polemically insists on). The polemic forces Thompson's hand. He is obliged to overshoot and short-circuit real issues. This leaves us uncertain as to the status of his own discourse. When the polemical dust settles, isn't there, after all, a problem about "empiricism"—especially the unconscious empiricism of a good deal of English historiography? Aren't there, in Marxism, real difficulties about the relation of "theory" and "practice"? Or between the "logic of argument" and the "'logic' of history"? Thompson perfectly well knows these questions exist. By failing to do justice to his adversary, Thompson ends up by not doing justice to himself.

For example, polemic has the effect of obscuring certain real underlying convergences with Althusser. Both, after all, are concerned to rebut the real tendencies to reductionism and economism in orthodox Marxism. Both are concerned with the real specificity of different practices. The attempt to recognise this, while also holding to some notion of a "complex totality," is brought together, by Althusser, under the concept of "relative autonomy." Anyone familiar with Thompson's historical work knows that, for him too, "relative autonomy" is the name of the game—his problematic, to give it the fancy Althusserian title. They both recognise the importance of Engels's contribution, at the end of his life, in raising, in his letters, the problem of "economism" in Marxism. They both acknowledge that, though Engels correctly put this problem on the agenda, he did not succeed in offering an adequate theoretical solution. Yet, because "relative autonomy" is identified with Althusser's influence, Thompson is driven by his polemic to play fast and loose with the concept: now assigning it to some ninth circle of damned concepts ("a kind of oratorical sauce to season our researches with"), now offering it a last-minute reprieve ("a helpful talisman against reductionism"). This produces real theoretical fluctuations and incoherences in *The Poverty*—not recouped by such disingenuous concessions in the form of "Yes, yes, and perhaps all this is so"—which makes a mockery of serious intellectual argument.

The Poverty of Theory, however, stands or falls, not only on the brilliance of its polemic, but on the cogency of its theoretical and political alternatives. On this score, too, there are serious questions which must be posed, even at the risk of finding oneself caricatured into place in the direct line of fire.

The Althusserians got themselves into an indefensible position about history. All the same, there are real problems with Thompson's defence of that "dialogue between model and evidence" which, for him, constitutes the basis of the historical method. Whence do the "models" arise? They cannot arise from the evidence itself, since this is what they are tested against. Either they are heuristic constructions—like Weber's ideal types; or the question must be faced as to how concepts are constructed, and the necessity to any form of theorising, Thompson's included, of modes of abstraction. And there we are, once again, with the problem of "theory" and "practice." Althusser took this too far in his propositions about the autonomy of "theoretical practice." But he wasn't idiotic to recognise that a problem exists. As Marx himself says, chemists have reagents and botanists microscopes: the historian of society has only one "instrument"—the procedure of abstraction. Thompson cannot acknowledge this, except half-heartedly. To him, since history presents itself as a complex "lived" whole, any conceptualisation of it must be a reduction of the "evidence." But this is tantamount to saying that "the evidence" speaks its meaning transitively, without the mediation of concepts: it provides its own "models." Like it or not, this represents, theoretically, a conflation of "thought" and "the real." It entails an "empiricist" theory of knowledge—in the proper, not simply the "theoreticist" sense. Thompson does acknowledge that historical facts cannot speak for themselves. But, elsewhere, he frequently advances history as its own author: historical "experience" as the test of its authenticity. He is thus driven to declare every part of Marx's *Capital* which is not "historical" as a form of "Hegelianism" trapped in the abstractions of logical deduction. Whatever concessions are made, this in fact dissolves the real problem of abstraction—and Marx's *Capital* is organised in terms of a complex set of types of abstraction of a more "abstract" and more concretely determinate character—in an empiricist manner.

This problem is compounded, in *The Poverty of Theory*, by two other related ones: the status of history as such; and the problem of "experience." In *The Poverty* Thompson's History is counterposed to Althusser's Theory. Thompson speaks of a unified "historical method" which unites all historians: an odd, "professionalised" construction for a Marxist historian who has polemicised vigorously against many professional colleagues. His "History," like Althusser's "Theory" is erected into an absolute. He criticises Althusser, correctly, for applying to specific historical cases an abstract, formal framework based on the clear separation of their different aspects into "instances." Less convincingly, he says this leads Althusser into ascribing some practices—for example, the law—simply and unproblematically to "the superstructures." His own work on eighteenth-century law and crime, he argues, shows that sometimes the law was "superstructural," securing the dominance of a ruling class; sometimes directly imbricated with the economy; sometimes "running free" of all determination. Still, Marxists cannot be satisfied with this positing of an endless series of contingent "particularities"—even if they also have to be intensely careful about how cases are generalised from. For then there would be no "general theoretical framework" at all, which might provide insights into the (same or different) position of the law in other societies or at other conjunctures (for example, today). This would have the theoretical effect of establishing history as final arbiter and judge: since only "History" could say, in any instance, whether the law was determined, relatively determined, running free or standing on its head. This certainly saves history: but it dissolves Marxism into it. This question is quite inadequately dealt with in Thompson's book.

It is related to the problem about "experience." Thompson has made himself the undisputed master of a history which recaptures and recovers the lived historical experience of classes which official history banished from the record. This work stands as a permanent rebuke to those Althusserians who read their Master as saying that experience was *purely* ideological and unconscious and that a truly theoretical history was one which treated classes as mere "bearers" of the historical process, without agency: and historical process itself as a process "without a subject." But there is no way in which the category of "experience" can be an unproblematic one for Marxism. All experience is penetrated by cultural and ideological categories. This does not render it "false consciousness." But it must undermine the notion that "experience" can simply be read for its meaning, rather than being interrogated for its complex interweaving of real and ideological elements. Reductive Marxism treated class consciousness as paradigmatic with the economic position. It tempted the analyst to "read off" the former from the latter. The new social history, led by Thompson, has gone very far in correcting against this deformation, restoring the centrality of culture and consciousness to any account of historical transitions. Still, for Marxism, the problem remains: how to combine, in any analysis, the structural and the historical elements of a Marxist explanation. To absorb or elevate structural "conditions" into the level of "experience" is to dissolve the dialectic at the heart of the theory. Thompson constantly evokes the classical Marxist dialectic between "being" and "consciousness." But he does, *sometimes*, treat the former "experientially"—reading social formations from the perspective of "experience." Whilst militantly refusing any criticism of his work from this viewpoint, he now acknowledges that his category of "experience" is not an adequate one, precisely because it conflates things which, of course, "in reality" (lived experience) occur together, but which have, analytically, to be distinguished. His attempt to overcome this by speaking of two "experiences"—experience I (conditions) and experience II (how these are appropriated in consciousness)—is, however, still theoretically quite unsatisfactory. You do not facilitate the difficult process of thinking the relation *between* two terms by naming them with *the same* concept. This simply blurs distinctions which have to be kept conceptually separate.

This is a theoretical argument: but it has quite immediate political consequences. If class consciousness is itself an historical process, and cannot be simply derived from the economic position of class agents (a really non-reductive Marxism), then the whole problem of Marxist politics is caught in the related but not necessarily corresponding connections between class-in-itself and class-for-itself. To resolve both into the catch-all category of "experience" is to imply—despite all the complexities of any particular analysis—that "the class" is always *really* in its place, at the ready, and can be summoned up "for socialism." Something very like this is often inscribed in, for example, History Workshop's notion of "people's history"—as if, simply to tell the story of past oppressions and struggles is to find the promise of socialism already there, fully constituted, only waiting to "speak out." It is also, often, implied in Thompson's eloquent invocations of the traditions of the "free-born Englishmen" and of "the common people," which live on in popular tradition if only they can be free from their bourgeois constituents. But the whole record of socialism, up to and especially in the present moment, is against this too-simple "populism." A non-reductive Marxist theory must entail facing up to all that is involved in saying that socialism has to be constructed by a real political practice, not merely "rediscovered" in a recuperative historical reflection. The latter can deeply inform, but not replace, the former. This may seem a paradoxical point to put to an historical practice which has, correctly, stressed agency and struggle over structure and position. But "theory," despite its "poverty," lays funny, unexpected traps for all of us. Somewhere in there is a real difference between the hard road towards the building up, today, of different sites of struggle into a broad popular and democratic movement in the direction of a non-statist socialism; and what I think of as a sometimes too-easy invocation of an existing and unsullied radical "populism," which can be a heartening thought in dark times, but may not prove to be as available a force, ready and waiting in the wings, as is sometimes supposed.

In general, I think *The Poverty of Theory*, despite its magisterial polemic, its correct engagement with "vulgar Althusserianism," its socialist passion and the rich historical imagination on which it draws, does, in the end, evade these difficult issues, both of theory *and* politics, today. Humanism and the "agenda of 1956" require defence against their idiotic detractors: but they cannot simply be moved back into place. Between them and us, so far as the left is concerned, lies that complex moment of "1968"—a contradictory inheritance which has to be neither simply revived nor simply denigrated but reckoned with. It has, after all, inflected every element popular and socialist—out of which a popular democratic socialist politics has to be constructed today. Thompson's commitment to "1956" and his brutal dismissal of everything that has happened, politically and theoretically since—the "lumpen-intelligentsia" busy "doing its own thing"—is a striking blindness in so sophisticated and subtle a historian. The attempt to bury and obliterate, not only the worst excesses of "vulgar Althusserianism," but also the real theoretical gains made in the interval, arises from the same, over-hasty and ill-tempered reaction. It does not do the current struggle much service. It leaves us with a set of matching sectarianisms—the theoretical absolutism of Althusser's Theory, the implicit absolutism of Thompson's "Poverty." Against both, we need Gramsci's "pessimism of the intellect, optimism of the will," but Gramsci knew better than to equate "pessimism"—a realistic appraisal of the real situation before us, using every available intellectual and political resource we could muster—with theoretical impoverishment.

NOTES

This essay first appeared in *People's History and Socialist Theory*, ed. Raphael Samuel (London: Routledge and Kegan Paul, 1981), 378–85.

1 E. P. Thompson, *The Poverty of Theory and Other Essays* (London: Merlin, 1978); *The Making of the English Working Class* (Harmondsworth, UK: Pelican, 1968); *Whigs and Hunters: The Origin of the Black Act* (London: Allen Lane, 1976).

2 Louis Althusser, "Contradiction and Overdetermination," in *For Marx* (London: Allen Lane, 1969); Louis Althusser and Étienne Balibar, *Reading Capital* (London: New Left Books, 1970); Louis Althusser, "Ideology and Ideological State Apparatuses," in *Lenin and Philosophy and Other Essays* (London: New Left Books, 1971).

CHAPTER 10

Authoritarian Populism:
A Reply to Jessop et al.

In *New Left Review* 147, Bob Jessop, Kevin Bonnett, Simon Bromley and Tom Ling contributed a long and important article, "Authoritarian Populism, Two Nations and Thatcherism."[1] This article took issue with "authoritarian populism" (hereinafter, alas, AP) and the use of that concept in my work on Thatcherism; and proposed some wide-ranging alternative theses. I should like myself to take issue with some aspects of their argument, not so much to defend my work as, through mutual discussion and debate, to advance our understanding of the phenomenon of Thatcherism.

My view, briefly, is that in their genuine desire to produce a *general* and definitive account of Thatcherism as a global phenomenon, Jessop et al. have been led to mistake my own, more delimited project for their own, more ambitious one. In so doing, they obscure or misread many of my arguments. They produce, in the end, a rather confused tangle of important arguments and spurious debating points. Let me say categorically that "authoritarian populism" has never been intended to, could not possibly have been intended and—I would claim—has never been used in my work, to produce a *general* explanation of Thatcherism. It addresses, directly, the question of the forms of hegemonic politics. In doing so, it deliberately and self-consciously *foregrounds* the political-ideological dimension. Thatcherism, however, is a multi-faceted historical phenomenon, which it would be ludicrous to assume could be "explained" along one dimension of analysis only. In that basic sense, I believe the Jessop et al. critique to have been fundamentally misdirected. The misunderstanding begins, so far as I can see, with their partial and inadequate account of the genealogy of the concept.

AP first emerged, as they acknowledged, from the analysis of the political conjuncture, mid-1960s/mid-1970s, advanced by myself and others in *Policing the Crisis*.[2] That analysis accurately forecast the rise of Thatcherism, though it was researched in the mid-1970s and published in 1978. It pointed, *inter alia*, to a shift taking place in the "balance of social and political forces" (or what Gramsci calls the "relations of force"), pinpointed in the disintegration of the social-democratic consensus under Callaghan and the rise of the radical right under Thatcherite auspices. It argued that the corporatist consensus—the form of politics in which Labour had attempted to stabilise the crisis—was breaking up under internal and external pressures. However, the balance in the relations of force was moving—in that "unstable equilibrium" between coercion and consent which characterises *all* democratic class politics—decisively towards the "authoritarian" pole. We were approaching, it argued, a moment of "closure" in which the state played an increasingly central "educative" role. We noted, however, the degree to which this shift "from above" was pioneered by, harnessed to, and to some extent legitimated by a populist groundswell below. The *form* of this populist enlistment—we suggested—in the 1960s and 1970s often took the shape of a sequence of "moral panics," around such apparently non-political issues as race, law-and-order, permissiveness and social anarchy. These served to win for the authoritarian closure the gloss of populist consent.[3]

Development of the Concept

The actual term "authoritarian populism," however, only emerged in 1978 after I read the concluding section to Nicos Poulantzas's courageous and original book, *State, Power, Socialism*, which was also—tragically—his last political statement. There, Poulantzas attempted to characterise a new "moment" in the conjuncture of the class democracies, formed by "intensive state control over every sphere of socio-economic life, combined with radical decline of the institutions of political democracy and with draconian and multiform curtailment of so-called 'formal' liberties, whose reality is being discovered now that they are going overboard."[4] (I especially relished that final phrase, since it put me in mind of how often the fundamentalist left is scornful of civil liberties until they find themselves badly in need of some.) More seriously, I thought I recognised in this account, and in my brief conversations with Poulantzas at the time, many similarities between his characterisation and those I had been struggling to formulate in *Policing the Crisis*, "Drifting into a Law-and-Order Society," and so on.

Poulantzas called this the moment of "authoritarian statism" (AS). He added, *inter alia*, that it was linked with "the periodisation of capitalism into distinct stages and phases"; that it existed "in the form of regimes that vary according to the conjuncture of the country concerned"; that it covered, specifically, *both* "the political crisis and the crisis of the state"; that it was intended to help us periodise "the relationship between the state and the political crisis." He insisted it was *neither* the birth pangs of fascism nor an "exceptional form of the capitalist state" nor even "the fulfilment of the totalitarian buds inherent in every capitalist state." Indeed, the importance of AS was that it represented a new combination of coercion/consent, tilted towards the coercive end of the spectrum, while maintaining the outer forms of democratic class rule intact. It did, he argued, relate to "considerable shifts in class relations" (not, devotees of [the journal] *Class Politics* please note, to the so-called "disappearance of class or the class struggle," whatever that entirely fictional construction of theirs might mean). But also, that it coincided with the generalisation of class conflict and other social struggles to "new fronts." It thus represented a fundamental shift in the modalities through which ruling blocs attempt to construct hegemony in capitalist class democracies. That was its explicit field of reference. There is little need to elaborate on AS further, if only because Bob Jessop must be thoroughly familiar with it since he is one of Poulantzas's most meticulous and accomplished commentators and critics, as his forthcoming study will show.

Poulantzas's concept seemed to me extremely useful—but weak in two major respects. It misread the emerging strategy, since one of the fundamental things which seemed to me to be shifting was precisely the abandonment of the "corporatist" strategy central to Labourism, and its replacement by an "anti-statist" strategy of the "New Right." (An "anti-statist" strategy, incidentally, is not one which refuses to operate through the state; it is one which conceives a more limited state role, and which advances through the attempt, ideologically, to *represent itself* as anti-statist, for the purposes of populist mobilisation.) I assumed that this highly contradictory strategy—which we have in fact seen in operation under Thatcherism: simultaneously, dismantling the welfare state, "anti-statist" in its ideological self-representation *and* highly state-centralist and dirigiste in many of its strategic operations—would inflect politics in new ways and have real political effects.

Secondly, I believed that Poulantzas had neglected the one dimension which, above all others, has defeated the left, politically, and Marxist analysis theoretically, in every advanced capitalist democracy since the First World War: namely, the ways in which popular consent can be so constructed, by a historical bloc seeking hegemony, as to harness to its support some popular discontents, neutralise the opposing forces, disaggregate the opposition and really incorporate *some* strategic elements of popular opinion into its own hegemonic project.

These two arguments led me to build on Poulantzas's insights, but to shift the characterisation of the conjuncture from "authoritarian statism" to "authoritarian populism." I hoped by adopting this deliberately contradictory term precisely to encapsulate the contradictory features of the emerging conjuncture: a movement towards a dominative and "authoritarian" form of democratic class politics—paradoxically, apparently rooted in the "transformism" (Gramsci's term) of populist discontents. This was further elaborated in my article "Popular-Democratic versus Authoritarian Populism," where I drew on the seminal work of Ernesto Laclau, and his notion of "populist rupture." But I distanced my more delimited use of the term "populism" from his more inclusive one, attempting thereby to distinguish the genuine mobilisation of popular demands and discontents from a "populist" mobilisation which, at a certain point in its trajectory, flips over or is recuperated into a statist-led political leadership.

Levels of Abstraction

I grant that this genealogy is nowhere fully laid out; though I would claim that it is plain enough from the context and sequence of my work. I also grant that there was too little rigorous or logical "construction of concepts" here. The concepts, I am afraid, were generated in the heat of conjunctural analysis—I was trying to comprehend the shift towards Thatcherism as it was taking place. So, admittedly, the theorisation is a bit rough and ready. I explored the idea of "passive revolution," for example; and I still believe it has something to contribute to our understanding of populist (as opposed to popular) strategies. But I could not at the time bring off the link and have not been able to do so since. Like many of Gramsci's most fruitful concepts, AP remains "over-descriptive." Perhaps I have caught his disease. I suspect that a more fundamental disagreement divides my position from that of Jessop et al. here. I do not believe that all concepts operate at the same level of abstraction—indeed, I think one of the principal things which separates me from the fundamentalist Marxist revival is precisely that they believe that the concepts which Marx advanced at the highest level of abstraction (e.g., mode of production, capitalist epoch) can be transferred directly into the analysis of concrete historical conjunctures. My own view is that concepts like that of "hegemony" (the family or level of abstraction to which AP also belongs) are of necessity somewhat "descriptive," historically more specific, time-bound, concrete in their reference—because they attempt to conceptualise what Marx himself said of "the concrete": that it is the "product of many determinations." So I have to confess that it was not an error or oversight which determined the level of concreteness at which AP operates. It was quite deliberately and self-consciously *not* pitched at that level of "pure" theoretical-analytic operation at which Jessop et al. seem to assume *all* concepts must be produced. The costs of operating at this level of abstraction are clear. But to me—in the wake of the academicising of Marxism and the theoreticist deluge of the 1970s—so are the gains.

I would argue, therefore, that I have only used AP at the level of abstraction and with the range of reference outlined above. I have never claimed for it the general explanatory sweep which Jessop et al. attempt to graft on to it. I am therefore not at all surprised to find that AP is only a partial explanation of Thatcherism. What else *could* it be? It was an attempt to characterise certain strategic shifts in the political/ideological conjuncture. Essentially, it refers to changes in the "balance of forces." It refers directly to the modalities of political and ideological relationships between the ruling *bloc*, the state and the dominated classes. It attempts to expand on and to begin to periodise the internal composition of hegemonic strategies in the politics of class democracies. Theoretically—if anyone is interested—it is part of a wider project to develop and expand on the rich but too condensed concept of hegemony. It is a sort of footnote to Gramsci's "Modern Prince" and "State and Civil Society." It references, but could neither characterise nor explain, changes in the more structural aspects of capitalist social formations. I do not understand how, even grammatically, AP could have been misunderstood as a concept operating at the latter level. "In this field, the struggle can and must be carried on by developing the concept of hegemony," Gramsci observed, in *The Prison Notebooks*. AP is a response to that fateful injunction.

Jessop et al. are certainly in need of no further instruction from me about the concept of hegemony. However, I cannot resist pointing out, at this stage in the argument, that I have *never* advanced the proposition that Thatcherism has achieved "hegemony." The idea, to my mind, is preposterous. What I have said is that, in sharp contrast to the political strategy of *both* the Labourist and the fundamentalist left, Thatcherite politics are "hegemonic" in their conception and project: the *aim* is to struggle on several fronts at once, not on the economic-corporate one alone; and this is based on the knowledge that, in order really to dominate and restructure a social formation, political, moral and intellectual leadership must be coupled to economic dominance. The Thatcherites know they must "win" in civil society as well as in the state. They understand, as the left generally does not, the consequences of the generalisation of the class struggle to new arenas and the need to have a strategy for them too. They mean, if possible, to reconstruct the terrain of what is "taken for granted" in social and political thought—and so to form a new common sense. If one watches how, in the face of a teeth-gritting opposition, they have steadily *used* the unpopularity of some aspects of trade union practice with their own members to inflict massive wounds on the whole labour movement, or how they have steadily not only pursued the "privatisation" of the public sector but installed "value for money" at the heart of the calculations of *every* Labour council and every other social institution—health service, school meals, universities, street cleaning, unemployment benefit offices, social services—one will take this politico-ideological level of struggle somewhat more seriously than the left currently does. That is the *project* of Thatcherism—from which, I am sufficiently in apostasy to believe, the left has something to learn as to the conduct of political struggle. But I do *not* believe and have nowhere advanced the claim that the project has been delivered.

Indeed, I have several times pointed out the yawning discrepancy between Thatcherism's ideological advances and its economic failures. I have consistently argued against the view that Thatcherite neo-monetarism could provide solutions to Britain's structural economic crisis. As the authoritarian face of Thatcherism has become—in line with my analysis—more and more pronounced, it seems to me self-evident that Thatcherism remains *dominant* but *not* hegemonic. It must impose—because it cannot lead. But I have also tried quite carefully to define what we might mean by its "success." In "Thatcherism—A New Stage?" I said *inter alia*: "It is beset by internal contradictions and subject to real limits. It won a measure of electoral support. . . . It cannot deliver on them all. . . . It is not touching the structural economic problems at home . . . and it is powerless to ward off the savage effects of a global capitalist recession."[5] But I also warned that Thatcherism had won power on "a long leash" and would not be blown off course "by an immediate crisis of electoral support." I added that it would be perfectly possible for Thatcherism to "fail" in delivering a solution to Britain's economic crisis, and yet to "succeed" "in its long-term mission to shift the balance of class forces to the right." Big capital, I suggested, has supported Thatcherism because it sees in it "the only political force capable of altering the relations of forces in a manner favourable to the imposition of capitalist solutions." In that sense, I argued, "the long-term political mission of the radical Right could 'succeed' even if this particular Government had to give way to one of another electoral complexion." To that extent, I concluded, "Thatcherism has irrevocably undermined the old solutions and positions." That analysis was offered in 1980, but I believe it to have been fundamentally correct and to have been confirmed by subsequent developments. In the face of that, it is ludicrous to suggest that I have argued that Thatcherism has already achieved hegemony.

"Ideologism"?

This brings us to the charges advanced by Jessop et al. of "ideologism." This is so impacted that it is hard to disentangle. First of all I think they are themselves at fault in eliding the levels of political and ideological struggle, and in suppressing what they must know well—the need for concepts which define their specificity. They may be right in saying that AP does not sufficiently distinguish between these two dimensions of struggle. However, I do hold to the position that, in my own work, I have consistently struggled *against* any definition of hegemony which identifies it as exclusively an ideological phenomenon. On the contrary, I have repeated *ad nauseam* Gramsci's argument about hegemony being impossible to conceptualise or achieve without "the decisive nucleus of economic activity." It is therefore particularly galling to be accused of advancing an explanation of Thatcherism as exclusively an ideological phenomenon, simply because I have drawn attention to features of its ideological strategy which are specific and important.

It seems well-nigh impossible on the left to affirm the importance and specificity of a particular level of analysis or arena of struggle without immediately being misunderstood as saying that, because it is important, it is the *only* one. I have tried in my own work not to make that easy slide. I work on the political/ideological dimension (a) because I happen to have some competence in that area, and (b) because it is often either neglected or reductively treated by the left generally and by some Marxists. But the idea that, because one works at that level, one therefore assumes economic questions to be residual or unimportant is absurd. I think the ideological dimension of Thatcherism to be critical. I am certain the left neither understands it nor knows how to conduct this level of struggle—and is constantly misled by misreading its importance. Hence I was determined to bring out this level of analysis—and AP in part served to do just that. But since AP was never advanced as a general or global explanation, it entailed no prescriptions whatsoever as to the other levels of analysis. The fact is that until these other dimensions are in place *alongside* the concept of AP, the analysis of Thatcherism remains partial and incomplete. But the "foregrounding" involved in AP was quite deliberate. "Bending the twig" towards the most neglected dimension, against the drift of current discussion, Althusser once called it. Jessop et al. have, I think, missed my tactical purpose; they have thereby robbed themselves of insights from which their own analysis might have profited.

When they do turn to the question of ideological foregrounding, I think they misrepresent the work done with AP. Even on the ideological front, Thatcherism has adopted other strategies—like the construction of an intellectual leadership, the formation of a new stratum of "organic" intellectuals, the level of the organisation of theoretical ideas in certain strategic academic, research and other intellectual sites—to which I have also drawn attention, but which have nothing whatsoever to do with the AP strategy and the construction of the popular consent to power. Thatcherism also has a distinct political strategy for the internal re-composition of the power bloc and the state machine which is not "purely" ideological—whatever that means—and has little to do with AP. It is true that, when I turn to describing the ideological *mechanisms*, I use the insights of "discourse theory." That is because I believe that discourse theory has much to tell us about how Thatcherism accomplishes the condensation of different discourses into its contradictory formation, and how it "works" so as to recruit people to its different, often contradictory, subject positions: even though it has only had partial success in its project to construct a new kind of political "subject." But I have long ago definitively dissociated myself from the discourse theoretical approach to the analysis of whole social formations, or even from the idea that the production of new subjectivities provides, in itself, an adequate theory of ideology (as opposed to a critical aspect of its functioning).[6] I have characterised that as a species—long familiar to the tradition of "Western Marxism"—of neo-Kantianism. In doing so, I have also tried carefully to demarcate the immensely fruitful things which I learned from Ernesto Laclau's

Politics and Ideology in Marxist Theory from the dissolution of everything into discourse which, I believe, mars the later volume, *Hegemony and Socialist Strategy*, despite its many insights.[7] These distinctions were widely debated in the so-called "Hegemony Group" in 1980–83, in which Jessop himself took a leading role, so I find it difficult to be now misidentified by Jessop et al. with the latter position.

I believe from what I have already said that it is also quite difficult to sustain the charge that I treat Thatcherism as an "uncontradictory monolith." The entire thrust of my work on the ideology of Thatcherism has been to try to show how Thatcherism has managed to stitch up or "unify" the contradictory strands in its discourse—"the resonant themes of organic Toryism—nation, family, duty, authority, standards, traditionalism, patriarchalism—with the aggressive themes of a revived neo-liberalism—self-interest, competitive individualism, anti-statism," as I put it in "The Great Moving Right Show."[8] In the same piece, I pointed to the highly contradictory subject-positions which Thatcherism was attempting to condense. I deliberately adopted Andrew Gamble's brief but telling paradox—"free market, strong state." How all this could be described as representing Thatcherism as an uncontradictory ideological monolith beats me. Nor do Jessop et al. score points by showing that many of these elements in Thatcherism are not new. "Some of these," I said in the very next sentence, "had been secured in earlier times through the grand themes of one-nation popular Conservatism: the means by which Toryism circumnavigated democracy." I thought this of particular importance in giving substance to Gramsci's argument that, often, ideological shifts take place, not by substituting one whole, new conception of the world for another, but by presenting a novel combination of old and new elements—"a process of distinction and of change in the relative weight possessed by the elements of the old ideology." I don't see how all that could conceivably be construed as endowing Thatcherism with an "excessively unified image."

The Keynesian Welfare State

For the reasons I have already advanced, there are many things which Jessop et al. argue in the succeeding sections of their article with which I wholeheartedly agree. Their analysis and mine are only, I am afraid, in competition with one another in the rather spurious atmosphere of polemical contestation which they quite unnecessarily generated. Nevertheless, I believe that the failures they show in understanding how AP works carry over into their own substantive analysis. Thus they repeat the now-familiar, lefter-than-thou argument that the break-up of the post-war consensus could not be of much political significance because the "Keynesian Welfare State" (KWS) was never "socialist." This is supposed to inflict further damage on the concept of AP. However, I am perfectly well aware that the KWS was not socialist. In *Policing the Crisis* I spent a great deal of space analysing the limits of the KWS and spelling out the contradiction of Labour in power, which I quite specifically characterised as "social democratic" not socialist in political content. The argument has, so far as I know, *never* been that the KWS was "socialist" and that we should therefore now go back to it. That is a figment of the fundamentalist left imagination. What I have argued and do argue is that the KWS was a contradictory structure, a "historic compromise," which both achieved something in a reformist direction for the working class *and* became an instrument in disciplining it. Why else should anyone on the left be now campaigning for the restoration of the cuts in the welfare state if it did *nothing* for the working class? I have also argued that, if we cannot mobilise a full-scale popular agitation around the limited demands of maintaining and expanding "welfare state reformism," on what grounds could we conceivably conceptualise the political conjuncture as one likely to lead to an "irreversible shift of power" towards immediate working-class power? I keep not getting an answer to this conundrum, and must presume this is because the symbolics of who can swear loudest at the reformism of Labour governments is more important on the left than hard analysis. It seems to be convenient to answer, not the question I pose but another, fictional one because the latter usefully demonstrates the degree of my apostasy! I am surprised to find Jessop et al. allowing themselves to drift into that vulgar exercise.

I have other problems with the analysis they advance, though on these I can be briefer. I do not find the "two nations" hypothesis at all convincing. "Good citizen" and "hard worker" seem to me poor characterisations of the critical points of reference in the Thatcherite strategy. Thatcherism deliberately—and from its viewpoint, correctly—eschews *all* reference to the concept of *citizenship*. "Worker" is also a difficult one for it to negotiate, and it constantly prefers "wealth creator." Jessop et al. pose the "hard" question of the relation of Thatcherism to specific class interests. But they fail to provide the non-class-reductionist articulation to class positions they call for. "An uneasy and unstable alliance of interests"? Amen—but we all got as far as that long ago. I also think that Jessop et al. are still too mesmerised by a problem which has long ago disappeared, in the sociological form in which it was carefully tended in the 1970s, into the oblivion. That is the question of "corporatism." The problems to which "corporatism" was a response in the 1970s remain. The corporatist strategy is in abeyance—one of Thatcherism's accomplishments: though a healthy dose of Kinnock-ism will undoubtedly revive its deeply undemocratic features and endow it with a life-after-death.

On many other aspects of the Jessop et al. analysis I do not substantially differ. But on the central thrust of the argument, I think their article sophisticated but mistaken. They have badly skewed their own analysis and our general understanding of the Thatcherism phenomenon by entering into a misconceived confrontation with my work and with the concept of AP. They have profoundly misread the entire Gramscian terrain in which, from beginning to end, the whole AP discussion has been rooted. I am afraid they have sometimes had their eye cocked more towards scoring points than deconstructing Thatcherism. Nevertheless, they have contributed substantially to our understanding of many of its perplexing aspects. Perhaps, now that the sound of conceptual gunfire has died away, we might all get back to the far more important task of understanding the real complexity of the Thatcherism phenomenon, the better to defeat and destroy it.

NOTES

This essay first appeared in *New Left Review*, I/151 (1985): 115–24.

1. Kevin Bonnett, Simon Bromley, Bob Jessop, and Tom Ling, "Authoritarian Populism, Two Nations and Thatcherism," *New Left Review*, I/147 (September/October 1984).
2. Stuart Hall, Chas Critcher, Tony Jefferson, John Clarke, and Brian Roberts, *Policing the Crisis: Mugging, the State and Law and Order* (London: Macmillan, 1978).
3. On the conceptual distinction between "popular" and "populist" mobilization, which Jessop et al. seem to ignore, see Stuart Hall, "Popular-Democratic versus Authoritarian Populism," in *Marxism and Democracy*, ed. Alan Hunt (London: Lawrence and Wishart, 1980).
4. Nicos Poulantzas, *State, Power, Socialism* (London: New Left Books, 1978), 203.
5. *Marxism Today*, February 1980.
6. See, *inter alia*, "Recent Developments in Language and Ideology," in *Culture, Media, Language*, ed. Stuart Hall, Dorothy Hobson, Andrew Lowe, and Paul Willis (London: Hutchinson/CCCS, 1980).
7. Ernesto Laclau, *Politics and Ideology in Marxist Theory* (London: New Left Books, 1977); Ernesto Laclau and Chantal Mouffe, *Hegemony and Socialist Strategy* (London: Verso, 1985).
8. In Stuart Hall and Martin Jacques, eds., *The Politics of Thatcherism* (London: Lawrence and Wishart, 1983).

CHAPTER 11

When Was "the Post-colonial"?
Thinking at the Limit

Necessarily, we must dismiss those tendencies that encourage the consoling play of recognitions.
—Michel Foucault, "Nietzsche, Genealogy, History"

When was "the post-colonial"? What should be included and excluded from its frame? Where is the invisible line between it and its "others" (colonialism, neo-colonialism, Third World, imperialism), in relation to whose termination it ceaselessly, but without final supersession, marks itself? The main purpose of this paper is to explore the interrogation marks which have begun to cluster thick and fast around the question of "the post-colonial" and the notion of post-colonial times. If post-colonial time is the time *after* colonialism, and colonialism is defined in terms of the binary division between the colonisers and the colonised, why is post-colonial time *also* a time of "difference"? What sort of "difference" is this and what are its implications for the forms of politics and for subject formation in this late-modern moment? These questions increasingly haunt the contested space in which the concept of the "post-colonial" now operates and they cannot be satisfactorily explored until we know more about what the concept means and why it has become the bearer of such powerful unconscious investments—a sign of desire for some, and equally for others, a signifier of danger.

This interrogation can most usefully be done by engaging with the case against the "post-colonial" which has been rapidly taking shape in a series of critical commentaries in recent months. Ella Shohat, whose work in this field has been exemplary for critical scholars, has taken it to task for a variety of conceptual sins. She criticises the "post-colonial" for its theoretical and political ambiguity, its "dizzying multiplicity of positionalities," its "a-historical and universalising displacements" and its "depoliticising implications."[1] The post-colonial, she argues, is politically ambivalent because it blurs the clear-cut distinctions between colonisers and colonised hitherto associated with the paradigms of "colonialism," "neo-colonialism" and "Third Worldism" which it aims to supplant. It dissolves the politics of resistance because it "posits no clear domination and calls for no clear opposition." Like the other "posts" with which it is aligned, it collapses different histories, temporalities and racial formations into the same universalising category. This is a critique shared by Anne McClintock, another of the original scholars working in this field, who criticises the concept for its linearity and its "entranced suspension of history."[2] For both critics, the concept is used to mark the final closure of a historical epoch, as if colonialism and its effects are definitively over. "Post," for Shohat, means *past*: definitively terminated, closed. But this too, for Shohat, is part of its ambiguity since it does not make clear whether this periodisation is intended to be epistemological or chronological. Does "post-colonial" mark the ruptural point between two epistemes in intellectual history or does it refer to "the strict chronologies of history *tout court*?"[3]

In his recent polemical contribution to this debate, the distinguished scholar of modern China, Arif Dirlik, not only cites many of the criticisms of Shohat and McClintock with approval—he too finds the concept "celebratory" of the so-called end of colonialism—but adds two substantial critiques of his own. The first is that the post-colonial is a post-structuralist, post-foundationalist discourse, deployed mainly by displaced Third World intellectuals making good in prestige "Ivy League" American universities and deploying the fashionable language of the linguistic and cultural "turn" to "rephrase" Marxism, returning it "to another First World language with universalistic epistemological pretentions." The second and related argument is that the "post-colonial" grossly underplays "capitalism's structuring of the modern world." Its notion of identity is discursive not structural. It repudiates structure and totality. Post-colonial discourse, he says blankly, is "a culturalism."[4] Lurking within the first of Dirlik's arguments is a refrain which is common to all these recent critiques: namely, the "ubiquitous academic marketability" of the term "post-colonial" (McClintock) and the prominent position in its deployment of "academic intellectuals of Third World origin . . . [acting as] pace-setters in cultural criticism" (Dirlik).

Let us leave aside the latter point, with its whiff of politically correct grapeshot and the unwelcome glimpse it unconsciously affords into (as well as the bizarre preoccupation of American-based critical intellectuals with) the "ins" and "outs" of American academia. There are larger issues hovering in the shadows here to which we will have to return—such as, for example, the reductionism of Dirlik's proposition that post-colonial criticism "resonates with the conceptual needs" of global relationships caused by shifts in the world capitalist economy (when last have we heard *that* formulation!) which, he says, explains why a concept which is intended to be critical "should appear to be complicitous in 'the consecration of hegemony.'"[5]

Of course, when one looks at these arguments carefully in context, there is less underlying agreement between them than sometimes appears. The "multiplicity of positionalities" which Shohat finds disquieting in the post-colonial may not be all that different from the "multiplicity" McClintock regards as a worrying absence: "I am struck by how seldom the term is used to denote *multiplicity*." The assault on post-structuralism in Dirlik does not actually square with what we know of McClintock's substantive work, which is profoundly "post-foundational" in inspiration.[6] Though Shohat ends her critique with the recognition that one conceptual frame is not necessarily "wrong" and the other "right," her criticisms are so extensive and damaging that it is difficult to know what of substance she would like to see rescued from the debris. But this is nit-picking. The case against the post-colonial advanced by these critics and others is substantial and must be taken seriously in its own terms.

A certain nostalgia runs through some of these arguments for a return to a clear-cut politics of binary oppositions, where clear "lines can be drawn in the sand" between goodies and baddies (Shohat's article starts with the "clarifying" instance of the Gulf War). This is not as compelling an argument as it seems at first sight. These "lines" may have been simple once (were they?), but they certainly are so no longer. Otherwise, how are we to understand the general crisis of politics on the left except as some sort of simple conspiracy? This does not mean that there are no "right" or "wrong" sides, no play of power, no hard political choices to be made. But isn't the ubiquitous, the soul-searing, lesson of our times the fact that political binaries do not (do not any longer? did they ever?) either stabilise the field of political antagonism in any permanent way or render it transparently intelligible? "Frontier effects" are not "given" but constructed; consequently, political positionalities are not fixed and do not repeat themselves from one historical situation to the next or from one theatre of antagonism to another, ever "in place," in an endless iteration. Isn't that the shift from politics as a "war of manoeuvre" to politics as a "war of position," which Gramsci long ago, and decisively, charted? And are we not all, in different ways, and through different conceptual spaces (of which the post-colonial is definitively one), desperately trying to understand what making an ethical political choice and taking a political position in a necessarily open and contingent political field is like, what sort of "politics" it adds up to?

There may indeed be differences of response here between the US and Britain. Without going to great lengths, I find myself insisting that what the Gulf War provided was not the clarifying political experience of "lines ... drawn in the sand" but the difficulties which arose in opposing the Western war in the desert when manifestly the situation in the Gulf involved *both* the atrocities which the Alliance committed in defence of Western oil interests under UN cover against the people of Iraq (in whose historic "underdevelopment" the West is deeply implicated); *and* the atrocities committed against his own people and against the best interests of the region, not to speak of those of the Kurds and the Marsh Arabs, by Saddam Hussein. There is a "politics" there; but it is not one from which complexity and ambiguity can be usefully expunged. And it isn't an untypical example, randomly chosen, but characteristic of a certain kind of political event of our "new times" in which *both* the crisis of the uncompleted struggle for "decolonisation" *and* the crisis of the "post-independence" state are deeply inscribed? In short, wasn't the Gulf War, in this sense, a classic "post-colonial" event?

Ella Shohat, of course, at one level, clearly understands this argument, if not endorsing all of its implications. The last three decades in the "Third World," she observes, have

> offered a number of very complex and politically ambiguous developments ... [including] the realisation that the wretched of the earth are not unanimously revolutionary ... and [that] despite the broad patterns of geo-political hegemony, power relations in the Third World are also dispersed and contradictory.

She refers to conflicts "not only between ... but also within nations, with the constantly changing relations between dominant and subaltern groups."[7] However, instead of this observation provoking an examination of the potential value of the term "post-colonial" in precisely referencing this shift theoretically, she ends this part of the discussion with a polemically negative observation about the visibility of the "post-colonial" "in Anglo-American academic cultural studies." In short, where she could easily have concluded with a conceptual reflection, she chose instead a polemical closure.

As to whether the concept "post-colonial" has been confusingly universalised: there is undoubtedly some careless homogenising going on, as the phrase has caught on and become widely and sometimes inappropriately applied. There are serious distinctions to be made here which have been neglected and which do weaken the conceptual value of the term. Is Britain "post-colonial" in the same sense as the US? Indeed, is the US usefully thought of as "post-colonial" at all? Should the term be commonly applied to Australia, which is a white settler colony, and to India? Are Britain and Canada, Nigeria and Jamaica "equally 'post-colonial'?," as Shohat asks in her article. Can Algerians living at home and in France, the French and the *pied noir* settlers, *all* be "post-colonial"? Is Latin America "post-colonial," even though its independence struggles were fought early in the nineteenth century, long before the recent stage of "decolonisation" to which the term more evidently refers, and were led by the descendants of Spanish settlers who had colonised their own "native peoples"? Shohat, in her article, exploits this weakness effectively and it is clear that, in the light of this critique, those deploying the concept must attend more carefully to its discriminations and specificities and/or establish more clearly at what level of abstraction the term is operating and how this avoids a spurious "universalisation." Anne McClintock also persuasively distinguishes between a number of different trajectories in global domination, in the course of making a valid and important general point about the need to think the "continuities and discontinuities of power" together.[8] Lata Mani and Ruth Frankenberg, in their carefully argued assessment, are particularly helpful here in reminding us that it need not follow that all societies are "post-colonial" *in the same* way and that in any case the "post-colonial" does not operate on its own but "is in effect a construct internally differentiated by its intersections with other unfolding relations."[9]

So, a more careful discrimination is in order between different social and racial formations. Australia and Canada, on the one hand, Nigeria, India and Jamaica on the other, are certainly not "post-colonial" *in the same way*. But this does not mean that they are not "post-colonial" *in any way*. In terms of their relation to the imperial centre, and the ways in which, as C. L. R. James put it about the Caribbean, they are "in but not of the West," they were plainly all "colonial," and are usefully designated now as "post-colonial," though the manner, timing and conditions of their colonisation and independence varied greatly. So, for that matter, was the US, whose current "culture wars," conducted throughout with reference to some mythicised Eurocentric conception of high civilisation, are literally unintelligible outside the framework of America's colonial past.

There are, however, some ways of discriminating between uses of the term which are not, in my view, helpful. Some would deny it to white settler colonies, reserving it exclusively for the non-western colonised societies. Others would refuse it to the colonising societies of the metropolis, reserving it for the colonies of the periphery only. This is to confuse a descriptive category with an evaluative one. What the concept *may* help us to do is to describe or characterise the shift in global relations which marks the (necessarily uneven) transition from the age of Empires to the post-independence or post-decolonisation moment. It may also help us (though here its value is more gestural) to identify what are the new relations and dispositions of power which are emerging in the new conjuncture. But as Peter Hulme has argued recently,

> If "post-colonial" is a useful word, then it refers to a *process* of disengagement from the whole colonial syndrome which takes many forms and is probably inescapable for all those whose worlds have been marked by that set of phenomena: "post-colonial" is (or should be) a descriptive not an evaluative term. . . . [It is not] some kind of badge of merit.[10]

This thought also helps us to identify, not only the level at which careful distinctions have to be made, but also the level at which "post-colonial" is *properly* "universalising" (i.e., a concept which is referring to a high level of abstraction). It refers to a general process of decolonisation which, like colonisation itself, has marked the colonising societies as powerfully as it has the colonised (of course, in different ways). Hence the subverting of the old colonising/colonised binary in the new conjuncture. Indeed, one of the principal values of the term "post-colonial" has been to direct our attention to the many ways in which colonisation was never simply external to the societies of the imperial metropolis. It was always inscribed deeply within them—as it became indelibly inscribed in the cultures of the colonised. This was a process whose negative effects provided the foundation of anti-colonial political mobilisation and provoked the attempt to recover an alternative set of cultural origins not contaminated by the colonising experience. This was, as Shohat observes, the critical dimension of anti-colonial struggles. However, in terms of any absolute return to a pure set of uncontaminated origins, the long-term historical and cultural effects of the "transculturation" which characterised the colonising experience proved, in my view, to be irreversible. The differences, of course, between colonising and colonised cultures remain profound. But they have never operated in a purely binary way and they certainly do so no longer. Indeed, the shift from circumstances in which anti-colonial struggles seemed to assume a binary form of representation to the present when they can no longer be represented within a binary structure, I would describe as a move from one conception of difference to another,[11] from difference *to différance*, and this shift is precisely what the serialised or staggered transition to the "post-colonial" is marking. But it is not only not marking it in a "then" and "now" way. It is obliging us to re-read the very binary form in which the colonial encounter has for so long itself been represented. It obliges us to re-read the binaries as forms of transculturation, of cultural translation, destined to trouble the here/there cultural binaries for ever.

It is precisely this "double inscription," breaking down the clearly demarcated inside/outside of the colonial system on which the histories of imperialism have thrived for so long, which the concept of the "post-colonial" has done so much to bring to the fore.[12] It follows that the term "post-colonial" is not merely descriptive of "this" society rather than "that," or of "then" and "now." It re-reads "colonisation" as part of an essentially trans-national and transcultural "global" process—and it produces a decentred, diasporic or "global" rewriting of earlier, nation-centred imperial grand narratives. Its theoretical value therefore lies precisely in its refusal of this "here" and "there," "then" and "now," "home" and "abroad" perspective. "Global" here does not mean universal, but it is not nation- or society-specific either. It is about how the lateral and transverse cross-relations of what Paul Gilroy calls the "diasporic" supplement and simultaneously dis-place the centre-periphery, and the global/local reciprocally re-organise and re-shape one another.[13] As Mani and Frankenberg argue, "colonialism" always was about, and "post-colonial" certainly is about, different ways of "staging the encounters" between the colonising societies and their "others"—"though not always in the same way or to the same degree."[14]

This argument connects with another strand of the critique—namely, the "post-colonial" as a form of periodisation, and what Shohat calls its "problematic temporality." What "post-colonial" certainly is not is one of those periodisations based on epochal "stages," when everything is reversed at the same moment, all the old relations disappear for ever and entirely new ones come to replace them. Clearly, the disengagement from the colonising process has been a long, drawn-out and differentiated affair, in which the recent post-war movements towards decolonisation figures as one, but only one, distinctive "moment." Here, "colonisation" signals direct colonial occupation and rule, and the transition to "post-colonial" is characterised by independence from direct colonial rule, the formation of new nation states, forms of economic development dominated by the growth of indigenous capital and their relations of neo-colonial dependency on the developed capitalist world, and the politics which arise from emergence of powerful local elites managing the contradictory effects of under-development. Just as significant, it is characterised by the persistence of many of the effects of colonisation, but at the same time their displacement from the coloniser/colonised axis to their internalisation within the decolonised society itself. Hence, the British, who were deeply implicated with the regional economies, the ruling factions and the complex politics of the Gulf States, Persia and Mesopotamia through the network of mandates and protected "spheres of influence" after World War One, withdrew in the decolonising moment "west of Suez"; and the "after-effects" of this pervasive type of indirect colonial hegemony is then "lived" and "re-worked" through the various "internal" crises of the post-colonial states and societies of the Gulf States, Iraq, Iran and Afghanistan, not to speak of Palestine and Israel. In this scenario, "the colonial" is not dead, since it lives on in its "after-effects." But its politics can certainly no longer be mapped completely back into, nor declared to be "the same" in the post-colonial moment as it was during the period of the British mandate. These complexities and re-stagings have become a common feature in many parts of the "post-colonial" world, although there have also been other "decolonising" trajectories, both earlier ones and ones with significantly different outcomes.

One could ask—it seems some of the critics are asking—why then privilege this moment of the "post-colonial"? Doesn't it, with its preoccupation with the colonised/colonising relationship, simply revive or re-stage exactly what the post-colonial so triumphantly declares to be "over"? Dirlik, for example, finds it strange that the post-colonial critics are so preoccupied with the Enlightenment and with Europe, the critique of which seems—oddly— to be their central task. McClintock also criticises the "recentering of global history around the single rubric of European time."[15] It is true that the "post-colonial" signals the proliferation of histories and temporalities, the intrusion of difference and specificity into the generalising and Eurocentric post-Enlightenment grand narratives, the multiplicity of lateral and decentred cultural connections, movements and migrations which make up the world today, often bypassing the old metropolitan centres. Perhaps, however, we should have been warned by other theoretical examples, where the deconstruction of core concepts undertaken by the so-called "post-" discourses is followed, not by their abolition and disappearance, but rather *by their proliferation* (as Foucault warned), only now in a "decentred" position in the discourse. The "subject" and "identity" are only two of the concepts which, having been radically undermined in their unitary and essentialist form, have proliferated beyond our wildest expectations in their decentred forms into new discursive positionalities.

At the same time, there is something to the argument that, as Lata Mani and Ruth Frankenberg remark in their critique of Robert Young's *White Mythologies*, sometimes the *only* purpose which the post-colonial critique seems to serve is as a critique of western philosophical discourse, which, as they observe, is like "merely [taking] a detour to return to the position of the Other as a resource for rethinking the Western Self." It would, as they say, be a turn-up for the books if the "key object and achievement of the Algerian War of Independence was the overthrow of the Hegelian dialectic"![16] In fact, in my view, the problem with *White Mythologies* is not that it sees the connection between the post-colonial and the critique of the western metaphysical tradition, but that it is driven by a Promethean desire for the ultimate theoretically correct position—a desire to out-theorise everyone else—and, in so doing, sets up a hierarchy from the "bad" (Sartre, Marxism, Jameson) through the "not-too-bad-but-wrong" (Said, Foucault) to the "almost-OK" (Spivak, Bhabha) without ever once putting on the table for serious critical inspection the normative discourse, the foundational figure—i.e., Derrida—in relation to whose absence/presence the whole linear sequence is staged. But that is another story—or rather the same story in another part of the forest...

Many of the critiques of the "post-colonial," then—paradoxically, given its post-structuralist orientation—take the form of a demand for more multiplicity and dispersal (though Dirlik, with his stress on the structuring force of capitalism, is deeply suspicious of this kind of post-structuralist flirtation). Yet, while holding fast to differentiation and specificity, we cannot afford to forget the overdetermining effects of the colonial moment, the "work" which its binaries were constantly required to do to *re-present* the proliferation of cultural difference and forms of life, which were always there, within the sutured and overdetermined "unity" of that simplifying, over-arching binary, "the West and the Rest." (This recognition goes some way to rescuing

Edward Said's *Orientalism* from the critique that it fails to discriminate between different imperialisms.)[17] We have to keep these two ends of the chain in play at the same time—overdetermination and difference, condensation and dissemination—if we are not to fall into a playful deconstructionism, the fantasy of a powerless *utopia* of difference. It is only too tempting to fall into the trap of assuming that, because essentialism has been deconstructed *theoretically*, therefore it has been displaced *politically*.

In terms of periodisation, however, the "post-colonial" retains some ambiguity because, in addition to identifying the post-decolonisation moment as critical for a shift in global relations, the term also offers—as all periodisations do—an alternative narrative, highlighting different key conjunctures to those embedded in the classical narrative of Modernity. Colonisation, from this "post-colonial" perspective, was no local or marginal sub-plot in some larger story (for example, the transition from feudalism to capitalism in western Europe, the latter developing "organically" in the womb of the former). In the re-staged narrative of the post-colonial, colonisation assumes the place and significance of a major, extended and ruptural world-historical event. By "colonisation," the "post-colonial" references something more than direct rule over certain areas of the world by the imperial powers. I think it is signifying the whole process of expansion, exploration, conquest, colonisation and imperial hegemonisation which constituted the "outer face," the constitutive outside, of European and then Western capitalist modernity after 1492.

This re-narrativisation displaces the "story" of capitalist modernity from its European centring to its dispersed global "peripheries"; from peaceful evolution to imposed violence; from the transition from feudalism to capitalism (which played such a talismanic role in, for example, Western Marxism) to the formation of the world market, to use shorthand terms for a moment; or rather to new ways of conceptualising the relationship between these different "events"—the permeable inside/outside borders of emergent "global" capitalist modernity. It is the retrospective re-phrasing of modernity within the framework of "globalisation" in all its various ruptural forms and moments (from the Portuguese entry to the Indian Ocean and the conquest of the New World to the internationalisation of financial markets and information flows) which is the really distinctive element in a "post-colonial" periodisation. In this way, the "post-colonial" marks a critical interruption into that whole grand historiographical narrative which, in liberal historiography and Weberian historical sociology, as much as in the dominant traditions of Western Marxism, gave this global dimension a subordinate presence in a story which could essentially be told from within its European parameters.

Colonisation, understood or re-read in this sense, was only intelligible as an event of global significance—by which one signals not its universal and totalising, but its dislocated and differentiated character. That is to say, it had to be understood then, and certainly can only be understood now, in terms, not only of the vertical relations between coloniser and colonised, but also in terms of how these and other forms of power-relations were *always* displaced and decentred by another set of vectors—the transverse linkages between and across nation-state frontiers and the *global/local* inter-relationships which cannot be read off against a nation-state template. It is in this reconstitution of the epistemic and power/knowledge fields around the relations of globalisation, through its various historical forms, that the "periodisation" of the "post-colonial" is really challenging. However, this point hardly surfaces in any of the critiques. And when it does (as in Dirlik), its effects are contradictory for the run of the argument, as I hope to demonstrate below. What's more, to jump several stages ahead for a moment, it is precisely because of this critical relay through the global that the "post-colonial" has been able to become so sensitively attuned to precisely those dimensions which Shohat, for example, finds problematic—questions of hybridity, syncretism, of cultural undecidability and the complexities of diasporic identification which interrupt any "return" to ethnically closed and "centred" original histories. Understood in its global and transcultural context, colonisation has made ethnic absolutism an increasingly untenable cultural strategy. It made the "colonies" themselves, and even more, large tracts of the "post-colonial" world, always-already "diasporic" in relation to what might be thought of as their cultures of origin. The notion that only the multicultural cities of the First World are "diasporaised" is a fantasy which can only be sustained by those who have never lived in the hybridised spaces of a Third World, so-called "colonial" city.

In this "post-colonial" moment, these transverse, transnational, transcultural movements, which were always inscribed in the history of "colonisation," but carefully overwritten by more binary forms of narrativisation, have, of course, emerged in new forms to disrupt the settled relations of domination and resistance inscribed in other ways of living and telling these stories. They reposition and dis-place "difference" without, in the Hegelian sense, "overcoming" it. Shohat observes that the anti-essentialist emphasis in "post-colonial" discourse sometimes seems to define *any* attempt to recover or inscribe a communal past as a form of idealisation, despite its significance as a site of resistance and collective identity. She makes the very valid point that this past *could* be negotiated differently, "not as a static fetishised phase to be literally reproduced but as fragmented sets of narrated memories and experiences."[18] I would agree with this argument. But this is to take the double-inscriptions of the colonising encounter, the dialogic character of its alterity, the specific character of its "difference" and the centrality of questions of narrative and the imaginary in political struggle seriously.[19] However, isn't that precisely what is meant by thinking the cultural consequences of the colonising process "diasporically," in non-originary ways—that is, *through*, rather than around, "hybridity"? Doesn't it imply trying to think the questions of cultural power and political struggle *within* rather than against the grain of "the post-colonial"?

The way difference was lived in the colonised societies after the violent and abrupt rupture of colonisation, was and had to be decisively different from how these cultures would have developed, had they done so in isolation from one another. From that turning point in the closing decades of the fifteenth century forwards, there is, of course, no "single, homogeneous, empty (Western) time." But there are the condensations and ellipses which arise when all the different temporalities, while remaining "present" and "real" in their differential effects, are also rupturally convened *in relation to*, and must mark their "difference" in terms of, the overdetermining effects of Eurocentric temporalities, systems of representation and power. This is what is meant by placing colonisation in the framework of "globalisation" or rather by the assertion that what distinguishes modernity is this overdetermined, sutured and *supplementary* character of its temporalities. Hybridity, syncretism, multidimensional temporalities, the double inscriptions of colonial and metropolitan times, the two-way cultural traffic characteristic of the contact zones of the cities of the "colonised" long before they have become the characteristic tropes of the cities of the "colonising," the forms of translation and transculturation which have characterised the "colonial relation" from its earliest stages, the disavowals and in-betweenness, the here-and-theres, mark the *aporias* and re-doublings whose interstices colonial discourses have always negotiated and about which Homi Bhabha has written with such profound insight.[20] It goes without saying that they have, *of course*, always to be set within and against the overdetermining power-knowledge discursive relations by which imperial regimes were stitched or laced together. They are the tropes of supplementarity and *différance* within a dislocated but sutured global system which only emerged or could emerge in the wake of the onset of the colonising expansionist process which Mary Louise Pratt calls the Euro-imperial adventure.[21]

Since the sixteenth century, these differential temporalities and histories have been irrevocably and violently yoked together. This certainly does not mean that they ever were or are *the same*. Their grossly unequal trajectories, which formed the very ground of political antagonism and cultural resistance, have nevertheless been impossible to disentangle, conceptualise or narrate as discrete entities: though that is precisely what the dominant western historiographical tradition has often tried to do. No site, either "there" or "here," in its fantasised autonomy and indifference, could develop without taking into account its significant and/or abjected others. The very notion of an autonomous, self-produced and self-identical cultural identity, like that of a self-sufficient economy or absolutely sovereign polity, had in fact to be discursively constructed in and through "the Other," through a system of similarities and differences, through the play of *différance* and the tendency of these fixed signifiers to float, to go "on the slide." The Other ceased to be a term fixed in place and time external to the system of identification and became, instead, a symbolically marked "constitutive outside," a positionality of differential marking within a discursive chain.

It is possible, now, to answer the question posed earlier about the "post-colonial's" preoccupation with Eurocentric time. The Enlightenment returns, in the discourse of the "post-colonial," in its decentred position, because it represents a critical epistemic shift within the colonising process, understood in this wider sense, whose discursive, power-knowledge, effects are still in play (how, in western discourses dominated by science and the social sciences, could it fail to be?). Until the Enlightenment, difference had often been conceptualised in terms of different orders of being—"Are they True Men?" was the question which Juan Ginés de Sepúlveda put to Bartholomé de Las Casas in the famous debate at Vallodolid before Charles V in 1550. Whereas, under the universalising panoptic eye of the Enlightenment, all forms of human life were brought within the universal scope of a single order of being, so that difference had to be recast into the constant marking and re-marking of positions within a single discursive system (*différance*). This process was organised by those shifting mechanisms of "otherness," alterity and exclusion and the tropes of fetishism and pathologisation, which were required if "difference" was ever to be fixed and consolidated within a "unified" discourse of *civilisation*. They were constitutive in the symbolic production of a constitutive outside, which however has always refused to be fixed in place and which was, and even more today is, always slipping back across the porous or invisible borders to disturb and subvert from the inside.[22]

The argument is not that, thereafter, everything has remained the same—colonisation repeating itself in perpetuity to the end of time. It is, rather, that colonisation so refigured the terrain that, ever since, the very idea of a world of separate identities, of isolated or separable and self-sufficient cultures and economies, has been obliged to yield to a variety of paradigms designed to capture these different but related forms of relationship, interconnection and discontinuity. This was the distinctive form of dissemination-and-condensation which colonisation set in play. It is in privileging this missing or downgraded dimension in the official narrative of "colonisation" that the discourse of "post-colonial" is conceptually distinctive. Although colonisation's particular forms of inscription and subjection varied in almost every other respect from one part of the globe to another, its general effects also require to be crudely but decisively marked, theoretically, alongside its pluralities and multiplicities. That, in my view, is what the anomalous signifier "colonial" is doing in the concept of the "post-colonial."

What, then, about the more troubling question of the prefix, the "post-"? Shohat, for example, acknowledges that the "post-" signals both the "closure of a certain historical event or age" and a "going beyond ... commenting upon a certain intellectual movement."[23] She clearly prefers the latter meaning to the former. For Hulme, however, the "post-" in "post-colonial"

> has two dimensions which exist in tension with each other: a temporal dimension in which there is a punctual relationship in time between, for example, a colony and a post-colonial state; and a critical dimension in which, for example, post-colonial theory comes into existence through a critique of a body of theory.[24]

Moreover, the tension, for Hulme, is productive, whereas for Shohat it produces a structured ambivalence. In this respect, she seems to argue that the "post-colonial" is different from the other "posts" in attempting to be both epistemic and chronological. It is both the paradigm and the chronological moment of the "colonial" which the "post-colonial" claims to be superseding.

However, it seems to me that, in this respect, the "post-colonial" is no different from the other "posts." It is not only "after" but "going beyond" the colonial, as post-modernism is both "going beyond" and "after" modernism, and post-structuralism both follows chronologically and achieves its theoretical gains "on the back of" structuralism. The trickier question is whether in fact these two could ever be separated, and what such a separation would imply about the way "colonisation" itself is being conceptualised. "Colonialism" refers to a specific historical moment (a complex and differentiated one, as we have tried to suggest); but it was always also a way of staging or narrating a history, and its descriptive value was always framed within a distinctive definitional and theoretical paradigm. The very succession of terms which have been coined to refer to this process—colonisation, imperialism, neo-colonial, dependency, Third World—shows the degree to which each apparently innocent descriptive term carried in its slipstream powerful epistemological, conceptual and indeed political baggage: the degree, in short, to which each has to be understood discursively. Indeed, the distinction which this critique seems to be trying to enforce between "power" and "knowledge" is exactly what the discourse of the post-colonial (or rather, what thinking both "the colonial" and "the post-colonial" discursively) has displaced. With "colonisation," and consequently with the "post-colonial," we are irrevocably within a power-knowledge field of force. It is precisely the false and disabling distinction between colonisation as a system of rule, of power and exploitation, and colonisation as a system of knowledge and representation, which is being refused. It is because the relations which characterised the "colonial" are no longer in the same place and relative position, that we are able not simply to oppose them but to critique, to deconstruct and try to "go beyond" them.

But what exactly might be meant by this "after" and "going beyond"? Shohat argues that "the operation of simultaneously privileging and distancing the colonial narrative, moving beyond it, structures the 'in-between' framework of the 'post-colonial.'"[25] She is not very sympathetic to this undecidability. But it is possible to argue that the tension between the epistemological and the chronological is not disabling but productive. "After" means in the moment which follows that moment (the colonial) in which the colonial relation was dominant. It does not mean, as we tried to show earlier, that what we have called the "after-effects" of colonial rule have somehow been suspended. It certainly does *not* mean that we have passed from a regime of power-knowledge into some powerless and conflict-free time zone. Nevertheless, it does also stake its claim in terms of the fact that some other, related but as yet "emergent" new configurations of power-knowledge relations are beginning to exert their distinctive and specific effects. This way of conceptualising the shift between these paradigms—not as an epistemological "break" in the Althusserian/structuralist sense but more on the analogy of what Gramsci called a movement of deconstruction-reconstruction or what Derrida, in a more deconstructive sense, calls a "double inscription"—is characteristic of all the "posts."

Gramsci, speaking about transformations in the field of practical common sense, observes that they have to be thought as

> a process of distinction and of change in the relative weight possessed by the elements of the old ideology.... What was secondary or even incidental becomes of primary importance, it becomes the nucleus of a new doctrinal and ideological ensemble. The old collective will disintegrates into its contradictory elements so that the subordinate elements amongst them can develop socially.[26]

What, in their different ways, these theoretical descriptions are attempting to construct is a notion of a shift or a transition conceptualised as the reconfiguration of a field, rather than as a movement of linear transcendence between two mutually exclusive states. Such transformations are not only not completed but they may not be best captured within a paradigm which assumes that all major historical shifts are driven by a necessitarian logic towards a teleological end. Lata Mani and Ruth Frankenberg make the critical distinction between a transition which is "decisive" (which the "post-colonial" certainly is) and one which is "definitive." To put this another way, all the key concepts in the "post-colonial," as in the general discourse of the "posts," are operating, as Derrida would put it, "under erasure." They have been subjected to a deep and thoroughgoing critique, exposing their assumptions as a set of foundational effects. But this deconstruction does not abolish them, in the classic movement of supersession, an *Aufhebung*. It leaves them as the only conceptual instruments and tools with which to think about the present—but only if they are deployed in their deconstructed form. They are, to use another, more Heideggerian, formulation, which Iain Chambers, for example, prefers, "a presence that exists in abeyance."[27]

In a now-famous exchange about "thinking at the limit"—which seems to me a good description of the status of "the post-colonial" as an episteme-in-formation—Derrida once defined the limit of philosophical discourse as "the episteme, functioning within a system of fundamental constraints, conceptual oppositions outside of which philosophy becomes impracticable." He spoke of "a necessarily double gesture ... marked in certain decisive places by an erasure which allows what it obliterates to be read, violently inscribing within the text that which attempted to govern it from without" and of trying to respect as rigorously as possible "the internal, regulated play of philosophemes... by making them slide... to the point of their nonpertinence, their exhaustion, their closure."

> To "deconstruct" philosophy, thus, would be to think—in the most faithful interior way—the structured genealogy of philosophy's concepts, but at the same time to determine—from a certain exterior that is unqualifiable or unnameable by philosophy—what this history has been unable to dissimulate or forbid.... By means of this simultaneously faithful and violent circulation between the inside and the outside of philosophy... there is produced a certain textual work...

When his interlocutor, Henri Ronse, asked him whether by this means there could be "a surpassing of this metaphysics," Derrida remarked,

> There is *not* a transgression if one understands by that a pure and simple landing into the beyond of metaphysics.... But, by means of the work done on one side and the other of the limit, the field inside is modified, and a transgression is produced that consequently is nowhere present as a *fait accompli*.[28]

The problem, then, is not that the "post-colonial" is a conventional paradigm of a logico-deductive type which erroneously confuses the chronological and the epistemological. Lying behind this is a deeper choice between epistemologies: between a rational and successive logic and a deconstructive one. In this sense, Dirlik is correct to pinpoint the question of the post-colonial's relation to what can be broadly called "post-structuralist" ways of thinking as a central issue which its critics find particularly troubling. Larger issues are thus "at stake" in this debate than the criticisms which have been widely signalled sometimes suggest.

Dirlik is particularly ferocious in this area and for reasons which are not difficult to identify. Discovering that the term "post-colonial" is applied to many writers who do not necessarily agree with one another, some of whom Dirlik likes and others he does not, he is driven to the polemical conclusion that the "post-colonial" is not the description of anything or anyone in particular but rather "a discourse that seeks to constitute the world in the self-image of intellectuals who view themselves or have come to view themselves as post-colonial intellectuals [and] ... an expression ... of [their] new-found power" in First World academia. This rather crude *ad hominem* and *ad feminam* name-calling disfigures the argument of a distinguished scholar of modern China and it would perhaps be wise to think of it as "symptomatic." But of what? We get a clue to an answer when he takes Gyan Prakash's elegant post-structuralist defence of the post-colonial, "Post-colonial Criticism and Indian Historiography," as his principal stalking horse.[29] Let us leave the many local criticisms of this article, some of which we have already mentioned, to one side. The main burden of the charge is that the post-colonial, like the post-structuralist discourse which provides its philosophical and theoretical grounding, is anti-foundational and, as such, cannot deal with a concept like "capitalism" and with "capitalism's structuring of the modern world." Moreover, the "post-colonial" is "a culturalism." It is preoccupied with questions of identity and the subject and hence cannot give "an account of the world outside the subject." Attention is shifted from national origin to subject position and "a politics of location takes precedence over politics informed by fixed categories (in this case the nation, though obviously other categories such as Third World and class are also implied)." The "post-colonial" presents the coloniser equally with the colonised with "a problem of identity."[30]

This is all going with a remarkable swing for twenty pages when, on page 347, a by now somewhat characteristic "turn" begins to reveal itself. "These criticisms, however vehement on occasion, do not necessarily indicate that post-colonialism's critics deny it all value." The "post-colonial" discourse turns out, after all, to have something to say about "a crisis in the modes of comprehending the world associated with such concepts as Third World and nation state." Nor, apparently, is it to be denied that

> as the global situation has become more blurred with the disappearance of the socialist states, with the emergence of important differences economically and politically between so-called Third World societies and the diasporic motions of peoples across national and regional boundaries, fragmentation of the global into the local has emerged into the foreground of historical and political consciousness.[31]

This may appear to innocent eyes like recuperating a good deal of already repudiated territory, apart from containing in itself some questionable formulations. (Some post-modern critics *may* believe that the global has fragmented into the local but most of the serious ones argue that what is happening is a mutual reorganisation of the local and the global, a very different proposition.[32] But let that pass.) For it is followed, in the second section of the article, by a long, detailed and persuasive account of some of the main features of what is "variously" described as "late capitalism, flexible production or accumulation, disorganised capitalism and global capitalism."

These include: the new international division of labour, the new global information technologies, a "de-centering of capitalism nationally," the linkage provided by the transnational corporation, the transnationalisation of production, the appearance of the capitalist mode of production, "for the first time in the history of capitalism," as an "authentically global abstraction," cultural fragmentation and multi-culturalism, the re-articulation of native cultures into a capitalist narrative (the example here being the Confucian revival amongst the rising South East Asian capitalist elite), the weakening of boundaries, the replication internally in once-colonial societies of inequalities once associated with colonial differences, the "disorganisation of a world conceived in terms of three worlds," the flow of culture which is "at once homogenising and heterogenising," a modernity which "is no longer just Euro-American," forms of control which cannot just be imposed but have to be "negotiated," the reconstitution of subjectivities across national boundaries, and so on . . . [33]

It is not only an impressive, and impressively comprehensive, list. It also, I think incontrovertibly, touches at some point every single theme which makes the "post-colonial" a distinctive theoretical paradigm, and marks decisively how radically and unalterably *different*—that is to say, how incontrovertibly *post-colonial*—is the world and the relations being described. And, indeed, to the reader's astonishment, this is also acknowledged: "Post-coloniality represents a response to a genuine need, the need to overcome a crisis of understanding produced by the inability of old categories to account for the world."[34] Is there a "post-colonial" critic in the house who would dissent from that judgement?

Two arguments could follow from this second half of the essay. The first is a serious one—indeed, the most serious criticism which the post-colonial critics and theorists have urgently now to face—and it is succinctly put by Dirlik. "What is remarkable . . . is that a consideration of the relationship between postcolonialism and global capitalism should be absent from the writings of postcolonial intellectuals." Let us not quibble and say of *some* post-colonial intellectuals. It *is* remarkable. And it has become seriously damaging and disabling for everything positive which the post-colonial paradigm can, and has the ambition to, accomplish. These two halves of the current debate about "late modernity"—the post-colonial and the analysis of the new developments in global capitalism—have indeed largely proceeded in relative isolation from one another, and to their mutual cost. It is not difficult to understand why, though Dirlik does not seem interested in pursuing this as a serious question (he does have a trivial answer to it, which is different). One reason is that the discourses of the "post" have emerged, and been (often silently) articulated against the practical, political, historical and theoretical effects of the collapse of a certain kind of economistic, teleological and, in the end, reductionist Marxism. What has resulted from the abandonment of this deterministic economism has been, not alternative ways of thinking questions about the economic relations and their effects, as the "conditions of existence" of other practices, inserting them in a "de-centred" or dislocated way into our explanatory paradigms, but instead a massive, gigantic and eloquent *disavowal*. As if, since the economic in its broadest sense, definitively does *not*, as it was once supposed to do, "determine" the real movement of history "in the last instance," it does not exist at all! This is a failure of theorisation so profound, and (with very few, still relatively sketchy, exceptions)[35] so disabling, that, in my view, it has enabled much weaker and less conceptually rich paradigms to continue to flourish and dominate the field. (Dirlik himself makes, at one point, an interesting observation that he prefers "the world system approach," even though, like the post-colonial, it "locates the Third World discursively,"[36] but this interesting and fruitful line of discussion is not pursued.)

Of course, it is not simply a matter that the relationship between these paradigms has been left to one side. This is itself partly an institutional effect—an unintended consequence, some would say, of the fact that the "post-colonial" has been most fully developed by literary scholars, who have been reluctant to make the break across disciplinary (even post-disciplinary) boundaries required to advance the argument. It is also because there may well be some conceptual incompatibility between a certain kind of post-foundationalism and the serious investigation of these complex articulations. But this cannot yet be accepted as an unbridgeable philosophical chasm, especially because, though they do not address the question of the conceptual role which the category "capitalism" may have in a post-foundationalist "logic," certain articulations of this order are *in fact* either implicitly assumed or silently at work in the underpinning assumptions of almost all the post-colonial critical work.

Dirlik has therefore put his finger squarely, and convincingly, on a serious lacuna in the post-colonial episteme. To have concluded with the implications for the future of the post-colonial paradigm of this critique would indeed have served a very important, timely and strategic purpose. And had this been the conclusion to his essay, one could have overlooked the curiously broken-backed and internally contradictory nature of the argument (the second half repudiating in effect much of the substance and all of the tone of the first half). However, it is not. His conclusion takes the second path. Far from just "representing a response to a genuine [theoretical] need," he ends with the thought that "post-coloniality resonates with the problems thrown up by global capitalism," is "attuned" to its issues and hence *serves its cultural requirements*. The post-colonial critics are, in effect, unwitting spokespersons for the new global capitalist order. This is a conclusion to a long and detailed argument of such stunning (and one is obliged to say, banal) reductionism, a functionalism of a kind which one thought had disappeared from scholarly debate as a serious explanation of *anything*, that it reads like a echo from a distant, primeval era. It is all the more disturbing because a very similar line of argument is to be found from a diametrically opposite position—the inexplicably simplistic charge in Robert Young's *Colonial Desire*[37] that the post-colonial critics are "complicit" with Victorian racial theory *because both sets of writers deploy the same term—"hybridity"—in their discourse!*

Here, then, we find ourselves between Scylla and Charybdis, between the devil and the deep blue sea. We always knew that the dismantling of the colonial paradigm would release strange demons from the deep, and that these monsters might come trailing all sorts of subterranean material. Still, the awkward twists and turns, leaps and reversals in the ways the argument is being conducted should alert us to the sleep of reason that is beyond or after Reason, the way desire plays across power and knowledge in the dangerous enterprise of thinking at or beyond the limit.

NOTES

This essay first appeared in *The Post-colonial Question: Common Skies, Divided Horizons*, ed. Iain Chambers and Lidia Curti (London: Routledge, 1996), 242–60.

1. Ella Shohat, "Notes on the 'Post-colonial,'" *Social Text*, nos. 31–32 (1992).
2. Anne McClintock, "The Angel of Progress: Pitfalls of the Term 'Post-colonialism,'" *Social Text*, nos. 31–32 (1992).
3. Shohat, "Notes on the 'Post-colonial,'" 101.
4. Arif Dirlik, "The Postcolonial Aura: Third World Criticism in the Age of Global Capitalism," *Critical Inquiry* 20, no. 2 (Winter 1994): 347.
5. Dirlik, "The Postcolonial Aura," 331, quoting Shohat; see also Masao Miyoshi, "A Borderless World? From Colonialism to Transnationalism and the Decline of the Nation State," *Critical Inquiry* 19, no. 4 (Summer 1993).

6. See, for example, Anne McClintock's brilliant essay "The Return of Female Fetishism and the Fiction of the Phallus," *New Formations* 19 (1993); see also Anne McClintock, *Imperial Leather* (London: Routledge, 1995).
7. Shohat, "Notes on the 'Post-colonial,'" 101.
8. McClintock, *Imperial Leather*, 294.
9. Ruth Frankenberg and Lata Mani, "Crosscurrents, Crosstalk: Race, 'Postcoloniality' and the Politics of Location," *Cultural Studies* 7, no. 2 (1993).
10. Peter Hulme, "Including America," *Ariel* 26, no. 1 (1995).
11. See Stuart Hall, "The Question of Cultural Identity," in *Modernity and Its Futures*, ed. Stuart Hall, David Held, and Tony McGrew (Cambridge: Polity, 1992).
12. See, on this historiographical point and its implications for a politics of the present, Catherine Hall, "Histories, Empires, and the Post-colonial Moment," in *The Post-colonial Question: Common Skies, Divided Horizons*, ed. Iain Chambers and Lidia Curti (London: Routledge, 1996).
13. Paul Gilroy, *The Black Atlantic: Modernity and Double Consciousness* (London: Verso, 1993).
14. Frankenberg and Mani, "Crosscurrents," 301.
15. McClintock, "The Angel of Progress," 86.
16. Frankenberg and Mani, "Crosscurrents," 301; Robert J. C. Young, *White Mythologies: Writing History and the West* (London: Routledge, 1990).
17. Edward Said, *Orientalism* (London: Routledge and Kegan Paul, 1978).
18. Shohat, "Notes on the 'Post-colonial,'" 101.
19. See, for example, Stuart Hall, "Cultural Identity and Diaspora," in *Identity*, ed. Jonathan Rutherford (London: Lawrence and Wishart, 1990).
20. Homi K. Bhabha, *The Location of Culture* (London: Routledge, 1994).
21. Mary Louise Pratt, "Imperial Eyes," in *Travel Writing and Transculturation* (London: Routledge, 1992).
22. Ernesto Laclau, *New Reflections on the Revolution of Our Time* (London: Verso, 1990); Judith Butler, *Bodies That Matter* (London: Routledge, 1993).
23. Shohat, "Notes on the 'Post-colonial,'" 101, 108.
24. Hulme, "Including America."
25. Shohat, "Notes on the 'Post-colonial,'" 107.
26. Antonio Gramsci, *Quaderni*, vol. 3 (1975), quoted in Chantal Mouffe, *Gramsci and Marxist Theory* (London: Lawrence and Wishart, 1979). See also Stuart Hall, *The Hard Road to Renewal: Thatcherism and the Crisis of the Left* (London: Verso, 1988), 138.
27. Iain Chambers, *Migrancy, Culture, Identity* (London: Routledge, 1994).
28. Jacques Derrida, *Positions* (Chicago: University of Chicago Press, 1981), 6–7, 12.
29. Gyan Prakash, "Postcolonial Criticism and Indian Historiography," *Social Text*, nos. 31–32 (1992).
30. Dirlik, "The Postcolonial Aura," 346, 336, 337.
31. Dirlik, "The Postcolonial Aura," 347.

32 See Doreen Massey, *Space, Place and Gender* (Cambridge: Polity, 1994); Kevin Robins, "Tradition and Translation: National Cultures in a Global Context," in *Enterprise and Heritage: Crosscurrents of National Culture*, ed. John Corner and Sylvia Harvey (London: Routledge, 1991); Stuart Hall, "The Question of Cultural Identity."
33 Dirlik, "The Postcolonial Aura," 350, 353.
34 Dirlik, "The Postcolonial Aura," 353.
35 See Laclau, *New Reflections*; also Michèle Barrett, *The Politics of Truth* (Cambridge: Polity, 1991).
36 Dirlik, "The Postcolonial Aura," 346.
37 Robert J. C. Young, *Colonial Desire* (London: Routledge, 1995).

CHAPTER 12

The Centrality of Culture:
Notes on the Cultural Revolutions of Our Time

Introduction

[...]

Why is culture at the centre of so many discussions and debates at the present time? In one sense, culture has always been important. The human and social sciences have long recognised its significance. In the humanities, the study of the languages, literatures, art forms, philosophical ideas, moral and religious systems of belief have long constituted the fundamental subject-matter, though the idea that these all composed a distinct set of meanings—a culture—has not been as common an idea as we might have supposed. In the social sciences, and in particular in sociology, what is said to be distinctive about "social action"—as distinct from behaviour which is purely instinctual or biologically and genetically programmed—is that it requires and is relevant to meaning. Human beings are meaning-making, interpretive beings. Social action is meaningful, both to those who perform it and to those who observe it; not "in itself," but because of the many and variable systems of meanings which human beings deploy to define what things mean and to code, organise and regulate their conduct towards one another. These systems or codes of meaning give significance to our actions. They allow us to interpret meaningfully the actions of others. Taken together, they constitute our "cultures." They help to ensure that all social action is "cultural," that all social practices express or communicate a meaning and, in that sense, are "signifying practices."

However, it does not follow from this that the social and human sciences have always given "culture" either the substantive centrality or the epistemological weight it deserves. This distinction between the substantive and the epistemological aspects of culture (introduced in du Gay, Hall, et al. 1997)[1] is worth bearing in mind throughout the rest of this chapter. By "substantive," we mean culture's place in the actual empirical structure and organisation of cultural activities, institutions and relationships of society at any particular historical moment. By epistemological, we refer to culture's position in relation to matters of knowledge and conceptualisation, that is how "culture" is used to transform our understanding, explanations and theoretical models of the world. In what follows, we deal with substantive aspects first.

The Centrality of Culture: The Global Dimension

In the twentieth century there has been a "cultural revolution" in the substantive, empirical and material senses of the word. Substantively, the domain constituted by the activities, institutions and practices we call "cultural" has expanded out of all recognition. At the same time, culture has assumed a role of unparalleled significance in the structure and organisation of late-modern society, in the processes of development of the global environment and in the disposition of its economic and material resources. In particular, the means of producing, circulating and exchanging culture have been dramatically expanded through the new media technologies and the information revolution. Directly, a much greater proportion of the world's human, material and technical resources than ever before go into these sectors. At the same time, indirectly, the cultural industries have become the mediating element in every other process. The old distinction which classical Marxism used to make between the economic "base" and the ideological "superstructure" is difficult to sustain in circumstances where the media both form a critical part of the material infrastructure of modern societies and are the principal means by which ideas and images are circulated. Today, they sustain the global circuits of economic exchange on which the worldwide movement of information, knowledge, capital, investment, the production of commodities, the trade in raw materials and the marketing of goods and ideas depend. As David Harvey observed, "The formation of a global stock market, of global commodity (even debt) futures markets, of currency and interest rate swops, together with accelerated geographical mobility of funds, meant, for the first time, the formation of a single world market for money and credit supply."[2] They have made a reality of what Marx only dimly foresaw—the emergence of a truly "global" market. The resources which once went into the "hardware" industries of the nineteenth-century industrial age—coal, iron and steel—are now, at the turn of the third millennium, being invested in the neural systems of the future—the "software" and digital communication technologies of the Cyber Age.

In terms of some absolute aesthetic standards of judgement and taste, the cultural products of this revolution may not compare in value with the achievements of other historical moments—the civilisations of Egypt or of ancient China, for example, or the art of the Italian Renaissance. But compared with the relative narrowness of the social elite whose lives were positively transformed by those earlier historical examples, the significance of the cultural revolutions at the end of the twentieth century resides in their global scope and scale, their breadth of impact, their democratic and popular character. The foreshortening of time and space—time-space compression, as Harvey calls it—which these new technologies make possible, introduce changes in popular consciousness, as we live increasingly in multiple and—even more disconcertingly—in "virtual" worlds. They truncate the speed at which images travel, the distances across which commodities can be assembled, the rate at which profits can be realised (reducing the so-called "turnover time of capital"), even the intervals between the opening times of the different stock markets around the world—minute time-gaps in which millions of dollars can be made or lost. These are the new "nervous systems" which thread together societies with very different histories, different ways of life, at different stages of development and dwelling in different time-zones. It is here, especially, that revolutions in culture at the global level impact on ways of life, on how people live, on how they make sense of life, on their aspirations for the future—on "culture" in the other, more local, sense.

These global cultural shifts are creating rapid social change—but also serious cultural dislocation, in about equal measure. As Paul du Gay notes,

> The new electronic media not only allow the stretching of social relations across time and space, they also deepen this global interconnectedness by annihilating the distance between people and places, throwing them into intense and immediate contact with one another in a perpetual "present," where what is happening anywhere can be happening wherever we are. . . . This doesn't mean that people no longer lead a local life—that they are no longer situated contextually in time and space. What it does

mean is that local life is inherently dislocated—that the local does not have an "objective" identity outside of its relationship with the global.[3]

One effect of this time-space compression is the tendency towards cultural homogenisation—the tendency[4] for the world, in effect, to become one place, not just spatially and temporally, but culturally: the syndrome which one theorist has termed the "McDonaldisation" of the globe. It is indeed hard to deny that the growth of the great transnational communications giants such as CNN, Time Warner and News International tends to favour the transmission of a set of standardised cultural products using standardised western technologies to every corner of the globe, eroding local particularities and differences and producing in their place a homogenised, westernised "world-culture." However, those of you who have followed these debates will know that the consequences of this global cultural revolution are neither as uniform nor as easy to predict as the more extreme of the "homogenisers" suggest. For it is also a characteristic feature that these processes are very unevenly distributed across the world—subject to what Doreen Massey has called a definite "power geometry"[5]—and that their consequences are profoundly contradictory. Thus, there certainly are many negative consequences—so far, without solution—in terms of the cultural exports of the technologically over-developed "West" weakening and undermining the capacities of older nation-states and emerging societies to define their own ways of life and the pace and direction of their development.[6] But there are also many countervailing tendencies which prevent the world from becoming a culturally uniform and homogeneous space.[7] Global culture itself requires and thrives on "difference"—even if only to try to convert it into another cultural commodity for the world market (such as ethnic cuisine). It is therefore more likely to produce "simultaneously, *new 'global'* and *new 'local'* identifications" than some uniform and homogeneous world culture.[8]

The result of cultural mixing, or syncretism, across old frontiers may not be the obliteration of the old by the new, but the creation of some hybrid alternatives, synthesising elements from both but reducible to neither—as is increasingly the case in the culturally diverse, multicultural societies created by the great migrations of peoples arising from war, poverty and economic hardship in the late twentieth century.[9] A good example would be the catalogue of *Translocations*, an exhibition which took place in 1997 at the Photographers Gallery in London. This showed new visual work, some of it digitally produced, by post-colonial artists and others living and working in the UK, which was instructive in this respect, capturing some of the complexities which shadow these processes:

> *Translocations* is a collection of images, ideas and meditations which seeks to explore contemporary notions of place, positioning and movement. The idea of "place" which *Translocations* seeks to explore is the concept of place as a series of processes, marked by fluidity, flux and movement, which impact on the ways we position ourselves within the world.... *Permanent Revolution II*, an interactive multimedia installation, is a first-time collaboration between Keith Piper and Derek Richards. By tracing the continual ebbs and flows of migrating people within what has been called "The Black Atlantic," Piper and Richards explore the role that the convergence of migrating peoples and the resulting fusions play in the development of new cultural forms. [It] poses an alternative to essentialist representations of cultural purity and homogeneity.... Roshini Kempadoo's photo installation examines the impact that time-space compression is having on those who are subject to, rather than in control of, its unequal flows and movements.[10]

The very pace and unevenness of global cultural change often produces its own resistances, which can of course be positive but are sometimes negative, defensive reactions, against a global culture and represent powerful tendencies towards "closure."[11] For example, the growth of Christian fundamentalism in the US, of Islamic fundamentalism in parts of the Middle East, of Hindu fundamentalism in India, the resurgence of ethnic nationalisms in Central and Eastern Europe, the anti-immigrant, "fortress" attitude and Euro-sceptic mood of many western European societies, and cultural nationalism in the form of reassertions of heritage and tradition,[12] though all *very different* in their detail and particulars, can be seen, in another sense, as conservative cultural responses, part of the retreat from the dissemination of cultural diversity by the forces of cultural globalisation.

All these factors, then, qualify and complicate any simplistic, purely celebratory response to cultural globalisation as the dominant form of cultural change in the foreseeable future.[13] They cannot, however, entirely negate the scale of the transformation in global relationships which the information and cultural revolution constitutes. Whether we like it or not, approve or not, the new forces and relationships which this process has set in motion are unravelling many of the patterns and traditions of the past. For good or ill, culture is now one of the most dynamic—and most unpredictable—elements of historical change in the new millennium. We should not be surprised, then, that struggles over power increasingly take a symbolic and discursive rather than simply a physical and compulsive form, and that politics itself increasingly assumes the form of a "cultural politics."[14]

[...]

The Final Frontier: Identity and Subjectivity

The impact of the cultural revolutions on global societies and on local, everyday life may seem significant and broad-ranging enough to justify the claim that the substantive expansion of "culture" in the late-twentieth century has been unprecedented. But the mention of its impact on "inner life" reminds us of another frontier which needs to be addressed. This concerns the centrality of culture for the constitution of subjectivity, of identity itself and of the person as a social actor. Until recently, this was regarded as the conventional line of distinction between the disciplines of sociology and psychology, even though it was always recognised that every sociological model carried within it certain psychological assumptions about the nature of the individual subject and the formation of "self"—and vice versa. However, in a significant way, this boundary line has been weakened and eroded by questions of "culture." Even the most sceptical have been obliged to acknowledge that meanings are both *subjectively* valid and at the same time *objectively* present in the world—in our actions, institutions, rituals and practices. The focus on language and meaning has had the effect of blurring, if not dissolving, the common-sense frontier between the two spheres of the social and the psychic.

Perhaps the easiest way to see what is at issue here is through an example. Suppose one were allowed only three images with which to explain to a young and intelligent person recently arrived from Mars what it means to "be English." Which images would we choose? Let us, for argument's sake, choose two sets, at the opposite extremes. In the first set, perhaps, changing the guards at Buckingham Palace, the Lake District and the Houses of Parliament. In the second set, Docklands, a cotton mill in Shipley and Wembley Stadium. There's no need to say in detail why each set was chosen. The first signifies (carries the meaning of) tradition, a stable and well-ordered society; the evocative landscape associated with the English love of Nature and most famous English poets—the Romantics; the proud heritage of parliamentary government, the quintessential sign of what it is about England that has survived through thick and thin—Big Ben; and so on. The second set—more modern, popular, up-to-date, thrusting, entrepreneurial: post-Thatcher Britain, face turned towards the competitive world; the triumphs of the industrial revolution on which Britain's greatness was based, Victorian values, the hard graft of work and labour which built its former prosperity; and, in popular sport, a testimony to "ordinary folk," the backbone of the nation, and to the nation coming together, across class and regional (racial and gender?) lines in the football stadium.

These may seem very oversimplified contrasting images. But we should not imagine that they do not refer to quite complex discursive and cultural formations. In an article in the *Guardian*, Martin Jacques discussed the contrasting images of "middle" and "multi-cultural" England and of the complex historical lineages behind each which, he suggested, were haunting the political discourses of both major political parties in the 1997 general election:

> There are two stories of Britain. One is about creative radicals and the other is about respectable conservatives. Both exist in the national psyche, both are authentic parts of what we are. But they command unequal recognition, one official and mainstream, the other unofficial and subterranean. The official culture warmly embraces Andrew Lloyd Webber, Cilla Black and Cliff Richard as authentically British: it treats our creative anarchists like [John] Lennon and [Vivienne] Westwood as phenomena, as freaks, taking a voyeuristic pleasure in their lives and activities rather than regarding them as one of us.
>
> From time to time, there is a rebirth of cultural energy, always starting on the periphery then working its way to the centre. Now is one such moment. In the capital, it has much to do with the emergence of London as a global city, perhaps the most global city in the world, certainly in Europe. London is now more open than ever before to a kaleidoscope of global influences from food to music, from ideas to business.
>
> And above all people: the ethnic minorities now figure in our cultural life like never before. Many of the key designers in London Fashion Week were from ethnic minorities. Immigrants are frequently a source of exceptional energy. Our cultural radicalism has much to do with being both an island and being culturally porous.

One might think that this explosion of energy would command the attention of our politicians. True, John Major proudly boasted about London's new vibrancy and Tony Blair is partial to Britpop. But for Major and Blair the rallying cry [was] not cultural radicalism but Middle England, the template of respectable conservatism. In 1964, Harold Wilson gave more than a nod in the direction of the Beatles. . . . Blair and Major preferred to walk on the other side of Britain's cultural street.[15]

It would be useless to ask, which of these two sets of images represents the "true" Englishness—for *both* are "true," in the sense of representing certain historical and present elements which have indeed been significant in the shaping of England, an English imaginary and an English identity. Let us leave aside for the moment the troubling complications of whether this is "English" or "British"—and thus of Scotland, Ireland (North and South), Wales, let alone the rest of the former British Empire—noting only that "English" as an identity exists and takes its place in this complicated, shifting, unsettled, overlapping but not interchangeable table of terms, refusing either to separate itself firmly from or to easily incorporate or accommodate the others. These are internal fault-lines—boundaries—around which differences are marked, and which are therefore the potential sites of a contestation over meaning, a "politics of identity." Both sets, then, are "true" (meaning is never finally fixed).[16]

But that does not mean that they are complete. Their meaning is defined, partly, in relation to each other; partly by what they leave out. Suppose, for example, you insisted on replacing one of those images with a shot of Brixton High Street—would this challenge existing assumptions about Englishness as an exclusive form of "whiteness"? Or with one of the scene outside any primary school in England at around 3:30 in the afternoon when mothers (and some fathers) collect their children—would this pose the question of whether the feminine and domestic is as adequate and compelling a way of signifying "the nation" as a more masculine scenario?

Each individual will feel more or less drawn to, more or less compelled by, each set of images. You may not feel perfectly or adequately "expressed" by either—something of "who you are" remains outside, a troubling remainder, something in excess of the meaning-system which these two sets of images attempt, between them, to capture. Left to itself, this excluded remainder or supplement could well, under the right conditions, become the focus for an alternative definition—a third set—precipitating a challenge to the cultural authority of the two sets already offered and representing the birth of a new contestation over the meaning of "Englishness," a different focus of identification—and thus, a new "politics of identity."[17] However, even if you are not fully *represented* by either of the image sets offered, you will probably feel pulled more towards one than the other, seeing yourself imaged or reflected (or, as they say, "summoned into place") more by one than the other. You have begun to invest in or *identify* with one or another meaning of "what it is to be English" and, by taking up that subject position, are becoming more *that* sort of English person yourself than the other.

This is one, rather common-sense and descriptive way of explaining how a *national identity* comes into being.[18] But it may be worth spelling out the implications of what we have said. Were you "English" in the sense defined here, in the core of your being—in your heart and soul, in your genes, in your blood—*before* you were offered the list? Or has your English identity undergone greater definition through the process of representation and identification just described? What this suggests is that identity emerges, not so much from the inner core of our "one, true, self" alone but in the dialogue between the meanings and definitions which are *represented to us* by the discourses of a culture, and our willingness (consciously or unconsciously) to respond to the summons of those meanings, to be hailed by them, to step into the subject positions constructed for us by one of the discourses on "Englishness"—in short, to invest our sympathies and feelings in one or other of those images, to *identify*.[19] What we call "our identities" are probably better conceptualised as the sedimentations over time of those different identifications or positionalities we have taken up and tried to "live," as it were, from the inside, no doubt inflected by the particular mix of circumstances, feelings, histories and experiences which are unique and peculiar to us as individual subjects. Our identities, in short, are culturally formed.

This, at any rate, is what is meant by saying that we should think of social identities as constructed *within* representation, *through* culture, not outside of them. They are the result of a process of identification which enables us to position ourselves within or to "subject ourselves" (inside) to the definitions which cultural discourses (outside) provide. Our so-called subjectivities, then, are, partly, discursively or dialogically produced. It is therefore easy to see why our understanding of this whole process has had to be thoroughly reconstituted by our interest in culture; and why it is increasingly difficult to maintain the traditional distinction between "inside" and "outside," between the social and the psychic, once culture has intervened.

Epistemological Aspects: The "Cultural Turn"

So far, we have been addressing the question of the "centrality of culture" in substantive terms, looking in particular at four dimensions: the rise of new domains, institutions and technologies associated with the cultural industries, which have transformed the traditional spheres of the economy, industry, society and culture itself; culture as a force for global historical change; the cultural transformation of everyday life; the centrality of culture in the formation of subjective and social identities. Now it is time to turn to the second aspect of culture's centrality: its *epistemological* dimensions.

As in the world and in social life, so also in terms of knowledge, theory and understanding. In recent decades, there has been a revolution in human thought around the idea of "culture." Within the human and social sciences we now accord culture a much greater significance and explanatory weight than used to be the case—though changing habits of thought is also a slow and uneven process, and not without its powerful rearguard actions (such as, for example, the ritual attacks launched against media or cultural studies by the traditional disciplines which feel somehow challenged or displaced by their very existence). Despite this, a major conceptual revolution is in the making in the human and social sciences. This goes beyond learning to put cultural questions more at the centre of our calculations, alongside economic processes, social institutions and the production of goods, wealth and services—important as this shift is. It refers to an approach to contemporary social analysis which has made culture a constitutive condition of existence of social life, rather than a dependent variable, provoking a paradigm shift in the humanities and social sciences in recent years which has come to be known as the "cultural turn."

Essentially, the "cultural turn" began with a revolution in attitudes towards language. Language has always been the subject of specialist interest among some literary scholars and linguists. However, the concern with language which we have in mind here refers to something broader—a concern with language as a general term for the practices of representation, giving language a privileged position in the construction and circulation of *meaning*. This "turn" involved

> a reversal of the relationship that has traditionally been held to exist between the vocabularies we use to describe things and the things themselves. The usual, common-sense assumption is that objects exist "objectively," as it were, "in the world" and as such are prior to and constraining of our

descriptions of them. In other words, it seems normal to assume that "molecules" and "genes" exist prior to and independently of scientists' models of them. Or that "society" exists independently of sociologists' descriptions of it. What these examples serve to highlight is the way in which language is assumed to be subordinate to and in the service of the world of "fact." However, in recent years the relationship between language and the objects it describes has been the subject of a radical rethink. Language has been promoted to an altogether more important role. Theorists from many different fields—philosophy, literature, feminism, cultural anthropology, sociology—have declared language to bring facts into being and not simply to report on them.[20]

What is involved here is the whole relationship between language and what we might call "reality." Don't objects exist in the world independently of our language about them? In one sense, of course, they do. To return to a familiar example: a stone still exists regardless of our descriptions of it.[21] However, our identification of it as a "stone" is only possible because of a particular way of classifying objects and making them meaningful (i.e., stone as part of a classificatory system which differentiates stone from iron, wood etc.; or, on the other hand, within a different classificatory system—a stone, as opposed to a boulder, a rock, a pebble etc.). Outside of these meaning-systems (each of which gives the thing—a "stone"—a different meaning), objects certainly exist; but they cannot be defined as "stones," or indeed as anything else, unless there is a language or meaning-system capable of classifying them in that way and giving them a meaning by distinguishing them from other objects:

> This idea that things only have meaning through their insertion within a particular classifying system or "language game," as the philosopher Wittgenstein would call it, has some very profound consequences. Taken-for-granted assumptions about the fixed or given "nature" and "essence" of things are immediately open to question, in any final or absolute sense, if one accepts that the meaning of any object resides not within that object itself but is a product of how that object is socially constructed through language and representation.[22]

What this has done is to prise open a gap between the *existence* and the *meaning* of an object. Meaning arises, not from things in themselves— "reality"—but from the language games and classifying systems into which they are inserted. What we think of as natural facts are therefore *also* discursive phenomena.

It is difficult to exaggerate the consequences of this for the philosophy and practice of the social sciences. Ever since the Enlightenment it has been accepted that the role of "science" was to offer an objective, impartial, rational and "true" account or knowledge of the world. A scientific approach, in which facts were independent of our descriptions of them, was regarded as an ultimate arbiter of truth to which the social sciences should, as far as possible, aspire:

> The idea that, whatever is the nature of the elements of which physical objects are constructed, "atoms" are a product of a classificatory or discursive practice—atomic theory, and that they are contextual and historically contingent, and are therefore open to different forms of classification which may emerge in the future, has undercut simple notions of accuracy, truth and objectivity, and opened the floodgates to what its critics see as a tide of relativism.[23]

The "cultural turn" is closely related to this new attitude towards language. For culture is nothing but the sum of the different classificatory systems and discursive formations, on which language draws in order to give meaning to things. The very term "discourse" refers to a group of statements in any domain which provides a language for talking about a topic and a way of producing a particular kind of knowledge about that topic. The term refers both to the production of knowledge through language and representation and the way that knowledge is institutionalised, shaping social practices and setting new practices into play. To say, then, that a stone is only a stone within a particular discursive or classificatory schema is not to deny that it has a material existence but it is to say that its *meaning* is the result not of its natural essence, but of its discursive character.

The "cultural turn" expands this insight about language to social life in general. It argues that because economic and social processes themselves *depend* on meaning and have consequences for our ways of life, for who we are—our identities—and for "how we live now," they too must be understood as cultural, as discursive practices. To take only one example, the question of creating an "enterprise culture" seems to have become *the* critical issue, not only for corporate economic and business success in the 1980s and '90s,[24] but also for personal and social life, for politics and for our collective moral well-being and definitions of "the good life." It is a topic about which management gurus address us in the language of hard-headed economic calculation on *The Money Programme* and in sober, moralistic voices on *Thought for the Day*, the daily religious slot on BBC Radio 4. What is this discourse about? Is it about economics, management, morality or personal self-improvement? Where does the "economics" stop, in this example, and the culture begin?

Giving "culture" a determinate and constitutive role in understanding and analysing all social relations and institutions is different from how it has been theorised for many years in the mainstream social sciences. So much so that the "turn to culture" is sometimes represented as a total rupture of the entire theoretical universe of the social sciences. This is probably too apocalyptic a view. There have always been traditions, even within mainstream sociology in the 1950s and 1960s, which privileged questions of meaning: for example, symbolic interactionism, deviancy studies, the concern in American social science with "values and attitudes," the legacy of Weberian approaches, the ethnographic tradition, much influenced by anthropological techniques, and so on.

So, the "cultural turn" is probably more accurately seen, not as total rupture, but as a reconfiguration of elements, some of which have always been present in sociological analysis, but coupled with new elements—in particular, the focus on language and culture as a substantive area, not just that which provided value-integration for the rest of the social system. Indeed, in some respects, the "cultural turn" could be read as representing a "return" to certain neglected classical and traditional sociological themes after a long period dominated by more structural, functionalist or empiricist concerns. It was, after all, one of the founding figures of modern sociology, Max Weber, who in his interpretive sociology defined the *subject* of sociological investigation—"social action"—as "action which is relevant to meaning"— though, for many years, this was not the most frequently referenced aspect of Weber's work. Durkheim and his *Année Sociologique* school in France, another founding formation in the early history of the human and social sciences, considered the centre-piece of sociology to be the study of relationships between "the social" and "the symbolic"; and much of their work concerned the study of the social meanings embodied in religion as well as in the classificatory systems of so-called "primitive societies." This idea was foundational for social anthropology and formed the basis of modern structuralism and semiotics.[25] Claude Lévi-Strauss, for example, in his inaugural lecture on "the scope of anthropology," which outlined the project of structuralist cultural analysis, referred to his own work as a "continuation of the programme first inaugurated by Durkheim and Mauss." However, this aspect of Durkheim was considered "too idealist" for mainstream sociology.[26] Even Marx, whose predominant emphases were, of course, on the primacy of the economic and the material over the cultural and the symbolic, was one of the first classical social scientists to recognise that what was distinctive about human social action, as contrasted with that of animals, was that human action and behaviour was guided and informed by cultural models. (As he observed, the worst of architects was cleverer than the best of bees because the former had to construct the *model* of a building conceptually in the mind before it could be built, whereas the industrious bees could only build in limited ways guided by instinct. Nowadays, we would call this a "discursive" or cultural conception of social practice!)

It was in the 1960s, with the work of Lévi-Strauss and Roland Barthes in France, and of Raymond Williams and Richard Hoggart in the UK, that the "cultural turn" began to have a major impact on intellectual and academic life, and a new interdisciplinary field of study organised around culture as the privileged concept—"cultural studies"—began to take shape, stimulated in part by the founding of the postgraduate research Centre for Contemporary Cultural Studies at the University of Birmingham in 1964. Many strands of theorising and analysis in the human and social sciences were selectively drawn on to provide the intellectual matrix out of which "cultural studies" developed. Without going into detail, in order to get some sense of the different theoretical discourses on which cultural studies drew, one would have to refer, *inter alia*, to the traditions of textual analysis (visual and verbal), literary criticism, art history and genre studies, social history, as well as linguistics and theories of language, in the humanities; in the social sciences, the more interactionist and culturalist aspects of mainstream sociology, deviancy studies and anthropology; critical theory (e.g., the French semiotic and post-structuralist theorists; Foucault; the "Frankfurt School"; feminist and psychoanalytic writers); film, media and communications studies, studies of popular culture. Also important were the many non-reductionist forms of Marxism (especially those associated with the work of Antonio Gramsci and the French structuralist school led by Althusser), and their preoccupation with questions of cultural hegemony, ideology and power.[27] Since those early days there has been both an enormous expansion in the teaching of, and the demand by students for, cultural studies, not just in the UK but internationally.[28] Just as significant, perhaps, has been the way in which elements of cultural studies have been incorporated into the more traditional disciplines, and the manner in which the "cultural turn" has influenced and inflected the practices of the academic mainstream—not least of all, sociology itself.

Recent commentators have begun to recognise not only the real breaks and paradigm-shifts, but also some of the affinities and continuities, between older and newer traditions of work: for example, between Weber's classical interpretive "sociology of meaning" and Michel Foucault's emphasis on the role of the "discursive." Foucault's work in the 1970s and '80s has been critically influential for the "cultural turn"—which is why, despite the criticisms offered of his work, our [Open University] *Culture, Media and Identities* project has kept returning to the debate with Foucault. What all this suggests is that the "cultural turn" is the product of a more complex genealogy than has been widely recognised and could be interpreted as a recovery—in a new key, so to speak—of some long-neglected and subordinated strands, in critical thought within the human and social sciences. Its overwhelming consequence has been, not—as its critics suggest—to replace one kind of reductionism (idealism) for another (materialism), but to force us to radically rethink the centrality of "the cultural" and the articulation between the material and the cultural or symbolic factors in social analysis. This is the intellectual point of reference from which "cultural studies" took its point of departure.

Is Everything Culture? Is There Nothing outside Discourse?

In part, then, in its epistemological sense, the centrality of culture lies in the paradigm shifts which the "cultural turn" has provoked within traditional disciplines, the explanatory weight which the concept of culture carries, and its constitutive rather than its dependent role in social analysis. One aspect of this is the expansion of "culture" to a wider, more inclusive range of institutions and practices. Thus we have spoken about the "culture" of corporate enterprises, the "culture" of the workplace, the growth of an enterprise "culture" in public and private corporate organisations,[29] the "culture" of masculinity,[30] the "cultures" of motherhood and the family,[31] a "culture" of home decoration and of shopping,[32] a "culture" of deregulation,[33] even a "culture" of the fit, and—even more disturbingly—a "culture" of the thin body.[34] What this suggests is that every social activity or institution generates and requires its own distinctive "world" of meanings and practices—its own culture. So, increasingly, the term is being applied to institutions and practices, which are manifestly not part of "the cultural sphere" in the traditional sense of the word. According to this emphasis, all social practices, in so far as they are relevant to meaning or require meaning for their operation, have a "cultural" dimension.

Where does this leave the traditional distinction, long a part of accepted conventional sociological wisdom, between "material" and "symbolic" factors, between "things" and "signs"? If "culture" is in everything and everywhere, where does it begin and end? Of course, this claim for the centrality of culture does not mean—as its critics have sometimes suggested—that there is nothing but "culture"—that everything is "culture" and that "culture" is everything; or, to paraphrase the now infamous observation by the deconstructionist French philosopher Jacques Derrida, "There is nothing outside the text"; or, as Foucault is sometimes thought to have said, "There is nothing but discourse." If this were what is being argued, it would certainly—and rightly—be exposed to the critique that, in this case, we had simply replaced the economic materialism or sociologism which once threatened to dominate these questions in the social sciences with a cultural idealism—i.e., substituting one form of reductionist argument for another. What is being argued, in fact, is not that "everything is culture" but that every social practice depends on and relates to meaning; consequently, that culture is one of the constitutive conditions of existence of that practice, that every social practice has a cultural dimension. Not that there is nothing but discourse, but that every social practice *has a discursive character*.

Thus, of course, there are *political* practices, which are concerned with the disposition and exercise of power, just as there are *economic* practices, which are concerned with the production and distribution of goods and of wealth. Each of these is subject to the conditions which organise and govern political and economic life in these societies. Now, political power has very real and palpable material effects. However, its actual operation depends on how people *define situations politically*. For example, until recently, the family, gender and sexual relations were defined as outside power: that is, spheres of life to which the term "politics" had no bearing or meaning. A "sexual politics" would have been impossible to conceive without some shift in the definition of what constitutes "the political." Likewise, it is only recently—since feminism has redefined "the political" (for example, "the personal is political")—that we have come to recognise that there is a "politics of the family." And this is a matter of *meaning*—the political *has a cultural dimension*.

Similarly, the distribution of economic wealth and resources has real and tangible *material effects* for rich and poor people in society. However, the question of whether the present distribution of wealth is "fair" or "unjust" is a matter of meaning—that is to say, it depends on how "justice" and "fairness" are defined; and our economic actions will be determined, in part, on what position we take up with respect to these definitions. Consequently, we can say that economic practices take place and have effects within the discursive framework of what is understood as fair and as unjust—they depend on and are "relevant to meaning" and are consequently "cultural practices." As Foucault might say, the operations of the economy depend upon the discursive formation of a society at any particular moment. Clearly, this does not mean that economic processes have been dissolved into discourse or language. It does mean that the discursive or meaning dimension is one of the constitutive conditions for the operation of the economy. The "economic," so to speak, could not operate or have real effects without "culture" or outside of meaning and discourse. Culture is therefore, in these examples, constitutive of "the political" and "the economic," just as "the political" and "the economic" are, in turn, constitutive of, and set limits for, culture. They are mutually constitutive of one another—which is another way of saying that they are *articulated* with each other. Thus, to be strictly accurate, we should really re-word the expanded claim about "culture" offered above as follows: every social practice *has cultural or discursive conditions of existence.* Social practices, in so far as they depend on meaning for their operation and effects, take place "within discourse," are "discursive."

[...]

NOTES

This essay first appeared in *Media and Cultural Regulation*, ed. Kenneth Thompson (London: Sage/Open University, 1997), 207–38.
1 Paul du Gay, Stuart Hall, Linda Janes, Hugh Mackay, and Keith Negus, *Doing Cultural Studies: The Story of the Sony Walkman* (London: Sage/Open University, 1997).
2 David Harvey, *The Condition of Postmodernity: An Enquiry into the Origins of Cultural Change* (Oxford: Blackwell, 1989).
3 Paul du Gay, "Some Course Themes," unpublished ms. (Milton Keynes, UK: Open University, 1994).
4 As extensively debated in Paul du Gay, "Organising Identity: Making Up People at Work," in *Production of Culture/Cultures of Production*, ed. Paul du Gay (London: Sage/Open University, 1997); Hugh Mackay, ed., *Consumption and Everyday Life* (London: Sage/Open University, 1997); and Kenneth Thompson, ed., *Media and Cultural Regulation* (London: Sage/Open University, 1997).
5 Doreen Massey, "Making Spaces, or, Geography Is Political Too," *Soundings* 1 (1995).

6 See John Tomlinson, "Internationalism, Globalisation and Cultural Imperialism," in Thompson, *Media and Cultural Regulation*.
7 See Stuart Hall, "The Question of Cultural Identity," in *Modernity and Its Futures*, ed. Stuart Hall, David Held, and Tony McGrew (Cambridge: Polity/Open University, 1992); Kevin Robins, "What in the World's Going On?," in du Gay, *Production of Culture/Cultures of Production*; Daniel Miller, "Consumption and Its Consequences," in Mackay, *Consumption and Everyday Life*.
8 Hall, "The Question of Cultural Identity."
9 See Paul Gilroy, "Diaspora and the Detours of Identity," in *Identity and Difference*, ed. Kath Woodward (London: Sage/Open University, 1997); and Bhikhu Parekh, "National Culture and Multiculturalism," in Thompson, *Media and Cultural Regulation*.
10 Photographers Gallery, *Great 11: Translocations*, exhibition catalogue, 1997.
11 See Woodward, *Identity and Difference*.
12 See Thompson, *Media and Cultural Regulation*.
13 See, for example, the critiques by Paul Hirst and Grahame Thompson in their *Globalisation in Question: The International Economy and the Possibilities of Governance* (Cambridge: Polity, 1996); and by David Goldblatt, David Held, Tony McGrew, and Jonathan Perraton, *Global Flows, Global Transformations: Concepts, Evidence and Arguments* (Cambridge: Polity, 1997).
14 See, for example, Glenn Jordan and Christine Weedon, *Cultural Politics* (Oxford: Blackwell, 1995).
15 Martin Jacques, "The Rebel Alliance of British Talents," *Guardian*, 20 February 1997, 17.
16 See Katherine Woodward, "Concepts of Identity and Difference," in Woodward, *Identity and Difference*; Stuart Hall, ed., *Representation: Cultural Representations and Signifying Practices* (London: Sage/Open University, 1997).
17 Judith Butler, *Bodies That Matter: On the Discursive Limits of "Sex"* (London: Routledge, 1993).
18 See Peter Hamilton, "Representing the Social: France and Frenchness in Postwar Humanist Photography," in Hall, *Representation*; Hall, "The Question of Cultural Identity"; and Homi K. Bhabha, ed., *Nation and Narration* (London: Routledge, 1990).
19 See Woodward, *Identity and Difference*.
20 Du Gay, "Some Course Themes."
21 See Stuart Hall, "The Work of Representation," in Hall, *Representation*, 45.
22 Du Gay, "Some Course Themes"; see also Woodward, "Concepts of Identity and Difference."
23 Du Gay, "Some Course Themes"; Gregor McLennan, "The Enlightenment Project Revisited," in *Modernity and Its Futures*, ed. Stuart Hall, David Held, and Tony McGrew (Cambridge: Polity/Open University, 1992).
24 See du Gay, *Production of Culture/Cultures of Production*.
25 See Hall, "The Work of Representation."

26 For example, that seminal text by Talcott Parsons, *The Structure of Social Action* (1937; repr., London: Collier-Macmillan, 1968). Parsons was at that time the leading American social theorist.
27 See Stuart Hall, "Cultural Studies and Its Theoretical Legacies," in *Cultural Studies*, ed. Lawrence Grossberg and Cary Nelson (London: Routledge, 1992).
28 See Grossberg and Nelson, *Cultural Studies*; Kuan-Hsing Chen, "Not Yet the Postcolonial Era," *Cultural Studies* 10, no. 1 (1996); and Ien Ang and John Stratton, "Asianing Australia," *Cultural Studies* 10, no. 1 (1996).
29 In du Gay, *Production of Culture/Cultures of Production*.
30 Sean Nixon, "Exhibiting Masculinity," in Hall, *Representation*.
31 Katherine Woodward, "Motherhood: Identities, Meanings and Myths," in Woodward, *Identity and Difference*.
32 Miller, "Consumption and Its Consequences."
33 Kenneth Thompson, "Regulation, De-regulation, Re-regulation," in Thompson, *Media and Cultural Regulation*.
34 Susan Benson, "The Body, Health and Eating Disorders," in Woodward, *Identity and Difference*.

EDITOR'S DISCUSSION OF THE PART III WRITINGS

Chapters 8 and 9 need no extra framing beyond that provided in my initial introduction. However, a further word on the "authoritarian populism" argument (chapter 10) is worthwhile, before turning our attention to the two writings that pose serious questions about the extent and longevity of Hall's Marxism.

Hall, Marxism, Thatcherism

Hall's "debate" on Thatcherism with Bob Jessop and his coauthors ran on—if indirectly—beyond Hall's response to their initial allegations regarding his "ideologism." The critics produced a rejoinder to that response (once more in *New Left Review*), detailing further their concern that Hall's analysis of Thatcherism lacked a sufficiently structural-economic dimension, but this time adding that even within Hall's highlighted realms of intervention and specificity—the political and ideological levels—his account came up short.[1] This supplementary challenge was every bit as cutting as the first, but rather than get entrapped in diminishing-returns polemic, Hall chose to handle it more comprehensively, through the form of presentation of his 1988 collection *The Hard Road to Renewal: Thatcherism and the Crisis of the Left*. In the synoptic introduction to that book, he steered clear of the contentious idea of authoritarian populism and reemphasized that Thatcherism could not possibly be understood except in terms of the interconnectedness of economic and ideological factors. Yet Hall also took the opportunity to dwell once more on the severe limitations of reemerging old-Marxist objections to the "new revisionism" around the phenomenon of Thatcherism, to the effect that class-theoretical analysis was being abandoned.

"Authoritarian populism" reappeared in the second part of *The Hard Road to Renewal*, four chapters of which were strategically compartmentalized as "Questions of Theory." Within this section, the article responding to Jessop and colleagues was placed alongside an earlier Hall discussion of "Two Ways of Taking Democracy Seriously," namely, authoritarian populism and the notion of the popular-democratic. This latter paper came from the same Hall phase as "Base and Superstructure" and "The Problem of Ideology" (our chapters 2 and 4), so the juxtaposition served to remind readers of two things: whether revisionist or not, Hall was not interested in shaping up as a post-Marxist, and his emphasis on the vital significance of ideology could not reasonably be equated with *ideologism*.

The theory section of *Hard Road* was headed by "State and Society, 1880–1930," coauthored with Bill Schwarz, and taken from what was, in effect, the last of the CCCS/Hutchinson former *Working Papers in Cultural Studies* series.[2] This was an interesting move, because that account was not at all theoretical in the standard sense of laying out thinkers and concepts and elaborating on the ones considered most useful. Rather, it was an applied Gramscian excavation of how the succession of political crises in that period had severely threatened "the hegemony of the dominant order" and gelled into an "epochal transition" involving "the recomposition of British society, politics and the state."[3] In describing how the realigned forces of collectivism and conservatism acted as powerful "strands in the dispersal of liberalism," Hall and Schwarz showed how a momentous passive revolution (Gramsci) got underway; without an understanding of that context, the Thatcher conjuncture itself could not properly be grasped. The authors made no apology for concentrating on the political level: both the crises and the transition, they insisted, were constituted by political forces. But again, we should not see this as amounting to "politicism," any more than the approach to Thatcherism represented "ideologism." The very use of "passive revolution," in both Gramsci and Hall, such that our own conjuncture must be perceived, organically, as stretching back in various ways to that late nineteenth-century moment, rules out any purely presentist or superstructuralist interpretation of what Hall was endeavoring to explain. But the political had to be given its due, just as giving the economic its due also required dedicated attention. For example, in another chapter in the collection in which "State and Society" appeared (titled "The Corporate Economy, 1890–1929"), Schwarz provided the sort of focus that he and Hall would have seen as necessarily interweaving with their chapter in *Hard Road*.[4]

As well as underlining the continuity between our chapter 7, "Variants of Liberalism," and Hall's approach in his Thatcherism book, the theory section of *Hard Road* works against the impression given in the Jessop critique that Hall was fixated on the immediate ideological novelty of Thatcherism; that he had a thin version of Gramsci; and that he was less attuned than he might have been to the contested nature of discourses and institutions that aspired to be hegemonic. Jessop and his coauthors produced their own longer project volume—*Thatcherism: A Tale of Two Nations*—in the same year as Hall's *Hard Road*.[5] Further efforts were made to emphasize that, despite their reservations, they were seeking constructively to build on Hall's seminal contribution, but by reproducing all three parts of the earlier encounter (including Hall's response) and by consistently streaming the nub of the exchange, as they saw it, throughout the rest of the book, the hint of personal animus could not be expunged, whatever their intention. Otherwise, Jessop and colleagues' *Thatcherism* was impressively comprehensive, and their critique of Far Left and traditionalist Marxist authors who fail to recognize the relative autonomy of the political and the ideological was indeed, in substantive terms, similar to Hall's. Such compatibility is also attested, at one remove, by Jessop's subsequent development of the analytical lenses of "critical discourse analysis" and "cultural political economy," both underpinned by a generous interpretation of Marxist categories and purposes. From the angle of the selection of Hall's writings in this book, perhaps what is most emphatically revealed by that whole episode of debate was that while Hall's forte as a mediator in the politics of theory involves strenuously synthesizing concepts and positions, it was ultimately the broad trajectories of thought and practice that mattered to him, rather than the kind of theoretical exactitude that could end up being divisive.

Beyond Our Existing Vocabularies?

Race, ethnicity, identity, postcoloniality, diaspora. These were major Hall concerns, and his thinking about them, together with his experience of them, are defining elements of his life and work. As such, they prompt appreciation and review in their own terms. Yet nothing about Hall makes for easy compartmentalization, and we have already seen in chapter 6 how his Marxism and his approach to race and ethnicity were spun from a single fabric of thought. The same could be said of two other pivotal papers already mentioned—"Race, Articulation and Societies Structured in Dominance" (1980) and "Gramsci's Relevance for the Study of Race and Ethnicity" (1986). These were included in the *Essential Essays* volumes, in which editor David Morley quotes Kobena Mercer's introduction to another prime Hall publication—*The Fateful Triangle: Race, Ethnicity, Nation*—in order to underscore that Hall's earlier neo-Marxist, sociologically minded theorizations, as exemplified by those two essays, provided the very grounding for the "more discursive approaches to these questions displayed in his later work."[6] This is well said, but we should not minimize the significant shift that took place in Hall's interests and in his sense of the politics of theory.

We might put it this way: ten years after "Gramsci's Relevance" it would be difficult to imagine Hall constructing a discussion of ethnicity and identity in the form taken by that paper, which involved no fewer than twenty-six pages on the concepts and importance of Gramsci before a seven-page "sketch" was presented of "some of the ways in which this Gramscian perspective could potentially be used... in the analysis of racism and related social phenomena."[7] To be sure, one decade on, the Gramscian story line had often been delivered, and its terms were part and parcel of Hall's very apparatus of perception—as many readers would have known. Elaborate exposition on that score may have been unnecessary. Yet into the 1990s Hall's range of reference broadened considerably in order to address more directly what he increasingly regarded as the ineluctably discursive aspect of thinking and being. Naturally, the categories of race and ethnicity could not simply be abandoned, any more than class itself could: their social substrates continued to be fundamental and it would be hard—indeed, bizarre—to think of them as exclusively subjective-ideational constructions. But Hall came to find problematical the *obviousness* of the assumption that those concepts represented definitively real social conditions and identities, outside the means and processes of their representation. In the terms of our discussion of the part I writings, the discursive sense of articulation was becoming, for Hall, at least as important as its societal meaning, and it was getting close to the point where the very distinction—so vital for his reading of the 1857 "Introduction"—was starting to slide. In that context, the more mobile, fluid ideas of the postcolonial and the diasporic greatly appealed. True, in some theoretical hands the new ways of thinking seemed to be endowed with an almost principled conceptual elusiveness and an evasive heterogeneity of purpose. At the same time, why would it *not* be the case that a transition into truly "global" thinking for the first time, together with a corresponding break with all unreflective modernist paradigms, would throw up significant sectors of ambivalence and compounded ways of proceeding? We might recall here Sartre's suggestive phrase about the progressive impulse in intellectual movements seeking to catch hold of "the profundity of the lived." At any rate, in "When Was 'the Post-colonial'? Thinking at the Limit" Hall fully engages with this train of thought.

In the handful of years prior to the writing of our chapter 11, Hall had produced searching reflections on "new ethnicities," "questions of cultural identity," and critiques of "essentialist" ways of understanding personal and political subjectivity, including the essentialist "black" subject. His thought was correspondingly marked by inclinations toward *hybridity* (cultural, social, intellectual) and he expressed (further) complexity regarding the interrelations between the political, the historical, the conceptual, and the psychic, both as layers of comprehension and as sensibilities. One important predecessor to "When Was 'the Post-colonial'?" was "The West and the Rest: Discourse and Power."[8] Because the latter was yet another outstanding Open University teaching text Hall did not wish to overcomplicate matters, but the title of that investigation immediately indicated that the binary distinction he was seeking to explore (West/Rest) represented an ideological "imaginary" as much as any preexisting real division in the world, while the trademark Foucauldian subtitle ("discourse and power") signaled Hall's intention to give greater credit than previously to that preeminent non-Marxist. And an important thesis in that regard was not only that standard modernist sociology, with its characteristic contraposition of advanced and primitive social types, was shot through with Eurocentric bias, but so, too, arguably, was Marxism itself. Among other reasons, this was because historical materialism took an oddly positive view of Western modernity (*in potentia* at least), since capitalism represented a necessary stage in humanity's progress toward "advanced Communism." Hall thus highlighted the congruence among sociology, Marxism, and European Enlightenment theories of the "stages" through which human civilization necessarily evolved, the lineaments of which were constructed on the back of colonialist convictions about the essential inferiority—or else the simple idyllic nobility—of the "savage" peoples of the world that were at that time rapidly being "discovered." It seemed, then, that Marxism had to be considered part of the dominant "regime of truth" (Foucault) in whose terms non-Western modes of living and thinking had been defined as necessarily backward (and, as such, systematically exploited/destroyed).

"The West and the Rest" is often read as though such critical considerations were being put forward by Hall as unequivocal *arguments*. As such, it would be hard to see how he could continue to express any kind of commitment to Marxism. But I think this misreads what he was doing. Hall wanted to advertise the crucial importance of Edward Said's famous book of 1978, *Orientalism*, in advancing discussions of colonial dominance and cultural power.[9] Yet as has been widely acknowledged, while Said brilliantly combined Foucault and Gramsci in understanding Western scholarly and governmental approaches to the Orient in (largely) the nineteenth century, he also had difficulty squaring their different theoretical emphases. The Marxian heritage of Gramsci continued to work, at least in part, against the poststructuralist bearings of Foucault. Said's text, then, while powerful and suggestive, was not altogether coherent. Aware of this, Hall adopted a *heuristic* approach to the thinkers he brought into play, not least because this might be the appropriate pedagogical approach. That way, all the featured lines of argument could be deemed important, providing food for critical thought; but no one of them was necessarily complete or exclusively right. It is also noteworthy that Hall drew on the Marxist economic historian R. L. Meek's book *Social Science and the Ignoble Savage* in framing the topic of "The West and the Rest."[10] Meek's argument, crucially, was twofold: *some* stadial theorizations of history in the eighteenth century were blatantly racist or supremacist, but others, even if faulty and ideologically tinged, supplied indispensable ingredients for any adequate comparative cultural and sociological understanding, without which the critique of "Eurocentrism" itself could not get off the ground. For Meek, and Hall too, this better line of Enlightenment inquiry eminently included, later, the ideas of Karl Marx.

"When Was 'the Post-colonial'?" is a more difficult essay, theoretically falling somewhere between "The West and the Rest" and Hall's significant paper of 2000, "The Multicultural Question." In the latter, he seeks to explain why the hybrid phenomena and agonistic demands (equality *plus* difference) of contemporary "multiculture"—not "multiculturalism," about which Hall remained skeptical—"appear to outrun our existing political vocabularies."[11] And that, clearly, includes our existing Marxist vocabularies. Again, though, we must be careful. Hall was not necessarily implying that in every respect Marxism had served its time. It might well still be *compatible*, after a fashion, with his focus on the radical insufficiency of all identities, and with the conundrum of retaining a grain of universalism while accepting that relationships between partial selves and multiple concrete "others" in our contemporary settings are constantly negotiated and intrinsically contingent. But put that way, while the connection to Marxism may not have been lost in principle, it was becoming in practice vanishingly thin. Accordingly, in "The Multicultural Question," it is Ernesto Laclau, Judith Butler, and, again, Foucault—theorists of the discursive—that Hall turns to, with Gramsci and Marx consigned to a couple of footnotes and asides.

That our chapter 11 opens up extremely tricky ground is signaled straight away by the fact that in its first five pages Hall clusters together as many as twenty rapid-fire, overlapping questions. Their gist, and that of the paper as a whole, is to convey that the notion of the postcolonial raises profound problems. First, regarding its periodization: *when* are we to think of "it" as taking place, vis-à-vis coloniality and modernity? Second, regarding its very status as a conceptual vector: Is the postcolonial to be considered a "real" compendium of forces and events, or is it not, instead, the name for a *way of seeing*, a problem space, through which many taken-for-granted ideas are going to have to be fundamentally reconsidered and indeed replaced? This involves interrogating anew at least three core concepts underpinning modern social understanding:

- Time—Is there such a single, politics-free, continuous, temporal medium as "history," at least as conventionally understood?
- Space—What happens once we see that traditional ideas about "geography," and the "world" itself, have been definitively imagined through Eurocentric eyes?
- The cultural politics of belonging—How can we continue to identify exclusively *either* with dominant white groups, nations, and cultures *or* with subordinate "local," "ethnic minority" ones, once we know that the very localism and ethnicism of the latter are largely the product of the dubious universalism of the former?

Hall poses such considerations as formidable not only in a conceptual sense but also because they are disturbing and unsettling in a deeply psychic way, something that rationalist approaches to philosophical commitment tend to play down. Finally, in Hall's perspective, all these difficulties, and the feelings of derailment and ambivalence that go with them, will frustrate white Western academics and political actors far more than "subaltern" or self-consciously hybrid groups and thinkers. For the latter, release from unambiguous stability in our previous positionings within and concerning the world represents, under the sign of the postcolonial, a dramatic new source of freedom and participation.

Throughout the "'Post-colonial'" essay, we should observe, Hall's ability as mediator is continuously exemplified—and being stretched. In a different context, social philosopher Bruno Latour makes the distinction between true mediators and mere "intermediaries." For Latour, the latter take problem fields as given, and assume that some preexisting state of "the social" itself is being transparently represented in arriving at a stable set of issues and, preferably, a definite verdict. Mediators, by contrast, for Latour, *reconstitute* the very concerns being addressed; in effect, they propose and coproduce a *new* "social" in and through their acts of problematization and the network effects they trigger. That is why Latour says that mediators, but not intermediaries, are "game-changers" and "track-switchers."[12] I find this helpful in appreciating what Hall is doing in "'Post-colonial,'" for there is a kind of genius in the way that he orchestrates such overviews. Engaging with existing literatures and debates, Hall proceeds to *reset* the postcolonial as, precisely, a series of concerns and problems rather than definite positions and oppositions. This then enables him to bring *inside* the engaged constituency some authors—for example, Ella Shohat—whose arguments are ostensibly directed against it.

The stickiest operation of that sort is Hall's protracted interaction with Arif Dirlik's critical assessment of postcolonialism. Hall views this as a prize instance of Marxist reductionism, so he takes time to counter Dirlik's caricature of postcolonial thought as little more than a variant of rampant, apolitical, academic—and Western!—postmodernism, the very creature of consumer capitalism itself. And if reductionism is mostly what Hall is countering here, he is also posing challenges to the Marxist problematic in its entirety. For Hall, it is mistaken to see postcolonialism as offering a new, rival totalization to that of Marxism; rather, it represents a disruption and "retrospective rephrasing" of modernity within the framework of an alternative globalization. If Marxism is not exactly being knocked out of the picture, it must necessarily be "dislocated." Hall knows that Marx was more aware of the role of colonial plunder and violence in creating the very conditions for Western capitalist modernity than is often granted in postcolonial circles, but even so, the Marxist tradition as a whole has insufficiently recognized the fundamental role and timing of capitalism's "constitutive outside."

Instead, the dominant image has been of a powerful dynamic *internal* to the relentless logic of capital itself, and this amounts to—or at least it can lead to—a blinkered, apologetic form of Eurocentric modernism. Moreover, under postcolonial lights, Marxism's claimed substantive validity—its correspondence with reality—cannot be stated or defended outside the culturally specific cast of its overall narrative structure and privileged categories. Such issues, for Hall, cannot easily be resolved; but no longer can they be brushed aside.

Determined to avoid swapping one kind of "polemical closure" for another, Hall then moves toward a more positive take on Dirlik's critique. This involves drawing attention to the latter's notable oscillations: on the one hand, Dirlik sets up postcolonialism as a sham, an irresponsible "culturalism"; on the other hand, he eventually accepts that it genuinely signals a crisis in traditional ways of understanding global conditions and syndromes. Hall seizes on this hiatus to commend Dirlik's "comprehensive list" of Marxist-phrased factors that shape the new structural situation. And he agrees that it is quite "remarkable"—indeed, a glaring deficit—that "the relationship between postcolonialism and global capitalism" has slipped the attention of at least some people working in this vein. Hall also neatly balances out his habitual rejection of reductionist Marxism by deriding attempts to position postcolonialism itself as the new unambiguously correct theoretical standpoint, including uniformly negative presentations of the entire Western philosophical tradition.[13]

Once again, it seems that all along Hall has been carefully plotting another of his typically satisfactory syntheses: postcolonialism and Marxism are not, after all, completely at odds with one another, and the differences between the epistemological norms of critical theory and the disruptive motifs of subaltern identities and temporalities can, with some effort, be mutually accommodated. In one sense, this *is* what Hall is seeking to achieve, and to good effect. But only in part, because unlike many other discussions of his, Hall senses that the tensions and counterpoints in this case should *not* be satisfactorily resolved: they should be lived with, mulled over, left to disturb, constantly be rethought. This is why the concept of *différance*, taken from Jacques Derrida, is central to his argument, referring to the impossibility of restabilizing notional unities once significant differences in thought and in substance have been introduced. Under the sign of *différance*, sociological and conceptual differences become recalcitrant, become incommensurables. To be sure, Hall remains as skeptical about the "fantasy of a utopia of difference" as he is about the fantasy of a progressive sameness. Still, he accepts that the "post-" in "postcolonial" signals a shift from thinking about things in a "rational-successive" way to a deconstructive mode of understanding. Thus, the concepts and purposes of the modernist paradigms that we have inherited must be put "under erasure": not altogether deserted, but fundamentally questioned and beset by all manner of alternatives, especially ones that derive from struggles, identities, and histories that are fundamentally different from the dominant ones. That the result is hard even cogently to think through is, for Hall, productive and salutary. Centers will not hold; multitudinous and marginalized diversity must be foregrounded. This is what Hall, following Derrida, is seeking to capture in the notion of thinking at the limit.

We may ask, in response: Is Hall's stream of thought through these twists and turns—in seeking to work with the coherence of incoherence, so to speak—convincing? This is debatable. On the one hand, he is not completely letting go of the forms of understanding that are being destabilized. Amid all the slippage, bifurcation, and complexity, Hall acknowledges, we probably cannot avoid reaching for some form of "overdetermined unity" in both theory and practice. It may even be politically remiss to drop that quest altogether. To that extent, despite "some conceptual incompatibility" between postfoundationalism and critical-modernist discourses, "this cannot yet be accepted as an unbridgeable philosophical chasm."[14] Equally, though, Hall is pushing us to see that the question of coherence quickly loops back on itself at a higher level: Is there, after all, such a clear distinction between coherence and disruption as some of us might (desire to) think? And might not the question of coherence/incoherence ultimately itself be a matter of political contestation rather than philosophical reasoning, especially concerning the postcolonial? This disquisition of Hall's, I think, consciously avoids giving firm answers to the questions it raises, including the question of Marxism. But it does seem to mark a transition in his personal and political odyssey, from *neo*-Marxism to *post*-Marxism.

Culturalism?

Chapter 12 illustrates another way in which, in the mid-1990s, Hall pursued his points of departure regarding Marxism. The chapter selection here omits two sections of the original. One of these, quite short, illustrates connections between the local and the global by way of transformations of culture in everyday life, bringing out the way in which the spheres of leisure, sports,

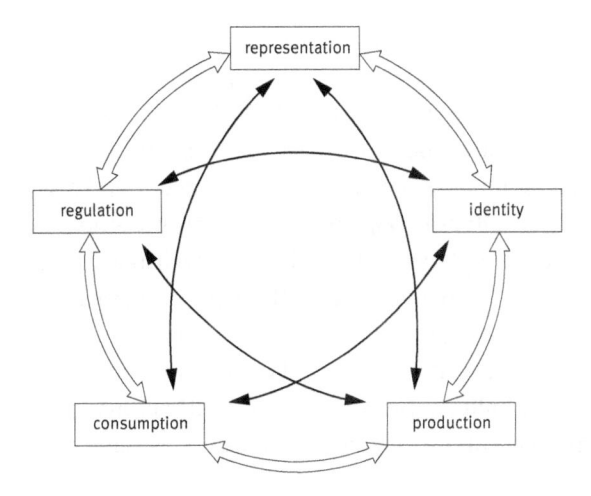

```
              representation
             /    |    \
    regulation    |    identity
             \    |    /
         consumption  production
```

domesticity, and lifestyles show how "culture creeps into every nook and crevice of contemporary social life."[15] A second, ten-page omission focuses on cultural regulation: the way that cultural spheres and initiatives—in the mass media, broadcasting, the arts, and so on—are *governed*, largely through navigation of policy paths through ethno-nationally defined public service, on the one hand, and commercial interests, on the other. The regulation section is valuable, but it does not depend on or follow the theoretical propositions that boldly front the Open University book series *Culture, Media and Identities* that Hall's essay concluded.

To see that organizing perspective more clearly, we can refer, as Hall does, to the introduction to the book on the Sony Walkman that kicks off this extensive OU project. Part of the thinking is captured in its "circuit of culture" diagram.[16] This schema was, in part, a development of Richard Johnson's theoretical map in "What Is Cultural Studies Anyway?"[17] Part of Johnson's purpose, as I indicated earlier, was to break with the Marxist emphasis on the priority of production, both *within* the circuit and in relation to placing culture generally in terms of the determinations of the social formation—not least via that other crucial visualization, "base and superstructure." Writing on behalf of the editorial team, Paul du Gay continues this theme by theorizing the circuit as an articulation of a "number of distinct processes," the outcome of whose interactions are "variable and contingent."[18] In effect, production is stripped of its privileged standing *outside* culture; then, when repositioned within the cultural circuit, it is conceived as having equal status with the other nodes, in a ceaseless process of mutual interaction (see the figure).

In our chapter 12, Hall reiterates the major premise laid down in the *Culture, Media and Identities* introduction: that culture, today, is central, not peripheral, both substantively and epistemologically. Substantive-historically, culture is *more* central today, owing to its dramatically increased influence on contemporary experience and interconnectivity. Epistemologically, social reality is culturally *constituted*; materiality, economic causation, and social practice cannot meaningfully be conceived as existing outside the symbolic codes and normative valences through which we represent them. By extension, the very categories of understanding by means of which analysts gain ordered social knowledge themselves intrinsically express social meanings and cultural preferences. As Hall summarizes: "Culture is nothing but the sum of the different classificatory systems and discursive formations."[19]

He goes on to exemplify the centrality of culture, both in the "global dimension" of contemporary society and along the "final frontier" of identity and subjectivity. Here Hall undoubtedly puts his finger on crucial phenomena of cultural and political life in the (post)modern era. The question is, however, whether their importance can be appreciated only on condition of acceptance of the twofold centrality of culture thesis, understood as *reversing* the (supposed) priorities of previous generations of sociologists and Marxists alike, in effect instituting a move from culture-as-derivative to culture-as-primary. In the end, Hall backs off from this strong statement of "culturalism," but the initial rhetoric pushes hard in that direction.

The case for the strong centrality thesis, in both its aspects, is not in my view greatly convincing. Is culture really more central than before? To take only the Victorian era of British capitalist modernity, providing many of the stock images of materialism-in-command: its production of wealth and goods, its machines, factories, and systems of land management were hardly less embroiled with, and overlaid by, cultural values than present-day "things"—Protestant ethics and religious revivals immediately come to mind; symbols and norms of respectability, thrift, industriousness, deference, and domesticity; changing ideals of health and leisure and imperial destiny (each partly driving the expansion of one of the defining forces of the age, the railway). Hall also mentions Egyptian civilization, ancient China, and the Renaissance, epochs that are even more frequently defined in essentially cultural terms rather than by whatever "material" factors produced or were produced by them. By the same token, today's *immaterial*, virtual, communicational society, in which imaginaries are allegedly in command, are the product of unprecedented levels of mass production of computerized hardware of every size (producing grotesque levels of material waste).

In any case, the "substantive" thesis is undermined by the "epistemological" thesis, because if social action and human existence alike are quintessentially meaning-laden, as Hall tells us in the first paragraph of chapter 12, then there cannot be times and places where this nostrum applies more and others where it applies less, or not at all. We can certainly say that new or different *forms* of cultural life, or communicative technologies, or styles of meaning-making, are vital today in a way that they were not previously. But that is not the same as saying that culture has become more socially significant.

The assumption that social action is intrinsically meaningful has long been invoked by sociologists and others in the human sciences to oppose "biologistic" imperialism in the understanding of behavior. Accordingly, at various points Hall recruits sociological classics like Durkheim and Weber to this cause. But it then seems curious that the epistemological dimension of the centrality of culture idea is intended above all to counter sociologists—as though it was a characteristic dogma of sociologists that social reality can indeed be specified and known in a way that makes culture definitively secondary. Even allowing for the fact that traditions of thought can be differently interpreted, this claim is questionable. According to du Gay's introductory assertion, backed by Hall, in the "explanatory hierarchy of the social sciences in general and sociology in particular . . . cultural processes were deemed rather ephemeral and superficial."[20] But this is tendentious. More likely, sociology stood in little need of a "cultural turn" because it was *always*, in the main, culturalist rather than materialist in its explanatory hierarchy.[21] This was certainly the shared assumption of keynote articles ranging across several CCCS volumes of *Working Papers in Cultural Studies*, in which sociologists were typified as excessively idealist, habitually tending to gloss over structural realities by dwelling on attitudes, norms, and values.

Along those lines, in *Cultural Studies 1983*, Hall himself astutely summarized the work of Talcott Parsons, doyen of sociological theory in the twentieth century.[22] Parsons too, Hall knew, was centrally concerned with "the importance of the realm of the symbolic in the integration of different social groups." The trouble was, though, that in his characteristically abstract thinking about culture in general, Parsons gave "very little concrete elaboration . . . around which cultural values the integration is made," proceeding as though "cultural relations function outside of the impact of economic relations, of social structures, and especially power." This is an excellent point, but one made at a time when Hall felt no compulsion definitively to prioritize the centrality of culture as such. Indeed, one irony of the later, revised argument is that the OU team's "circuit of culture" bears a striking resemblance to Parsons's own oft-diagrammed, multinodal, cultural conception of society's "generalized media of exchange."

We should conclude from this that it was probably not mainstream sociology at all but, once again—under cover—orthodox Marxism that Hall and du Gay most had in their sights—perhaps quite specifically a handful of 1970s–80s neo-Marxist sociologists of the media. For all that, against the run of the presentation, the ostensibly strident argument about the primacy of culture is not finally pushed to its conclusion. After all, it was not so long ago that Hall's own theorizing and grasp of events was, in effect, close to that of Marx-respecting sociologists—as amply evidenced in "Race, Articulation and Societies Structured in Dominance."[23] Also, Hall could not entirely embrace the full implications of the discursive turn. As he put it in an interview with *Radical Philosophy* published in the same year as "Centrality of Culture": "Everything is within the discursive, but nothing is only discourse or only discursive."[24] This chimes with other statements of his explaining why, although he accepted something of poststructuralism and especially its more political variant in the form of Laclau's work, such affiliation was never complete. Thus, in our chapter 12, Hall proceeds to compromise the epistemological argument about the centrality of culture by allowing that— "of course"—the latter could not possibly mean that "that everything is 'culture' and that 'culture' is everything." If this were so, Hall conceded, it would rightly be open to the criticism that "we had simply replaced the economic materialism or sociologism which once threatened to dominate these questions in the social sciences with a cultural idealism." So, in the end, it is not a question of making a total break with previous mainstreams at all; rather, it is a matter of a returning to some neglected elements of modern social thought. The argument then becomes that "every social practice has a discursive character"—a significantly different and notably mediational rendering of the cultural revolutions of our time.[25]

A second edition of *Doing Cultural Studies* was produced in 2013, without Hall's direct involvement. Self-critically, Paul du Gay felt that in the intervening time the focus on culture in the original book/OU project had rightly been problematized by way of subsequent "turns" to practice and to materiality. The foundational circuit of culture diagram—especially its "representation" node—was now considered far from adequate, and even the driving theorization behind the whole circuit conception, namely the cultural turn, "like its near cousin, 'social constructionism' has increasingly lost its foothold," having been "subject to considerable critique."[26]

As the 2000s progressed, Stuart Hall's sense of rage about neoliberalism, alongside his partial recovery of a more straightforward register of ideology-critique, meant that his writings of the later 1990s and early 2000s represented the furthest points from which he had moved away from his previous bottom-line commitment to Marxist problem-formation. In a notable change of emphasis, he ended what proved to be his last interview with the consideration that, as a product of the constant opposition to economism and reductionism within cultural studies, "we drifted off into the cultural institutions and discourses and discursive analyses *etc.*, as if the economy didn't exist." But in 2013, looking "at a society like Britain today," Hall reflected, "almost every feature of the culture—public culture, every feature of social life and I sometimes think every aspect of the inside of a lot of people's heads are influenced, shaped by what I would call the 'economic.'"[27] His point was not to retract altogether the centrality of culture claim; rather, it was, once again, decisively to link together "both ends of the chain."

NOTES

1 Relatedly, more recently, Perry Anderson in effect cancels out his stated appreciation of Hall's creative use of Gramsci by faulting its neglect of the coercion/domination dimension of "hegemony," and by finding that in Hall's account of Thatcherism "the popular moment effaces, all but completely, the national." See Anderson, "The Heirs of Gramsci," *New Left Review*, II/100 (July/August 2016): 74–78. Both points are contestable.

2 Mary Langan and Bill Schwarz, eds., *Crises in the British State, 1880–1930* (London: CCCS/Hutchinson, 1985).

3 Stuart Hall, *The Hard Road to Renewal: Thatcherism and the Crisis of the Left* (London: Verso, 1988), 95–96.

4 Bill Schwarz, "The Corporate Economy, 1890–1929," in Langan and Schwarz, *Crises in the British State*, 80–103.

5 Bob Jessop, Kevin Bonnett, Simon Bromley, and Tom Ling, *Thatcherism: A Tale of Two Nations* (Cambridge: Polity, 1988).

6 Stuart Hall, *Essential Essays*, vol. 2, *Identity and Diaspora*, ed. David Morley (Durham, NC: Duke University Press, 2019), 17; and Stuart Hall, *The Fateful Triangle: Race, Ethnicity, Nation*, ed. Kobena Mercer (Cambridge, MA: Harvard University Press, 2017).

7 Hall, *Essential Essays*, 2:47.
8 Stuart Hall, "The West and the Rest: Discourse and Power," in *Formations of Modernity*, ed. Stuart Hall and Bram Gieben (Cambridge: Polity, 1992), 275–331.
9 Edward Said, *Orientalism* (London: Routledge and Kegan Paul, 1978).
10 R. L. Meek, *Social Science and the Ignoble Savage* (Cambridge: Cambridge University Press, 1975).
11 Hall, *Essential Essays*, 2:120.
12 Bruno Latour, *Reassembling the Social: An Introduction to Actor-Network-Theory* (Oxford: Oxford University Press, 2005), 37–42. I should add that, for Latour, neither mediators nor intermediaries are necessarily single agents or humans.
13 This volume, p. 311, 301.
14 This volume, p. 312.
15 Stuart Hall, "The Centrality of Culture: Notes on the Cultural Revolutions of Our Time," in *Media and Cultural Regulation*, ed. Kenneth Thompson (London: Sage, 1997), 215.
16 Paul du Gay, "Introduction," in Paul du Gay, Stuart Hall, Linda Janes, Hugh Mackay, and Keith Negus, *Doing Cultural Studies: The Story of the Sony Walkman* (London: Open University/Sage, 1997), 1–5, 3.
17 Richard Johnson, "What Is Cultural Studies Anyway?," CCCS Stencilled Paper No. 74, University of Birmingham, reproduced in *CCCS Selected Working Papers*, vol. 1, ed. Ann Gray, Jan Campbell, Mark Erikson, Stuart Hanson, and Helen Wood (Abingdon, UK: Routledge, 2007), 655–93.
18 Du Gay, "Introduction," 3.
19 This volume, p. 327.
20 Du Gay, "Introduction," 1.
21 See Gregor McLennan, "Sociology, Cultural Studies and the Cultural Turn," in *The Palgrave Handbook of Sociology in Britain*, ed. John Holmwood and John Scott (Houndmills, UK: Palgrave Macmillan, 2014), 510–35.
22 Stuart Hall, *Cultural Studies 1983: A Theoretical History*, ed. Jennifer Daryl Slack and Lawrence Grossberg (Durham, NC: Duke University Press, 2016), 17–18.
23 Reproduced in Stuart Hall, *Essential Essays*, vol. 1, *Foundations of Cultural Studies*, ed. David Morley (Durham, NC: Duke University Press, 2019).
24 Stuart Hall, "Interview: Culture and Power," *Radical Philosophy* 86 (1997): 24–41.
25 This volume, p. 328, 331.
26 Paul du Gay and Anders Koed Madsen, "Introduction to the Second Edition," in Paul du Gay, Stuart Hall, Linda Janes, Anders Koed Madsen, Hugh Mackay, and Keith Negus, *Doing Cultural Studies: The Story of the Sony Walkman*, 2nd ed. (London: Open University/Sage, 2013), xi–xxvii, xvii.
27 Stuart Hall, "Interview," in *Cultural Studies: 50 Years On*, ed. Kieran Connell and Matthew Hilton (London: Rowman and Littlefield, 2016), 287–304, 304.

INDEX

actor-network theory, 350n12. *See also* Latour, Bruno

Althusser, Louis, 2–3, 11, 158, 160–61, 165–76, 249; "Althusser group," 261–62, 265; and Balibar, 166; and "base/superstructure" theory, 67–68, 73, 84–88, 99, 121, 140, 278; on *Capital*, 63; on *The Communist Manifesto*, 97–98; on determinacy, 36, 69, 86–87, 122, 131, 139; emphasis on articulation, 166; on *The German Ideology*, 68, 72–73; and Gramsci, 85, 168, 249, 307, 329; Hall and, 160, 168, 172–73, 176n35, 176n36, 249, 276, 289; Hall's 1972 paper on Gramsci and Althusser, 168; as idealist, 11, 39, 168; on "ideological state apparatuses," 85, 87, 139–40, 186, 262, 267, 275; on ideology, 130, 139, 140; influence on Laclau, 170; key phrasings, 11; periodization of Marx's work, 92; and Poulantzas, 261–62; in the *Reading Capital* period, 87, 94, 122, 139; and "symptomatic reading" of Marx, 93; and "theoretical practice," 277–78; use of "conjuncture" concept, 158; use of terms from psychoanalysis, 140. *See also* Althusserians and Althusserianism; Balibar, Étienne; Gramsci, Antonio; Hall, Stuart; Poulantzas, Nicos; Rancière, Jacques; *individual works*

Althusserians and Althusserianism, 84, 88, 139, 166–68, 261–62, 265, 271, 276–78; Althusserian structuralism, 6, 46, 307, 329; British, 273–77; "classical Althusserianism," 266; "vulgar Althusserianism," 275, 280. *See also* Althusser, Louis

American Revolution, 228, 237. *See also* United States

Anderson, Perry, 89n23, 135, 273, 349n1

anticolonial struggles, 298–99. *See also* colonialism; imperialism; neocolonialism; postcolonialism and "the postcolonial"

anti-theory, 274. *See also The Poverty of Theory*

aristocracy, 75, 76, 182; bourgeois, 218; financial, 116; of labor, 217. *See also* class; nobility articulation, 36, 76, 94, 270, 291, 311, 330, 345; in Althusser, 11, 86, 97; double, 57, 185; Hall's use of concept, 8, 165–67, 169, 170, 251, 338; Jameson on, 175n24; in Marx, 8, 41–44, 47, 120–22, 128; of social relations, 70. *See also* "Race, Articulation and Societies Structured in Dominance"

Asia: labor migration from, 223

Australia, 297

authoritarian populism (AP), 8, 270, 282–86, 288–92, 335–36

"Authoritarian Populism, Two Nations and Thatcherism" (Jessop et al.), 6, 7–8, 282–92

authoritarian statism, 270, 284–85

Bakunin, Mikhail, 20, 124

Balibar, Étienne, 122, 166, 262, 265, 266, 270. *See also* Althusser, Louis; *Reading Capital*

Barthes, Roland, 329

"base and superstructure" metaphor, 3, 7, 11, 15n15, 54, 98, 117, 130–31, 135, 139, 254, 266; Althusser and, 67–68, 73, 84–88, 99, 121, 140, 278; Gramsci and, 82, 114; Hall on, 62–88, 160–62, 166, 186, 211, 236, 317, 336, 345

Bentham, Jeremy, 81, 144

Bhabha, Homi, 2, 301, 304

Birmingham, 248

Birmingham school, 5. *See also* Centre for Contemporary Cultural Studies; University of Birmingham

"Black Crime, Black Proletariat" (Hall), 199–223, 250–52

Black Liberator, 211, 212, 213, 215, 217, 220, 251. *See also* Cambridge, A. X.

Black Lives Matter movement, 252

Black Panthers, 248

Blair, Tony, 323

Bolte, Friedrich, 111, 113

Bonapartism. See *The Eighteenth Brumaire of Louis Bonaparte*; France

Bonnett, Kevin, 6, 282. *See also* "Authoritarian Populism, Two Nations and Thatcherism"; *Thatcherism*

bourgeoisie, 55, 102, 110, 126, 218, 241, 279; bourgeois aristocracy and proletariat, 112, 218; bourgeois political economy, 23, 57, 142, 146; bourgeois thought and society, 81, 95–96, 100, 116–18, 134–38, 141–45, 153, 184, 197, 201, 228, 240, 244, 267; French, 120, 125; industrial, 75–76, 108, 116–17, 176n36, 182; law and the, 76; vs. peasantry, 119; petty bourgeoisie, 104, 116–18, 129, 153, 202–3, 264; political power of the, 71, 113, 115–16, 123, 152, 241; Portuguese, 263; vs. proletarians, 96–97, 99, 101, 201. *See also* class; France

Braverman, Harry, 208, 223, 264

Britain, 1, 129, 153–54, 179, 210, 216, 220, 236, 239, 255, 265, 296–97; British Mandate period, 300; capitalist modernity in, 346; "Englishness," 323–24; government of, 129, 228, 233, 240–43; Marx on British politics, 73–76, 79, 96, 103, 123, 126, 203; post-Thatcher, 322–23, 349; working-class culture in, 188. *See also* English Revolution; Thatcher, Margaret; Tory Party; Whig Party

Bromley, Simon, 6, 282. *See also* "Authoritarian Populism, Two Nations and Thatcherism"; *Thatcherism*

Burke, Edmund, 47

Butler, Judith, 341

Cabral, Amilcar, 219

Caesarism, 83, 264

Callinicos, Alex, 3

Cambridge, A. X., 211, 212, 213, 215, 216, 251

Canada, 297
Capital (Marx), 46, 60n31, 62–63, 65–68, 73–82, 91–95, 99, 104–5, 108, 110, 114, 128, 137, 146, 148, 277; capitalist and laborer personifications in, 128; crime in, 202; echo of *The Communist Manifesto* in, 160; "fetishism of commodities" discussion in, 22, 60n55; and Hegel, 171; labor and surplus value discussion in, 205–6, 209–10, 222; "Machinery and Modern Industry" chapter, 104, 127; methodology of, 22–23, 43, 48–52, 56–58; place of within Marx's oeuvre, 158, 164, 203–4; social capital in, 211. *See also* Marx, Karl; *Reading Capital*
capitalism, 8–10, 23, 33, 44, 47–51, 57–58, 79–81, 83–84, 126, 137, 158, 160, 182, 200, 209, 301; British, 79, 241; and class relations, 101, 108, 112–13, 127, 153, 252; and crime, 202; development of, 83–84, 106, 217, 221–23, 284, 302, 310–13, 339, 342–43; early, 21, 74–75, 97, 211; Fordist production techniques, 211; French, 114, 124–25; laissez-faire, 79, 84; the market in, 143, 147; modern, 203, 206, 270. *See also* colonialism; globalization; labor; liberalism
Carchedi, Guglielmo, 133n43, 264
Caribbean culture and labor, 209, 210, 213–15, 220, 223, 297
Carver, Terrell, 175n30
caste, 75, 123, 209–10, 218. *See also* class
Catholicism: Catholic Europe, 229; Marx on, 69
Centre for Contemporary Cultural Studies (CCCS; University of Birmingham), 1, 4, 13, 164, 168, 173, 248–56, 329, 336; CCCS Marxism/neo-Marxism, 252–55; Hall/CCCS archives, 175n27; seminars at, 19, 164, 248; *Working Papers in Cultural Studies*, 165, 347
Chambers, Iain, 308

Chambers, Samuel A., 176n36
China, 219; ancient, 318, 346; Chinese Revolution, 199; modern, 294, 309
Civil War in France, The (Marx), 92, 113, 123, 124
Clarke, John, 169
class, 10, 13; as central in Marxism, 9; class conflict, 53, 91–98, 188–89, 200–201, 284; class relations, 83, 91, 100–101, 122, 125, 127, 130, 187, 189, 197, 208, 220–21, 268–69, 284; underclass, 219. *See also* bourgeoisie; middle class; proletariat; working class
Classes in Contemporary Capitalism (Poulantzas), 263, 264
Class Struggles in France, The (Marx), 73, 91, 95, 113
CND (Committee for Nuclear Disarmament), 196
Cohen, Phil, 195
Colletti, Lucio, 46, 47; *Marxism and Hegel*, 165
colonialism, 210, 220, 293–94, 299, 307, 339. *See also* imperialism; neocolonialism; postcolonialism and "the postcolonial"
commodity fetishism. *See* fetishism
communism, 9, 83, 114, 161, 240, 252, 339. *See also* Communist Party
Communist Manifesto, The (Marx and Engels), 4, 57, 74, 91, 97–99, 101–10, 112, 114, 124–25; class struggle in, 93, 95; echoed in *Capital*, 160
Communist Party, 13, 162, 261, 265. *See also* communism
Communist University of London (CUL), 161
conjuncture, concept of, 86, 116–18, 123–24; and concept of overdetermination, 46; Hall's use of, 158
consciousness, 9, 201, 202, 241, 318; class, 112, 137, 139, 141, 146, 279; generational, 180, 193–94; Hegel on

consciousness (*continued*)
    self-consciousness, 27, 66; ideological, 81; Marxist conception of, 50, 53–54, 65–73, 136–42, 145–52, 254; mythology as a form of, 54; political, 102, 109, 219, 250, 310; social, 67, 70, 82, 235. *See also* false consciousness
conservatism, 290, 323, 336
corporatism, 213, 283, 284, 292
crime, 249, 278; black, 199, 207, 214; criminal subculture, 184, 201–2; Marxist theory of, 201–5; petty, 217; and political struggle, 199–201
Critique of Hegel's Philosophy of Right (Marx), 76
Critique of the Gotha Programme (Marx), 124, 125
"Critique of the Hegelian Dialectic and Philosophy as a Whole" (Marx), 20, 28, 30
culturalism, 7, 8, 14, 15n15, 169, 294, 310, 343, 344–46
Cultural Studies 1983 (Hall), 1, 11, 15n15, 175n27, 347
cultural theory, 10, 13, 247
cultural turn, 325–30, 347, 349. *See also* culturalism; cultural theory; culture
culture: "centrality of culture" thesis, 8, 279, 321, 325, 330–32, 346–49; cultural power, 181–83, 304, 340; English, 188, 321–24; epistemological aspects of, 325–30; formation of through football, 190, 194, 196, 198n19, 322; globalization and, 317–21; and identity politics, 323–24; "parent" cultures, 183–85, 191, 193–96; substantive vs. epistemological aspects of, 317; US "culture wars," 298. *See also* culturalism; cultural turn
"Culture, Media and Identities" (Open University), 8, 330, 345, 346

Dalla Costa, Mariarosa, 208
Darstellung (representation), 79, 86, 130

Debray, Régis, 262, 265
deconstruction, 134, 302, 331. *See also* Derrida, Jacques
Derrida, Jacques, 8, 301, 308–9, 331, 344; concept of *différance*, 299, 304, 305, 343
determinism/determinacy, 146, 220; for Althusser, 86, 98; Marxist view of, 30–34, 36, 70–72, 86, 98–99, 139, 142, 155–56, 163, 275, 312. *See also* overdetermination/overdeterminacy
Dews, Peter, 268–69
dialectic: classical Marxian, 20, 22, 36, 43, 54, 58, 68, 159, 207, 279; "Critique of the Hegelian Dialectic and Philosophy as a Whole" (Marx), 20, 28, 30; cultural, 183, 185; Hegelian, 20, 23, 35, 72, 169, 301
diaspora and diasporic perspectives, 1, 299, 303–4, 310, 337, 338
dictatorships, 119, 263; "dictatorship of the proletariat," 113, 124, 265, 266, 270. *See also* fascism
Dietzgen, Joseph, 20
différance, 299, 304, 305, 343
Dirlik, Arif, 294–95, 300, 301, 303, 309, 311–12, 342–43
discourse and the discursive, 5, 137, 140, 149, 151–52, 162, 327–32, 337, 339, 344, 348–49; of bourgeois political economy, 137, 146, 267; discourse theory, 289; Foucault and, 267–68, 330; liberal, 228, 232, 241; of the market, 143, 150; Marxist, 169, 248; Western, 301, 305, 308
"double relation," 65, 70
du Gay, Paul, 318, 345, 347–48
Durkheim, Émile, 328–29, 347
Dworkin, Dennis, 254

Economic and Philosophic Manuscripts of 1844 (Marx), 20, 92, 97–98
economism, 236, 266, 269, 349; in Marxism, 14, 102, 126, 139, 159, 276, 312

Egypt, 54, 318, 346
Eighteenth Brumaire of Louis Bonaparte, The (Marx), 73, 74–77, 95, 111, 113–14, 117–18, 122–25, 129, 131, 153, 159–60, 203
Elster, Jon, 160
Engels, Friedrich, 39, 75, 76, 82, 111–12, 267; and "asymptotic movement," 47; *The Condition of the Working Class in England*, 203; and "economism," 276; as guardian of the Marx/Engels legacy, 71; letters on historical materialism, 71–74; letters to and from Marx, 20, 93, 218; Letter to Schmidt, 121–22; *Ludwig Feuerbach and the End of Classical German Philosophy*, 76; and Marx, 3, 12, 58, 63–64, 65, 123, 126, 136–39, 171, 203, 213, 216–17, 220, 235, 261, 263. See also *The Communist Manifesto*; *The German Ideology*; Marx, Karl
England. See Britain
English Revolution, 239–40; Civil War, 228, 232, 236, 239–41, 243, 255; "Glorious Revolution" of 1688, 233, 241–43, 255
Enlightenment, 300, 305, 327, 339, 340
environmentalism, 10
Essays in Self-Criticism (Althusser), 131, 140
ethnicity. See race and ethnicity; workers: black
Eurocentrism, 298, 300, 341; Eurocentric bias, 339–41; Eurocentric modernism, 343; Eurocentric temporalities, 304, 305
Europe, 95, 200, 229, 265, 300, 320; capitalist societies in, 135, 199, 212, 223, 302
Euro-skepticism, 320

false consciousness, 139, 141, 146, 147, 149, 162, 236, 278. See also consciousness
Fanon, Frantz, 219, 248
fascism, 264, 270, 284; in 1930s Germany, 203; in 1930s Italy, 82

Fateful Triangle: Race, Ethnicity, Nation, The (Hall), 338
feminism and feminist thought, 10, 14, 207, 209, 242, 250, 251, 255, 258n8, 326, 329, 331; women's subordination, 255
Fernbach, David, 75, 89n17, 114, 126
fetishism, 60, 79–81, 147, 190, 193, 305; commodity fetishism, 50
Feuerbach, Ludwig, 29, 64, 98, 172, 245n11. See also *Ludwig Feuerbach and the End of Classical German Philosophy*; *Theses on Feuerbach*
financial aristocracy, 116
First World, 220, 294, 303; academia in, 309
football in cultural formation, 190, 194, 196, 198n19, 322
Foucault, Michel, 6, 140, 228, 265–70, 301, 329, 332, 339; and the "cultural turn," 330; *Discipline and Punish*, 269; on the discursive, 330, 331; poststructuralism of, 340–41
France, 76, 203, 228, 261, 265; Algeria and, 297; development of capitalism in, 114–21, 124–25; Marx's understanding of, 75, 103, 115–20; Napoleonic state and Bonapartism in, 77–78, 115, 119, 124, 125, 129, 159, 264; "New Philosophers" in, 266–68; peasants in, 78, 118–19; royalism in, 116; social sciences in, 328–29. See also *The Civil War in France*; *The Class Struggles in France*; *The Eighteenth Brumaire of Louis Bonaparte*
Frankenberg, Ruth, 297, 301, 308
Frankfurt School, 329
French Revolution, 228. See also France
Freud, Sigmund, 86, 93, 140, 147; Lacanian revision of, 87

Gamble, Andrew, 238, 290
gender. See feminism and feminist thought; intersectionality; workers: female and domestic

General Council of the International, 111
"General Formula for Capital" (Marx), 52
Geras, Norman, 168
German Ideology, The (Marx and Engels), 31, 64–75, 79, 82, 91, 101, 110, 137–40, 235
Gilroy, Paul, 299
globalization, 128, 217–18, 222, 248, 263–64, 287, 295–99, 302–4, 317, 342–43; and rise of religious fundamentalism and ethnic nationalism, 320
Glucksmann, André, 168
Godelier, Maurice, 49, 52–53, 160
Gorz, André, 264
Gouldner, Alvin, 201
Gramsci, Antonio, 16n26, 103–4, 138, 139, 158–59, 235, 253, 255, 283, 329; and "base/superstructure" theory, 78, 82–85, 114; on "common sense," 307–8; and "conjuncture" concept, 158, 180, 201; Hall and, 2, 5, 7, 12–13, 162, 168, 249, 336–41, 349n1; and hegemony, 186–88, 197, 286; as historicist, 85; and the idea of "national identity," 153–54; on "ideological state apparatuses," 186–87; and ideology, 151–52, 154; "pessimism of the intellect, optimism of the will," 280; on politics as a "war of position," 296; and Poulantzas, 261, 263–64; *Prison Notebooks*, 160, 286. *See also* Althusser, Louis; Hall, Stuart
Gray, Ann, 174n19, 254
"The Great Moving Right Show" (Hall), 290
Greece, 261, 263; Marx on ancient Greek civilization, 54–55. *See also* Poulantzas, Nicos
Grossberg, Larry, 1, 169
Grundrisse (Marx), 4, 19, 21–22, 47–48, 66, 91, 99, 122, 164; 1857 "Introduction" to, 4, 19–59, 66, 69, 80, 99, 163–66, 168, 174n19, 175n28, 176n36, 254, 338; and "law of uneven development," 76

Gulf War, 294, 295
Gutzmore, Cecil, 211, 212, 213, 216

Hall, Stuart: and Birmingham CCCS, 5, 164, 175n27, 252–55, 336; *Cultural Studies 1983* (ed. Grossberg and Slack), 1, 11, 15n15, 175n27, 347; *Essential Essays* (ed. Morley), 1, 5, 338; as Gramscian, 12–13; on Gramsci and Althusser, 11–12, 158, 160, 166–68, 176n36, 249, 307, 329; "The Great Moving Right Show," 290; *The Hard Road to Renewal*, 335–37; and Hegel, 169–72, 174n17, 176n35; as Marxist mediator, 14, 162, 169, 172, 250, 251, 255, 337, 342; "The Multicultural Question," 5, 340, 341; and neoliberalism, 250, 349; "The Neo-liberal Revolution," 6; and *New Left Review*, 248; "Notes on the Cultural Revolutions of Our Time," 8; and Open University, 5, 255–57; *Policing the Crisis*, 5, 248, 283, 284, 291; on race and ethnicity, 1, 5, 14, 165, 205, 208–20, 251–54, 283, 294, 297, 313, 322, 337–338, 348; *Resistance through Rituals*, 5, 248; as revisionist (or neo-) Marxist, 3–4, 10–14, 158–63, 247, 253; and Thatcherism, 335–36; "Variants of Liberalism," 227–45, 255–57; "The West and the Rest" (Hall), 301, 339–40; use of close reading method, 4; use of recent writings, 165. *See also* Centre for Contemporary Cultural Studies; University of Birmingham
Handsworth (area of Birmingham), 248
Hard Road to Renewal, The (Hall), 335–37
Harlem, 248
Harvey, David, 317, 318
Hayek, Friedrich A., 232, 257
Hegel, G. W. F., 20, 23, 25–30, 32, 35, 38, 40, 42, 45, 53; anti-Hegelian "inversion," 66; Hegelian analyses, 29, 33, 34, 40, 50, 53, 56, 58, 54, 98, 139, 165,

169–72; Hegelian dialectic, 20, 28, 30, 35, 72, 301; Hegelianism, 25, 72, 138, 142, 277; Left Hegelians, 56, 64, 91; Marx's relation to, 56, 58, 141–42, 147, 165, 167, 169–72, 174n17, 176n35. See also *Marxism and Hegel*

hegemony, 8, 77, 115, 140, 168, 181, 284–88, 295, 296, 336, 349n1; colonial, 300; cultural, 329; Gramsci's concept of, 83, 154, 162, 186–88, 197, 263

Heidegger, Martin, 308

Hindess, Barry, 274

Hippies and Hippie culture, 196, 196

Hirst, Paul, 130, 131, 161, 202, 274; *lumpenproletariat* notion of, 213

historical materialism, 13, 23, 57, 58, 63, 65, 120, 161, 168, 202, 339; Engels on, 71–73

historicism, 102, 169, 173, 221; "antihistoricist" interpretation of Marx, 60n55; Gramsci and, 85; Marx and, 24, 41, 42, 45, 67–71, 88, 97; "structural," 46, 49

History and Class Consciousness (Lukács), 102

History Workshop, 6, 273, 279

Hobbes, Thomas, 230, 236–37, 257

Hobsbawm, Eric, 49, 200–201, 217, 218

Hoggart, Richard, 194, 329

housework, 207–11, 251

Howe, Darcus, 213–16, 251

Hulme, Peter, 298, 306

humanism, 71, 88, 97–98, 164, 274, 275, 280

Hunt, Alan, 261, 264

hybridity, 303–4, 313, 339. See also colonialism; neocolonialism; postcolonialism and "the postcolonial"

identity, cultural, 16n15, 193, 305, 346. See also culture

identity, national, 134, Gramsci and, 153–54. See also culture

identity relation, 60n25, 125

ideological state apparatuses, 85, 130, 186. See also ideology

ideologism, 7–8, 14, 159, 288, 335–36. See also ideology

ideology, 3, 5, 9, 12, 23, 69, 211, 232, 240, 244, 329; Althusser on, 130; Hall on debates about, 134–55, 159, 161–63, 255–58, 289, 336, 349; and class struggle, 152, 189, 241–44; Hall's definition of, 136; function of, 140; Marxist formulations of, 74–77, 82, 84, 87, 122, 135, 137–40, 145, 235, 245, 250, 255; in France, 77, 119, 159; and hegemony, 186–88; discursive conception of, 140, 143; vs. culture, 182, 190–91; vs. science, 142, 150; mystifying effects of, 149; Foucault and, 140; liberalism as, 227–28, 235–37, 241; Gramsci and, 187, 290, 308; "distortions" of, 141, 143, 146–50. See also false consciousness; ideological state apparatuses; ideologism

"Ideology and Ideological State Apparatuses" (Althusser), 85, 87, 130, 139, 140, 262, 275

imperialism, 8, 127, 215–18, 263–64, 293, 299, 302, 307; age of Empires, 298; "biologistic," 347. See also colonialism; neocolonialism; postcolonialism and "the postcolonial"

India, 219, 297, 320

intelligentsia, 83, 183; "lumpenintelligentsia" (Thompson), 280

International, 124, 126; General Council of, 111; Second, 71, 72

intersectionality, 251–52

Iraq, 296; and other Gulf States, 300

Italy, 82, 187, 228, 265, 318; Marxist theory in, 211. See also Gramsci, Antonio

Jacques, Martin, 322

Jamaica, 214, 297

James, C. L. R., 209, 297
James, Selma, 208, 209, 210
Jameson, Fredric, 175n24, 301
Jefferson, Tony, 249. See also *Resistance through Rituals*
Jessop, Bob, 6, 7–8, 284, 290, 335–37. See also "Authoritarian Populism, Two Nations and Thatcherism"; *Thatcherism*
Johnson, Richard, 7, 171, 176n37, 253, 276, 345
Jones, Gareth Stedman, 10
Joseph, Keith, 256

Kant, Immanuel, 170; Kantian Marxist analysis, 165
Keynes, John Maynard: Keynesian economic management, 211; Keynesian welfare state, 290–91
Kline, G. L., 172
Korsch, Karl, 24, 52

labor, 9, 21, 27, 31, 54, 59n22, 65, 79; "abstract," 23, 212; "aristocracy of labor," 217, 218; capital vs. labor, 12, 52, 98, 118, 124–26, 128, 182, 188; discussed in *Capital*, 205–6, 209–10, 222; division of, 65, 70, 88, 103–7, 127, 199, 207–9, 267, 311; exploitation of, 102, 113, 137, 144, 204; factory/industrial, 49–52, 107–9, 190, 217; forced, 192; free, 96, 100; Locke and, 244; organized, 188, 200, 223, 287; productive vs. unproductive, 24, 88, 183, 202, 204–7, 216, 222, 234, 251, 264; reserve army of, 104, 205, 208, 210, 212, 215–16, 220–23, 251; socialization of, 105, 107; surplus, 68, 148, 199, 204–5; theoretical, 44, 46, 55, 57–58, 91, 138; wages and wage-labor, 34–39, 80–81, 93, 96, 103–4, 130, 143, 145, 148–49, 204, 210–12, 234. See also labor movement; trade unions; workers
laborers. See workers

labor movement, 188, 200, 233. See also labor: organized; trade unions
Labour Party (UK), 129, 252, 283, 287, 291. See also Britain
Lacan, Jacques, 87, 140, 271
Laclau, Ernesto, 150, 170, 176n36, 228, 285, 289, 341, 348
Larrain, Jorge, 235
Laski, Harold, 238
Laslett, Peter, 243
Latin America, 199, 223, 248, 297
Latour, Bruno, 342, 350n12
Lenin, Vladimir, 82, 83, 85, 98, 112, 113, 124, 126, 217–18, 235, 263, 271; Leninist Marxism, 10, 127, 209, 265, 266, 270. See also *State and Revolution*
Letter to Friedrich Bolte (Marx), 111, 112
Letter to Schmidt (Engels), 121–22
Lévi-Strauss, Claude, 328–29
liberalism, 5; and class, 239–45; core concepts, 227–34; and "free market" competition, 22, 80, 100, 103, 119, 143–50, 204, 231–34, 237–38, 255, 290; historically situated, 234–39; Nature and natural rights in, 229–31, 237, 242, 244; and science, 238–39. See also capitalism; globalization; Locke, John; neoliberalism
Ling, Tom, 6, 282. See also "Authoritarian Populism, Two Nations and Thatcherism"; *Thatcherism*
Locke, John, 228, 231, 232, 237, 242–44, 255
Long Revolution, The (Williams), 7
Louis-Napoleon. See *The Eighteenth Brumaire of Louis Bonaparte*; France
Ludwig Feuerbach and the End of Classical German Philosophy (Engels), 76
Lukács, György, 47, 102, 139, 235, 261, 274
Lukes, Steven, 186
lumpenproletariat. See proletariat

Macherey, Pierre, 262
Macpherson, C. B., 233

Major, John, 323
Mani, Lata, 297, 301, 308
Martynov, Alexandr, 126
Marx, Karl: and class, 50, 53–54, 65–73, 91, 136–42, 145–52, 162, 254; biography of, 10; and Hegel, 20, 23–32, 38, 40, 42, 45, 53, 56, 58, 141–42, 147, 165, 167, 169–72; and historicism, 24, 41, 42, 45, 67–71, 88, 97; and Ricardo, 21, 55, 58, 137, 146–47; as structuralist, 43, 48, 87, 94, 164. *See also* Engels, Friedrich; individual works by Marx, Marx and Engels
Marxism: central elements of, 9–10, 250–51; classical, 11, 139, 235, 268, 317; contemporary, 10, 247, 253, 344; *Marxism and the Interpretation of Culture* (ed. Nelson and Grossberg), 11; neo-Marxism, 5, 16n19, 253, 255, 344; post-Marxism, 14, 134, 162–63, 336, 344; structuralist, 6, 8, 40, 48, 52, 85, 87–88, 271, 329; vulgar, 12; Western, 2, 10–11, 82, 135, 289, 302. *See also* Marx, Karl
Marxism and Hegel (Colletti), 165
Marxism and the Interpretation of Culture (Nelson and Grossberg), 11
Marxism Today, 180, 265
Massey, Doreen, 319
Mauss, Marcel, 329
McClintock, Anne, 294–95, 297, 300
McLellan, David, 164
mediation, 12–13, 54, 138; Hall as dialectical mediator, 14, 162, 169, 172, 250, 251, 255, 337, 342; Marx and, 30, 166, 169–70, 277; mediators vs. intermediaries (Latour), 342, 350n12; Sartre and, 13–14, 16n30
Meek, R. L., 340
Mepham, John, 19, 59n6
Mercer, Kobena, 338
metaphysics, 169, 171
middle class, 75, 103, 183–84, 195–97. *See also* class

Miliband, Ralph, 262
Mill, John Stuart, 27
modernism, 238, 249, 306, 339, 343–44. *See also* postmodernism
modes of production, 54, 77, 93, 100, 115, 120, 128, 166; advanced, 211; phases of, 9, 42, 44, 65, 251
"Modern Prince" (Gramsci), 13, 296
money, 48, 49–50, 54, 80, 81, 244, 287; as abstract vs. concrete concept, 43, 150; economy based on, 33, 143, 148. *See also* bourgeoisie; capitalism
Morley, David, 1, 338
multiculturalism, 311, 340
"The Multicultural Question" (Hall), 5, 340, 341

Napoleon III (Charles-Louis Napoléon Bonaparte). See *The Eighteenth Brumaire of Louis Bonaparte*; France
neocolonialism, 293–294. *See also* colonialism; imperialism; postcolonialism and "the postcolonial"
neoliberalism, 144, 232, 250, 255, 290, 349; "The Neo-liberal Revolution" (Hall), 6
neo-Marxism, 5, 16n19, 253, 255, 344; of Hall, 10, 160, 247, 338, 348
New Left Review, 7, 89n23, 165, 248, 282, 335
Nicolaus, Martin, 19, 24, 52, 164, 174n17
nobility, 229, 240–41, 339. *See also* aristocracy
"Notes on the Cultural Revolutions of Our Time" (Hall), 8

Open University (OU), 5, 8, 255–56, 330, 339, 345
Orientalism (Said), 302, 340
overdetermination/overdeterminacy, 9–10, 35–36, 86, 96, 99, 114, 120, 128, 191, 216, 301, 302, 304; Althusser on, 121; and class, 194, 262; Hall on "overdetermined unity," 344. *See also* determination/determinacy

INDEX | 359

Paine, Tom, 237, 255
Paris Commune, 112, 113, 124. *See also* France
Parsons, Talcott, 334n26, 347–48
patriarchy of the wage, 211
pauperism, 222
Phenomenology of Spirit, The (Hegel), 20, 27
Philosophy of Right, The (Hegel), 20, 42
Policing the Crisis (Hall et al.), 5, 248, 283, 284, 291
political economy, bourgeois, 23, 57, 142, 146
populism, 280, 292n2; authoritarian, 8, 270, 282–86, 288–92, 335–36
postcolonialism and "the postcolonial," 8, 10, 14, 293–313, 319, 337–44; anticolonial struggles, 298–99; as term vs. process, 298. *See also* colonialism; imperialism; neocolonialism
post-Marxism, 14, 134, 162–63, 336, 344
postmodernism, 249, 306, 310, 342. *See also* modernism
poststructuralism, 2, 250, 294–95, 301, 306, 309–10, 329, 340, 348; Hall as poststructuralist-in-waiting, 2
Poulantzas, Nicos, 6, 82, 87, 152, 162, 261–71, 282–85; and Althusser, 85, 186; on class, 162; *Classes in Contemporary Capitalism*, 263, 264; and Gramsci, 85; on "ideological state apparatuses," 186; *State, Power, Socialism*, 283
Poverty of Philosophy, The (Marx), 25, 27, 37, 110, 112, 138, 202
Poverty of Theory, The (Thompson), 6, 273–80
Prakash, Gyan, 310
Pratt, Mary-Louise, 305
proletariat, 96–97, 102–4, 112, 115, 118, 126, 199, 204, 217; black, 215–16; bourgeois, 218; and bourgeoisie, 110, 117, 202, 203; British, 218; cohesion of the, 107–8, 211; colonial, 218–19, 222; "dictatorship of the proletariat," 113, 124, 265, 266, 270; as fundamental revolutionary class, 102, 200, 202; lumpenproletariat, 116, 201–3, 205, 210, 213, 216, 219–20, 222, 251; sub-proletariat, 215–16, 218, 220

property, 31, 81, 116, 117, 128, 143–44, 230; feudal, 46, 119, 238; landed, 34–35, 46, 49, 75, 115–16, 240; people without, 241–42, 243; private, 23, 27, 42, 211; property rights, 145, 232, 234, 237–38, 243
Proudhon, Pierre-Joseph, 25–26, 37, 50, 55
psychoanalysis and psychoanalytic theory, 14, 140, 147, 162, 250, 329

race and ethnicity: Black Panthers, 248; black youth, 199, 212; Hall on, 1, 5, 14, 165, 205, 208–20, 251–54, 283, 294, 297, 322, 337–338, 348; racial exploitation and oppression, 212, 215–16; Victorian racial theory, 313. *See also* workers: black
"Race, Articulation and Societies Structured in Dominance" (Hall), 165, 338, 348
Rancière, Jacques, 87, 262, 265
Reading Capital (Althusser et al.), 85–88, 94, 122, 139, 262, 266, 275
reductionism, 236, 295, 313, 330, 349; in Marxism, 11, 12, 72, 84, 98, 131, 138–39, 145, 250, 276–77, 342
religion, 65, 66, 69, 70, 116, 138, 156, 233, 235, 328; the church, 83, 186, 187, 229, 238, 240; fundamentalism in, 320; Puritanism, 229, 237, 240–42; Reformation, 229, 237, 238, 240
"reserve army" of labor, 104, 205, 208, 210, 212, 215–16, 220–23, 251
resistance, 108, 183, 187–88, 200, 212, 221, 269; anticolonial, 294, 303–5
Resistance through Rituals (Hall and Jefferson), 5, 248

Ricardo, David, 21, 55, 58, 137, 142, 147; Ricardian theory of wages, 56
rights, 81, 144, 229–34, 237, 240–44; property rights, 145
Rosdolsky, Roman, 21
Rousseau, Jean-Jacques, 21
Rusher, Robin, 168
Rustin, Michael, 2

Said, Edward, 301, 302, 340
Sartre, Jean-Paul, 13–14, 16n30, 261, 301, 339; *Search for a Method*, 13
Schwarz, Bill, 336–37
Science of Logic (Hegel), 20, 29, 170
science, 45, 46, 50, 79, 106, 142, 154, 305, 327; Althusser's understanding of, 168; in liberalism, 237–39; Marxist political economy as, 51–58, 62, 72, 81, 88, 109, 156, 161, 175n28. *See also* social sciences
Seccombe, Wally, 207–8, 213
Second International, 71, 72
Shohat, Ella, 294–99, 303, 306–7, 342
Slack, Jennifer Daryl, 1
slavery, 23, 35, 37, 95, 99, 100
Smith, Adam, 21, 55, 142, 228, 237, 255
social class. *See* class
socialism, 9, 279–80; democratic, 270–71; transition to, 9, 159, 202, 264–66, 270; utopian, 101, 110
social sciences, 305, 316, 327, 356; "cultural turn" in, 325, 328–31, 347–48. *See also* sociology
sociology, 9, 98, 249, 316, 321, 326, 328–30, 339, 347–48; of knowledge, 5, 161; Weberian, 302, 328, 330. *See also* social sciences
Sparks, Colin, 2
Spinoza, Baruch, 30, 170
Spivak, Gayatri, 301
Stalinism, 10, 265, 273
State, Power, Socialism (Poulantzas), 6, 261–71

"State and Civil Society" (Gramsci), 85, 286
State and Revolution, The (Lenin), 83, 124
Stedman Jones, Gareth, 10
structuralism, 14, 43, 46, 169, 253, 262, 266, 274–76, 306–7, 328; Marx and, 164, 273; structuralist Marxism, 6, 8, 40, 48, 52, 85, 87–88, 271, 329. *See also* poststructuralism
subcultures, 179–97, 247, 249, 258n8; Beats, 196; countercultures, 195–97; defined, 183–84; Hippies, 195, 196–97; middle-class, 195–97; Skinheads, 185, 190, 195; Teddy Boys and Mods, 185, 190; working-class culture, 189–97, 253–54; youth, 179–94, 248–50
surplus value, 52, 56, 68, 79, 104, 108, 137, 145, 202, 204, 206; Absolute vs. Relative, 109; produced by black workers, 210, 212, 215

Thatcher, Margaret, 8, 130, 144, 256, 322; and "regressive modernization," 8. *See also* Thatcherism
Thatcherism, 7–8, 142, 255, 270, 274, 349n1; Hall on, 282–92, 335–37. *See also* Thatcher, Margaret
Thatcherism (Jessop et al.), 337
theoretical practice, 28, 39, 86, 94, 277; *Theoretical Practice* journal, 168. *See also* Althusser, Louis
Therborn, Goran, 10
Theses on Feuerbach (Marx), 39, 172
Third World, 218–20, 223, 248, 293, 295–96, 303, 307, 310, 312; "Third Worldism," 294
Thompson, E. P., 6–7, 89n23, 273–80
Tory Party (UK), 75; Toryism, 290. *See also* Thatcher, Margaret
trade unions, 96, 102, 112, 126–27, 287
Translocations (exhibition), 319–20
Two Treatises on Government (Locke), 237, 243

Uchida, Hiroshi, 175
underclass, 219
unemployment, 187, 190, 192, 215, 219–23, 287; among young blacks, 210, 214
unions. *See* trade unions
United Kingdom. *See* Britain; English Revolution
United States, 297, 298, 311, 320; academia, 294–95, 297, 328; American Revolution, 228, 237; economy, 208, 223; government, 232, 233; Gulf War and, 296
University of Birmingham, 4–5, 7, 13, 175n27, 248–52, 329. *See also* Centre for Contemporary Cultural Studies
Utilitarians, 255
Utopian Socialism, 101, 110

"Variants of Liberalism" (Hall), 227–45, 255–57
Victorian era, 255, 346
Vilar, Pierre, 20, 39–40, 165, 171
Volosinov, V. N., 151
Volpe, Galvano Della, 175n28

Weber, Max, 238, 277, 302, 328, 330, 347
West, the: Western academics, 341; Western capitalist modernity, 342; Western Marxism, 2, 10–11; Western modernity, 5, 339; Western philosophical tradition, 343
"The West and the Rest" (Hall), 301, 339–40

What Is to Be Done? (Lenin), 112, 126, 271
Whig Party (UK), 75, 233, 242, 243; and Locke's philosophy, 243
Williams, Gwyn, 74, 95, 114
Williams, Raymond, 4, 7; "culturalism" of, 15n15
Wilson, Harold, 323
Women's Studies Group, 255. *See also* feminism and feminist thought
workers, 37, 81, 104, 128, 204, 207; agricultural, 202, 222, 239; black, 199, 205, 210–12, 215–16, 220–23, 251; deskilling of, 103–4, 106, 211, 220, 222; female and domestic, 207–11, 213, 223; "mass," 211–12, 220; migrant, 212, 220, 223; serfs, 37, 95, 99; skilled, 150. *See also* labor; proletariat; trade unions
working class, 13, 75, 102, 105–13, 129–30, 135, 199, 202–22, 264, 273, 291; Marxism and working-class struggle, 9, 71, 106, 111–13, 123–26; working-class consciousness, 141; working-class culture, 183–85, 188–97, 253–54
Working Papers in Cultural Studies (WPCS), 13, 165, 168, 171, 172, 174n19, 175n27, 176n35, 254–55, 258n17, 336, 347
Wright, Erik Olin, 264

Young, Robert, 301
youth. *See* race: black youth; subcultures: youth

Zeleny, Jindrich, 175n28

PLACE OF FIRST PUBLICATION

Chapter 1: "Marx's Notes on Method: A 'Reading' of the '1857 Introduction,'" in "Cultural Studies and Theory," *Working Papers in Cultural Studies*, no. 6 (Birmingham: Centre for Contemporary Cultural Studies, University of Birmingham, 1974), 132–70. An earlier, longer version was published informally as CCCS Stencilled Paper No. 1 (Autumn 1973), with a slightly different title: "A 'Reading' of Marx's *1857 Introduction* to the *Grundrisse*." The differences between the versions are significant, as elaborated in "Editor's Discussion of the Part I Writings."

Chapter 2: "Rethinking the 'Base and Superstructure' Metaphor" (under the title "Re-thinking the 'Base-and-Superstructure' Metaphor"), in *Class, Hegemony and Party*, ed. Jon Bloomfield (London: Lawrence and Wishart, 1977), 43–72.

Chapter 3: "The 'Political' and the 'Economic' in Marx's Theory of Classes," in *Class and Class Structure*, ed. Alan Hunt (London: Lawrence and Wishart, 1977), 15–60.

Chapter 4: "The Problem of Ideology: Marxism without Guarantees," in *Marx: A Hundred Years On*, ed. Betty Matthews (London: Lawrence and Wishart, 1983), 57–85.

Chapter 5: "Subcultures, Cultures and Class: A Theoretical Overview" (with John Clarke, Tony Jefferson, and Brian Roberts), in "Resistance through Rituals: Youth Subcultures in Post-war Britain," ed. Stuart Hall and Tony Jefferson, *Working Papers in Cultural Studies*, nos. 7–8 (Birmingham: Centre for Contemporary Cultural Studies, University of Birmingham, 1975), 9–74.

Chapter 6: "Black Crime, Black Proletariat," in Stuart Hall, Chas Critcher, Tony Jefferson, John Clarke, and Brian Roberts, *Policing the Crisis: Mugging, the State, and Law and Order* (London: Macmillan, 1978), 362–81.

Chapter 7: "Variants of Liberalism," in *Politics and Ideology*, ed. James Donald and Stuart Hall (Milton Keynes, UK: Open University Press, 1986), 34–69.

Chapter 8: "Nicos Poulantzas: State, Power, Socialism," in *New Left Review*, I/119 (1980): 60–69.

Chapter 9: "In Defence of Theory," in *People's History and Socialist Theory*, ed. Raphael Samuel (London: Routledge and Kegan Paul, 1981), 378–85.

Chapter 10: "Authoritarian Populism: A Reply to Jessop et al.," in *New Left Review*, I/151 (1985): 115–24.

Chapter 11: "When Was 'the Post-colonial'? Thinking at the Limit," in *The Post-colonial Question: Common Skies, Divided Horizons*, ed. Iain Chambers and Lidia Curti (London: Routledge, 1996), 242–60.

Chapter 12: "The Centrality of Culture: Notes on the Cultural Revolutions of Our Time," in *Media and Cultural Regulation*, ed. Kenneth Thompson (London: Sage/Open University, 1997), 207–38.